"Bryan brings a straightforward, conversational, and modern take on traditional recipes. *Pan y Dulce* is a lightning rod for pan-Latin baking traditions and history, and Bryan's pride in his heritage and exploration of the baking traditions of the Latin world shine through. He masterfully blends traditions culled from Indigenous cultures with the baking customs of the colonizers, creating a unique and rich fusion of flavors and techniques. Complemented by lush photography, this book is a feast for the eyes as well as the palate."

—JIM LAHEY, JAMES BEARD AWARD–WINNING BAKER AND AUTHOR OF *MY BREAD*

"*Pan y Dulce* offers so much more than just delicious baked goods; it takes you on a sweeping journey through history, from the origins of bread through its transformation by Black, Brown, and Indigenous hands across Latin America. From the jalapeño quesillo bolillo filled with creamy Oaxacan cheese to coconut milk tortillas de harina (which have set a new standard for any future tortilla I'll ever eat), Bryan's recipes are layered with comfort and a deep gratitude for the past. This is an essential cookbook for new and experienced bakers alike, teaching not just *how* to bake but also *why* we bake."

—FRANKIE GAW, AUTHOR OF *FIRST GENERATION*

"Bryan Ford brings a much-needed and refreshing perspective to the world of baking with this thoughtful and inspired compilation of Latin American baking traditions. *Pan y Dulce* pays tribute to the vast and deep historical and cultural significance bread has throughout the continent. This remarkable cookbook provides a harmonious blend of classic and innovative recipes of extensive breads and pastries, captivating and essential for home and professional bakers alike."

—ARTURO ENCISO, HEAD BAKER, GUSTO BREAD

PAN Y DULCE

PAN Y DULCE

THE LATIN AMERICAN BAKING BOOK

PASTRIES, DESSERTS, RUSTIC BREADS, SAVORY BAKING, AND MORE

Bryan Ford

Photographs by Brittany Conerly
Location photographs by Lizzie Ford-Madrid

VORACIOUS
Little, Brown and Company
New York Boston London

I dedicate this book to my parents.

To my father, Glen Carl Ford-Bodden, who passed away on October 31, 2022, during the writing of this book.

The first loaf of bread I ever baked was a cinnamon raisin loaf for him, and while it underwent zero fermentation and was completely burned, he ate the whole thing and enjoyed it.

I know that he was always so proud of me. I miss you, Pa.

To my mother, Herling Madrid, who is my biggest fan and biggest supporter. There is no one that I look up to more than you, Ma, and I would have never had the honor of writing this book without all of your continued hard work over the years. To many more sunrises and sunsets together.

CONTENTS

INTRODUCTION   xi

HOW TO USE THIS BOOK SUCCESSFULLY   xiii

PART 1
BAKER'S GUIDE

CHAPTER 1
INGREDIENTS AND TOOLS

Grains and Roots	4
Sugars, Spices, and Chocolate	6
Other Ingredients	8
Weight Conversions	9
Tools	9

CHAPTER 2
TECHNIQUES

Leavening	14
Converting Between Yeasted and Sourdough Recipes	18
Mixing, Shaping, and Baking Bread	20
Pastry and Dessert Techniques	25
Temperature, Climate, and Altitude	27

CHAPTER 3
YEASTED AND HYBRID DOUGHS

Bolillo	34
Bolillo Integral	37
Jalapeño Quesillo Bolillo	40
Pan Michita	43
Pirujos	46
Pãozinho	48
Pebete	51
Pan Mojicón	53
Pan Cubano	56
Pan de Media Noche	59
Pan Sobao	62
Tripleta on Pan Sobao	65
Pan de Yema Peruano	67
Pan Sarnita	68
Cachitos de Espinaca y Ricota	71
Cachitos de Jamón	72
Pan de Cemita	75
Cemita Milanesa de Pollo	77

CHAPTER 4
SOURDOUGH
Rustic, Savory, and Sweet

Pan Casero	82
Pan Casero Integral	85
Pan de Tres Puntas	88
Pan Chuta	90
Sheca	92
Pan de Cazuela	95
Birote Salado	98
Torta Ahogada	101
Marraquetas	102
Pan Chapla	105
Pan Rústico de Sorgo y Amaranto Tostado	106
Pan de Plátano a la Parrilla	108
Blue Masa Sourdough	111
Pan de Molde con Ajonjolí	113
Pan de Molde 100% Integral	116
Roles de Pimiento Asado	119
Fugazza	120
Fugazzeta	122
Stuffed Fugazzeta	125
Fugazzeta de Vegetales	126
Pizza de Jamón y Morrones	129
Pizza al Molde Napolitana	130
Pan Trenza	133

Mogolla Chicharrona	134
Mogolla Integral	137
Hallullas	138
Galletas de Campana	141
Concha Tradicional	143
Concha de Chocolate y Jamaica	147
Semita de Yema Integral	149
Semita Hondureña de Maíz	152
Semita Hondureña de Arroz	154
Mallorca de Chocolate with Guava Glaze	157
Medialunas	159
Golfeados	163
Roscón de Arequipe	166
Pan de Coco Tradicional	168
Roasted Ginger and Caramelized Pineapple Pan de Coco	170
Banana and Rum Raisin Pan de Coco	172
Pan de Muerto	175
Rosca de Reyes	177
T'anta Wawa	180
Roles de Canela with Mango Cream Cheese Frosting	182
Pan de Yema	185
Pan de Jamón	187
Pan Payaso	190

CHAPTER 5

DESSERTS AND PASTRIES

Tres Leches Tradicional	194
Chocolate Tres Leches de Coco	196
Torta de Ricota	199
Bizcocho de Ron	200
Mantecada con Masa Madre	203
Arepa Dulce de Maíz	204
Bizcocho de Naranja	207
Dulce de Camote	208
Dulce de Papaya	209
Dulce de Leche	210
Alfajores Chilenitos	213
Alfajores de Maicena	214
Alfajores Blancos y Negros with Dulce de Papaya	217
Naturally Leavened Alfajores con Dulce de Camote	218
Alfajores de Miel	221
Pudín de Pan	222
Champurradas	225
Torta Rogel	226
Suspiros	228
Coyotas	231
Galletas de Boda	232
Churros Tradicionales	234
Chocolate Churros	237
Churros de Masa Madre	238
Picos	241
Rosquillas	242
Tustacas	245
Flan de Coco	246
Quesadilla Ecuatoriana	249
Brazilian Bombocado	250
Brigadeiros	253
Curau de Milho	254
Galletas Cucas	257
Chocotorta	258
Pastafrola	260
Volcán de Dulce de Leche	263
Quesadilla Hondureña/Salvadoreña	264
Cocadas	267
Semita de Piña	268
Picarones	271
Masa Hojaldre	272
Pastelitos de Guayaba y Queso	274
Pastelitos de Piña	276
Pastelitos de Camote y Mole	279
Pastelitos de Papaya y Queso	280
Orejas	283
Pastelitos Criollos	284

Tortillas de Maíz	290
Tortillas de Harina de Trigo	292
Tortillas de Harina Integral	294
My Mom's Tortillas de Harina	296
Sourdough Discard Tortillas	298
Baleadas	301
Salsa Roja	302
Curtido	305
Chimichurri	307
Arepas de Queso Colombianas	308
Arepas Reina Pepiada	311
Pupusas de Frijol con Queso	312
Empanada Dough—Flour	315
Empanada Dough—Whole Grain Flour	317
Empanada/Pastelito Dough—Corn	318
Empanadas de Pino	321
Empanadas de Carne Cortada al Cuchillo	322
Empanadas Jugosas de Pollo	324
Empanadas Salteñas	327
Empanadas de Jamón y Queso	331
Empanadas de Pabellón Criollo	332
Pastelitos de Perro	335
Tequeños	336
Sopa Paraguaya	339
Salt Cod Pâté Haïtien	340
Pastelitos de Carne	342
Pastelitos de Gandules y Hongos	345
Pão de Queijo	346
Cuñapés	349
Pandebonos	350
Gluten-Free Sourdough Starter	353
Gluten-Free Bolillo	354
Pan de Amaranto	356
Pan de Sorgo	359
Chocolate Quinoa Bread	360
Beiju de Tapioca	363

SUGAR, THE DOUBLE-EDGED MACHETE	7
PAN FRANCÉS THROUGHOUT LATIN AMERICA	32
TAINO TRADITION AND THE MODERN CUBANO	55
THE NOSTALGIA OF BIROTE	97
THE MANY FACES OF PAN DULCE	142
FROM AL-HASÚ TO ALFAJOR	212
THE REAL "BREAD" OF LATIN AMERICA	288
ENCURTIDO AL LAGO DE YOJOA	304
THE EMPANADA	314

FURTHER READING	368
ACKNOWLEDGMENTS	371
INDEX	373

INTRODUCTION

Welcome to the world of pan y dulce—the world of bread and sweetness.

One single book cannot possibly capture the full range and magic of Latin American baking, but it can give an intoxicating taste. Here I've done my best to introduce you to my interpretation of the delicious local specialties that express creativity across this richly varied region. Among these 150 or so recipes are baked goods that touch each of the thirty-three countries that are commonly known as comprising Latin America, extending from México to Central and South America and into the Caribbean.

"Latin America" is itself an odd concept that begins to fall apart once you start to think about it. Although it's a useful term in that it helps understand a group of countries and their people who have many commonalities and shared roots of language and geography, it is also a by-product of colonization and the Atlantic slave trade. Why are these areas considered "Latin"? It's because of the European languages that came to dominate these lands, alongside their occupiers. That's why Jamaica is not part of Latin America despite being so close to Cuba, Haiti, and the Dominican Republic in the Caribbean: it was colonized by people who spoke English, not Romance languages.

But for the purposes of this book, Latin America is a world unto itself. When I say Latin American baking, I'm talking about the artisan-style loaves you may know me for, soft sandwich rolls, and classic renditions of loaves that capture a regional expression, like Pan de Cazuela (page 95) from Oaxaca. In this world of baking you'll also find empanadas and tortillas in a variety of styles (and you'd better not sleep on my Baleadas, page 301). Medialunas (page 159), flaky and sweet. You'll find cakes from Chocolate Tres Leches de Coco (page 196) to Chocotorta (page 258). Cookies from Alfajores (pages 213–221) to Champurradas (page 225). Flan de Coco (page 246). And flatbreads like the Argentinian Fugazzeta (page 122).

Sharing the stories behind these recipes and how to make them is part of my mission: to expand the common understanding in the United States about what, and who, can make stellar baked goods.

It is impossible for any single culture to be the true or only source of baking expertise. Culinary ideas, ingredients, and traditions flow from culture to culture, changing over time and in response to regional opportunities and requirements. For me, much of the beauty in baking comes from using historically significant ingredients and flavors related to those roots and traditions. The most exciting baking of my life happened while I researched and developed these recipes.

In Latin America, precolonial baking traditions did not use wheat, a crop that was not Indigenous to the region. The domestication of wheat and the baking of wheat bread is believed to have originated in the Fertile Crescent, specifically Ancient Egypt. This practice spread to other parts of the world, which led to European colonizers bringing wheat to the Americas in the 1500s. That resulted in the extraordinary and diverse baked goods you can now find throughout Latin America. Of course, there is more to the story.

One of the first known harvesters of wheat in the Americas was Juan Garrido, who was born in West Africa and made his way to Spain as a young man where he joined the expedition to what was called Hispaniola. Juan Garrido, a name that he took after converting to Catholicism, is thought to be the first known African to arrive in present day North America. After joining Cortés in the siege of Tenochtitlán, he settled as a farmer and began planting wheat. As a byproduct of this, a few different bread varieties were produced and sold by Indigenous women, some with refined white flour and some with wheat bran. The colonizers' desire to cultivate wheat and make bread the way it was made in Europe was indeed a factor in the development of these early bread-making methods. But baking in México today is by no means a simple reimagining of the European institution.

Over time, Mexican baking has been transformed by an Indigenous cultural mixture. The brief French occupation opened the door to the creation of regional pan dulce, or sweet bread, with some linked to traditions like Pan de Muerto (page 175) or the Rosca de Reyes (page 177). Pan dulce has spread widely in Latin America, and every country has versions that are closely tied to its customs, climates, traditions, and the hands of its people. From Shecas (page 92) with a hint of molasses and anise in Guatemala to the various Semitas (pages 149–154) of Honduras, there is no shortage of delicious pan dulce.

There is much to explore beyond traditions that include wheat. Ambato, Ecuador, was said to have had some of the most delicious bread tasted by colonists. Indigenous bread was made with yuca and quinoa flours mixed with finely ground white corn. It was said to have texture and flavor on par with what they were accustomed to in Europe. After wheat was introduced, the standard of bread has remained very high in Ambato. Due to complications from the high altitude, bakers in the city developed a rigorous triple-rise process. Today, some of the best bread in Ecuador is still found along the Ambato River.

Many more intriguing stories accompany the recipes in this book. You may not have heard many of them because European baking culture has dominated the food media and our restaurant industry in the United States for quite some time. When new artisanal bakeries open here, they most often focus on selling croissants, baguettes, focaccias, and pizzas. This perpetuates the idea that the gold standard for a

successful, experienced baker is to be able to master French and Italian products and techniques. But oddly enough, many of the bakers laboring behind the scenes at successful bakeries in the United States are Hispanic, Black, or both—like me.

Don't get me wrong: croissants and pizza are dope. But they are just one part of the story. And if you limit your own baking to those traditions, you will miss out on something very special indeed.

Many of the most interesting and delicious baked goods in the world today come from Latin America. Learning about them is exciting. But many of their stories are not straightforward. Some of those items trace their roots back to Indigenous ingredients or traditions; others arose as a complex reaction to the often painful legacy of European colonialism. Others were influenced by West African traditions, as a result of the practice of chattel slavery.

I did not anticipate that my work would become part of an important conversation in the food world about topics such as inclusivity, representation, and diversity—buzz words that simply mean we need more Black, Brown, and Indigenous hands and faces representing the world of artisanal baking. I hope books like this one will help readers recognize the fundamental value and impressiveness of their own cultures and expand the minds of both new and experienced bakers.

When I first visited Honduras as a child, I remember my whole life changing as my palate expanded beyond what I knew from the United States. New colors, aromas, and cooking styles presented themselves before my eyes. My goal with these recipes is for you to experience something similar. Whether you are a seasoned or new baker, I want to open your eyes to the beauty of Latin America. I want your kitchen to fill with joy, happiness, and deliciousness. I hope that this book will help you bake bread and pastries no matter your skill level.

As you bake your way through this book, I hope you will be swept away by the deliciousness of all of Latinoamérica. I wish you a happy journey filled with many delicious bakes with your friends, family, and loved ones.

How to Use This Book Successfully

My aim is to deliver practical baking know-how along with relevant history and cultural insight, so there are occasional essays that explore interesting details about recipes, along with a substantial section at the front of the book about tools, ingredients, and techniques. Novice bakers might want to start with the introductory materials, move on to simpler cookies and yeasted breads, and finally work their way up to hybrid and full sourdough recipes.

The recipe chapters begin with the breads that I believe are truest to their form as a straight dough, meaning there is just one stage of mixing with a form of commercial yeast, or as a hybrid, where I use a preferment (typically sourdough) to enhance the flavor while still using commercial yeast for its contribution to texture. A chapter of pure sourdough recipes follows. I believe these recipes are true to their traditional spirit and essence, from a flavor and texture perspective, while being naturally leavened. Then we explore many, many delicious desserts and pastries from Latin America. And finally, the last recipe chapter shares savory bakes and several delicious gluten-free recipes, an homage to the way Latin America baked before wheat was introduced.

In these recipes I also tried to capture the essence of my background as an Afro-Honduran baker located in the United States, in order to share with you the way I enjoy making each recipe. This means that in some cases, I've made a sourdough version of a bread that is traditionally made with commercial yeast, because I prefer that result. If you wish to convert from commercial yeast to sourdough or back, the guide on page 18 will show you how.

As a professional baker, I am hopelessly devoted to the practice of measuring my ingredients by weight. While this does require a cheap digital kitchen scale, the practice will give you an instant upgrade from baking volumetrically, by which I mean using measuring cups and tablespoons. But because I realize that not all home bakers are with me yet, I have included conversions by volume. If you have questions about a particular conversion, consult the conversion guide on page 366. Note that gram weights will always deliver the more precise result, so when in doubt, pull out that scale.

Finally, note that when an ingredient is used to taste, I mark it as "al gusto."

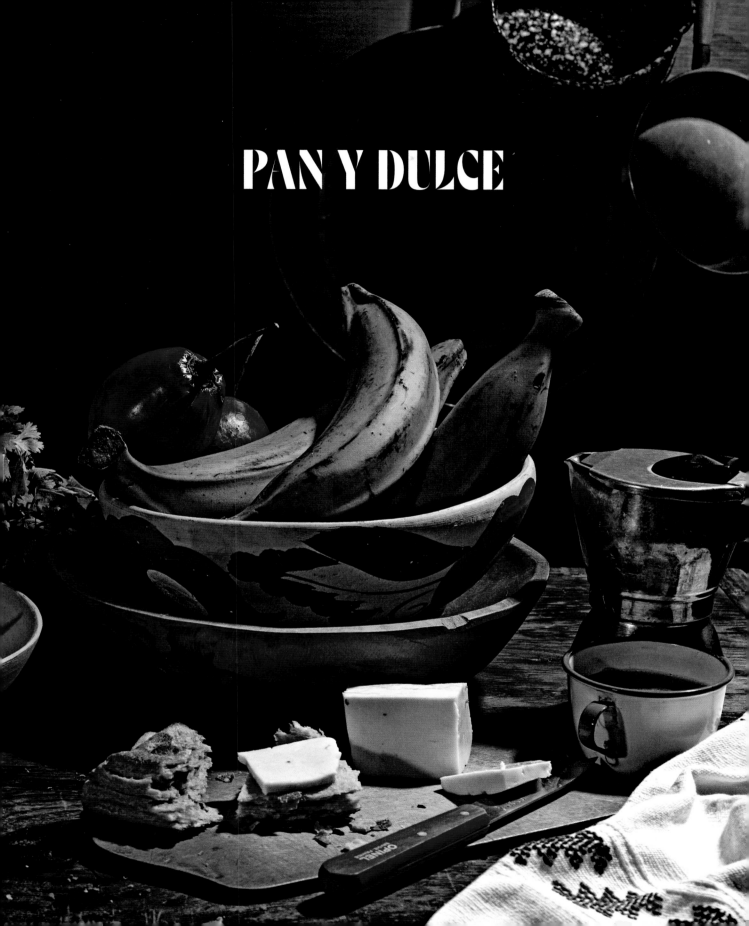

PAN Y DULCE

BAKER'S GUIDE

INGREDIENTS AND TOOLS

While ingredients like flour and sugar might seem basic, their history in Latin America is part of a complicated, problematic story. Today, nations in Latin America are often referred to as underdeveloped, but the fact is that they have been overexploited. Lands once lush with resources now see some inhabitants unable to eat or afford the very produce that grows on their native land. The destabilization caused by exporting resources to the rest of the world—rather than use the resources domestically to create a better quality of life for the home populations—has left some Latin American countries in shambles.

Historically, colonizers had a nasty habit of planting things where they did not belong. In Brazil, sugarcane absolutely devastated some of the natural, lush lands filled with orange and mango plantations. In México, maíz and amaranth are native grains, but wheat was planted when the Spaniards arrived. Before the introduction of wheat, cooking and baking largely centered on the available grains, spices, and roots. Yet today, some really great quality wheat exists in Latin America. It has never been a more exciting time to bake in this part of the world.

Let's take a closer look at some of the main grains, spices, sugars, and roots used in Latin American baking that you can stock your kitchen with.

GRAINS AND ROOTS

~~~~~

ARROZ (RICE)

In the 1500s, rice arrived in México by way of the Spanish and in Brazil by the Portuguese. Rice is such a versatile grain that you can cook it using a variety of techniques; every culture has a staple rice dish that is dear to its people. From arroz con pollo to pelao guayanés or bolinho de arroz, rice is a daily staple in most of Latin America today, just as it was for our ancestors.

From a baking perspective, rice flour is often used in Western baking to dust proofing baskets, but I love to incorporate small percentages of rice flour into the mix for an extra nutty taste and to soften the dough. Brown rice flour is a great addition when making gluten-free breads, as you will see near the end of chapter 6.

CASSAVA

Cassava, also referred to as yuca, manioc, or tapioca, is easily one of the most important crops in Latin America because of its use by many Indigenous populations. When colonists arrived in the Antilles, they did at first end up eating local cassava-based breads and cakes, but described them as essentially inedible and hard. Cassava is obviously "gluten-free," which means that the process to get it from the starch stage to an edible stage is much different than what colonists were used to. However, some precolonial cassava-based breads like pão de queijo were improved upon once dairy became available, as it helped soften the texture during the baking process. Today, you can find different versions of cassava in your grocery store, mainly cassava flour or tapioca starch, the difference being that the former incorporates the whole root and the latter is just the starchy part. Keep an eye out for these flours in chapter 6, "Savory and Gluten-Free."

MAÍZ (CORN)

It is impossible to talk about food in Latin America without talking about the most important ingredient in all the land: maíz. This word, *maíz*, is a slightly altered version of the word *mahiz* from the Indigenous, precolonial Taino language. Maíz originated around nine thousand years ago in what is now central México

and grew throughout the Americas long before colonists made contact—although the crop as we know it today did not necessarily exist. A wild grass known as teosinte was first encountered by Indigenous people in the region that is now southeast México, and it is believed to be the wild ancestor of corn.

Maíz is commonly consumed in the form of masa. It is made into masa through a process called nixtamalization, which involves cooking corn in a mixture of alkali and water, before grinding it into a wet dough. Today, you can find masa in a dry form called masa harina. In parts of South America, corn is precooked, but not nixtamalized, to form masarepa.

From tortillas in México and arepas in Venezuela, to pan de maíz in República Dominicana, Indigenous corn varieties play a major factor in the cuisine of most Latin American and some Caribbean countries. In this book, look out for the use of both **masa harina** and **masarepa** to supplement some recipes, in addition to serving as the major player in some sweet and savory treats. Recently, in New York City, I have been serving a beautiful sourdough loaf that I infuse with freshly made blue corn masa from a local restaurant. This masa is added to a mixture of whole grain flour, water, and sourdough preferment, tossed in roasted corn flour, and then baked on dried corn husks. See page 111 for the recipe—it's a favorite!

QUIHUICHA/AMARANTO (AMARANTH)

Amaranth, or quihuicha as it is known in the high Andes region of Perú, is an edible seed that originated in South America and is considered one of the healthiest of the Andean superfoods. Sometimes called "mini quinoa," amaranth contains betacyanin, a rich antioxidant, and is gluten-free. Amaranth is loaded with fiber, antioxidants, all nine vital amino acids, and many proteins not found in other grains. Amaranth is often ground, toasted, or popped. It is used in tortillas, bread, and other baked goods. It features a unique flavor that can overpower a dish on its own. Expect to see a healthy amount of it used throughout the recipes in this book.

QUINOA

Known as the "golden grain of the Andes," quinoa is referred to as a superfood because it is high in protein, low in fat, and full of vitamins and minerals. Quinoa is native to South America and was first grown around Lake Titicaca near both Perú and Bolivia, then domesticated by Indigenous people throughout the Americas approximately six thousand years ago. Today, Perú is the world's largest producer of the grain.

Quinoa has a mellow flavor, a unique, crunchy texture with flavor notes that are nutty and earthy. Unlike most grains, quinoa's germ—a tiny tail it sprouts when cooked—and bran are not discarded. I love to use quinoa cooked and whole in some recipes, as well as adding small percentages of the ground flour into a dough mix. If using whole quinoa, make sure it's cooked thoroughly, so it doesn't soak up all the water in your dough!

SORGO (SORGHUM)

Sorghum is a grain that originated in West Africa and arrived to the Americas in the middle of the nineteenth century, although it was initially met with little real interest in terms of cultivation. However, in the 1960s and '70s, sorghum production in Central America and México began to take off. Several Central American countries use this grain in their cooking practices, although it is often used as animal feed and a secondary crop in case maíz fails. Sorghum is an amazing source of protein, vitamins, niacin, and iron, which makes it valuable in countries where adequate nutrition is a challenge. Sorghum can be ground into flour and used to make a variety of baked goods; it is great for gluten-free baking. I love incorporating the whole cooked grain or toasted ground flour into the mix.

TRIGO (WHEAT)

The initial contact that colonizers had with the soil of the Americas and the Caribbean is believed to have been in the Antilles. Although they carried with them the seeds to plant and cultivate wheat, it was not known whether the crop would survive. The results in the Antilles were quite poor due to the humid, tropical conditions, which is not an ideal climate for wheat to thrive. In areas like México, maíz was the dominant crop, and still is today—however, wheat has become a major part of the average Latin American diet.

Admittedly, wheat itself has struggled to thrive as a crop in much of Latin America. One of the strongest and most popular types of wheat, white Sonoran wheat, is found in northwest México and is believed to be one of the oldest varieties of wheat to have survived in North America. Sonoran wheat was an important factor in the development of the flour tortilla due to its soft, elastic properties, and it plays a key role in baking in this region of North America.

In South America, Argentina's climate has allowed it to become the largest producer of wheat in the region, which has been a big factor in a surge of artisanal bakeries producing high-quality breads and pastries. Meanwhile, Brazil has been working diligently to develop wheat varieties that can thrive in tropical climates—if successful, Brazil could be a player in the conversations about being one of the world's largest wheat exporters.

For wheat to become flour, it is harvested and put through several stages of processing before it can end up in your mixing bowl. The berries of wheat are first analyzed and sorted through to remove foreign objects such as sticks, rocks, and debris before being tempered—a process where moisture levels are altered, which affects the grinding consistency. Finally, the grain can be milled and sifted, if desired. The amount of the wheat sifted out will determine the extraction rate of the flour. If you see a flour that is 100 percent extraction, it implies that the flour is composed of the entirety of the wheat berries grinded. An 85 percent extraction flour implies that 15 percent of the weight was sifted out, and so on and so forth.

Another important metric to understand about flour is its protein content and how that affects the baked goods that you make. To keep it simple, the higher the protein content of a flour, the stronger it will be in terms of allowing you to make things that need structure, like bread.

All things considered, Latin America is just one part of the world and you may not be living in it. So what type of wheat should you buy? It largely depends on where you live exactly, but following are general guidelines for the types of wheat that you should be able to find readily available at your local grocery stores and farmers' markets.

All-purpose Flour
The most common and versatile type of flour you can find is all-purpose flour, but not all of it is made the same. You want to make sure that you are using unbleached and unbromated flour—like the one produced by King Arthur Baking Company—to ensure that you are not consuming any chemicals. Typically, the type of wheat that is milled to make all-purpose flour varies, from hard wheat to a mixture of hard and soft wheats. After the milling process, the bran and germ are removed, leaving only the endosperm, which is what makes the flour lack any color. Once you have a good quality all-purpose flour, the possibilities of what you can make with it are endless.

Bread Flour

Like with all-purpose flour, ensure that you are buying bread flour that is neither bleached nor bromated. The main difference between these two "white" flours is that true bread flour will have a higher protein content, which results in your baked goods having the potential for more rise, structure, and chewiness. These are characteristics that one might want for different types of breads, but not necessarily for cakes or pastries. One thing to note is that I may use all-purpose flour and bread flour rather interchangeably in some bread recipes—I have become quite comfortable baking all types of bread with all-purpose flour, but if you cannot find an all-purpose flour that is strong enough, I would recommend you use bread flour for the bread recipes in this book.

Whole Wheat or Whole Grain Flour

As the name implies, a true whole wheat (or whole grain—I use these terms interchangeably) flour has none of the bran and germ sifted out and, therefore, utilizes the whole grain. This is the most delicious type of flour to bake with because its flavor and nutritional value are intact. I use whole grain flour in various increments for different recipes, but I encourage you to use it as desired and replace percentages of white flour with whole grain when possible. When it comes to feeding your sourdough starter, you definitely want to incorporate whole grain flour to keep it active and vigorous.

Rye Flour

While rye is not wheat, it is in the same family and has very similar functionalities. You can often find a few different types of rye flour, all dependent on how it was milled: light rye has less of the bran and germ intact, whereas whole grain rye flour includes it all. There is also medium rye, which is the middle ground and has characteristics of both light and dark rye. I recommend keeping rye flour in your kitchen, particularly for the maintenance and creation of your sourdough starter, since it is so nutrient-dense and potent. While not indigenous to Latin America, it is a common and commercially available flour that you are bound to come across.

Whole Spelt Flour

Spelt is thought to have been first cultivated in the Middle East and is one of the most widely used ancient grains that you can find today for making bread. Spelt has a weaker protein content than wheat, but offers soft and elastic textures to bread and pastries. When you use whole spelt, you can count on beautiful color and delicious, nutty flavor. Feel free to replace all-purpose flour in 10 percent increments to experiment with spelt.

Pastry and Cake Flour

Pastry flour and cake flour are both low in protein and therefore ideal for making cakes, quick breads, hojaldres, and any other delicate pastry. That said, I have to admit that I rarely keep either of these in stock at home since they are so specific to making certain things, and all-purpose flour does the job just fine. However, if you are making anything in chapter 5, chances are you can sub the all-purpose flour with pastry or cake flour.

SUGARS, SPICES, AND CHOCOLATE

A lot of pantry items that appear in almost every kitchen, like sugar and chocolate, may seem simple enough. But how often do you stop mid-recipe, hands coated in dough, a baked-goods aroma infusing your kitchen, to think about where these ingredients come from? I'm no historian, but I have been fascinated by the story associated with these baking staples.

ACHIOTE

Also known as annatto, achiote is native to the tropical areas of the Americas and is used to add color to foods. The flavor is deep and earthy, and I like to use it in the dough of pastelitos or empanadas, like Pastelitos de Perro (page 355) and Empanadas Salteñas (page 327). You can find it in most grocery stores in both paste and powdered form. One thing to note is that there is no good substitute for achiote, so if you really want to get that flavor, you've got to get the real thing! Head on over to a Central American grocery store ASAP.

Sugar, the Double-Edged Machete

Sugar provides much happiness to the modern-day consumer of baked goods. It is an ingredient that is consumed (often excessively) in several forms and is the backbone of countless desserts and pastries around the world. But our obsession with sugar, and all the delicate treats that are born of it, sits alongside the reality of what it took to create the modern multibillion-dollar sugar industry.

I could use this space to write about the different sugars I like to use when I bake, what makes them different in flavor and texture, and more of the usual cookbook ingredient monologue. But the story of sugar is integral in understanding the history of enslaved people in the Americas, and how that ultimately impacted our baking culture. (I will still talk to you about the different sugars that I use in this book, but that will come later. For now, class is in session.)

There is a dark, intense history behind the production of sugar in the Americas as it goes hand in hand with the perpetuation and expansion of slavery and the commodification of African and Indigenous people. Sugarcane production is one of the most laborious agricultural undertakings; there's a reason Europeans had not really attempted to do it back on their own land. Once they arrived to the "new" lands of the Americas, the colonists ultimately decided to use the labor of enslaved African people to catapult this industry into existence. In Brazil, Guyana, and Cuba, for example, once-fertile lands were devastated, and Indigenous and African lives were destroyed by the creation of sugar plantations.

Over time, Brazil became a major player in the sugar game via the Portuguese influx. They were able to afford more African people to enslave, which transformed the northeast of the land. Cane growers had crews of enslaved African people who would process the cane and deliver it to the mill as a way for the mill owners to cut costs. Today, Brazil is often the largest producer of sugarcane in the world (together with India, another world leader in sugarcane production), turning a treacherous past into a lucrative present and future—but lucrative for whom is something I cannot speak to.

In the late 1800s, there was a historically high number of enslaved people being transported across the Atlantic. Not so coincidentally, this was concurrent with increasingly high demand for sugar in Europe and the United States. Cuba had been doubling its sugar production year after year, and plantation owners were adamant about the continuation of the slave trade. Even after the United States abolished this form of slavery, Cuba continued to enslave African people up until 1886, due to the high demand for, and reliance on, sugar production. This ultimately created a fractured relationship among the ethnicities of people who lived on the island.

When it comes to contemporary sugar use in Latin America, there is a molded version of sugarcane extract that is present at any market you visit. Panela (also known as piloncillo in México because there is a cheese called panela) is made through an artisanal process where sugarcane juice is boiled and poured into molds to cool and harden. It is my favorite form of sugar to use while baking, and it makes a delicious syrup that you will see in some of the recipes in this book. In recipes, panela is usually grated or chopped before use. If grating, use the large holes of a box grater; do not use the finer side, because the small holes make a mushy paste. If you're measuring volumetrically (instead of by weight), lightly pack the grated panela into a measuring cup. Grating works better for uniform results, but a rough chop is much quicker if you're pressed for time.

If you don't have access to panela, you can use other sugars that are typical in baking, like granulated white sugar, light brown sugar, or dark brown sugar. I use these sugars interchangeably, depending on the flavor profile I'm seeking.

ANISE SEED

Anise seed is used around the world to flavor confections, alcohol, savory dishes, and baked goods. Native to Asia and the Middle East, the seed found its way to Latin America and has thrived there. Several recipes in this book include anise seed, not to be confused with star anise, although they both have notes of black licorice. Some of the most iconic baked goods and pastries of Latin America include anise seed, such as pan de muerto, picarones, and shecas. Stock up on anise as you bake your way through this book!

CANELA (CINNAMON)

True cinnamon is native to Sri Lanka, but it is now cultivated in several countries around the world. The Portuguese and Dutch attempted to establish monopolies on the spice within native cinnamon areas, but eventually these monopolies disappeared once cultivation in other parts of the world was known to be possible—for example, cinnamon trees can be successfully grown in South America and the West Indies. Interestingly, Mexican Cinnamon, known as canela, is imported from Sri Lanka, and the flavor profile suits the balance of Mexican cuisine. The versatility of cinnamon extends from savory cooking to sweet baking, and there are many dishes that rely on it.

CHOCOLATE

It's hard to imagine the world of baking without chocolate. It's actually hard to imagine the world *in general* without chocolate. But it is unfortunate that unhealthy, commercialized versions of chocolate take up the most space in our markets and our minds. But exactly where does chocolate come from, and how did it get to be such a widely produced product today? The answer lies in precolonial Mesoamerican civilizations, specifically the Maya and the Olmec.

Etymologists believe the origin of the word chocolate originates from an Aztec word, *xocoatl*, which roughly translates to "bitter water" and is the word used to describe what they used to make with cacao beans. For a long period of history, cacao beans were used to make drinks with no additional sugar, and the beans themselves are thought to have served as valuable currency. Colonists did not enjoy the version of cacao that was presented to them, so they began to add honey and sugar to the mix. This is the origin of the sugar-laden chocolate industry we know today—along with

the work of a Dutch chemist who created a powdered form of chocolate.

When it comes to baking at home, there are several chocolate types that you might encounter at the grocery store. I typically use semisweet chocolate that has roughly 50 percent cacao solid content. Every now and then I'll use a darker chocolate for a deeper flavor profile, usually around 70 percent, but it really is about personal preference. Both semisweet and dark chocolates are great for the recipes in this book that call for chocolate.

VANILLA

One of the most popular ingredients used in baking around the world is vanilla. It can be used in many forms when you are baking, such as an extract or paste. The initial cultivation of vanilla is believed to have come from the Indigenous Totonac in the region currently known as Veracruz. The Totonac were ultimately conquered by the Aztec and the vanilla game was taken to a new level: vanilla and cocoa together! This combination was the key to making xocolatl, which is similar to what we now know as hot chocolate, and is the reason that Europeans ultimately fell in love with vanilla.

At this point, there was an attempt to transplant vines from México to other tropical areas to see if vanilla could grow there. Ultimately, it was discovered that a particular bee in México is the only one able to pollinate the vanilla orchard; it does not exist anywhere else in the world. But the code was finally cracked by an enslaved boy named Edmond Albius, who created a hand pollination technique that allowed vanilla to flourish in other parts of the world.

If you are in the store and looking for the best type of vanilla to use, you will likely come across several options, and the best options tend to be quite pricey. It's okay to use a cheaper vanilla extract if needed. But I currently enjoy using a Bourbon vanilla paste—which draws its name from the group of islands that have excellent vanilla growing capabilities and not the whiskey.

OTHER INGREDIENTS

FATS

Fat can create a rich texture in your bakes, whether by creaming sugar with butter to make cookies or infusing lard into dough for a creamy loaf. In this book you will see lard used frequently, as it is common in

Latin America to enrich bakes with animal fat. (If you don't eat meat, use vegetable oil as a substitute.) Butter is one of the most premium and delicious fats that we have in existence, and you will see quite a bit of it in the enriched sourdough and dessert sections. I always use unsalted butter so that the salt content in the bake can be controlled. Olive oil is also a great fat to use when baking breads as it offers its own flavor when infused into the dough, and it aids in creating a crisp, crackling crust on the exterior of bakes, if desired.

When making bread with a mixer, I like to add fat into the mix after the initial gluten structure has developed and is strong enough to absorb properly without tearing the dough or disrupting the gluten formation process. If mixing by hand, a ratio of half fat up front and half later on, once there is some structure in the mix, is my go-to method, as adding a high percentage of fat by hand into dough can be quite challenging.

MILKS

Throughout this book you'll see doughs made with milk or coconut milk, as the extra fat content creates a stable environment for dough that's heavily enriched or laminated with butter. This creates softer, flakier baked goods. If you want a substitute for cow's milk in a recipe that calls for it, my preference is to use canned full-fat coconut milk. I don't advise using oat, soy, flax, or other milks that do not tend to have enough fat in them to do the job correctly.

SALT

Salt plays several roles in the baking process, and there are a variety of different salts out there that you can use when baking. When baking bread, the percentage of salt that is added to recipes is typically quite low (usually around 2 percent of the amount of flour used) but it has a tremendous impact on the end product.

These recipes have been tested using Diamond Crystal kosher salt, but you can use sea salt or any fine salt that isn't iodized. If you use another type of salt, I suggest you weigh it with a scale for consistent salinity, as the same weight of various salts may fill a measuring spoon differently.

WATER

One of the most important ingredients in baking is water, as it is responsible for the distribution of ingredients such as yeast and dictates the fermentation of dough through its temperature. I have baked in many different cities and countries using water straight from the tap, and have found it to make perfectly delicious baked goods. If I'm drinking water somewhere, I always assume that it is good for baking.

While I don't usually take the temperature of the water when I bake, it is a good idea to do so if you want to have more control and feel more secure as a baker (see the Temperature, Climate, and Altitude section on page 27 for more guidance). At the end of the day, I recommend leaning into your intuition and instinct while baking. For example, is it a cold day in your kitchen? If so, use some warm water. What does warm mean? Well, when you touch it, it doesn't feel too hot and it doesn't burn you, but it is also not cold. You get the idea.

WEIGHT CONVERSIONS

As mentioned elsewhere in the book, these recipes were developed using gram weights. Weighing your ingredients is the most precise way to bake. I've included volumetric conversions to measuring cups and spoons within each recipe. You can find a chart of all the conversions we made on page 366. In some cases, this means that a cup of flour may be treated as weighing slightly more or less from recipe to recipe, in order to avoid cup measurements that are unwieldy.

Note that the recipes that use preferments, including the sourdough starter, always have you make a little more than the recipe will call for. We use 200 g per cup of sourdough starter as a guide. But as always, if you are concerned about precision, weigh the ingredients!

TOOLS

BAKING PANS

Loaf Pans
Loaf pans (or tins) come in many shapes and sizes and are important for making quick breads and sandwich loaves, or pan de molde. I recommend a loaf pan that measures 9 by 5 inches and is 2.8 inches tall—but you can adapt any recipe to any loaf pan by using your instincts. For example, if you are going to bake a loaf,

your dough or batter should fill the pan a little over halfway—not overflowing or close to the top—when you start the proofing process. If you are making a quick bread, such as the bizcocho de naranja, the pan should also be just shy of more than halfway full.

Having these pans is a great way to bake off any dough that might have overproofed in your kitchen or had a shaping issue, because it will hold the dough in place and create a useable shape for your loaf.

Other Baking Pans

I was at a friend's house once and noticed that he had several types of baking pans: round, square, flat, rimmed...so many it felt like I was in a bakery for a second. I was curious because I didn't know that he baked. When I asked him what he used the pans for, he responded that he didn't know, he never used them, and that he doesn't understand how there could be so many different types of pans for baking. Perhaps you, too, don't really understand why there are different shapes, sizes, and types of baking pans.

Starting with the basics, a round cake pan is obviously used to bake round cakes. If you get a few of them and put your batter in them, you can make a multilayer cake. I'm not an obsessive cake baker, but the round cake pan is important to me for all the delicious Argentine pizzas in the sourdough chapter of this book. A 12-inch round cake pan works perfectly for making them, but of course there are several sweet treats in this book for which having a round cake pan comes through pretty clutch, like the Quesadilla Hondureña/Salvadoreña (page 264). Having size options helps. The most common pan diameter is 9 inches.

In general, I like to get baking pans that are not coated with nonstick material. I also like my rimmed sheet pans to be regular-degular. For loaf and cake pans, I do like nonstick. I like the heavier ones because you can slam them down to help release your cakes and loaves.

BAKING STONE OR STEEL

I prefer to bake exclusively on a baking stone or steel in my home oven and not deal with the fuss of cast-iron pots and pans. I've made this choice because I'm not too interested in the aesthetic result of my loaves (although to be fair they still come out top-notch). To properly cook many artisanal-style loaves, having that concentration of high heat is important in getting your oven spring (when the dough expands upon contact with heat), and I've found that a high-quality stone or steel in a home oven with some ice to create moisture works perfectly fine. I would opt for a stone or steel at least 12 by 12 inches but it really depends on your oven size. A bigger oven means a bigger stone or steel, which means you can really crank things up and get a few loaves in there.

BENCH AND DOUGH SCRAPERS

It was only recently that I realized the difference between a bench and a dough scraper, when my friend Serhan was over and we were making pizza. He asked me for a dough scraper, so I reached into the drawer and pulled out my trusty wooden-handled metal bench scraper. I handed it to him, and he said, "Bryan...that's a bench scraper. Don't you have a dough scraper?" Since that day, I have indeed purchased a dough scraper, which is a flexible plastic tool that is used to scrape dough out of mixing bowls effectively so that you don't leave any dough scraps behind. The bench scraper is critical for different applications, as it is made of metal and typically has a sturdy handle that allows you to divide your dough after it ferments as well as clean off the "bench"—which is probably just your kitchen countertop.

BOWLS AND TUBS

It is ideal to have bowls and tubs to put your dough in after it has been mixed. Bakers have different preferences, but at home I use a large glass mixing bowl so that I can see the activity in the dough as it ferments. In my bakery, glass is not ideal as it can pose danger during production if broken. So at work I use bus tubs, Cambros, or other nonbreakable containers to ferment my doughs. Feel free to use the classic metal mixing bowls that you can find in most stores, but make sure you have something deep enough to fit lots of dough.

DIGITAL SCALE

If you want to bake excellent and delicious things at home, the most important tool in your kitchen is a food scale. You've now heard me say this multiple times, but using a scale to weigh your ingredients is going to give you the most accurate measurements when baking. In my opinion it is also way easier to measure by weight than to figure out the different cups and spoons one might need. In any case, I have provided the recipes in this book in gram, and cup, and spoon measures so that no matter your preference, you'll be able to bake. Just note that the weighed measurements will always be the most accurate since they are the baseline.

FLAX LINEN CLOTH

When it comes to proofing bread, there are several ways you can get it done at home. My preferred method is to use either a cutting board or a flax linen cloth. You can find these online or at a fabric store, and you can cut the cloth to whatever size works for you. The reason I love to use a linen canvas cloth is because it helps the loaf retain its shape and takes up less space in the fridge than having multiple baskets. For example, if I shaped four loaves, I could line a sheet pan with canvas cloth and dust it with wheat bran and place the loaves on the cloth, dividing as I go (see the Techniques section on page 22–23 for some photographs of this). That sheet pan will fit cleanly on one shelf in the fridge with no issues. Additionally, I can size my loaves however I want, and not have the size of a basket dictate my shaping process.

LOADING PEEL

Because I opt to bake with a stone or steel, I need a way to get the dough into the oven while it's piping hot. A wooden loading peel is the way for me, but if you have a thin wooden cutting board, you can use this, too, with the right technique. I once worked at a bakery where we loaded loaves on upside-down sheet pans when times got tough!

PARCHMENT PAPER

It is important not to put any of your doughs directly on a sheet pan, to prevent them from sticking and burning. The most common solution to this problem is using unbleached parchment paper. You can also use a little bit of baking spray before you put the parchment paper on the pan to help it stay put, but this is mostly effective if you have a convection fan that blows the paper around.

PIPING BAG WITH TIPS

From piping churros into hot oil to filling your alfajores, piping bags and tips help create a stress-free dessert-making experience. That said, if you don't have these on hand, use a sturdy ziplock bag with a bottom corner carefully cut off.

ROLLING PIN

A good rolling pin goes a long way—whether I am making medialunas or masa hojaldre, a solid pin with handles is the way I like to get down. The heavy weight of the pin means you have to apply less force. There are several rolling pin styles from tapered edges to straight pine. Find one that suits your style and gets you baking often.

SPATULAS

There are several recipes in this book that require the use of a heat resistant spatula. It's important to have these spatulas to fold batters, stir dulces (jams) while they cook, or even spread frostings on tortas (cakes) and galletas (cookies). For optimal results in spreading batters and frostings, an offset spatula is your best bet.

STAND MIXER

One of the most important tools in my kitchen is a high-quality stand mixer that can mix dough repeatedly without overheating. The mixer I use has a seven-quart bowl and 500 watts of power. If you can't invest in a high-quality stand mixer, don't worry! You can use the mixing techniques in the next chapter to get through any of the recipes in this book with just your two hands.

THERMOMETERS

I recommend having a few types of thermometers so that you can make sure you are on top of different temperatures—let's not forget that temperature is one of the most important variables in baking. I grew up in the South, but if you live in an area with real changes in the seasons, it might be wise to keep a general room thermometer showing the ambient temperature in your kitchen. In terms of baking, it's important to make sure your stone/steel/cast iron is exactly as hot as it needs to be, so an infrared thermometer gun is helpful. Finally, you'll be frying a few delicious treats, such as Peruvian picarones, so it is important to have a stick thermometer to make sure the oil temperature is right where it needs to be.

CH 2

TECHNIQUES

Baking is a combination of technique and intuition. There truly is no right or wrong way to go about baking, but what follows is my roadmap for how I approach the many different steps that you encounter when baking breads, pastries, and savory treats.

I encourage you to take your time and seek to really understand this section, but know that you do not need to master anything here to get started with this book. The best teacher is experience.

LEAVENING

~~~~~

There are various ways to make baked goods rise, and none of them are right or wrong. In Latin America, commercial yeast is very common and is used for several quintessential breads, like bolillos and pan dulce. In fact, commercial yeast is used all over the world to make lots of spectacular baked goods, and it's something that I find myself using more often than not.

As a baker, I prefer to use the leavening method that yields the most pleasant result when it comes to taste and texture, given the type of baked good I am making. Sometimes that is a packet of active dry yeast, sometimes that is a preferment (a mixture of water and flour that has already started its fermentation process and is subsequently added into your mix—I'll get into more detail on this later).

You will find the breads in this book to be a mix of straight doughs (yeast and no preferment), hybrid doughs (using preferments and yeast at the same time), and sourdoughs (meaning there is only a mixture of flour and water with no added commercial yeast). I wrote these recipes based on my personal preference when making each type of bread, while trying to attain a traditional texture and appearance.

YEASTS

Instant Yeast
For the fastest results, turn to instant yeast. This is commercially processed, dried yeast that can be added straight into the flour during the mixing process. There is no need to rehydrate or proof this yeast, making it a convenient option for new bakers or those needing to bake quickly. Instant yeast works well for both sweet and rustic doughs. To store, it must be refrigerated after opening and generally lasts several months in the fridge. You can find instant yeast at most grocery stores.

Active Dry Yeast
Similar to instant yeast, active dry yeast can be found at most grocery stores and provides an easy leavening method for baked goods. The difference is that this type of yeast technically needs to be rehydrated and proofed before it is used (I say *technically* because I have also had success just throwing active dry yeast into a mix). To rehydrate active dry yeast, whisk a bit of warm water with your desired yeast amount in a small bowl and wait for it to become frothy. Active dry yeast must be refrigerated and, like instant yeast, keeps for several months.

Fresh Yeast

Fresh yeast is also known as cake yeast and is less commonly found at grocery stores, although bigger specialty stores may carry it. You can find it online but before you order it, be aware that it only lasts for a couple of weeks in your fridge. Fresh yeast is used widely in bakeries because it has advantages when it comes to longer, slower fermentation. The activity of the yeast in this variety lasts longer and, in turn, will assure you get a nice rise at different stages in the dough-making and baking process. I absolutely love using fresh yeast when possible as it creates softer textures in the dough and milkier flavors.

PREFERMENTS

If you are comfortable baking straight, yeasted doughs, you might be craving a little more flavor in your bread. There are several ways to add more complex texture and flavor to your dough, and my favorite approach is a preferment. As the name suggests, this is a mixture of flour, water, and yeast that is fermented ahead of time. Once the mixture reaches its peak, it is added to the final dough mix.

In this book, you will see preferments used with hybrid doughs. This means that the doughs are made using a combination of yeast and a preferment, as opposed to just one or the other. The recipes that use preferments will have the exact measurements specific to that recipe, but here are some simple examples of what a preferment mixture looks like.

Yeasted Preferment, liquid

This preferment is made twelve hours before you intend to start the final dough-mixing process using instant, active dry, or fresh yeast. This is a relatively wet mixture, so do not be concerned if it seems very sticky. Using a yeasted preferment offers a milky, creamy, and slightly tangy flavor profile in bread. It also gives dough a light, airy interior and aids in the development of a nice, crisp crust. For best results, use either all-purpose flour or bread flour.

    100 g (¾ c + 1 Tbsp) all-purpose flour
    100 g (¼ c + 3 Tbsp) warm water
    1 g (¼ tsp) instant yeast (just a pinch)

Combine ingredients in a jar or bowl that has a lid, and mix until it is all incorporated and there is no dry flour left. Cover and let rest in a warm place, ideally between 70° and 80°F, for 12 hours. Use according to the instructions in the recipe.

Yeasted Preferment, stiff

This preferment is made six hours before you intend on starting the final dough-mixing process using instant yeast. This will be a relatively dry mixture, so do not be concerned if it seems a little stiff. This works well when you do not want too high a water content in your dough, while still strengthening the gluten structure as well as offering those creamy, funky flavor notes.

    100 g (¾ c + 1 Tbsp) all-purpose flour
    50 g (3½ Tbsp) warm water
    1 g (¼ tsp) instant yeast

Combine ingredients in a jar or bowl that has a lid, and mix until it is all incorporated and there is no dry flour left.

Cover and let rest in a warm place, ideally about 70°F, for 6 hours.

Use according to the instructions in the recipe.

Mixing a stiff yeasted preferment

Sourdough Preferment

This is your sourdough starter, which uses no form of commercial yeast in the mixture. Rather, the wild yeasts that exist in the air are harvested and cultivated to create natural fermentation. It will take you roughly five days to get sourdough starter ready to go (see the Temperature, Climate, and Altitude section on page 27 for more detail). From there you will need to create the preferment that goes into the final dough mix, which means taking the active starter and adding flour and water to it, and letting it sit for a little while. The specifics vary from recipe to recipe, so check the instructions for the timing on when it will be ready to mix into the dough.

The sourdough starter you will create in this book is made of whole wheat flour with a pinch of amaranth flour—the earthiness of the amaranth will help get things going very quickly and aid in achieving a nice, funky flavor.

Day One: To start making your sourdough, use any cereal bowl or small container with a lid. You don't need to stress about this. People have been doing this for thousands of years. Make sure that you weigh your container—this will make future feedings easier since you can subtract the container weight at any point in time to know how much your mixture weighs. I typically mix with a fork or with my bare hand, depending on the size of the container.

Mix 25 g (3 Tbsp) whole wheat flour, 5 g (2 tsp) amaranth flour, and 20 g (1½ Tbsp) water. Cover and leave at room temperature for 24 hours. The ideal room temperature is between 72° and 85°F. The ideal water temperature is between 80° and 85°F. By no means do you need to stress out about these temperatures—use them as a guide.

Day Two: You will probably see some sort of activity depending on how warm your kitchen is. The smell of the starter at this point may not be so pleasant, but do not let this concern you. Keep half of the mixture and feed it another 25 g (3 Tbsp) whole wheat flour, 5 g (2 tsp) amaranth, and 20 g (1½ Tbsp) water. Cover and let rest another 24 hours.

Day Three: You may see the markings from a "rise and fall" of the new starter, along with nice bubbles and pockets. This is good. The smell should be getting a bit more bearable. Repeat the Day Two process: keep half the mixture and add 25 g (3 Tbsp) whole wheat flour, 5 g (2 tsp) amaranth, and 20 g (1½ Tbsp) water.

Day Four: There will be a good volume increase and a consistent amount of bubbling and air pockets. You should have a somewhat sweet and sour smell that is pleasant. You're in the home stretch. Repeat the steps in Day Two one more time.

Day Five: By now, you have a ripe and sweet-smelling sourdough starter. You should see some movement of the bubbles when you move the container and a structure when you stir it. You are now ready to build a sourdough preferment: the sourdough mixture that goes directly into your final dough mix and makes your bread rise. There are many, many ways to build a sourdough preferment, so make sure to read each specific recipe. While each recipe will have a distinct build, here is an example of a reliable feeding.

Mixing a sourdough preferment

SAMPLE SOURDOUGH PREFERMENT MIX

50 g (¼ c) mature sourdough starter
75 g (scant ⅔ c) all-purpose flour
25 g (3 Tbsp) whole wheat flour
75 g (¼ c + 1 Tbsp) warm water

Mix all ingredients in a container with a fork and let rest at room temperature*. Depending on your climate and room temperature, it should double in size in 3 to 4 hours. You can use it immediately or put it in the fridge and use it later. Pay close attention to the recipe for instructions on when to use the specific build.

*Note that the ambient temperature for both these processes is ideally 72° to 80°F.

SOURDOUGH PREFERMENT—SWEET AND STIFF

When making enriched sourdough bread, it can be important to counterbalance the acidity that builds up in your sourdough starter with a little bit of sugar. This helps neutralize any overly "sour" flavor that might be present in your preferment and allows you to enjoy the sweet and smooth texture of your enriched sourdough bread, for example a concha or a semita.

I usually mix this preferment as a stiffer mixture with a 1-to-1-to-2 ratio (by weight) of starter, water, and flour, plus sugar equal to 15 percent of the flour weight. For example, to 50 g of sourdough I would add 50 g of water, 100 g of flour, and 15 g of sugar.

A Note on Chemical Leaveners

There are other ways to make baked goods rise that do not include any yeast whatsoever. Typically, you'll see tortas (cakes) and galletas (cookies) made with baking soda or baking powder. These agents utilize carbon dioxide by trapping it into your mixture, which in turn causes doughs and batters to rise in the oven. In this book, you will see the use of these chemical leavening agents specifically in the "Desserts and Pastries" chapter.

CONVERTING BETWEEN YEASTED AND SOURDOUGH RECIPES

~~~~~

I love to bake with sourdough starter. The depth of flavor that I am able to achieve combined with how fun the overall process is makes me happy. However, many breads and leavened pastries in Latin America are not traditionally made with sourdough. Each recipe in this book is written to include the leavening technique that gives the final bake a texture, color, and flavor that, *in my opinion*, best suits that particular baked good.

You may not be ready to make something only with sourdough as you are just starting your baking journey. Or you might be an experienced baker and might not want to use commercialized yeasts. So, I believe it is important that *you* as a baker are able to make any of this book's bread recipes with your preferred method of leavening. This section will show how I convert recipes to use different types of yeast, regardless of how they are written.

Keep in mind that this is not an exact science, and you must use your intuition to determine how the dough looks and feels when moving on to the next step in your baking process.

These conversions only make sense when measuring by weight.

COMMERCIAL YEASTS:
INSTANT YEAST ↔ ACTIVE DRY YEAST ↔ FRESH YEAST

First, let's start with a simple conversion between the three types of commercial yeast. They each have different potency but get you to the same place in the end. Use the chart below to make conversions from one to another. Active dry yeast is 25 percent less potent than instant yeast, so you need to use 25 percent more of it. You need to use three times as much fresh yeast as instant yeast.

INSTANT	ACTIVE DRY	FRESH
3 g	3.75 g	9 g
1 tsp	1¼ tsp	1 Tbsp (3 tsp)

SOURDOUGH ↔ COMMERCIAL YEASTS

In addition to converting from one type of yeast to another, you can also replace commercial yeast with sourdough preferments. How much you need of the preferment depends not only on how much flour you have in the recipe, but whether the dough is enriched or not. Enrichment refers to incorporating sugar, fat, eggs, or dairy into the dough.

For non-enriched dough, meaning a dough made primarily of flour, water, and salt, I use the following formula to convert from yeast to sourdough:

(Flour called for in recipe) × 0.2 = amount of sourdough preferment to use.

For example, if the recipe calls for 300 g of flour, use 60 g of sourdough preferment in place of the commercial yeast requested in the recipe.

For enriched dough, the percentage is higher. This is because the enriching items disrupt gluten development and fermentation. For a yeasted enriched dough, I take 35 percent of the flour amount and that is the amount of sweet, stiff preferment I use.

(Flour called for in recipe) × 0.35 = amount of preferment to use.

So the 300 g of flour in an enriched dough would need 105 g of preferment.

To convert from sourdough preferment to commercial instant yeast, I use the following formula:

(Flour called for in recipe) × 0.005 = amount of instant yeast to use.

For instance, if the recipe calls for 300 g of flour, I would use 1.5 g of instant yeast.

Fermentation and proofing times

So, the above solves the issue of how much yeast or sourdough to use. Now it is time to adjust the fermentation and proofing times. You will learn more about what to look for when it comes to initial fermentation and proofing in the next technique section, but following are some general guidelines.

Rustic Sourdough: This typically needs a 4- to 5-hour bulk fermentation, which is the initial rise where the dough rises in bulk. This is then usually followed by a minimum 12-hour cold proof in the refrigerator, ideally around 40°F, or a 3- to 4-hour room temperature proof, in the 75° to 80°F range.

Enriched Sourdough: Any enriched sourdough will benefit from a fermentation in the refrigerator. It typically needs a 4- to 5-hour bulk fermentation at room temperature. That is followed by either an 8- to 12-hour cold fermentation in bulk that is then shaped and proofed at room temperature for 3 more hours, or skip the cold bulk fermentation and immediately divide and shape the dough, followed by proofing at room temperature for 3 hours.

Rustic Yeasted: Typically needs a 2- to 3-hour bulk fermentation at room temperature, followed by shaping and then a 2-hour proof.

Enriched Yeasted: Typically needs a 2- to 3-hour bulk fermentation at room temperature, followed by shaping and then a 2-hour proof.

All these theories are temperature dependent. Later, you will learn about how temperature, climate, and altitude might affect your baking.

MIXING, SHAPING, AND BAKING BREAD

～～～～～

In the bread chapters of this book, I specify my preferred mixing method for each recipe. Remember that this is just my preference, and you do not need to stress about doing it the way that I prefer. Hand mixing is the oldest bread baking technique out there, and I believe that mixing dough by hand should be the entry point to anyone who wants to bake bread.

If a dough feels too wet, don't be afraid to get it into your stand mixer with a dough hook attachment, add a little more flour, and get it strengthened. (Working dough activates the gluten, making it "stronger.") While each recipe gives you specifics on how to bring the dough together, following are some general tips.

I'm going to break this up into two parts: **rustic bread**, like bolillos or pan chuta, and **enriched loaves**, like semitas or conchas. Each baked good in this book can be made without the assistance of a machine, as long as you are patient and pay attention to the variables at hand.

RUSTIC BREAD

Hand Mixing

Hand mixing dough is one of the most relaxing things I've ever done in my life. From quiet moments in my home kitchen, to adapting to a new climate in the Andes Mountains, to dealing with a broken mixer during an overnight shift at a large bakery, I've had plenty of moments to work on my hand-mixing technique.

Adding the preferment

Adding flour

Incorporating flour, preferment, water

Adding salt

Squeezing salt

Kneading

The most basic form of bread that you can make is what I call pan rústico, or rustic bread—essentially any loaf that has only three or four total ingredients, or anything without high percentages of enriching items like milk, eggs, or fat. There are two ways you can start these mixes:

1. In a mixing bowl, add a percentage of the final water amount along with any preferment that is being called for, or

2. Add a percentage of the final water being called for along with the flour amount (no preferment).

First, let's address why you would want to withhold water from the mix. I typically find it easier to mix by hand if I gradually add the water into the mix over time, as opposed to incorporating it all at once. This will allow for easier initial gluten formation and prevent you from ending up with a soupy mess. **For each recipe, pay attention to the amount of water to withhold when starting your mix.**

In step 1 above, adding the preferment in the beginning stage means that as soon as the flour is mixed in, your bulk fermentation time has started. In step 2, letting the flour set with the water allows the dough to build up considerable strength before fermentation begins—once you later add the preferment, you can start your timer on fermentation.

Once your initial mix is done and you have let the dough rest, you can start gradually adding in some water, always reserving the last bit of water to add with your salt. Salt competes for hydration and I find that adding it at the end works best for me. When mixing by hand to add water and salt, I squeeze the dough with both hands until the side of my mixing bowl runs clean and you can tell it has been fully absorbed. You do not necessarily want to knead these doughs, as the resting time will help strengthen them.

For rustic doughs that are only slightly enriched with lard or oil, it is best to add the enrichments right before adding the salt or with the salt—by hand, I like to just lather the fat over the surface of the dough and squeeze/turn the dough until it is absorbed and the dough surface smooths out again.

Finalizing the Mix

One of the most important things at the end stage of mixing for me is the transfer of the dough to a clean vessel—a bowl, a tub, a Cambro container. Whatever bowl I mix it in will have clumps of hardened dry dough and flour. The bowl is not oiled so the dough sticks.

I like to transfer the dough to a clean, lightly oiled bowl. It makes it easier to remove the dough for stretches and folds, or to divide it, without sticking to the bowl and ripping up the gluten network.

Depending on the bread and dietary preferences (the oil you use can impact the flavor), I typically have neutral oils like canola, grapeseed, or sunflower on deck. Olive oil can work but know that it will add a slight amount of flavor into your dough. For enriched doughs, I grease my bowl with softened butter. The dough already has butter in it, so why introduce a different fat?

Always cover during the bulk ferment. I use containers that come with lids, but you can use a damp kitchen cloth or plastic wrap. If going into the fridge to ferment overnight, or during the winter, use plastic wrap and seal completely so the cold air does not form a skin on it or dry it out.

Machine Mixing

If you have a reliable stand mixer with at least a six-quart bowl capacity, machine mixing your dough makes life easy. I typically will only mix 1 kilogram of flour at a time with the dough hook, but it gets the entire mixing process done in under 10 minutes. I usually start by adding the preferment, water, and flour in all at once. Unless it is a dough heavy in whole grains, I won't bother letting the flour and water rest since the machine can strengthen the dough very quickly. After a brief mix on low speed, I'll slowly add the remaining water and salt, increasing to a high speed at the end until the dough is smooth. Make sure to check each recipe for specific instructions.

Stretching and Folding

If there's commercial yeast in the dough, I tend not to bother with stretching and folding to help build the gluten network. But natural leavening and wetter doughs (80%+) tend to need some assistance in developing their gluten networks, and that's where stretches and folds come in handy during bulk fermentation.

For a dough that has no commercial yeast in it, the natural fermentation process takes a long time to build the gluten network. You can strengthen the dough by stretching and folding it into itself. In a bowl, I'll use one hand to reach toward the bottom of the dough, pull it up as high as I can, without tearing or breaking, and fold it so that the tip of that dough lands on the surface of the rest of the dough. I'll rotate the bowl and do that about 4 times total around the circumference of the dough. I'll then cover it again and let it keep fermenting. Depending on the recipe, some breads need more strengthening than others. But the more you do it, in increments of 30 to 45 minutes at room temperature, the stronger your dough becomes. However, you don't want to do too many folds as this will ultimately just rip up the developing network of gluten.

Shaping

There's a lot that goes down when it comes to shaping. The objective of shaping is to give the dough structure again, before the bake, but after it's been cut and divided. One of the most important things that I've realized when it comes to shaping is that you really have to allow yourself to become fearless when handling the dough itself. If you are new to baking, it is definitely not something that will happen right away; you will need to develop a little bit of an instinct when it comes to handling dough to shape it.

The more dough you shape, the better you will become. At one bakery I worked in, there were thousands of pieces of bread shaped each shift and it was done at an alarmingly fast pace. My first couple of weeks were terrifying as I didn't want to make mistakes. I was a decent shaper, but not even close to the speed of my colleagues. Over time, that fear turned to confidence and speed, and I shaped happily ever after. Lucky for you, there is no pressure to perform as a shaper in your home kitchen, so you can take your time and learn at your own speed. Here are some of my favorite shapes, but keep in mind that each recipe will give you guidance on any specific requirements.

One thing to note is the concept of *pre-shaping*, which is what it sounds like: a shape before the final shape. This step is entirely optional, in my opinion, but can be helpful if you are struggling to attain a nice, tight, uniform shape. After dividing your dough, you can lightly shape it into a round circle, applying only a light amount of tension (enough to smooth out the top of the surface). Let the dough rest and relax for up to 45 minutes before applying the final shape. This allows the dough to relax after being cut, and creates more elasticity within the dough so that shaping, especially a wetter dough, becomes easier.

Turning dough out after fermentation

Dividing the dough

Folding both sides in

Rolling to create tension

Pinching ends to make final shape

Large Round: For larger rustic breads like Pan Rústico de Sorgo y Amaranto Tostado or Pan Casero (pages 106 and 82) shaping and proofing in a round shape is one of the easier things you can do. Simply take your dough, flour your work surface, and place the smoother side of the divided dough on the floured work surface. Next, fold multiple sides of the dough into the middle so that the dough starts to take on a round shape around the edges. Flip it upside down so that the smoother part of the dough is on top. Use your hands to tighten the seam on the bottom by pulling it toward you and rotating it. Repeat the tightening process and you now have a round dough shape.

Oval: The most common shape for a rustic loaf of bread is an oval, and there are a few ways you can get there. The most important thing to remember is that you should keep it simple and shape with confidence—flour can be your friend, but too much will prevent the dough from sealing up properly.

Oval shape 1—no preshape: After dividing your dough, do your best to pat it down on a lightly floured work surface and form into triangle shape. Roll the dough into a cylinder and apply tension using your thumbs to seal it up.

Oval Shape 2—preshape: Preshape the dough into a round shape and let it rest until it expands slightly. Flour the top of the dough and flip over. Form into a triangle shape and roll into a cylinder while applying tension using your thumbs.

Proofing

The proofing stage starts after you apply the final shape to your dough, which means it is the second rise that a dough gets (essentially the second stage of fermentation). Before you bake your bread, you want to proof the dough until it is slightly bouncy and has increased in size. If you are proofing your bread at room temperature, you will most likely notice a more significant difference in the size of the dough after it has fully proofed. Conversely, a cold proof (also known as "retarding") will yield a much less significant size change in the dough, but you will notice it become full, smooth, and slightly bouncy to the touch. The two most important things to take away when it comes to proofing is recognizing when something is either underproofed or overproofed.

Overproofed: As the name implies, the dough has gone over the time needed for a proper bake. The dough will start to collapse immediately if you touch or move it. If it's increased more than double in size and is difficult to handle, touch, or score, then the dough is most likely overproofed and your bake will turn out flat.

Underproofed: The dough will feel stiff, a little firm, and might not be very bouncy. If you poke the dough, it will bounce all the way back, and will feel heavy and small.

Proofing dough on a bran-dusted cloth

Folding the cloth to separate

Alternatively, proof on a bran-dusted cutting board

Baking

My favorite part of the baking process is, well, baking! You will notice in a lot of the recipes in this book for rustic style breads that I use either a pizza stone, steel, or cast-iron pot to bake bread. Lots of bakers around the world use these tools to make delicious, crunchy breads.

Pizza Stone/Steel: To bake in your home oven on a stone or steel, it is critical that you place it in the oven before you preheat your oven. This ensures that you get the hottest possible surface to load your breads onto and get good oven spring. Additionally, steaming a home oven can be difficult since these ovens are not meant to retain steam the way a professional bread oven does, but some steam is better than none. Steam is important in that it allows the bread to grow without the crust hardening too quickly. To steam a home oven with a pizza stone/steel inside, I typically drop ice onto the stone/steel and load a tray of ice into the bottom of the oven right before loading the bread.

Cast Iron: Baking bread in a cast-iron pot is a tried and true way of making high-quality breads at home. The best type of cast iron to get is a Dutch oven with a lid. Like the pizza stone/steel, preheating this in your oven for a solid hour before baking is the best way to make sure you get fantastic oven spring out of your loaf. The biggest benefit is that the lid creates a steamy environment for your bread, and you don't have to worry about the steam escaping the oven.

ENRICHED BREAD

Hand Mixing

Enriched doughs are those that contain high amounts of sugars and fats, allowing your bread to have a sweet, soft, and creamy texture. The key to mixing these doughs by hand is knowing when to incorporate the fat, as adding it all at once can impede your gluten development. Combining the flour and water or milk first can help create a strong network at the beginning, then you can add eggs and sugar, squeezing and kneading until incorporated. You'll want to add your butter in chunks, making sure it is softened. Some of these recipes call for a good amount of butter and I prefer to machine mix them, but you can do it by hand by being patient and knowing what to look for.

First, the dough should always smooth out after you add anything to it and work it for a few minutes. You don't want to continue adding butter or fat if the dough has not smoothed back out after working it. Second, kneading is your friend for these doughs to kick-start things, and once the butter content makes the dough too sticky to knead, you can stretch it and fold it to create strength. The key here is to keep a bowl of water next to your mixing station so that you can wet your hands and handle the dough without it sticking to you.

Adding proofed dough to parchment-lined peel

Scoring

Loading onto preheated stone or steel

Machine Mixing

The most important part in mixing enriched breads with your stand mixer is making sure you don't add all the fat at once. If you are mixing a recipe that calls for a lot of butter, for example, I will typically withhold a portion of it and add it at the end of the mix on a higher speed with the salt to finish off the dough. This allows the dough to develop strength without being overloaded by fats or salt, which will compete for hydration and potentially hinder the creation of a strong, smooth dough.

Shaping

Enriched doughs can be sticky if they are heavily enriched with eggs and butter, but most often they are slightly stiffer than rustic doughs. The most common types of shapes for enriched breads are bun-size rounds or cylinders that fit into a loaf pan. Don't be afraid to flour your work surface when it comes to shaping enriched doughs; this will keep the dough from sticking to your hands. For braided doughs, or doughs with a special shape that need to be elongated, it's best to divide the dough and let it rest and relax before attempting to lengthen it. The recipes where this is applicable will walk you through those steps when needed.

Baking

Most often, an enriched dough will be baked on either a sheet pan or a loaf pan and at lower temperatures than rustic breads. Since we are not looking for a hardened crust but a more soft and tender bake, high heats are not necessary for enriched breads. These bakes will range anywhere from 350° to 400°F, but make sure you pay attention to each specific recipe for the exact temperature and time.

PASTRY AND DESSERT TECHNIQUES

MIXING

The primary ingredient when making different types of desserts is flour. There are several different types of flours out there that are highly effective and optimal for baking things like tortas (cakes), bizcochos (quick breads), or galletas (cookies), such as pastry flour and cake flour. These low-protein flours offer a soft tenderness to your baked good, but note that they are not at all necessary and I rarely ever use or keep them in stock in my kitchen or bakery. All-purpose flour, whole wheat flour, and even spelt flour are great options to use to make delicate desserts.

When mixing baked goods, such as galletas (cookies), bizcochos (quick breads), or tortas (cakes), there are times when a recipe will call for you to separate the dry ingredients from the wet ones, which can be critical in terms of managing when the leavening agents activate. Once baking powder or baking soda is added to the wet ingredients, the first part of a chemical reaction occurs and the mixture will begin to bubble. This reaction concludes when the dough is placed in a preheated oven and your mixtures rise or expand.

CREAMING

Several dessert and pastry recipes will call for the butter and sugar to be creamed together before adding eggs and dry ingredients. It's important not to use cold butter or to microwave butter to soften it. You want to use butter that is at room temperature, soft to the touch, and pliable.

The creaming process creates an aerated mixture that allows your bakes to be light, crisp, and airy. To do this by hand, having a sturdy whisk and mixing bowl is key, although you can also cream fat and sugar together with a spatula. When it is time to add the dry ingredients to the mix, this is best done with a folding motion. When using a stand mixer, it is best to use the paddle attachment.

LAMINATING

Lamination is the process of folding a block of dough together with a block of butter repeatedly until several layers form. This creates light, flaky, and buttery pastries that melt in your mouth. Sounds easy, right? While each recipe in this book that requires lamination will have the exact instructions for you, here are some tips to keep in mind when you need to laminate dough in your kitchen:

Keep a sturdy rolling pin on hand. The heavier your rolling pin, the more success you will have with lamination. I personally do not prefer rolling pins that have handles, so a thick rolling pine is my preferred tool for lamination. If it is too light in weight, you will not be able to press your dough and butter forward efficiently.

Keep your kitchen cool. If you plan to laminate dough, make sure your kitchen is not any warmer than 70°F. However, if your kitchen is too cold, you can see your dough dry out. Finding the temperature sweet spot so that you don't end up with butter exploding out of your dough is key.

Consistency of butter and dough. The consistency of your dough and butter should be roughly the same, and I have the most success when my butter is pliable enough to bend and wobble without it cracking or smearing onto my hands.

Refrigerating and resting. If you run into trouble while laminating, the fridge is your best friend—but never freeze! The fridge can help things cool down and relax, while the freezer will alter the consistency of the butter and dough differently and you will end up with fragmented pieces of butter inside of your dough.

BAKING AND COOLING

While bake times vary depending on the dessert or pastry, it can be important to understand the type of bakeware that you use. The most effective type of bakeware is made of anodized aluminum, so if possible and you can afford it, aim to stock up on those. But don't worry, I use whatever is available, especially since I travel so much and stay in places that have all types of bakeware. Things turn out fine as long as you keep an eye on your bakes. For example, if you are using bakeware that is dark in color, know that it will retain much more heat than the lighter counterparts. That will affect the consistency of your bakes since the outside will bake much faster than the middle of your cake or loaf.

TEMPERATURE, CLIMATE, AND ALTITUDE

~~~~~

One of the most important variables in baking is temperature, and I'm not talking about what you set your oven to. The ambient temperature of your kitchen, plus the temperature of water you use to mix dough and batters, the flour itself, and your city's climate are all factors that play a part every time you bake. When you're at a higher altitude, your dough can dry out quickly, and in humid environments, your dough can take on extra moisture. I've baked in the rainy mountains of Medellín, the humid Sula Valley of Honduras, the tropics of Panama, and several other parts of Latin America.

Growing up in the US South, I am familiar with making adjustments in my baking due to the fluctuations between altitude and humidity. Admittedly, adapting to the cold is not something that comes naturally to me, but now that I live in New York City, I have managed to figure out the tips and tricks needed to bake successfully in colder, drier environments. Here are the tips I like to keep on hand for myself when dealing with new environments or trying to improve the quality of my bakes in my own environments.

HUMIDITY

Humidity is not something that you feel only when you walk outside. That moisture finds its way inside your kitchen too. Your basic pantry staples, and your doughs and batters themselves, absorb that extra moisture. If you are baking in a humid climate or time of the year and notice your doughs, preferments, and batters feel wet and loose, you can do a couple of things to fix that. First, keep dry ingredients like flour and sugar in the fridge, which will prevent them from absorbing any moisture. Second, when mixing doughs and preferments, you can add 5 to 10 percent less water into your mix, depending on how severely the humidity is affecting them.

ALTITUDE

When I was in Quito, Ecuador, the second highest capital city in the world at 9,350 feet, my eyes were opened to what life in a big city at a high altitude is like. The air is thinner, and evaporation happens much quicker than at sea level. This means that you need *more* water than usual in your mixes as well as longer bake times. Truthfully, I do not think there is a special formula to figure out exactly how to do this, and each specific environment requires its own testing.

If you are from a high-altitude area, it is likely that you won't realize these differences as much as someone like myself who is visiting. When consulting for a bakery in Medellín, at an altitude of roughly 5,000 feet, there was a noticeable difference in the dough mixes and bake times, but the air there is not as dry as in a place like Denver. In any case, if you are moving around and end up trying to bake in a high-altitude city, look out for dryness and add a little extra water into your doughs, batters, or preferments.

COLD

Baking in colder temperatures is not my favorite. However, I use a simple approach to solving my issues and I have had much success—except for the time I did a bakery pop-up during a blizzard and it was definitely way too cold in the basement kitchen I was operating in. Proofing and fermentation are usually the problematic areas when dealing with a cold kitchen, so I typically like to create makeshift environments for my dough to rest. I put my fermenting doughs on my countertop in tall, clear plastic bags (usually used for collecting your recycling) along with a pot of boiled water (allowing it to cool slightly, as just-boiled water will let off a lot of steam and add extra moisture to the dough—but that might be necessary depending on how dry your space is. If you have room on your patio, you can cold ferment your dough outside, instead of in your fridge, if you are in the 38° to 45°F range, just for fun.

GENERAL TEMPERATURE GUIDANCE

There is inherent math involved with baking because the process is chemical in nature. However, I like to do some basic things to keep up with my overall environment and make decisions using my intuition and experience as a baker (which is what you will do, too, the more you bake).

In the kitchen, keep a room thermometer so that you can immediately know your ambient temperature. Over time, you'll just be able to feel it and know what you need to do on any given day. For your mixes, measure your water temperature and make sure you are at an optimal range—too hot (greater than 120°F) and you will kill off your yeasts, and you don't ever want to do that. I find that between 77° and 82°F is a great temperature range for your water before mixing.

PART

2

RECIPES

YEASTED AND HYBRID DOUGHS

The goal of this section is to teach you to bake breads using a combination of yeasts and leavening techniques, including instant yeast, active dry yeast, a yeasted preferment, and/or a sourdough preferment.

Yeasted and hybrid doughs use commercial yeast as their only or primary leavening agent, and are generally simpler to make and bake than doughs made with your sourdough starter.

These yeasts are widely used in Latin America to achieve soft, spongey qualities in different breads. But among many bakers who prefer natural leavening methods that help make the gluten network inside wheat flour more digestible and impart more complex flavors, commercial yeast has fallen out of favor. Still, breads made with commercial yeast can be excellent.

The key is often to use smaller quantities of commercial yeasts and allow your doughs to rest longer; the result is quite flavorful and pleasant bread. In many cases, I recommend combining leavening techniques to achieve what I consider to be the best of both worlds: a traditional texture and more interesting flavor.

Pan Francés
Throughout Latin America

In Latin America, the name "pan francés" (Spanish for "French bread") pays homage to the origin of certain baking techniques brought to the Americas by colonizers. These airy, crispy loaves are popular all over the continent, where several countries have their own naming conventions, techniques, and ingredient variations that have transformed the colonists' imposition into cultural elegance. In fact, Latin American breads boast a variety of culinary innovations that fuse Indigenous tradition with the knowledge absorbed during the period of colonization. This fusion of cultures brought about new bread varieties like bolillos, pirujos, pão francés, and pan michita that have exciting qualities for bakers and customers alike.

So how did bread baking make its way all the way from Africa, through Europe, and to Mesoamerica? When Europeans arrived in the Greater Antilles and México, they forced Indigenous peoples to plant new crops, which in turn disrupted the local agriculture—requiring haciendas to be modified so that maíz (corn) and native crops could grow alongside wheat, rice, and sugarcane. In fact, the first person to plant wheat in America was Juan Garrido, a West African conquistador who was formerly enslaved but ultimately accompanied Juan Ponce de León to Florida. At some point, Ponce de León gave Juan a few grain seeds and told him to plant them, and thus the first wheat in the Americas was born.

The general consensus among food historian is that pan francés originated from a French baguette recipe adapted by the chefs of Austrian Archduke Ferdinand Maximilian, installed as emperor of México by French Emperor Napoleon III in 1864. In the early nineteenth century, French culture was all the rage. The first wave of European immigration to México and other parts of Latin America, along with the empire of Maximilian and the presidency of Porfirio Díaz in México, were all influential in promoting la comida afrancesada ("Frenchified" cooking.)

> "I am also a great admirer of excellent cookery, and generally find that everything must be eaten in season and at the right moment. One must not be too exclusive or partial in cookery, nor in anything in the world."
>
> —EMPEROR MAXIMILIAN I OF MÉXICO

Ferdinand Maximilian Joseph Maria von Habsburg-Lothringen was the emperor of the Second Mexican Empire from 1864 to 1867, and his tragic reign had a lasting effect on the food culture of Latin America. Maximilian is often remembered as a pawn of Napoleon III in la segunda intervención francesa en México (The Second French Intervention). México achieved independence from Spain in 1810 but remained in upheaval through the early 1860s. The ruling class in México had enough of the liberal reforms implemented by the government of Benito Juárez, who had abolished special privileges of the clergy and military as well as instituted civil marriage. The royalists, Catholic church, and other conservative groups conspired with Napoleon III to install Emperor Maximilian and his wife, Carlota, as the new rulers of México in 1864.

The new emperors proved to be a disappointment to their royalist supporters as their policies were also deemed too liberal and progressive. Maximilian wanted to spread French culture to the Mexican people and took to adopting some Mexican traditions. He loved fine French food and brought with him Hungarian head chef József Tüdös. Tüdös ran the palace kitchens, making extravagant menus featuring braised filet in Richelieu sauce, lamb cutlets and jardinière, and diplomat pudding. While Maximilian's charm offensive failed to connect with the Mexican people, the Mexican bourgeois were quick to adopt French culture. More than 100 patisseries opened and the emperor hosted frequent balls and banquets in Chapultepec.

After Maximilian's execution in 1867 came the presidency of Porfirio Díaz, who modernized México with liberal reforms while also concentrating wealth among a few and mostly foreign elite. The Mexican elite spared no expense in competing to see who could be the most French, even employing French chefs and governesses to elevate their status. French restaurants and bakeries flourished in México City. The bolillo is emblematic of how Mexican bakers incorporated this colonial mindset to create a uniquely Latin American bread.

YEASTED PREFERMENT

60 g (½ c) all-purpose flour
60 g (¼ c) warm water
1 g (¼ tsp) instant yeast

DOUGH

410 g (1¾ c) water
100 g (½ c) yeasted preferment
258 g (2 c) all-purpose flour
158 g (1¼ c) bread flour
**100 g (¾ c + 1 Tbsp) whole
    wheat flour**
1 g (¼ tsp) instant yeast
10 g (1 Tbsp) kosher salt
Wheat bran, for proofing

BOLILLO

The tortilla has long been considered the most significant food in Mexican cuisine—a symbol of cultivating Indigenous ingredients to create a distinct cultural delicacy. However, after the introduction of wheat to México, bakers began to turn inherited techniques into reimagined new ones. A new staple spread to dinner tables and street corners all over México: the bolillo.

Like all bread, the bolillo is comprised of two components: the migajón, or interior crumb, and the corteza, or crust. With a soft, tender interior and a crackling light-brown crust, the bolillo is the backbone of countless meals, tortas (by the way, in México a torta is a sandwich!), and molletes. Sometimes the migajón is removed from the bolillo so that the torta can be fully stuffed, yet remain supported by the corteza. There are plenty of different tortas you can make with a bolillo, like a guajolota, or torta de tamal, a common street food—simply add a tamal into the bolillo and enjoy.

My bolillo recipe combines a yeasted preferment with a pinch of instant yeast, to give it that familiar crispy and light texture with a milky tang.

YEASTED PREFERMENT

In a tall jar or large container with a lid, mix the flour, water, and yeast with your hand or a fork. Ensure that no dry flour remains at the bottom of the jar and that there are no clumps of flour either.

Cover the container and let it rest at room temperature (ideally between 70° and 80°F) for a minimum of 12 hours. It should become a creamy, bubbly, and funky mixture that more than doubles in size.

DOUGH

In a large mixing bowl, add 325 g (1⅓ c) of the water and the yeasted preferment. Mix together until the preferment has dissolved. Next, add the flours and instant yeast to the bowl and give it a rough mix, until it comes together and there isn't much dry flour left at the bottom of the bowl. Let this rest for 20 minutes.

Add the salt by spreading it over the top of the dough, along with the remaining water and squeeze until it is incorporated. Transfer to a clean bowl and let the dough ferment, covered by a clean cloth, at room temperature for 30 minutes. After the first 30 minutes, strengthen the dough by lifting one side from the bowl and stretching it into itself a few times. Cover the bowl with a lid or plastic wrap and put in the fridge for 12 hours.

(CONTINUED)

Once the dough is done fermenting in the fridge, flour your work surface lightly and dump out the dough. Divide into eight 120-g pieces (about the size of a lemon), and lightly shape them into oval balls. Let them rest for 5 minutes.

To shape the bolillo, flip each oval ball over so the smooth side is on your work surface and the oval shape is horizontally aligned in front of you. Starting from the top of the oval shape, use your fingertips to fold a small portion into the middle area of the dough. You should do 2 to 3 of these folds while making sure to apply pressure to create tension in your bolillo. Using the palms of your hands on the outside ends of the bolillo, push the tips down and roll back and forth to create a slightly pointed end.

Prepare your linen proofing cloth with a light dusting of wheat bran and place each bolillo, seam side down, onto the cloth, two per row. Lift up the cloth to create a division between the next two bolillos. Dust the tops with a small amount of all-purpose flour and let proof at room temperature for 2 hours. During the last hour of the proofing stage, preheat your oven with a stone or steel inside to 500°F.

Transfer your bolillos to a sheet of parchment paper on a loading peel or thin wooden cutting board.* Slash your bolillos down the middle with a serrated knife or razor blade.

Using a spray bottle, mist the bolillos so they are moist and then load into the oven. Use the spray bottle to spray the inside of the oven. Add ice cubes to a small baking pan and place the pan in the back or bottom of the oven during the bake to create a little bit of steam.

After loading, lower the temperature of the oven to 465°F. Bake for 20 minutes or until golden brown, being mindful to switch the bolillos from the front to the back of the baking stone/steel to get an even bake. Let cool on a cooling rack if desired for 10 to 15 minutes before eating.

*Alternatively, bolillos can be baked with no issue on a parchment-lined sheet pan. You may not get the full amount of oven spring and volume, but they will still bake up nice and crisp.

BOLILLO INTEGRAL

Traditionally, most bolillos are made entirely from white flour, which does not have the health benefits or flavor that whole grain wheat flour offers. So I experimented with incorporating a higher amount of whole grain flour as well as a sourdough preferment to create a heartier bolillo for your sandwich and table bread needs. To take things to an even more earthy level, I've added a pinch of amaranth, a grain native to México and Central America, to really make the heartiness come through; if you haven't had time to get your amaranth yet, simply replace it with whole grain wheat flour.

YEASTED PREFERMENT

In a tall jar or large container with a lid, mix the whole wheat flour, bread flour, amaranth flour, water, and mature sourdough starter with your hand or a fork. Ensure that no dry flour remains at the bottom of the jar and that there are no clumps of flour either.

Cover the container and let it rest at room temperature (ideally between 70° and 80°F) for 4 hours. It should double in size and have a firm, bubbly structure on the top. Once the preferment is ready to use, you can start baking straight away or place it in the fridge for later use (up to 2 days).

DOUGH

In a large mixing bowl, add 315 g (1⅓ c) of the water and the sourdough preferment and mix until the preferment has dissolved.

Add the whole flour, amaranth flour, bread flour, an additional 60 g (¼ c) water, and the instant yeast to the bowl and give it a rough mix, until it comes together and there isn't much dry flour left at the bottom of the bowl. Let rest for 20 minutes.

Spread the salt over the top of the dough, along with the remaining 50 g (scant ¼ c) water, and squeeze until it is incorporated. Transfer to a clean bowl, give it a nice stretch, flip until it is smooth, cover, and place in the fridge for 12 hours.

Once the dough is done with the cold bulk fermentation, flour the work surface lightly and dump out the dough. Divide into 130-g pieces (about the size of a lemon), and lightly shape them into oval balls. Let them rest for 5 minutes.

To shape the bolillo, flip each oval ball over so the smooth side is on your work surface and the oval shape is horizontally aligned in front of you. Starting from the top of the oval shape, use your fingertips to fold a small portion into the middle area of the dough. You should do 2 to 3 of these folds while making

(CONTINUED)

SOURDOUGH PREFERMENT
25 g (3 Tbsp) whole wheat flour
20 g (2½ Tbsp) bread flour
5 g (1 Tbsp) amaranth flour
50 g (3 Tbsp + 1 tsp) warm water
25 g (2 Tbsp) mature sourdough
    starter

DOUGH
425 g (1¾ c + 1 Tbsp) water
120 g (heaped ½ c) sourdough
    preferment
300 g (2½ c) whole wheat flour
15 g (2½ Tbsp) amaranth flour
200 g (1⅔ c) bread flour
1 g (¼ tsp) instant yeast
10 g (3 tsp) kosher salt
Wheat bran, for proofing

sure to apply pressure to create tension in your bolillo. Using the palms of your hands on the outside ends of the bolillo, push the tips down and roll back and forth to create a slightly pointed end.

Prepare your linen proofing cloth with a light dusting of wheat bran and place each bolillo, seam side down, onto the cloth. Dust the tops with a small amount of all-purpose flour and let proof at room temperature for 1½ to 2 hours. The bolillos should expand in size slightly, and remain firm but fluffy when touched with your fingertips. During the last hour of the proofing stage, preheat the oven with a stone or steel inside to 500°F.

Transfer your bolillos to a sheet of parchment paper on a loading peel or thin wooden cutting board.* Slash your bolillos down the middle with a serrated knife or a razor blade.

Using a spray bottle, mist the bolillos so they are moist and then load into the oven. Use the spray bottle to spray the inside of the oven. Add ice cubes to a small baking pan and place the pan in the back or bottom of the oven during the bake to create a little bit of steam.

After loading, lower the temperature of the oven to 465°F. Bake for 20 minutes or until golden brown, being mindful to rotate the bolillos from the front to the back of the baking stone/peel to get an even color. Let cool on a cooling rack if desired for 10 to 15 minutes before eating.

*Alternatively, the bolillos can be baked with no issue on a parchment-lined sheet pan. You may not get the full amount of oven spring and volume, but they will still bake up nice and crisp.

JALAPEÑO QUESILLO BOLILLO

To have a bit more fun with bolillos I incorporated ingredients that are native to México. The jalapeño, named by the Spanish in the city of Xalapa, is one of the most common peppers in the world. You most likely are able to grow them in your garden or find them at any grocery store. This recipe calls for the removal of the seeds, because those seeds are a bit too spicy to get lost in a dough mix (make sure you wear gloves!).

I had been making these with cheddar cheese, but after spending time in Oaxaca, I realized how much more fun and delicious it would be to instead fold fresh, creamy quesillo into this dough. If you can't find quesillo, cube up any lower-moisture cheese and incorporate it as a direct replacement in this recipe. The jalapeños are not roasted before going into the dough because during the baking process they typically roast to the perfect consistency. However, feel free to experiment with roasting the peppers beforehand to suit your palate (or keep the seeds in there if you are really brave). Use these to make sandwiches, toast up with butter, or eat on their own.

YEASTED PREFERMENT

50 g (⅓ c + 1 Tbsp) all-purpose flour
50 g (3½ Tbsp) warm water
1 g (¼ tsp) instant yeast

SOURDOUGH PREFERMENT

30 g (¼ c) bread flour
20 g (2½ Tbsp) whole wheat flour
50 g (3½ Tbsp) warm water
25 g (2 Tbsp) mature sourdough starter

DOUGH

410 g (1¾ c) water
50 g (¼ c) sourdough preferment
50 g (¼ c) yeasted preferment
258 g (2 c) bread flour
200 g (1⅔ c) all-purpose flour
60 g (½ c) whole wheat flour
10 g (1 Tbsp) kosher salt
158 g (1 c) chopped jalapeños
364 g (2½ c) quesillo, cubed

YEASTED PREFERMENT

In a tall jar or large container with a lid, mix the flour, water, and yeast with your hand or a fork. Ensure that no dry flour remains at the bottom of the jar and that there are no clumps of flour either.

Cover the container and let it rest at room temperature (ideally between 70° and 80°F) for 12 hours. It should become a creamy, bubbly, and funky mixture that expands in size.

SOURDOUGH PREFERMENT

In a tall jar or large container with a lid, mix the bread flour, whole wheat flour, water, and mature sourdough starter with your hand or a fork. Ensure that no dry flour remains at the bottom of the jar.

Cover the container and let it rest at room temperature (ideally between 70° and 80°F) for 4 hours. It should double in size and have a firm, bubbly structure on the top. Once the preferment is ready to use, you can start baking straight away or place it in your fridge for later use (up to 2 days).

(CONTINUED)

DOUGH

In a large mixing bowl, add 325 g (1⅓ c) of the water and both the sourdough and yeasted preferments and mix until the preferment has dissolved. Next, add the bread flour, all-purpose flour, and whole wheat flour to the bowl and give it a rough mix, until it comes together and there isn't much dry flour left at the bottom of the bowl. Let rest for 20 minutes.

Spread the salt over the top of the dough, add the remaining water, and squeeze the dough until it is incorporated. Let it rest for 30 minutes after adding the salt. Transfer the dough to a clean, lightly oiled bowl.

After the dough has rested, add half of the jalapeños and quesillo chunks to the surface and fold the sides of the dough into the middle, covering the additions. Flip the dough over and add half of the remaining jalapeños and quesillo to the dough and repeat the folding to fully incorporate. (To be clear, you've added ¾ of the total amount of jalapeño and quesillo, reserving ¼ for a step to come during the bake.) Cover and place in the refrigerator for 12 hours.

After the dough ferments, divide into eight 190-g pieces, and shape into ovals with pointy edges. Place the bolillos evenly spaced on a parchment-lined sheet pan. Spritz the bolillos with olive oil so they don't dry out.

Let the bolillos proof for 2 hours at room temperature. Thirty minutes before they are done proofing, preheat the oven to 500°F. Spray the top of the proofed dough with more olive oil and slash down the middle with a knife or razor blade.

Lower the heat to 465°F, place the bolillos in the oven, and bake for 20 minutes. Halfway through the bake, top each bolillo with the remaining quesillo chunks and jalapeños. Keep an eye on the sheet pan and rotate from top to bottom in the middle of the bake to prevent the bottoms from burning.

Let cool before eating so the cheese isn't piping hot.

PAN MICHITA

When the French arrived to construct the Panama Canal, it is thought that they attempted to create miche, or micha bread, which may have loosely ended up translating into michita—but the exact origins of this bread are not precisely known. In any case, the Panamanian version of pan francés loaves are baked close together, and forgo the scoring process to create an extremely flaky and soft interior. This recipe uses a yeasted preferment and a sourdough preferment without the addition of any more yeast in the dough. I recommend making both these preferments before bed so that they are ready to go in the morning. Michita are often enriched with vegetable oil but feel free to substitute with melted butter or lard.

YEASTED PREFERMENT

In a tall jar or large container with a lid, mix the flour, water, and yeast with your hand or a fork. Ensure that no dry flour remains at the bottom of the jar.

Cover the container and let it rest at room temperature (ideally between 70° and 80°F) for 10 hours. It should become a creamy, bubbly, and funky mixture that expands in size.

SOURDOUGH PREFERMENT

In a tall jar or large container with a lid, mix the bread flour, whole wheat flour, water, and mature sourdough starter with your hand or a fork. Ensure that no dry flour remains at the bottom of the jar.

Cover the container and let it rest at room temperature (ideally between 70° and 80°F) for 10 hours. It should double in size and have a wet, bubbly structure on the top.

DOUGH

In a large mixing bowl, combine the sourdough and yeasted preferments with the water. Add the all-purpose flour, whole wheat flour, and the panela to the bowl and mix until there is no dry flour left. Let rest for 15 minutes at room temperature, covered with a clean cloth.

Add the oil and squeeze into the dough until it is fully incorporated and the surface of the dough smooths out again. This might take 5 to 7 minutes.

Spread the salt on the dough and add a splash of water. Squeeze until the salt and water are incorporated and the dough smooths out one more time, about 5 minutes.

(CONTINUED)

Makes
10 LOAVES

YEASTED PREFERMENT

50 g (⅓ c + 1 Tbsp) all-purpose flour
50 g (3½ Tbsp) warm water
1 g (¼ tsp) instant yeast

SOURDOUGH PREFERMENT

30 g (¼ c) bread flour
20 g (2½ Tbsp) whole wheat flour
50 g (3½ Tbsp) warm water
15 g (1 Tbsp) mature sourdough starter

DOUGH

100 g (½ c) sourdough preferment
100 g (½ c) yeasted preferment
365 g (1½ c + 1 Tbsp) water
500 g (4 c) all-purpose flour
50 g (scant ½ c) whole wheat flour
25 g (2 Tbsp packed) grated panela
25 g (2 Tbsp) vegetable oil
10 g (1 Tbsp) kosher salt

Dump the dough onto an unfloured work surface. With wet hands, pick the dough up and slap it down onto your work surface and fold it over itself a few times until you get a smooth, round dough.

Place it in a lightly oiled bowl, cover, and let ferment for 3 hours at room temperature. Then transfer the dough to the fridge for 12 hours.

After the cold fermentation, on a floured work surface, divide the dough into ten 110-g pieces (the size of small lemons). Shape into small, tight logs with pointed ends and place on a parchment-lined baking sheet, arranged 2 by 5, with the ends of the dough facing the wide part of the sheet pan.

Allow the pan michita to proof for 2½ hours, or until the dough is bouncy to the touch. After the first 2 hours of the proof elapses, place the oven rack in the middle of the oven and preheat to 500°F.

Mist the dough with water or brush on with a pastry brush. Without scoring the dough, place in the oven and bake at 500°F for 8 minutes, then reduce the heat to 475°F and bake for 12 minutes more. You are looking for a nice brown exterior and for each pan michita to have connected with the others to create a soft, warm interior.

PIRUJOS

Pirujo is the name used in Guatemala for the regional version of pan francés. There is a unique scoring technique sometimes used with multiple shallow diagonal cuts that create a distinct look compared to other panes franceses in Central America. In addition, there is a hint of fat in the dough; I use a blend of butter and lard to maximize the creaminess and flavor profile. For the leavening, a hybrid of sourdough and instant yeast achieves a bouncy yet crunchy loaf that is suitable to eat alone with butter or as a sandwich. In Guatemala, they make some bangin' breakfast sandwiches with pirujos, complete with scrambled eggs, black beans, and different types of sausage.

SOURDOUGH PREFERMENT

In a tall jar or large container with a lid, mix the bread flour, whole wheat flour, water, and mature sourdough starter with your hand or a fork. Ensure that no dry flour remains at the bottom of the jar and that there are no clumps of flour either.

Cover the container and let it rest at room temperature (ideally between 70° and 80°F) for 4 hours. It should double in size and have a firm, bubbly structure on the top. Once the preferment is ready to use, you can start baking straight away or place it in your fridge for later use (up to 2 days).

DOUGH

In a large mixing bowl, combine the sourdough preferment with the water and mix until dissolved.

Add the all-purpose flour, bread flour, whole wheat flour, panela, and instant yeast and mix until you have a shaggy/rough dough but all water is absorbed. Let rest for 10 minutes.

Add the melted butter, melted lard, and salt, then squeeze into the dough with your hands until the dough absorbs it all and it has a smooth surface again. This might take anywhere between 5 and 10 minutes. Let rest for 10 minutes.

Transfer to a work surface and dust with flour. Knead until smooth by using your fingers to bring the dough into itself in the middle and the palm of your hand to push it back out. The dough might be slightly sticky, so dust with flour, if needed. Rotate your dough and repeat the kneading process until you have a smooth dough. If it starts to tear, you have kneaded it too much. Transfer to a clean, oiled bowl and cover.

Let the dough ferment at room temperature for 2½ hours, or until roughly doubled in size.

Makes

SOURDOUGH PREFERMENT
25 g (3 Tbsp) bread flour
25 g (3 Tbsp) whole wheat flour
25 g (1 Tbsp + 2 tsp) warm water
25 g (2 Tbsp) mature sourdough starter

DOUGH
100 g (½ c) sourdough preferment
365 g (1½ c + 1 Tbsp) water
345 g (2¾ c) all-purpose flour
125 g (1 c) bread flour
55 g (scant ½ c) whole wheat flour
15 g (1 Tbsp + 1 tsp packed) grated panela
2 g (½ tsp) instant yeast
20 g (1½ Tbsp) unsalted butter, melted
5 g (1 tsp) melted lard
10 g (1 Tbsp) kosher salt
Wheat bran, for proofing

Divide into eight 120-g pieces (about the size of a lemon) and shape tightly into cylinders, using the palms of your hands to point the edges out.

Dust a linen proofing cloth with wheat bran and transfer the shaped dough to the cloth. Let proof for 2 hours. During the last hour of the proof, add the baking steel or stone to the oven and preheat it to 500°F.

Transfer the pirujos to a parchment-lined loading peel and make several diagonal scores on each one.

Spritz the pirujos with water, and place in the hot oven. Then, using a spray bottle, spray the inside of the oven and lower the temperature to 450°F.

Bake for 15 to 20 minutes, being mindful about the bottoms. If necessary, transfer from the bottom to the top to get an even bake.

PÃOZINHO

In Brazil, you are bound to encounter a crisp, delicate white bread that is typically referred to as pão francés, or French bread. Wealthy travelers in the early twentieth century returning to Brazil from Western Europe yearned for something similar to a crispy white baguette and instructed their cooks to replicate it. However, the bakers created a bread that is creamier and crispier, due to the sugar and fat typically added to this dough. Every household seeks out warm, fresh bread as part of their daily meals, and depending on what region of Brazil you are in, these breads are actually called different names and can sometimes have slight variations in ingredients and texture. In São Paulo this bread is also known as pãozinho, and quite frankly it is my favorite word to pronounce. For this recipe, I've used panela as the sugar, which goes by the name of rapadura in Brazil, and melted butter to give the bread a very creamy and light interior.

SOURDOUGH PREFERMENT

50 g (⅓ c + 1 Tbsp) bread flour
30 g (2 Tbsp) warm water
25 g (2 Tbsp) mature sourdough starter

DOUGH

450 g (3⅔ c) all-purpose flour
50 g (scant ½ c) whole wheat flour
50 g (3½ Tbsp) unsalted butter, melted
12.5 g (1 scant Tbsp packed) grated panela
365 g (1½ c + 1 Tbsp) water
2 g (½ tsp) instant yeast
100 g (½ c) sourdough preferment
10 g (1 Tbsp) kosher salt

SOURDOUGH PREFERMENT

In a tall jar or large container with a lid, mix the bread flour, water, and mature sourdough starter with your hand or a fork. Ensure that no dry flour remains at the bottom of the jar.

Cover the container and let it rest at room temperature (ideally between 70° and 80°F) for 4 hours. It should double in size and have a firm, bubbly structure on the top. Once the preferment is ready to use, you can start baking straight away or place it in your fridge for later use (up to 2 days).

DOUGH

In a large bowl, combine the all-purpose flour, whole wheat flour, melted butter, panela, water, instant yeast, and sourdough preferment. Mix with your hands by squeezing and turning until there is no dry flour left. Allow the dough to rest for 20 minutes. Add the salt with a splash of water and squeeze until the salt is thoroughly combined.

Transfer to a clean, oiled bowl, cover, and let ferment for 3 hours at room temperature, or until the dough is doubled in size and is bouncy. On a floured work surface, divide the dough into eight 130-g pieces (about the size of medium tomatoes). Shape each piece into a tight cylinder by using your fingers to tuck the dough into itself starting from the top and pushing it into the middle. Repeat until you have the shape of a log and use your palms to point the ends slightly.

Place on a floured cutting board, linen cloth, or sheet pan dusted with wheat bran and a little whole wheat flour. Let proof for 1½ hours. During the last 45 minutes of proofing, place a baking stone or steel inside the oven and preheat to 500°F.

Transfer your pãozinhos to a parchment-lined loading peel or thin wooden cutting board, mist each piece with water, and slash down the middle with a serrated knife or razor blade.

Load onto the stone or steel in the oven, lower the temperature to 450°F, and bake for 25 minutes, or until you have a nice golden-brown crust and a slightly browned bottom.

PEBETE

Ah, pebete de jamón y queso—music to my ears because of its simplicity. But what does that mean? In Argentina, the word *pebete* is slang for little kid, with this bread seeming to pay homage to one's childhood. Pebete is a silky, soft, freshly baked bread that can be stuffed with fresh ham, cheese, tomato, and mayo. In Argentina and Uruguay, this small roll is extremely popular and serves as a quick snack with coffee or as a meal in itself, if you eat enough of them. Pebetes benefit from a good proof and a tight bake so that they flake away from each other once they are done. I love using fresh yeast because the optimal texture is extremely soft and smooth, as well as the subtle milky flavors that fresh yeast brings to the table. Plus, you'll want to be able to bake these up quickly to always have around the house.

This recipe yields 24 pebetes, but feel free to cut the recipe in half if you'd like to make a smaller batch. If you make the full batch, use two half sheet pans (18 by 3 by 1 inches). Using a stand mixer makes it easier to incorporate the butter, however if you are mixing by hand, be patient and make sure you squeeze the butter in until it is fully absorbed. Once you have incorporated the butter, the dough might feel wet or sticky, but can be strengthened by slapping it down on your work surface and folding it over repeatedly.

In the bowl of a stand mixer fitted with the dough hook attachment, add the all-purpose flour, water (except for 80 g, or ⅓ c), sugar, fresh yeast, and 2 of the eggs. Mix on low speed until a rough dough forms.

Slowly add the remaining water and switch to medium speed while doing so. The dough will come apart but let it keep mixing until it comes back together with the water, about 3 minutes.

Once the water is incorporated, add the butter 50 g (3½ Tbsp) at a time and switch to high speed. Make sure the butter is incorporated before adding more. With the last bit of butter, add the salt. Let the mixer continue on high speed for 4 to 5 minutes until you get a smooth, creamy dough.

Transfer to a clean, buttered bowl, cover and let ferment for 4 hours. After the initial fermentation, dump the dough onto a floured work surface and divide it into twenty-four 80-g pieces (about the size of clementines). Shape into balls and then use the palms of your hands to roll into tight logs, about 3 inches long.

Place the rolls on parchment-lined sheet pans, 3 by 4, cover with a plastic bag or a large damp cloth, and proof for 2 hours.

Combine the remaining egg with a pinch of salt and whisk rigorously until homogenous. Brush each pebete with the egg wash and bake for 25 minutes at 375°F. They should have a nice, dark brown shine to them when they are done.

DOUGH

1000 g (8 c) all-purpose flour
600 g (2½ c + 1 Tbsp) water
100 g (½ c) granulated sugar
12 g (1½ Tbsp) fresh yeast
3 large eggs
200 g (14 Tbsp) unsalted butter, softened
8 g (2½ tsp) kosher salt, plus a pinch for the egg wash
2 g (½ tsp) vanilla extract

PAN MOJICÓN

In Colombia, like many other countries in Latin America, wheat comes in as the number two dietary staple after colonizers planted wheat in and around Bogotá and the surrounding areas. Bread culture was interesting in the past: the poor were only able to access some whole grain breads while the rich ate processed white breads. Since then, the major cities in Colombia, such as Medellín, Cali, and Bogotá, have developed several delicious bread recipes including these sweet and soft mojicones. In the capital, they're eaten at any time of day and the aroma near the bakeries is heavenly. They are dusted liberally with a coat of cinnamon and sugar before going into the oven, and after the bake the buttery flakiness is out of this world. I use a sweet preferment for these because sugar helps tame bacterial growth in the preferment, which in turn makes the flavor profile less sour.

SWEET SOURDOUGH PREFERMENT

In a tall jar or large container with a lid, mix the bread flour, whole wheat flour, panela, water, and mature sourdough starter with your hand or a fork. Ensure that no dry flour remains at the bottom of the jar.

Cover the container and let it rest at room temperature (ideally between 70° and 80°F) for 4 hours. It should double in size and have a firm, bubbly structure on the top. Once the preferment is ready to use, you can start baking straight away or place it in your fridge for later use (up to 2 days).

DOUGH

Combine the active dry yeast with 50 g (3½ Tbsp) of the warm water in a small container and whisk until frothy. Set aside for 5 minutes.

In the bowl of a stand mixer fitted with the dough hook attachment, add the milk, panela, sugar, eggs, all-purpose flour, bread flour, and sweet sourdough preferment and mix on low speed until combined.

Switch to medium speed and slowly add the yeast mixture until fully incorporated. This should take 2 to 3 minutes.

Add the butter 50 g (3½ Tbsp) at a time and switch to medium-high speed (whichever mixer you're using, put the speed knob between halfway and maximum speed). Make sure all butter is incorporated before adding more. With the last bit of butter, add the salt. Let the mixer continue on high speed for 4 to 5 minutes until you get a smooth, creamy dough.

SWEET SOURDOUGH PREFERMENT

155 g (1¼ c) bread flour
50 g (scant ½ c) whole wheat flour
50 g (scant ¼ c packed) grated panela (or granulated sugar)
100 g (¼ c + 3 Tbsp) water
100 g (½ c) mature sourdough starter

DOUGH

2 g (½ tsp) active dry yeast
200 g (⅔ c + 3 Tbsp) warm water
300 g (1¼ c) whole milk, warm
10 g (2 tsp packed) grated panela
100 g (½ c) granulated sugar, plus more for sprinkling
2 large eggs
405 g (3¼ c) all-purpose flour
600 g (4 c) bread flour
250 g (heaped 1 c) sweet sourdough preferment (see above)
150 g (10½ Tbsp) unsalted butter, softened
8 g (2½ tsp) kosher salt
Cinnamon, for sprinkling

(CONTINUED)

Transfer to a clean, buttered bowl, cover, and let ferment for 3 hours at room temperature. After the initial fermentation, dump onto a floured work surface and divide into sixteen 120-g pieces (about the size of a lemon). Shape into balls and place the rolls on a parchment-lined sheet pan, 4 by 4, and proof for 2½ hours. Preheat your oven to 375°F during the last 30 minutes of the proof.

Baste the rolls with melted butter and sprinkle with cinnamon and sugar. Bake for 25 minutes at 375°F. The mojicones will have a nice, dark shine and toasty cinnamon sugar top when done.

Taino Tradition and the Modern Cubano

The origin story of the Cuban sandwich is hotly contested. Some say it was created by the Taino tribe in Cuba more than five hundred years ago, predating European colonization. The Taino tribe ate unleavened cassava (casabe) bread made from the yuca root, which can be poisonous if not prepared correctly; the bread itself might have been more like a cracker. Naturally this was gluten-free. The Taino might have used fish, vegetables, and game fowl for the filling. The Cuban sandwich as we know it today evolved when the Spanish arrived with pork, ham, and wheat. Once these ingredients were forced onto the land, they became incorporated into native diets.

Other people believe that the Cuban sandwich's origins lie in the midnight cafés of Havana. Still others argue that it began in Cuban cafés in Key West. The most enduring origin story lies in Ybor City, where a community of Cuban immigrants settled in Tampa, Florida, in the 1800s. Ybor City was founded by Vicente Martínez-Ybor in 1886. After his cigar factory in Key West burned down, he moved to Tampa and established Ybor City as a safe place for cigar manufacturers to set up shop. It became the home to a thriving Cuban community and was known as the "Cigar Capital of the World" from 1886 up to the early 1930s. Waves of immigrants arriving in the city to work created a fierce demand for fast and cheap lunch options.

La Joven Francesca Bakery in Ybor is said to have invented "Cuban bread" in 1896 and by the year 1900, the cafés of Ybor began offering the Cuban sandwich, which was called "mixto" because of the mixture of meats. Due to the large-scale immigration of the 1800s, there were also Italian and Spanish settlers in Tampa at the time, which may provide some explanation as to how Genoa salami made its way onto the Tampa version of the Cuban sandwich, which was removed from the sandwich when it traveled down to Miami.

PAN CUBANO

I met my good friend Danny, who is Cuban, in New Orleans and one of the first things I noticed about him was his use of the word *sanguich*—a pronunciation of *sandwich* that is common in his home town of Miami. After I moved to Miami, I noticed how people absolutely love their pan cubano and the sanguiches made with it. The bread is so crispy, light, and perfect for toast with breakfast or for a cubano—they remind me why it's important to keep the purpose of a type of bread in perspective.

Every type of bread, in every culture, is made with intention. Pan cubano is particularly enjoyable because of the tangy, sweet flavor and crispy exterior that provides a simple vessel with which to enjoy the rich flavors of Cuban cuisine. Something really fun about making pan cubano is that this bread is baked with a single palm leaf right down the middle of the dough surface to create steam and an even bake, a tradition dating back as far as the 1800s. If you have access to palm leaves, give it a try! If not, you can always use kitchen twine, making sure to remove it all before eating. At the end of the day, without this bread, the breakfasts and cubanos I've come to enjoy simply would not taste the same.

YEASTED PREFERMENT

YEASTED PREFERMENT
80 g (⅔ c) all-purpose flour
80 g (⅓ c) warm water
1 g (¼ tsp) instant yeast

DOUGH
1 g (¼ tsp) active dry yeast
365 g (1½ c + 1 Tbsp) water
125 g (heaped ½ c) yeasted preferment
300 g (2⅓ c + 1 Tbsp) all-purpose flour
200 g (1⅔ c) bread flour
10 g (2½ tsp) granulated sugar
15 g (1 Tbsp) lard
10 g (1 Tbsp) kosher salt
2-4 palm leaves, or 2-4 (12-inch) pieces of cotton twine

In a tall jar or large container with a lid, mix the flour, water, and yeast with your hand or a fork. Ensure that no dry flour remains at the bottom of the jar.

Cover the container and let it rest at room temperature (ideally between 70° and 80°F) for 12 hours. It should become a creamy, bubbly, and funky mixture that expands in size.

DOUGH

In a small bowl, combine the active dry yeast and 25 g (1½ Tbsp) of the water and whisk together. Set aside 5 minutes, until frothy.

In a large mixing bowl, combine the remaining water with the preferment and active dry yeast mixture. Add the all-purpose flour, bread flour, and sugar and mix until there is no dry flour left. Cover and let the dough rest for 30 minutes.

Place the lard on top of the dough and spread it out. Then perform a stretch and fold to your dough, and squeeze in the lard at the same time. You may need to add a splash of water here. Add the salt during this squeezing process. The goal is to start building strength and also incorporate the lard at the same time. This may take a few minutes of stretching and squeezing but trust the process.

(CONTINUED)

You need not perform any more stretch and folds with this dough. Let the initial rise continue for 1 additional hour then transfer to the fridge overnight, or for at least 12 hours.

After the cold fermentation period, it's time to divide and shape the pan cubano. Divide your dough into 2 or 4 pieces, depending on your preferred loaf size.

Take each piece and roll into a small log. Try to apply as much tension as possible when rolling it. Once you have a small log, cover with a damp towel and let the dough rest for 25 minutes, which will allow it to relax before lengthening.

After the brief rest, start from the middle with both hands and roll it back and forth while pushing your hands outward. You want your pan cubano to get longer, so once you have your desired length you can stop. No need to make pointy ends on these loaves like the bolillos. The signature of a nice pan cubano are the rounded edges.

Brush one of the loaves with water. Take a long palm leaf or string of twine and place it on your canvas proofing cloth or cutting board. Flip your dough so that the seam is facing up and the palm leaf or twine covers the length of the smooth side of the dough, right down the middle. Repeat with your other loaf or loaves.

Let your dough proof for 2 hours. During the last 30 minutes, place the baking steel or stone in the oven and preheat to 500°F.

Flip the loaves onto a parchment-lined loading peel so that the leaf/twine is now on the top side and load into the oven. (Alternatively, you can bake them on a sheet pan, following the same directions below.)

Steam the oven by misting it with a spray bottle of water, if possible, or simply use a pan with hot water in the oven to generate some steam. Lower the heat to 465°F.

Bake the pan cubano loaves for 15 to 20 minutes, depending on your color preference. I prefer to bake it dark, but if you're using the bread for the pressed sanguich, you can bake it light so that it can keep toasting during the sandwich-making process.

PAN DE MEDIA NOCHE

At the ventanitas in Miami (the small windows where you order your goodies at Cuban cafés), you can find yourself a solid meal at any time of day. Breakfasts, lunches, and of course, sanguiches. But if you thought all Cuban bread was the same, think again. If you have had your fix of cubanos and tripletas, but want to continue to explore Caribbean sandwich culture, look no further than the little sibling of the cubano: the media noche. With a creamier, softer, and more buttery bread, the texture and complexity of the sandwich change completely when using this rather than pan cubano. I opted to use a slightly sweet sourdough preferment to balance out the acidity of the bread but still provide a mild, tangy flavor. The fillings for the sandwich are largely the same, although I have found media noches to be cheesier than cubanos. A recipe for the sandwich follows.

SWEET SOURDOUGH PREFERMENT

In a tall jar or large container with a lid, mix the flour, water, panela, and mature sourdough starter with your hand or a fork. Ensure that no dry flour remains at the bottom of the jar.

Cover the container and let it rest at room temperature (ideally between 70° and 80°F) for 4 hours. It should double in size and have a firm, bubbly structure on the top. Once the preferment is ready to use, you can start baking straight away or place it in your fridge for later use (up to 2 days).

DOUGH

In a small bowl, combine the active dry yeast with 50 g (3½ Tbsp) of the warm water and whisk until frothy. Set aside for 5 minutes.

In the bowl of a stand mixer with the dough hook attachment, add the whole wheat flour, all-purpose flour, bread flour, eggs, milk, sugar, and sourdough preferment and mix on low speed until combined.

Switch the mixer to medium speed and slowly add the yeast mixture until fully incorporated. This should take 3 to 4 minutes.

After the dough smooths back out, add the butter and switch to high speed. Make sure all the butter is incorporated before moving on to the next step. This will take 2 to 3 minutes depending on your mixer.

Add the salt and a splash of water. Let the mixer continue on high speed for 4 to 5 minutes until you get a smooth, creamy dough. It should not fall apart, but it should be very elastic.

Transfer the dough to a clean, lightly buttered bowl, cover, and let ferment for 3 hours at room temperature.

(CONTINUED)

Makes
4 LOAVES

SWEET SOURDOUGH PREFERMENT

50 g (⅓ c + 1 Tbsp) bread flour
25 g (1½ Tbsp) warm water
10 g (2 tsp packed) grated panela (or 1 Tbsp granulated sugar)
25 g (2 Tbsp) mature sourdough starter

DOUGH

1 g (¼ tsp) active dry yeast
165 g (scant ¾ c) warm water
25 g (3 Tbsp) whole wheat flour
310 g (2½ c) all-purpose flour
250 g (2 c) bread flour
3 large eggs
1 egg yolk
110 g (scant ½ c) whole milk
30 g (2½ Tbsp) granulated sugar
100 g (½ c) sweet sourdough preferment
80 g (5½ Tbsp) unsalted butter, room temperature
Pinch kosher salt

After the initial fermentation, dump the dough onto a floured work surface and divide evenly into 4 pieces. Shape each piece into a long tube, applying tension, and place each one on a parchment-lined sheet pan, horizontally. Proof for 2 hours at room temperature.

Mix 1 egg with 1 egg yolk, brush the loaves with the egg wash, and bake at 375°F for 20 minutes, until light brown.

MEDIA NOCHE SANDWICH

The main difference between the two most popular and delicious Cuban sandwiches lies in the bread used, as the filling for each is largely the same: juicy, slow-cooked pork shoulder that was marinated in a citrusy, garlic forward mojo criollo; thick sliced ham; dill pickles; and lots of melty Swiss cheese. I'm not trying to reinvent the wheel here or make any kind of trendy version of these sandwiches. This is straight to the point and true to the simple but elegant nature of what you find in Cuban neighborhoods. Use the rustic Pan Cubano (page 56) to make a sanguich cubano, and the softer Pan de Media Noche for a media noche! If you don't have a sandwich press, improvise by using a heavy cast-iron skillet to press the sandwich down while cooking.

I've been known to take one of these down all on my own, but you might want to split it in half and share.

If you have a sandwich press, heat it up and coat it with lard. If you don't have one, heat two cast-iron skillets on your stove over high heat until they're as hot as possible, coating the one you intend to place the sandwich on with lard. If you don't have one that is big enough to press the sandwich, you can cut it in half after assembling and press one half at a time.

Slice open the loaf of Pan de Media Noche making sure to keep it hinged. Spread both sides with the mustard and add the ham onto the bottom side. Then add the roasted pork shoulder and top with the cheese. Finally, add the pickles and close the sandwich.

Transfer to your heated sandwich press or cast-iron skillet. If using the cast-iron skillets, brush the top of the loaf with lard and place the second hot cast-iron skillet directly on top of the sandwich, applying a slight amount of pressure. After about 3 minutes, flip the sandwich over and repeat. If using the sandwich press, let it cook and sizzle until it flattens to about half of the original size, about 8 minutes, making sure all the cheese melts. Serve immediately.

Makes
1 LARGE SANDWICH

100 g lard
1 loaf Pan de Media Noche or Pan Cubano (page 56)
Yellow mustard, al gusto
6 slices ham
455 g (1 lb) roasted pork shoulder
6 slices Swiss cheese
Pickles, al gusto

PAN SOBAO

One thing about the buzzing streets of Puerto Rico is that you can't stop seeing and smelling freshly baked breads. One particular rustic loaf, pan sobao, caught my eye as it was used so commonly for sandwiches and also sold on its own. On a visit to Guaynabo, my good friend Ricky took me to several places to eat, and whether we were having pinchos fresh off the grill, breakfast, or stuffing our face with sandwiches after a night out, pan sobao was there. This loaf is creamy, soft, and slightly sweet on the inside and crispy on the outside, which helps counterbalance the salty, fatty elements that often accompany it. I made this pan sobao with a yeasted preferment and a sourdough preferment, to bring the qualities I like about this loaf in addition to some extra funk and flavor. I especially love this for a tripleta sandwich; that recipe follows.

YEASTED PREFERMENT

In a tall jar or large container with a lid, mix the flour, water, and yeast with your hand or a fork. Ensure that no dry flour remains at the bottom of the jar.

Cover the container and let it rest at room temperature (ideally between 70° and 80°F) for 12 hours. It should become a creamy, bubbly, and funky mixture that expands in size.

SOURDOUGH PREFERMENT

In a tall jar or large container with a lid, mix the bread flour, whole wheat flour, water, and mature sourdough starter with your hand or a fork. Ensure that no dry flour remains at the bottom of the jar.

Cover the container and let it rest at room temperature (ideally between 70° and 80°F) for 4 hours. It should double in size and have a firm, bubbly structure on the top. Once the preferment is ready to use, you can start baking straight away or place it in your fridge for later use (up to 2 days).

DOUGH

In a small container, whisk together the active dry yeast with the water. Set aside for 5 minutes, or until it becomes frothy at the top.

In the bowl of a stand mixer with the dough hook attachment, combine the yeasted and sourdough preferments with the milk and dissolve.

On low speed, mix in the all-purpose flour, whole wheat flour, and the sugar until just combined.

Moving up to medium speed, slowly add the active dry yeast mixture to the dough. It might take a few minutes to fully absorb and become a smooth dough again.

(CONTINUED)

YEASTED PREFERMENT

60 g (½ c) all-purpose flour
60 g (¼ c) warm water
1 g (¼ tsp) instant yeast

SOURDOUGH PREFERMENT

30 g (¼ c) bread flour
20 g (2½ Tbsp) whole wheat flour
50 g (3½ Tbsp) warm water
25 g (2 Tbsp) mature sourdough starter

DOUGH

1 g (¼ tsp) active dry yeast
60 g (¼ c) warm water
16 g (1 Tbsp + 1¼ tsp) granulated sugar
100 g (½ c) yeasted preferment
100 g (½ c) sourdough preferment
240 g (2 c) whole milk
485 g (3¾ c + 2 Tbsp) all-purpose flour
15 g (2 Tbsp) whole wheat flour
15 g (1 Tbsp) lard
15 g (1 Tbsp + 2 tsp) kosher salt
Wheat bran, for dusting

Once the yeast mixture is fully absorbed, move up to medium-high speed and add the lard all at once. Allow the dough to mix and incorporate the fat for 3 to 4 minutes.

Add the salt with a splash of water, again making sure the dough comes back together and there is no moisture on the sides of the mixing bowl.

Transfer to a clean, oiled bowl, cover, and let rest for 4 hours at room temperature.

After the initial fermentation stage, divide evenly into 2 or 4 pieces depending on the size of the loaf you desire.

Shape the loaves into long cylinders, applying tension as you roll each one into itself and seal the seam with the palm of your hand. You are aiming for the loaves to be 16 to 18 inches each in length, regardless of whether you are making 2 or 4 loaves.

Line a sheet pan with parchment paper and dust with wheat bran. Transfer the loaves, seam side up, onto the sheet pan. Let the loaves proof for 2 hours at room temperature.

During the last hour of the proof, preheat the oven to 500°F.

Spray the loaves gently with water. Do not slash these loaves. Then place the sheet pan in the oven and lower the heat to 450°F. Bake for 25 minutes, or until golden brown, being mindful to swap your loaves to the top/bottom depending on your oven.

TRIPLETA ON PAN SOBAO

The nightlife in Puerto Rico is phenomenal, and even though I love a good bar or dance floor as much as the next person, those aren't the things that make me crave a night out. In fact, the only reason I want to party all night is to eat the most delicious, mouthwatering sandwich afterward and have it feel as though I somehow deserved it. Enter the tripleta—the bluntly named sandwich on soft, slightly sweet pan sobao that boasts three different types of meat as its filling: lechón (roasted suckling pig), grilled steak, and ham. If that's not enough to draw you in, the sandwich is also stuffed with fries and fully dressed with cheese, lettuce, tomato, mayo, and ketchup. I've gone to the most popular places to try tripletas, stumbled into unknown street corners for some, and had a remixed version called the "burripleta," which skips the pan sobao and loads it all into a fresh flour tortilla. Either way, after your kitchen is filled with the aroma of your own freshly baked pan sobao, you won't need a night out dancing to feel like you deserve to make this sandwich.

If you don't have time to roast your own pork shoulder, go to a grocery store and get it from the hot food section. There's often some kind of pulled pork in the dinner bar.

2 filets of cube steak, tenderized
Kosher salt, al gusto
Freshly ground black pepper, al gusto
Onion powder, al gusto
6 cloves garlic, minced
Juice of 1 orange
55 g (¼ c) olive oil
15 g (1 Tbsp) lard (or unsalted butter)
1 loaf Pan Sobao (page 62)
Mayonnaise, al gusto
Ketchup, al gusto
455 g (1 lb) roasted pork shoulder (any style), shredded
6 slices ham
6 slices Swiss cheese
200 g canned or precooked potato sticks (from about 1 large potato)
20 g (⅓ c) shredded lettuce
1 tomato, sliced thick

Season the cube steak with salt, pepper, and onion powder to your liking. In a small bowl, add the minced garlic, orange juice, and olive oil. Mix well and then pour over the cube steak. Cover and place in the fridge for at least 1 hour.

In a large cast-iron skillet or griddle over medium-high heat, add the lard or butter. Sear the cube steak until tender and soft but slightly pink in the middle, about 2 minutes per side. Remove from the heat and set aside.

Leave the skillet over medium-high heat, slice the pan sobao in half, press down onto the skillet, and toast in the lard that was used to fry the steak, about 1 minute.

Once the pan sobao is toasted, assemble the sandwich by spreading the mayonnaise and ketchup on the inside of the pan sobao and layering the pork, steak, ham, and cheese. If you want to melt the cheese, at this stage you can pop it under the broiler for a few minutes or use a torch over the cheese.

To finish the tripleta, add the potato sticks, lettuce, and tomato. Enjoy!

PAN DE YEMA PERUANO

If you've ever had a teatime or lonche in Perú, you probably ate a few rolls of pan de yema to go along with it. This soft, slightly sweet bread made with a high quantity of egg yolks goes perfectly with a variety of foods and beverages. In Perú, anise is frequently used in baking and pan de yema is no exception. When you make the dough, you should clearly see the anise seed in each little loaf before they go into the oven. This bread is rolled up and brushed with more egg yolk then topped with sesame seeds to achieve a wonderfully brown color during the bake. Your kitchen is going to be full of a beautiful scent when you bake these, and your lunches and tea and coffee breaks will be infinitely enhanced.

SOURDOUGH PREFERMENT
- 30 g (¼ c) bread flour
- 20 g (2½ Tbsp) whole wheat flour
- 50 g (3½ Tbsp) warm water
- 25 g (2 Tbsp) mature sourdough starter

DOUGH
- 1 g (¼ tsp) active dry yeast
- 250 g (1 c + 1 Tbsp) water
- 520 g (4 c + 3 Tbsp) all-purpose flour
- 50 g (3½ Tbsp) whole milk, warm
- 32 g (2½ Tbsp) granulated sugar
- 4 egg yolks plus 1 egg for the egg wash
- 15 g (1 Tbsp) unsalted butter
- 3 g (1½ tsp) whole anise seeds
- 120 g (heaped ½ c) sourdough preferment
- 12 g (1 Tbsp + 1 tsp) kosher salt
- 200 g (1⅓ c) sesame seeds

SOURDOUGH PREFERMENT

In a tall jar or large container with a lid, mix the bread flour, whole wheat flour, water, and mature sourdough starter with your hand or a fork. Ensure that no dry flour remains at the bottom of the jar.

Cover the container and let it rest at room temperature (ideally between 70° and 80°F) for 4 hours. It should double in size and have a firm, bubbly structure on the top. Once the preferment is ready to use, you can start baking straight away or place it in your fridge for later use (up to 2 days).

DOUGH

In a small bowl, dissolve the active dry yeast with 50 g (3½ Tbsp) of the water. Whisk together and let rest for 5 minutes until frothy.

In the bowl of a stand mixer fitted with the dough hook attachment, add the flour, milk, remaining water, sugar, egg yolks, butter, and anise seed. Mix on low speed until a rough dough forms and there is no dry flour left on the bottom.

Once all the ingredients are incorporated, switch the mixer speed to medium and slowly add the active dry yeast mixture, the sourdough preferment, and the salt and mix until all the water is absorbed and the dough smooths out.

Transfer to a lightly oiled bowl and let ferment for 3 hours at room temperature. After the initial fermentation period, divide into ten 110-g pieces (about the size of small lemons). Shape each piece into a small triangle and roll it up into a slight crescent shape. Brush with an egg wash and sprinkle with the sesame seeds.

Proof the dough on a parchment-lined sheet pan for 1½ hours. During the last 30 minutes, preheat the oven to 375°F. Place the sheet pan in the oven and bake the rolls for 20 minutes, or until a light brown color is achieved.

PAN SARNITA

Bolivia has the lowest wheat yield among the countries in its region and some of the highest altitudes in South America, which might make you think it does not have a delicious bread culture. Baking at a high altitude can be challenging because of how quickly water evaporates—leading to longer bake times as well as high chances of dough drying out while resting. But even with the challenge of altitude and needing to import so much wheat, there are several different breads that are commonly consumed in Bolivia. One especially delicious bread makes all this effort worthwhile: pan sarnita, a slightly cheesy roll that you will find at every panadería or on the kitchen table as a family's "pan casero," or homemade bread. The mozzarella cheese on top of the flattened out dough gives it a distinct, salty bite that complements the fluffy interior.

SOURDOUGH PREFERMENT

In a tall jar or large container with a lid, mix the bread flour, whole wheat flour, water, and mature sourdough starter with your hand or a fork. Ensure that no dry flour remains at the bottom of the jar.

Cover the container and let it rest at room temperature (ideally between 70° and 80°F) for 4 hours. It should double in size and have a firm, bubbly structure on the top. Once the preferment is ready to use, you can start baking straight away or place it in your fridge for later use (up to 2 days).

DOUGH

In a large mixing bowl, add the water and sourdough preferment and dissolve. Then add the bread flour, whole wheat flour, egg, instant yeast, panela, butter, and salt and mix until you have a rough dough with no dry flour left at the bottom of the bowl.

Turn the dough out onto a floured work surface and knead with your hands until smooth, 4 to 5 minutes. Place the dough in a lightly oiled bowl and let ferment for 4 hours at room temperature.

After the initial fermentation period, divide the dough into ten 105-g pieces (about the size of small lemons). Take each piece and roll it into a loose ball shape and let rest for 5 minutes.

Grease your hands with a little bit of oil, flatten the dough balls into disks, and transfer them to a parchment-lined sheet pan to start the proofing process. Let them rest at room temperature for 2 hours. During the last 30 minutes, preheat your oven to 400°F.

Brush the surface of each roll with water and spread 50 g of queso fresco over the top of each, pressing it down into the dough.

Bake the pan sarnita for 15 to 20 minutes, or until golden brown and the cheese is nice and melted.

SOURDOUGH PREFERMENT

30 g (¼ c) bread flour
20 g (2½ Tbsp) whole wheat flour
50 g (3½ Tbsp) warm water
25 g (2 Tbsp) mature sourdough starter

DOUGH

295 g (1¼ c) water
100 g (½ c) sourdough preferment
470 g (3¾ c) bread flour
50 g (scant ½ c) whole wheat flour
1 large egg
1 g (¼ tsp) instant yeast
50 g (¼ c packed) grated panela
30 g (2 Tbsp) unsalted butter
10 g (1 Tbsp) kosher salt
490 g (3½ c) queso fresco (farmer's cheese), crumbled

CACHITOS DE ESPINACA Y RICOTA

1 batch Cachitos de Jamón dough (page 72)
130 g (½ c) cooked spinach, squeezed dry
130 g (½ c + 2 tsp) ricotta
3 large eggs
5 g (1 tsp) onion powder
10 g (2 tsp) kosher salt
10 g (2 tsp) freshly ground black pepper
Pinch ground cinnamon
Pinch ground nutmeg
10 g (3 Tbsp) finely grated Parmesan cheese
100 g (⅓ c + 1½ Tbsp) melted unsalted butter for finishing

Cachitos can be filled with several other things besides ham, and one of the most common is the combination of spinach and ricotta. For this recipe, create the filling as described below and follow the steps from the preceding Cachitos de Jamón recipe (page 72) to make the dough, replacing the ham mixture with the ricotta and spinach mixture.

Follow the steps in the Cachitos de Jamón recipe (page 72) to create the dough. Once the dough is fermenting in the fridge, make the filling.

It is important to squeeze the cooked spinach dry so that there is no excess moisture in the filling mixture. In a medium bowl, combine the spinach, ricotta, 2 of the eggs, onion powder, salt, pepper, cinnamon, nutmeg, and Parmesan cheese and whisk together until creamy and thick. Place in the fridge overnight with your dough.

Dump the dough onto a floured work surface and use a rolling pin to flatten the dough out into a big circle. Next, use a pizza cutter or a chef's knife to cut the circle into 8 triangles, as if you were slicing a pizza.

Preheat the oven to 375°F.

Pull the base of the triangle of one piece of dough lower than the two corners to the left and right of the base. Add the spinach filling and use the two left/right corners to stretch over the top and create a seam.

Next, in one motion, roll the spinach mixture forward and tighten it.

Elongate the rest of the dough, and roll the base filled with the mixture to the right side, creating a diagonal fold. Repeat this going toward the left side and continue alternating until the last tip of the dough is folded underneath. You should end up with a small log that has 2 to 3 diagonal seams.

Place each cachito on a parchment-lined sheet pan. Combine the remaining egg with a pinch of salt and brush on each cachito. Let the cachitos rest for 30 minutes.

Place the sheet pan in the oven and bake for 20 to 25 minutes or until golden brown. Hot out of the oven, brush your cachitos with melted butter and serve warm.

CACHITOS DE JAMÓN

Portuguese influence played an important role in the history of Venezuela, and amid that influence came culinary ideas and new traditions. But it was not just the Portuguese—they facilitated the arrival of thousands of enslaved West Africans, which in turn led to their culinary traditions becoming a part of the overall culinary experience that you find in the present day. It's possible that the filled roll known as the cachito is rooted in this influence, although it is also said the cachito is a derivative of the Venezuelan Christmas speciality, pan de jamón. Cachitos are umami bombs, with a savory mouthful that will have you eating one after the other. Traditionally made with a nice semisweet but soft dough, they are typically filled with diced or chopped ham and a touch of tocino, or bacon. I first had cachitos during my time in Miami, as the Venezuelan population there is large and they have an overwhelming amount of options to choose from when it comes to bakeries. This is obviously one of my favorite recipes that I created because of how tasty they are. The passion that my Venezuelan followers have is incredibly high, and every time I share my thoughts, posts, or videos making traditional Venezuelan baked goods, I receive lots of feedback. I've included a sweet sourdough preferment in this dough, and I recommend that you use a stand mixer as it gets quite sticky when the butter is added.

SWEET SOURDOUGH PREFERMENT

In a tall jar or large container with a lid, mix the bread flour, whole wheat flour, panela, water, and mature sourdough starter with your hand or a fork. Ensure that no dry flour remains at the bottom of the jar.

Cover the container and let it rest at room temperature (ideally between 70° and 80°F) for 4 hours. It should double in size and have a firm, bubbly structure on the top. Once the preferment is ready to use, you can start baking straight away or place it in your fridge for later use (up to 2 days).

DOUGH

Combine the active dry yeast with 50 g (3½ Tbsp) of the warm milk in a small container and whisk until frothy. Set aside for 5 minutes.

In the bowl of a stand mixer fitted with the dough hook attachment, combine the remaining milk, all-purpose flour, whole wheat flour, sweet sourdough preferment, egg, panela, and vanilla extract and mix on low speed until the mixture becomes crumbly.

Switch to medium speed and slowly add the yeast mixture until fully incorporated. This should take 3 to 4 minutes.

Add the butter and the salt and switch to high speed for 4 to 5 minutes until you get a smooth, creamy dough.

(CONTINUED)

SWEET SOURDOUGH PREFERMENT

155 g (1¼ c) bread flour
50 g (scant ½ c) whole wheat flour
10 g (2 tsp packed) grated panela
100 g (⅓ c + 1½ Tbsp) water
100 g (½ c) mature sourdough starter

DOUGH

2 g (½ tsp) active dry yeast
100 g (⅓ c + 1½ Tbsp) whole milk, warm
250 g (2 c) all-purpose flour
20 g (2½ Tbsp) whole wheat flour
75 g (⅓ c + ½ Tbsp) sweet sourdough preferment
1 large egg
35 g (2½ Tbsp packed) grated panela
Dash of vanilla extract
50 g (3½ Tbsp) unsalted butter
4 g (1¼ tsp) kosher salt
400 g (14 oz) cubed ham
4 slices par-cooked bacon, finely chopped
1 large egg yolk, for brushing
100 g (⅓ c + 1½ Tbsp) melted unsalted butter for finishing

Transfer to a clean, buttered bowl, cover, and let ferment for 3½ hours at room temperature. Then transfer the dough to your fridge for 15 hours, or overnight.

Dump the dough onto a floured work surface and use a rolling pin to flatten the dough out into a big circle, about 12 inches in diameter. Next, use a pizza cutter or a chef's knife to cut the circle into 8 triangles, as if you were slicing a pizza.

Preheat the oven to 375°F.

Grab one triangle and pull the base lower than the two corners to the left and right of the base. Add ⅛ of the ham and bacon, and use the two left/right corners to stretch over the top of the filling and create a seam.

Next, in one motion, roll the ham mixture forward and tighten it. Elongate the rest of the dough, and roll the base filled with the mixture to the right side, creating a diagonal fold. Repeat this going toward the left side, and continue alternating until the last tip of the dough is folded underneath. You should end up with a small log that has 2 to 3 diagonal seams. Repeat this step to make the rest of the cachitos.

Place the cachitos on a parchment-lined sheet pan. In a small bowl, whisk together the egg yolk and a pinch of salt. Brush the cachitos with the egg wash and let rest for 30 minutes.

Place the sheet pan in the oven and bake for 20 to 25 minutes or until golden brown. Hot out of the oven, brush your cachitos with melted butter and serve warm.

PAN DE CEMITA

Sandwiches have become a big part of Mexican food culture. We have talked about bolillos and and the types of tortas (sandwiches) you can make with the bolillo. A cemita, however, is in a class of its own. Made with a round, crunchy, yet soft sesame bun, you can find many different cemita styles across México as well as in food trucks in the United States. The bread has an airiness to it, oftentimes with the addition of lard to give it a fuller flavor. This bread is special to me because it epitomizes the simplicity of what a sandwich bun can be, and it is consistently made across Mexican eateries. I used two preferments in this recipe to create balance between the milkiness and airiness of the yeast with the creaminess and tang of the sourdough. You also want to make sure you use salvaje, or wheat bran, on the bottom of these while baking to give them a nice, crisp bottom with some extra flavor from the toasted bran.

YEASTED PREFERMENT

In a tall jar or large container with a lid, mix the flour, water, and yeast with your hand or a fork. Ensure that no dry flour remains at the bottom of the jar.

Make sure the container is covered and let it rest at room temperature (ideally between 70° and 80°F) for 12 hours. It should become a creamy, bubbly, and funky mixture that expands in size.

SOURDOUGH PREFERMENT

In a tall jar or large container with a lid, mix the bread flour, whole wheat flour, water, and mature sourdough starter with your hand or a fork. Ensure that no dry flour remains at the bottom of the jar.

Cover the container and let it rest at room temperature (ideally between 70° and 80°F) for 4 hours. It should double in size and have a firm, bubbly structure on the top. Once the preferment is ready to use, you can start baking straight away or place it in your fridge for later use (up to 2 days).

DOUGH

In the bowl of a stand mixer with the dough hook attachment, combine the yeasted and sourdough preferments with 250 g (1 c + 1 Tbsp) of the water (and milk, if using) and dissolve.

Next, on low speed, mix in the all-purpose flour, whole grain flour, white rice flour, sugar, and milk powder (if using) until just combined. Moving up to medium speed, slowly add the fresh yeast to the dough. It might take a few minutes to fully absorb and become a smooth dough again.

(CONTINUED)

YEASTED PREFERMENT

50 g (⅓ c + 1 Tbsp) all-purpose flour
50 g (3½ Tbsp) warm water
1 g (¼ tsp) instant yeast

SOURDOUGH PREFERMENT

30 g (¼ c) bread flour
20 g (2½ Tbsp) whole wheat flour
50 g (3½ Tbsp) warm water
25 g (2 Tbsp) mature sourdough starter

DOUGH

100 g (½ c) yeasted preferment
100 g (½ c) sourdough preferment
350 g (1½ c) water
425 g (3½ c) all-purpose flour
75 g (½ c) whole grain flour
60 g (½ c) white rice flour
15 g (⅛ c) granulated sugar
7 g (1½ tsp) milk powder (If you don't have milk powder, replace half of the called-for water with whole milk)
1 g (½ tsp) fresh yeast
15 g (3 tsp) lard or softened unsalted butter
11 g (1 Tbsp) kosher salt
300 g (2⅓ c + 1 Tbsp) sesame seeds, for topping

Once the fresh yeast is fully absorbed, move up to medium-high speed and add the lard all at once. Allow the dough to mix and incorporate the fat for 3 to 4 minutes.

Add the salt with a splash of water, making sure the dough comes back together and there is no moisture on the sides of the mixing bowl. Transfer to a clean, oiled bowl, cover, and let rest for 3 hours at room temperature. Transfer to the fridge for at least 8 hours, or overnight.

After the cold fermentation stage, divide into eight 150-g pieces (about the size of medium tomatoes). Shape the pieces into round balls and place on a parchment-lined sheet pan, 3 by 3. Let the buns proof for 2 hours at room temperature.

During the last 30 minutes of proofing, preheat the oven to 450°F. Spritz the dough with water and sprinkle with sesame seeds. Place the sheet pan with the buns in the oven and bake for 25 minutes or until golden brown.

CEMITA MILANESA DE POLLO

The cemita milanesa de pollo is one of the most iconic Mexican tortas you can find. Originating in Puebla, México, it features a key ingredient that really distinguishes it from other tortas: papalo. This ancient Mexican herb is quite prevalent in Pueblan cooking, and is often described as having the fresh, bold flavor of cilantro and the slight bitterness of arugula. The papalo is a much needed textural, refreshing element in this cemita, as it is loaded with a perfectly crisp chicken cutlet, spicy chipotles in adobo, salty quesillo, and avocado. I love to go out to New York City neighborhoods in Queens, like Corona and Sunnyside, to get my fix, as there is a very strong and delicious Mexican food scene in these areas. As mentioned in the preceding recipe, the cemita bread is absolutely critical to the success of a cemita, because the light and airy texture lends itself as the perfect accompaniment to various fillings.

Heat the canola oil in a skillet over medium heat until it reaches roughly 375°F.

You will need three separate bowls for your dredge. In one bowl, add the all-purpose flour. In the second bowl, whisk together the eggs with the milk. In the third bowl, add the plain breadcrumbs, cayenne pepper, dried oregano, salt, and black pepper.

Dip one chicken cutlet into the all-purpose flour, then into the egg mixture, and finally into the breadcrumb mixture. Repeat with the second chicken cutlet. Place each cutlet in the skillet with the hot oil and fry both sides for roughly 5 minutes per side, or until the internal temperature reaches 165°F.

Remove the chicken cutlets and place them on a cooling rack or a paper towel–lined plate and set aside.

Slice your pan de cemita rolls in half and spread the mashed avocado on each bottom. Add a splash of lemon juice and a sprinkle of flaky salt and cracked black pepper. Add a chicken cutlet on each bottom, a handful of shredded quesillo, a heaping tablespoon (or two) of the chipotles in adobo, the papalo, onion, and the top bun. Smash your cemitas down slightly and enjoy!

Makes
2 SANDWICHES

110 g (½ c) canola oil
125 g (1 c) all-purpose flour
2 large eggs
30 g (2 Tbsp) whole milk
105 g (1 c) plain breadcrumbs
2 g (1 tsp) cayenne pepper
1 g (1 tsp) dried oregano
3 g (1 tsp) kosher salt
6 g (1 Tbsp) freshly ground black pepper
2 chicken breast cutlets
2 Pan de Cemita rolls (page 75)
1 whole ripe avocado, mashed
Juice of 1 lemon
Pinch flaky sea salt
Pinch cracked black pepper
240 g (2 c) quesillo (queso Oaxaca), pulled apart
1 can chipotles en adobo
1 bunch papalo, or any leafy green if you cannot find
1 half white onion, sliced into rings

NOTE: To make breadcrumbs, take any bread that's a few days old, like a bolillo or pan de tres puntas, tear it into pieces, and pulverize it in a blender. I like something with a nice, bold, and rustic crust. A small blender of the kind you make a smoothie with is ideal; a food processor can leave you with crumbs that are too coarse.

SOURDOUGH
Rustic, Savory, and Sweet

Baking bread with sourdough is not a trend or a fad. It is also not exclusive to any one culture or class, nor is it designed to be a bread baking technique with gatekeepers. The art of baking bread without any commercially cultivated form of yeast dates back thousands of years and spans several continents, most notably Africa and the Middle East. Making simple, rustic, and flavorful bread at home using only natural leavening does not need to be an intimidating math problem or science formula. The truth is that you can easily bake successful, delicious loaves for your friends and family.

Although some of these breads might not typically be made with sourdough in everyday life in the regions where they are best known, I do believe that historically, a lot of bread in Latin America was indeed naturally fermented, like the first whole grain versions of pan de coco baked in wood-fired ovens, pan chapla made with a corn ferment called chica de jora, or the original pan de Ambato made with pea flour. I also genuinely believe that it is the most fun way to bake bread because of how magical it feels to create a preferment and use it to make your bread rise. In this chapter, you will not only find rustic loaves and loaves with flavorful additions, but also a lot of sweet treats like the typical pan dulces found throughout several countries.

As a point of reference when baking sourdough, here is a snapshot of the time frame that I typically use when baking at home. There are several different stages of fermentation to take into consideration, and while each recipe does vary, I am usually starting the process two days before I want to bake my bread (this assumes you have gone through the process of building your sourdough starter and it is ready for use, which you can read about on page 16).

MONDAY

The first thing I'll do before baking my sourdough breads is build my sourdough preferment. Each recipe will have a distinct build, and admittedly these builds have a little buffer built into them, meaning there should be some extra. I do this for a couple of reasons:

1. Imagine accidentally spilling or throwing away your preferment. Not fun! If there was some extra built, you can rest assured that you will have something to add to your mix.

2. Having extra sourdough preferment means you have some extra to feed for later builds. Each recipe will call for a build, but then also call for an exact amount to add to the dough. Make sure you are adding what the final dough recipe calls for and save the extra to feed later.

I love to give my sourdough preferment build an overnight fermentation, so I will typically feed it, let it rest at room temperature for roughly 4 hours, then transfer it to the fridge so that I can do my mix the next day:

4:00 p.m.: Feed sourdough preferment according to the recipe, cover, and let rest at room temperature.

8:00 p.m.: Place the sourdough preferment in the fridge overnight.

TUESDAY

I like to mix right at noon because it gives me flexibility to ferment the dough slightly longer if necessary. I don't like getting caught shaping dough super late, but if that's your thing, go for it!

12:00 p.m.: Start the mix. Every recipe in this chapter will have different mixes and rest times, but ultimately most bulk fermentation times will be somewhere between 4 and 5 hours.

4:00 to 5:00 p.m.: Divide and shape your dough, if it is a rustic dough. Some doughs call for an overnight cold bulk, so you would simply transfer the dough to the fridge overnight.

WEDNESDAY

I love to let any shaped dough get at least 12 hours of fermentation in the fridge. The longer, the better, up to 18 hours in a fridge that is somewhere between 39° and 45°F.

8:00 a.m. (Rustic dough): Place a dutch oven or pizza steel or stone in the oven and preheat it.

8:00 a.m. (Enriched dough): Remove cold bulked dough from the fridge, shape, and proof. Follow the instructions of each specific recipe for exact timing on the proof and bake.

9:00 a.m. (Rustic dough): Bake your rustic loaf of bread!

11:00 a.m. (Enriched dough): Bake your panes dulces!

Keep in mind this is a general timeline. Each recipe will have specific timing to follow that you will also need to adapt to your environment.

PAN CASERO

Fresh, rustic table bread is one of the most fulfilling things you can make in your own kitchen. In Latin America, there are several different versions of pan casero, translated roughly as "homemade bread." If you want a simple starting point to making a "country" style sourdough loaf, this method will take you there. This recipe is a guideline, and I encourage you to make modifications to the type of flour you use, the amount of water you use, and any of the other ingredients or techniques that are listed as you become more comfortable baking it. Put another way, making pan casero is the perfect way for you to learn how to think like a baker and develop the confidence you need to bake other types of loaves that you might not be as familiar with.

I recommend using *up to* 750 g (3 c + 3 Tbsp) of water for a basic loaf of bread that is hand mixed. If you are new to baking, you can use as little as 650 g (2¾ c) of water for the dough. This will allow you to get comfortable handling dough and working with fermentation. The amount of water you use depends on your ambition or skill level. If you are new to baking, sometimes trying to incorporate too much water too quickly can be detrimental to your bake—the more water you incorporate, the greater the possibility of working with a soupy mess. However, using higher percentages of water will result in a crispier, lighter loaf of bread, which is worth pursuing. For these reasons, I recommend adding water in stages for it all to incorporate properly.

SOURDOUGH PREFERMENT

In a tall jar or large container with a lid, mix the bread flour, whole wheat flour, water, and mature sourdough starter with your hand or a fork. Ensure that no dry flour remains at the bottom of the jar.

Cover the container and let it rest at room temperature (ideally between 70° and 80°F) for 4 hours. It should double in size and have a firm, bubbly structure on the top. Once the preferment is ready to use, you can start baking straight away or place it in your fridge for later use (up to 2 days).

DOUGH

In a mixing bowl, combine 600 g (2½ c + 1 Tbsp) of the water with the sourdough preferment and dissolve it. It may not dissolve completely, which is fine. Slowly add the bread flour, whole wheat flour, and all-purpose flour with one hand while mixing with the other. At some point, both hands will be needed. The goal is to incorporate the water into the flours. Once it starts to come together and feels like a dry, rough dough, let it rest for 5 minutes.

SOURDOUGH PREFERMENT

50 g (⅓ c + 1 Tbsp) bread flour
50 g (scant ½ c) whole wheat flour
100 g (¼ c + 3 Tbsp) warm water
50 g (¼ c) mature sourdough starter

DOUGH

750 g (3 c + 3 Tbsp) warm water
210 g (1 c) sourdough preferment
600 g (4¾ c + 1 Tbsp) bread flour
200 g (1⅔ c) whole wheat flour
200 g (1½ c + 1½ Tbsp) all-purpose flour
20 g (2 Tbsp + ½ tsp) kosher salt

82   PAN Y DULCE

Add 50 g (3½ Tbsp) of the water to the dough, squeezing and mixing until it gets fully absorbed and there isn't any water streaking the sides of the bowl. Let the dough rest for 5 minutes. Repeat this step one more time with another 50 g (3½ Tbsp) of the water. Let the dough rest for 10 minutes.

Adding the water in increments, mixing, and letting the dough rest is the method that I find most effective for making bread with a decent amount of water in it.

Add the remaining 50 g (3½ Tbsp) of water and the salt and incorporate for one final time. Squeeze the water and salt into the dough, but don't tear it. The water and salt will absorb with squeezing and gentle folding for 5 to 7 minutes. At first it may seem like the water will not incorporate, but trust the process and be patient.

Once there is no dry flour and the dough is silky and smooth, transfer to another tub or bowl and let rest for an hour at room temperature. It's wise to transfer from the mixing bowl because it will start to get dried-up flour particles that will later interfere with your folds.

After transferring the dough, strengthen it by stretching it from each side and folding it into the middle every 30 minutes, for a total of 2 times. You can also get away with no stretches if you aren't a perfectionist and just want to eat good bread.

Let your dough ferment for a total of 4½ hours, which started the moment the sourdough preferment was added to the water. Signs to look for at the end of this initial fermentation period are a smooth surface, bubbles, elasticity when you pull at the top, and a slight weblike structure at the bottom when you turn the dough out on the table.

Once you're ready to shape, flour the work surface and divide the dough into 2 pieces. You can shape the loaves into round shapes or into tube shapes, just make sure you are applying tension to the dough.

Proof on a linen baker's cloth or cutting board, seam side up, for about 30 minutes at room temperature, then place in your fridge overnight (8 to 12 hours). You can leave uncovered as the seam side will be the bottom side so any skin that forms will get baked off and help form the bottom crust. Alternatively, you can cover with a simple plastic bag or dust with wheat bran and cover with a kitchen towel.

Place a baking stone, steel, or cast-iron skillet inside the oven and preheat to 500°F. If you are using a stone or steel, add a baking pan in the bottom of the oven for ice when loading.

Load into the oven depending on your baking vessel of choice. If using a cast-iron skillet, cut out a piece of parchment that fits the bottom of the skillet, place the dough on it, seam side down, slash the dough with a knife or blade, cover, and put the hot skillet back in the oven.

If you are using a baking stone or steel, place a piece of parchment on a loading peel, place the dough on it, and slash the dough with a knife or blade. Load onto the stone or steel, add ice to the baking pan, and use a spray bottle to spray the surface of the loaves and the inside of the oven.

Lower the heat to 465°F and bake for 20 minutes.

Let the steam out by uncovering the cast-iron skillet or simply opening the oven door if the loaves are on a stone or steel. Bake for 25 more minutes. I like to bake dark, so sometimes I go a little extra, and I finish my bake with the oven door open to let all the moisture out during the last couple of minutes.

Let cool on a wire rack before slicing, or eat warm out of the oven.

PAN CASERO INTEGRAL

I love to provide a whole grain version of staple breads so that you have a guide for mixing things up. This dough uses 50 percent whole wheat flour, honey, and a bit more water in the dough, as whole wheat absorbs more water during the mixing process. As you progress in your baking journey, feel free to use more or less flour and water to suit your baking style. Additionally, I added a touch of amaranth and brown rice flour to this one, but not too much as it accelerates the fermentation process. This dough pairs well with the flavors and aromas of banana leaf, so if you have it available, I recommend you proof and bake on a banana leaf.

SOURDOUGH PREFERMENT

In a tall jar or large container with a lid, mix the bread flour, amaranth flour, brown rice flour, whole wheat flour, water, and mature sourdough starter with your hand or a fork. Ensure that no dry flour remains at the bottom of the jar.

Cover the container and let it rest at room temperature (ideally between 70° and 80°F) for 4 hours. It should double in size and have a firm, bubbly structure on the top. Once the preferment is ready to use, you can start baking straight away or place it in your fridge for later use (up to 2 days).

DOUGH

In a mixing bowl, add 675 g (2¾ c + 2 Tbsp) of the water, the bread flour, whole wheat flour, all-purpose flour, brown rice flour, and amaranth flour and mix thoroughly until there isn't much dry flour left. This part is important in order to get a good start to the gluten development. Cover and let this mixture rest for 1 hour.

Next, add the sourdough preferment, honey, and 50 g (3½ Tbsp) of the water to the dough, squeezing and mixing until it gets fully absorbed and there isn't any water streaking the sides of the bowl. Let the dough rest for 10 minutes. Add another 50 g (3½ Tbsp) of the water to the dough, squeezing and mixing until it gets fully absorbed, and let it rest for 10 more minutes. During this mixing process it is important that you are patient and that you ensure the water absorbs into the dough each time. (If at any time it feels too wet or you do not think you can add more water, simply add the salt and move on to the fermentation stage).

Add the remaining 25 g (1 Tbsp + 2 tsp) of water and the salt and incorporate one final time. Squeeze the water and salt into the dough, but don't tear it. The water and salt will absorb with squeezing and gentle folding after 5 to 7 minutes.

(CONTINUED)

SOURDOUGH PREFERMENT

40 g (⅓ c) bread flour
5 g (1 Tbsp) amaranth flour
5 g (2 tsp) brown rice flour
50 g (scant ½ c) whole wheat flour
100 g (¼ c + 3 Tbsp) warm water
50 g (¼ c) mature sourdough starter

DOUGH

800 g (3⅓ c + 1 Tbsp) warm water
250 g (2 c) bread flour
500 g (4 c + 2½ Tbsp) whole wheat flour
200 g (1⅔ c + ½ Tbsp) all-purpose flour
25 g (3 Tbsp) brown rice flour
25 g (¼ c) amaranth flour
210 g (1 c) sourdough preferment
15 g (2 tsp) honey
20 g (2 Tbsp + ½ tsp) kosher salt
Wheat bran, for dusting

Once there is no dry flour and the dough is silky and smooth, transfer to another lightly oiled bowl. After transferring the dough, strengthen the dough by stretching it from each side and folding it into the middle every 30 minutes, for a total of 2 times.

Let your dough ferment for a total of 4½ hours, which started the moment the sourdough preferment was added to the dough. Signs to look for at the end of this initial fermentation period are a smooth surface, bubbles, elasticity when you pull at the top, and a slight weblike structure at the bottom when you turn the dough out on the table.

Once you're ready to shape, flour the work surface and divide the dough into 2 pieces. You can shape your loaves into round shapes or into tube shapes, just make sure you are applying tension to the dough.

Dust a cutting board or a canvas baking cloth liberally with wheat bran. Place your dough seam side up and dust the bottom of the dough with more wheat bran. Let proof at room temperature for about 3 hours, or until the dough slightly bounces back when poked.

Place a baking stone, steel, or cast-iron skillet inside the oven and preheat to 500°F. If you are using a stone or steel, add a baking pan in the oven at the bottom for ice when loading.

Load into the oven depending on your baking vessel of choice. If using a cast-iron skillet, cut out a piece of parchment that fits the bottom of the skillet, place the dough on it, seam side down, slash the dough with a knife or blade, cover, and put the hot skillet back in the oven.

If you are using a baking stone or steel, place a piece of parchment on a loading peel, place the dough on it, seam side down, and slash with a knife or blade. Load onto the stone, add ice to the baking pan, and use a spray bottle to spray the surface of the loaves and the inside of the oven.

Lower the heat to 465°F and bake for 20 minutes.

Let the steam out by uncovering the cast-iron skillet or simply opening the oven door if the loaves are on a stone or steel. Bake for 25 more minutes. I like to bake dark, so sometimes I go a little extra, and I finish my bake with the oven door open to let all the moisture out during the last couple of minutes.

Let cool on a wire rack before slicing or eat warm out of the oven.

PAN DE TRES PUNTAS

Makes
4 LOAVES

SOURDOUGH PREFERMENT
25 g (3 Tbsp) bread flour
25 g (3 Tbsp) whole wheat flour
50 g (3½ Tbsp) warm water
25 g (2 Tbsp) mature sourdough
starter

DOUGH
365 g (1½ c + 1 Tbsp) water
250 g (2 c) bread flour
250 g (2 c) whole wheat flour
100 g (½ c) sourdough
preferment
40 g (3 Tbsp packed) grated
panela
15 g (1 Tbsp + 2 tsp) kosher salt
Wheat bran, for dusting

With hundreds of different types of breads baked in Perú, it is no surprise that you will encounter some loaves that look unlike any others. Pan de tres puntas, or "bread of three points," is a special loaf. Shaped like a puffy, rustic triangle with slash marks on the surface, this bread is commonly eaten on Sundays in the city of Arequipa.

Why is it shaped like this? It's a big debate among the people of Arequipa. Some residents claim it represents the Holy Trinity—Perú is 85 to 90 percent Catholic. Some say the three points reference the three distinct volcanoes in the region: Chachani, Pichu Pichu, and Misti. Bakeries in the city make pan de tres puntas with traditional techniques, such as using a wood-fired oven and paying close attention to the grains used as well as the fermentation. There is no better way to spend the weekend than with a hearty pork stew and this delicious, freshly baked loaf. My version includes a sourdough preferment and a good percentage of whole grains to capture the earthy flavor reminiscent of mountain living.

SOURDOUGH PREFERMENT

In a tall jar or large container with a lid, mix the bread flour, whole wheat flour, water, and mature sourdough starter with your hand or a fork. Ensure that no dry flour remains at the bottom of the jar.

Cover the container and let it rest at room temperature (ideally between 70° and 80°F) for 4 hours. It should double in size and have a firm, bubbly structure on the top. Once the preferment is ready to use, you can start baking straight away or place it in your fridge for later use (up to 2 days).

DOUGH

In a large bowl, combine the water, bread flour, whole wheat flour, sourdough preferment, and panela. Mix with your hands by squeezing and turning until there is no dry flour left. Allow the dough to rest for 20 minutes.

Add the salt with a splash of water and squeeze until the salt is thoroughly combined.

Transfer to a clean, lightly oiled or greased bowl and cover. Let ferment for 4 hours, or until the dough is doubled in size and bouncy. Cover and transfer to the fridge for 15 hours.

On a floured work surface, divide the dough into 4 pieces, roughly 250 g each, and loosely shape into a ball (about the size of a large orange). Dust with flour or wheat bran and let the 4 pieces rest for an hour at room temperature to loosen up.

Flatten the balls of dough and shape each piece into a triangle by using your fingers to fold and tuck the dough into itself and form a triangle. Roll out each of the three points on the triangle to strengthen and tighten the shape.

Place on a canvas cloth dusted with wheat bran and a little whole wheat flour and let proof for 2 hours.

During the last hour, place a baking stone or steel inside the oven and preheat it to 500°F.

Transfer the loaves to a parchment-lined loading peel or thin wooden cutting board and load onto the stone or steel. Make two diagonal slashes in the middle with a serrated knife or razor blade and mist each loaf with water.

Load into the oven, lower the heat to 450°F, and bake for 30 minutes. The bread will be a nice deep brown color when done, with a crisp bottom that sounds hollow when tapped. Let cool and serve.

PAN CHUTA

Many people are familiar with Cusco, the old capital of the Incan empire and popular tourist destination for exploring the surrounding mountains and ruins. But did you know that just 15 miles away, deep in the Andes Mountains, lies the proclaimed bread capital of Perú? Oropesa, a district in the Quispicanchi province, is so deeply entrenched with artisanal baking that it is renowned for being the most delicious bread destination in the country. A large percentage of the citizens bake bread for a living. Sounds like my kind of town.

The most desired bread made in the city, pan chuta, is claimed to be so unique that it can't be replicated elsewhere due to the use of the water from the Apu Pachatusan, the highest mountain in the Cusco valley. Shaped like a big disk, pan chuta has a delicious, anise-infused flavor and creamy texture on the inside that is highly desirable at any time of day, but particularly for breakfast. Oftentimes, bran is used on the outside to create more texture and flavor, and some ovens are brushed with eucalyptus leaves before the bake for more layers of aroma and flavor. From my understanding, shortening can be used in pan chuta for a creamier texture, but I choose to use either butter or coconut oil.

This is one of my favorite breads to make fully with sourdough because of the complexity in flavor and texture that can be achieved when forgoing the use of instant yeast or any other type of preferment—besides, we aren't all lucky enough to have water from Apu Pachatusan, so we've got to find that extra flavor somewhere.

SOURDOUGH PREFERMENT

In a tall jar or large container with a lid, mix the bread flour, whole wheat flour, water, and mature sourdough starter with your hand or a fork. Ensure that no dry flour remains at the bottom of the jar.

Cover the container and let it rest at room temperature (ideally between 70° and 80°F) for 4 hours. It should double in size and have a firm, bubbly structure on the top. Once the preferment is ready to use, you can start baking straight away or place it in your fridge for later use (up to 2 days).

DOUGH

In a large mixing bowl, combine 645 g (2¾ c) of the water with the sourdough preferment, the eggs, and the vanilla. Whisk everything together until evenly combined and then add the bread flour, whole wheat flour, anise seed, and cinnamon. Use both hands to mix until most of the flour is absorbed and the dough is roughly incorporated. Let rest for 10 minutes.

Add the fat (butter or coconut oil) by rubbing it over the surface of the dough and using your hands to squeeze it in. This process might take about

SOURDOUGH PREFERMENT

50 g (⅓ c + 1 Tbsp) bread flour
50 g (scant ½ c) whole wheat flour
100 g (¼ c + 3 Tbsp) warm water
50 g (¼ c) mature sourdough starter

DOUGH

705 g (3 c) water
250 g (heaped 1 c) sourdough preferment
2 large eggs
1 g (¼ tsp) vanilla extract/essence/paste
710 g (5⅔ c) bread flour
295 g (2½ c) whole wheat flour
6 g (1 Tbsp) ground anise seed
2 g (1 tsp) ground cinnamon
50 g (3½ Tbsp) unsalted butter or coconut oil
20 g (2 tbsp + ½ tsp) kosher salt
Wheat bran, for dusting

10 minutes, but be patient and continue to squeeze and mix the dough until it becomes smooth and there is no noticeable fat left. Let the dough rest for another 10 minutes.

Finally, add the salt and the remaining 60 g (¼ c) of water. Apply the same technique used for the fat to incorporate the salt and water into the dough for about 10 minutes, or until it smooths out again. You should end up with a dough that is slightly sticky, but smooth to the touch. Transfer from this bowl to another clean, lightly oiled bowl or container. Let the dough rest for 30 minutes.

Next, strengthen the dough by stretching each corner and folding it into the center. When you have stretched each side, flip the dough over completely. Cover the dough and let it ferment for 3½ hours at room temperature. Ideally, your kitchen should be somewhere between 70° and 80°F. If you have a colder or warmer kitchen, use the information found in Temperature, Climate, and Altitude (page XX) to make the necessary adjustments to your timing.

Once the dough is finished fermenting in bulk, dump it onto a floured work surface and divide it into 3 pieces. Lightly shape the dough into round balls, but not with too much tension. Dust the dough with the wheat bran and cover with kitchen towels. Let the dough proof for 3 hours at room temperature directly on the work surface.

Place a baking stone or steel inside the oven and preheat to 500°F.

Meanwhile, lightly flour a work surface and place one of the dough balls on it. The dough should have relaxed quite a bit but still be springy and strong. Flatten the dough into a disk, about 10 inches in diameter. Transfer the flattened dough of the first loaf to a parchment-lined loading peel and load into the oven once it is preheated.

Bake the first loaf of pan chuta for 5 minutes at 500°F, then decrease the heat to 465°F and bake for 30 minutes, or until the crust is a deep, caramel brown. Let the stone reheat for about 45 minutes and then repeat the baking process with the remaining two loaves.

SHECA

Nestled near the Santa María stratovolcano, the city of Quetzaltenango is an artisanal baking hub in the western highlands of Guatemala. The sheca, one of the most widely consumed breads throughout Guatemala, is said to have originated in this area although its exact origin is debated. In the La Ermita y la Esmeralda Valley, on the way to Quetzaltenango, the city of San Pedro Sacatepéquez is home to locals who call themselves "shecanos"—a nod to the fact that this bread was made in San Pedro even before the arrival of colonists.

With the subtle hints of anise and the perfect touch of sweetness, it's no wonder that these are highly sought after around the country. Shecas have a unique look because the base is shaped and then topped with a smaller piece of dough, which ultimately looks like a small knot and sets it apart from other breads.

SOURDOUGH PREFERMENT

In a tall jar or large container with a lid, mix the bread flour, whole wheat flour, water, and mature sourdough starter with your hand or a fork. Ensure that no dry flour remains at the bottom of the jar.

Cover the container and let it rest at room temperature (ideally between 70° and 80°F) for 4 hours. It should double in size and have a firm, bubbly structure on the top. Once the preferment is ready to use, you can start baking straight away or place it in your fridge for later use (up to 2 days).

DOUGH

In the bowl of a stand mixer with the dough hook attachment, combine the all-purpose flour, whole wheat flour, bread flour, anise, panela, honey, sourdough preferment, and 280 g (1 c + 3 Tbsp) of the water. Mix on low speed for 3 minutes, until the dough is just combined. Let the mixture rest for 5 minutes and then add 20 g (1½ Tbsp) of the water and the lard. Start on low speed for 2 minutes and increase to medium speed for 5 minutes, or until all the fat and water are combined into the dough.

Finally, add the salt and the remaining water while the mixer is on medium speed. Let the dough mix for 5 minutes and finish on high speed for 3 minutes. The dough should be smooth and elastic, holding its form and not runny or too sticky. Using wet hands, transfer the dough to a clean, lightly oiled bowl and cover. Let the dough rest at room temperature for 4 hours.

After the initial rise, flour a work surface and dump out the dough. Divide the dough into five 200-g pieces (about the size of large tomatoes) and shape them into round balls. Cover and let them rest for 30 minutes.

Next, grab each dough ball and gently pull up a portion of the dough from the center, but do not allow it to break. Once you have a little bit of slack, twist

the portion that has come up and nestle it back into the center of the dough. Essentially, you are creating a small ball of dough that sits on a bigger ball of dough, with a twisting portion that connects them.

Transfer your shecas to a parchment-lined loading peel dusted with wheat bran. Dust the top of the shecas with flour, and cover with a kitchen towel. Let them proof at room temperature for 3 hours.

Place a baking stone or steel inside the oven and preheat to 500°F. Once preheated, load the shecas into the oven and lower the heat to 465°F. Bake for 35 minutes, or until there's a nice crackling, dark brown crust on the outside. Let cool and serve with coffee or chocolate.

PAN DE CAZUELA

Makes
3 LOAVES

SOURDOUGH PREFERMENT
50 g (⅓ c + 1 Tbsp) bread flour
50 g (scant ½ c) whole wheat flour
50 g (3½ Tbsp) warm water
50 g (¼ c) mature sourdough starter

DOUGH
500 g (4 c) bread flour
310 g (2½ c) all-purpose flour
200 g (1⅔ c) whole wheat flour
10 g (1 Tbsp + 2 tsp) anise seed
1 g (½ tsp) ground cinnamon
705 g (3 c) warm water
200 g (1 scant c) sourdough preferment
20 g (2 Tbsp + ½ tsp) kosher salt
150 g (1 c) chocolate chunks
150 g (1 c) raisins

Travel magazines don't yet talk about visiting Oaxaca just to check out the bread baking scene, but in my visits, I have been amazed by the caliber and quantity of bread in different parts of this Mexican state. In the bustling markets, bread is a constant, and not just a few small stands with a couple of loaves, but vendor upon vendor with stacks piled high of different types of bread. In the Mercado Central de Abastos, the largest market in Oaxaca, you can easily get lost in the maze of goods being offered, like freshly made tortillas, molcajetes, and generally anything you'd ever need—including piles and piles of pan cazuela.

This rustic loaf is baked in the form of a big upward spiral, with a dark brown, caramelized crust and a creamy interior filled with raisins and chocolate. It's no surprise to find chocolate infused into the bread, as Oaxacan chocolate is an important part of the daily food and drink culture. Tearing into this loaf brings me pure joy. Hailing from the municipality of Tlacolula, roughly 20 miles from Oaxaca Centro, pan de cazuela was originally baked in clay pots. The local bakers say that it is best baked in a wood-fired oven, as any other type of oven causes it to lose its distinct flavor. Although it is eaten year-round, during Día de los Muertos production is increased as pan cazuela decorates the altars of the dead along with other seasonal breads. I wanted to make this with only a sourdough preferment without any additional yeast because it has such a unique flavor profile and dark, bold crust—my favorite type of loaves to make with sourdough.

SOURDOUGH PREFERMENT

In a tall jar or large container with a lid, mix the bread flour, whole wheat flour, water, and mature sourdough starter with your hand. This preferment will be stiff so you may need to knead it lightly on your work surface after mixing.

Cover the container and let it rest at room temperature (ideally between 74° and 78°F) for 4 hours. It should double in size and have a firm, weblike structure on the inside. Once the preferment is ready to use, you can start baking straight away or place it in your fridge for later use (up to 2 days).

DOUGH

In a large mixing bowl, combine the bread flour, all-purpose flour, whole wheat flour, anise seed, and cinnamon with 645 g (2¾ c) of the water and mix until you have a rough but sticky dough, with not much dry flour left in the bowl. Let the mixture rest for 1 hour at room temperature.

(CONTINUED)

After this initial rest, spread the sourdough preferment and the salt on the surface of the dough with the remaining 60 g (¼ c) of water and begin incorporating by squeezing and mixing. This process will take about 10 minutes. Make sure you are not completely tearing into the dough as you squeeze and mix, and look for the dough to smooth out with no sign of water on the sides of the bowl. To further build strength, dump the dough onto a work surface. Wet your hands thoroughly, pick the dough up, and slap it back down, stretching the sides as it impacts the work surface. Try this for a few minutes and you should see the dough come together.

Place the dough in a clean, lightly oiled bowl or dough container, cover, and let rest for 30 minutes at room temperature.

Spread half of the chocolate and half of the raisins on the surface of the dough. Lift the corners of the dough and fold into the center until the mixture is covered. Flip the dough over and add the remaining chocolate and raisins. Repeat the stretching process. Cover and let ferment for 4 hours at room temperature.

After the initial fermentation stage, flour a work surface lightly and dump the dough on it. Divide into 3 equal pieces and pre-shape into rounds. Let the dough rounds rest for 45 minutes.

After the dough has relaxed, shape each round into a cylinder and extend it out as thinly and as long as possible, being careful not to tear it. Roll the elongated dough into a spiral shape, place on a board or canvas cloth, and let proof overnight in the fridge (about 12 hours).

Preheat your oven to 500°F. There are two options for baking these loaves. If you are confident in your shaping and the dough is not falling apart, you can bake directly on a stone or steel in the oven. If the shaping was a little loose, you can put these in a 9-inch cake pan to help keep their form.

If using the stone or steel, place the loaves on a parchment-lined loading peel dusted liberally with wheat bran, load into the oven, and reduce the heat to 465°F. Bake for 40 minutes, until a dark brown color sets.

If using cake pans, grease each one with oil and simply transfer the dough from your proofing vessel into the pan and bake for 40 minutes. Let cool before serving.

The Nostalgia of Birote

When it comes to the birote, nostalgia is everything. At least that's how it feels to me when I walk through the Mexican neighborhoods of Los Angeles and go to any of the esteemed torta shops.

The distinct characteristics of a birote baked in Guadalajara are almost like folklore—a tender miga, or crumb, that is soft and spongy, a crackling dark brown crust from a bold bake, and a salty, sour flavor that makes it the perfect vessel for a juicy torta. But not just any torta—we are talking about the torta ahogada, the "drowned sandwich." A heaping portion of juicy, tender carnitas is packed tightly into the birote, which makes you realize just how important it is to have the right bread for this sandwich because it can soak up and contain the filling. But this isn't the only thing it soaks up, as it then gets drowned in two different salsas. The salty, sourdough flavor of a birote is also the perfect complement to the spicy and fatty elements of the torta, which are often topped with pickled onions as a final accent.

The residents in various parts of Los Angeles, especially those from Guadalajara, will say that the bread made in any other city is not a birote due to the unique climate and altitude in their hometown. How exactly does altitude and humidity influence the flavor of bread? Different environments can create different flavors because every city has unique bacteria and yeasts floating around. If every bakery in Guadalajara is making 100 percent sourdough versions of birote, there could be a case made that these conditions do in fact create a unique flavor profile. Alas, the use of commercial yeast complicates things due to the high volume demands and production of the birote.

So can you make an "authentic" birote anywhere else in the world? I am giving you a recipe, so my answer is yes, but it is not without some consideration. We as bakers must keep in mind that naming conventions, customs, and traditions evoke emotion, especially when it comes to food. I believe that nostalgia is what really rules our mind and body—the sensory experience triggered when you eat something that tastes like your mother's or grandmother's cooking, for example. Why would a business owner drive all the way from Los Angeles to Tijuana to pick up bread from Guadalajara in the middle of the night if there was not at least some evocation of nostalgia and added value for their patrons?

On the flip side, my good friend Arturo who runs the Mexican-inspired bakery Gusto Bread (my favorite bakery in the Los Angeles area) has successfully made his version of the bread for some very delicious tortas ahogadas. It boils down to having an open mind and using the ingredients in your environment to make traditional foods. Arturo uses only organic ingredients and his sourdough starter has a unique, delicious flavor profile—one can only imagine how good this bread tastes. What I would recommend to you is that you use the highest quality flour that you can find to maximize the flavor profile you get from these birote. While there are recipes and stories about birote containing egg, lime, and even beer, I find comfort in letting fewer ingredients and good fermentation do the talking.

The history of immigration and food spans far and wide, and many cultures have adapted traditional food to the ingredients of a new land. Where is the line that determines when something is or isn't what it was back home? Authenticity can come across as a buzzword these days, so determining what it really means can be tricky—and I don't have the answer. This is probably the most subjective question one can ask, but my response to you is this: just make some damn birote.

BIROTE SALADO

SOURDOUGH PREFERMENT

75 g (scant ⅔ c) bread flour
25 g (3 Tbsp) whole wheat flour
100 g (¼ c + 3 Tbsp) water
25 g (2 Tbsp) mature sourdough
   starter

DOUGH

750 g (6 c) all-purpose flour
150 g (1¼ c) whole wheat flour
50 g (⅓ c + 1 Tbsp) bread flour
725 g (3 c + 1½ Tbsp) water
250 g (heaped 1 c) sourdough
   preferment
25 g (2 Tbsp + 2 tsp) kosher salt

SOURDOUGH PREFERMENT

In a tall jar or large container with a lid, mix the bread flour, whole wheat flour, water, and mature sourdough starter with your hand or a fork. Ensure that no dry flour remains at the bottom of the jar.

Cover the container and let it rest at room temperature (ideally between 70° and 80°F) for 8 to 10 hours, or until doubled in size. It should have a firm, bubbly structure on the top. Once the preferment is ready to use, you can start baking straight away or place it in your fridge for later use (up to 2 days).

DOUGH

In a mixing bowl, combine the all-purpose flour, whole wheat flour, bread flour, and 650 g (2¾ c) of the water. Mix until there is a rough dough with not much dry flour left at the bottom of the bowl. Cover and let rest at room temperature for 45 minutes.

Add the sourdough preferment and 25 g (1 Tbsp + 2 tsp) of the water to the dough. The goal is to incorporate this until it is smooth again, so mix and squeeze with your hands until the bowl does not have water streaks and no water or sourdough is visible on the surface. This should take about 10 minutes. Then, let the dough rest for 20 minutes.

Repeat the mixing process with another 25 g of water (1 Tbsp + 2 tsp) and let rest for another 20 minutes. Finally, add the salt and the remaining 25 g (1 Tbsp + 2 tsp) of water and repeat the mixing process. After the mixing process has been completed and you have a smooth dough with no moisture lingering on the surface, bottom, or sides, transfer the dough to a clean, lightly oiled bowl and cover.

Let the dough ferment for 3½ hours, but after the first 30 minutes, strengthen the dough. Lift each side of the dough, stretching it slightly, and fold it into the middle. Repeat this process one more time at the hour mark of the 3½ hours. Remember that fermentation begins as soon as the sourdough preferment is added, so in total this dough will go through an initial fermentation period of roughly 4½ hours.

After the initial fermentation period, flour a work surface and divide the dough into six 300-g pieces. Gently shape the dough into rounds with minimal tension. Dust the surface of the dough rounds with flour and let them rest for 30 minutes.

To give them their final shape, turn each dough round over onto the top side directly in front of you. Next, use the balls of your fingers to take the top side of the dough and fold over quickly into the top of the dough to create tension.

(CONTINUED)

Continue using your fingers to fold the dough into itself, applying tension as you go, until you create a cylinder. Use the palms of your hands on the ends to create a tight, pointed edge, preferably a rounded ball-like edge.

After shaping the remaining dough rounds, dust a canvas baking cloth with flour or wheat bran and place it on a sheet pan. Place the shaped loaves seam side down on the pan, lifting the cloth to create a division between them. Cover them with a canvas cloth, a large plastic bag, plastic wrap, or kitchen towels. Put the sheet pan in the fridge for an overnight fermentation, preferably for 15 hours.

The next day, place a baking stone or steel inside the oven and preheat to 500°F. Gently transfer two of the birotes to a parchment-lined loading peel or thin wooden cutting board, slash the birotes with a knife or blade straight down the middle, and load into the oven. Add ice cubes directly on the stone or steel (or in a separate baking pan placed at the bottom of your oven) and use a spray bottle to spray the loaves and the inside of the oven with water to create some steam. Bake the birotes for 35 to 40 minutes, making sure to rotate them around the 20-minute mark. You want them to take on a nice, bold color. Let them cool on a wire rack. Repeat the baking process with the remaining 4 loaves.

TORTA AHOGADA

Now that you've got some freshly baked, crunchy birotes, you don't want to miss out on making this classic torta. Torta Ahogada translates to "drowned sandwich," since the torta is drenched in two types of salsa before serving—one spicy and one rather mild. The inside of the torta has a layer of frijoles on one side of the birote, which serve as an accent to the tender, juicy carnitas stuffed on top. I had the pleasure of making Tortas Ahogadas with Chef Christina Martinez at one of my popups in New York City—she took care of making the delicious carnitas filling, frijoles, and salsas and I did my part in making a crunchy, sturdy birote to hold it all together. I've got to say that this was one of the most fun and delicious times I've ever had, and helped me learn even more about how to construct a proper torta.

PREPARE THE CARNITAS

Rub the salt on the pork and let rest, uncovered, in the fridge for at least 1 hour. In a large, heavy pot over medium heat, add the lard. Sear the pork in the lard for 10 minutes per side, or until you have a lightly charred exterior. After 20 minutes, reduce the heat and add the onion, garlic, clove, oregano, cumin, pepper, bay leaves, milk, water, and orange juice. Cover and let simmer. Cook until the pork is tender and easily shredded, 2 to 3 hours. Shred the pork and set aside.

PREPARE THE SALSA PICANTE

Prepare the chilies: Toast the guajillo and arbol chilies in a dry skillet over medium heat until fragrant. Soak in hot water for 20 to 30 minutes until softened.

Make the sauce: Blend the softened chilies, garlic, onion, apple cider vinegar, salt, oregano, and cumin until smooth. Strain and cook over medium heat for about 10 minutes. Adjust seasoning to taste.

ASSEMBLE AND DROWN THE TORTAS

Cut each sourdough birote in half and spread a thin layer of refried beans on the bottom and fill with the shredded pork. Place the filled tortas in a deep dish.

Drown your torta: Pour the salsa roja over the tortas until "drowned" to your liking. Add the salsa picante over the top. Garnish with sliced onion, cilantro, lime wedges, and avocado slices.

FOR THE CARNITAS

30 g (1½ Tbsp) kosher salt
2 kg (about 2 lbs) pork shoulder, trimmed and cut into large pieces
400 g (1½ c + 3 Tbsp) lard
1 large white onion, peeled and quartered
4 cloves garlic, peeled
4 pieces clove
12 g (2 Tbsp) dry oregano
15 g (2 Tbsp) ground cumin
7 g (1 Tbsp) freshly ground black pepper
2 bay leaves
120 g (½ c) whole milk
120 g (4 oz) water
Juice of two small oranges

FOR THE DROWNING SAUCE

See Salsa Roja recipe on page 302

SALSA PICANTE

6 dried guajillo chilies, seeded and stemmed
2 to 3 dried arbol chilies (adjust for heat), seeded and stemmed
2 cloves garlic
1 small onion, quartered
28 g (2 Tbsp) apple cider vinegar
Kosher salt to taste
2 g (1 tsp) dried oregano
2 g (1 tsp) ground cumin

FOR THE TORTA

6 birotes (page 98)
210 g (1 c) refried red beans
1 thinly sliced white onion or pickled red onion
1 bunch fresh cilantro leaves
4 lime wedges
1 avocado, sliced

MARRAQUETAS

SOURDOUGH PREFERMENT

25 g (3 Tbsp) bread flour
25 g (3 Tbsp) whole wheat flour
50 g (3½ Tbsp) warm water
50 g (¼ c) mature sourdough
starter

DOUGH

200 g (1 scant c) sourdough
preferment
350 g (1½ c) water
155 g (1¼ c) bread flour
290 g (2⅓ c) all-purpose flour
55 g (scant ½ c) whole wheat
flour
10 g (1 Tbsp) kosher salt
Wheat bran, for dusting

One of the most popular breads sold in Chile is the marraqueta, which has an iconic look. It is traditionally composed of small rolls joined together during the proofing process and pressed down the middle with a thin rod to create a natural seam. Baked in high heat and using simple ingredients, this is the Chilean version of what typical table bread or pan francés might be in other countries.

This bread is so popular that there are competitions in Santiago to see which baker makes the best one, similar to a "best baguette" competition you may see in cities like New York. It is said that the French brothers named Marraquette arrived in Valparaiso and began baking loaves that ultimately evolved into this unique Chilean staple. To me, it is also a great candidate to make with only sourdough as the shaping process is already fun. I tinkered with the flavor profile by adding a little whole grain flour.

SOURDOUGH PREFERMENT

In a tall jar or large container with a lid, mix the bread flour, whole wheat flour, water, and mature sourdough starter with your hand or a fork. Ensure that no dry flour remains at the bottom of the jar.

Cover the container and let it rest at room temperature (ideally between 70° and 80°F) for 4 hours. It should double in size and have a firm, bubbly structure on the top. Once the preferment is ready to use, you can start baking straight away or place it in your fridge for later use (up to 2 days).

DOUGH

In the bowl of a stand mixer with the dough hook attached, combine the sourdough preferment with 295 g (1¼ c) of the water and dissolve. Add the bread flour, all-purpose flour, and whole wheat flour and mix on low speed for 5 minutes, or until a shaggy dough forms. Switch the mixer to medium-high speed, add the salt, and slowly drizzle in the remaining water, until it is all absorbed and the dough comes back together to form a smooth surface, 3 to 4 minutes. Transfer the dough to a clean, lightly oiled bowl and cover. Let ferment at room temperature for 4 hours.

On a lightly floured work surface, divide the dough into eight 130-g pieces and form them into balls. Place two of the dough balls together, touching, and let rest for 30 minutes, covered. You should have 4 pieces of conjoined dough balls. After the rest period, use a thin rod (like the handle of a silicone spatula) to create a deep seam down the middle, vertically, of the conjoined dough balls. This should intersect the natural seam of where the dough balls are touching. On a flour-dusted canvas cloth or directly on a cutting board, place the 4

marraquetas top side down. Dust the bottoms (which are facing up) with wheat bran and let them proof at room temperature for 3 hours or until they almost double in size.

Place a baking stone or steel inside the oven and preheat to 500°F. Flip over the marraquetas onto a parchment-lined loading peel or thin wooden cutting board, and load into the oven. Spray the oven with water and add ice in a baking pan placed at the bottom of the oven to help create a steamy environment that will develop the crisp, crackling crust. Lower the heat to 450°F and bake for 25 to 30 minutes or until the loaves are fully colored and the bottom sounds hollow when tapped.

PAN CHAPLA

Makes
8 LOAVES

150 g (1¼ c) whole wheat flour
155 g (1¼ c) all-purpose flour
195 g (1½ c + 1 Tbsp) bread flour
7 g (1 Tbsp) ground anise seed
25 g (2 Tbsp) granulated sugar
350 g (1⅓ + 2 Tbsp) chicha de jora
7 g (2¼ tsp) kosher salt

Wheat production ramped up in the city known as Huamanga after colonization, which led to new baking traditions in this south central Andes region of Perú. After a battle for independence in 1825, the city's name was changed to Ayacucho, and during this Republican period the first pan chapla was baked. In the Quechua language, chapla means "crushed" and the bread is traditionally prepared by several artisans, each of whom have a particular role. The flour that is used in the dough comes from the watatas, or stone mills, that have been constructed in neighboring areas.

Pan chapla uses neither baker's yeast nor sourdough. Instead, its leavening comes from chicha de jora, a by-product of yellow corn that is fermented in a process similar to making beer. The chicha, in addition to a hint of anise, gives pan chapla a unique flavor. It is one of the most interesting things I have ever baked. I highly recommend you seek out chicha de jora, which you can find online. If you are in a major city, you might find it in the South American section of an international grocery store.

In the bowl of a stand mixer with the dough hook attachment, combine the whole wheat flour, all-purpose flour, bread flour, ground anise, sugar, and 280 g (1 c + 3 Tbsp) of the chicha de jora and mix on low speed for about 3 minutes or until the ingredients come together into a rough dough. Switch the mixer to medium speed and slowly trickle in 45 g (3 Tbsp) of the chicha. The goal is to drizzle in the chicha, let the dough absorb it, and continue to add the liquid. The dough should fully absorb and smooth out before adding more. This process will take about 5 minutes.

Set the mixer to high speed and add the salt with the remaining 25 g (1 Tbsp + 2 tsp) of chicha. Remember to slowly pour it in so that it does not splatter everywhere. Mix for 5 to 6 minutes, or until the dough is silky and smooth.

With wet hands, transfer the dough into a clean, lightly oiled bowl and cover. Let this ferment overnight, or about 12 hours, at room temperature.

After this fermentation period, dump the dough onto a floured work surface, divide it into eight 100-g pieces (about the size of small lemons), and shape them into round balls. Let them rest at room temperature for an additional 3 hours.

During the last hour of the proofing period, place a baking stone or steel inside the oven and preheat to 500°F.

Using a rolling pin and a heavily floured work surface, roll each dough ball into a round disk, 6 to 7 inches in diameter (they can be any size you want, but this is the size I go for to bake 3 at a time). Depending on the size of your peel or stone, transfer the amount of loaves that can fit onto a parchment-lined loading peel or thin wooden cutting board and load into the oven. Lower the heat to 465°F and bake for roughly 25 minutes, or until they are puffed up and golden brown. Let cool and serve. Repeat the baking process with the remaining loaves.

PAN RÚSTICO DE SORGO Y AMARANTO TOSTADO

△△△△△△△△△△△△

Makes

1 LARGE LOAF

∽∽∽∽∽∽∽∽∽∽∽∽

SOURDOUGH PREFERMENT

25 g (3 Tbsp) bread flour
25 g (¼ c) amaranth flour
25 g (3 Tbsp) whole wheat flour
25 g (3 Tbsp) sorghum flour
85 g (⅓ c + 1 tsp) warm water
50 g (¼ c) mature sourdough starter

DOUGH

50 g (⅓ c + 2 tsp) sorghum flour
50 g (½ c) amaranth flour
400 g (1½ c + 3 Tbsp) water
150 g (scant ¾ c) sourdough preferment
50 g (scant ½ c) whole wheat flour
205 g (1⅔ c) all-purpose flour
195 g (1½ c + 1 Tbsp) bread flour
12 g (1 Tbsp + 1 tsp) kosher salt

I wanted to create a rustic sourdough loaf that incorporates some of the native and abundant grains of Latin America, but also uses wheat to get a nice chew and good oven spring. As you will see throughout this book, amaranth and sorghum are my go-to grains to create potent, earthy flavor. For this loaf, I toasted these flours and found it intensified the flavor and aroma even before mixing into the dough. You can experiment with varying amounts of these flours but I found that this percentage works best to balance the flavors and textures of the gluten-free and gluten-filled flours. I also use a sourdough preferment that is fed with these grains, to really make sure the flavors pop. The shape of this bread was born out of my own curiosity to create something that felt unique and could be pulled apart easily to enjoy in various ways.

SOURDOUGH PREFERMENT

In a tall jar or large container with a lid, mix the bread flour, amaranth flour, whole wheat flour, sorghum flour, water, and mature sourdough starter with your hand or a fork. Ensure that no dry flour remains at the bottom of the jar.

Cover the container and let it rest at room temperature (ideally between 70° and 80°F) for 4 hours. It should double in size and have a firm, bubbly structure on the top. Once the preferment is ready to use, you can start baking straight away or place it in your fridge for later use (up to 2 days).

DOUGH

In a medium skillet over medium heat, toast the sorghum and amaranth flours for 5 to 6 minutes, or until the flours change to a golden/toasted brown color. You should smell sweet, nutty aromas at this point, reminiscent of popcorn.

In a large mixing bowl, combine 295 g (1¼ c) of the water with the sourdough preferment, dissolve, and then add the toasted sorghum and amaranth flours, whole wheat flour, all-purpose flour, and bread flour and mix until a rough dough forms and not much dry flour is left at the bottom of the bowl. Let the dough rest for 5 minutes.

Add 55 g (scant ¼ c) of the water and mix and squeeze the dough with both hands until the water absorbs completely and the dough smooths out, 6 to 7 minutes. Let the dough rest for 5 minutes.

Add the salt and the remaining 50 g (3½ Tbsp) of water and repeat the mixing and squeezing process until the salt and water are completely absorbed and you have a smooth, silky dough. Transfer to a lightly oiled bowl and cover. Let the dough ferment at room temperature for 4 hours.

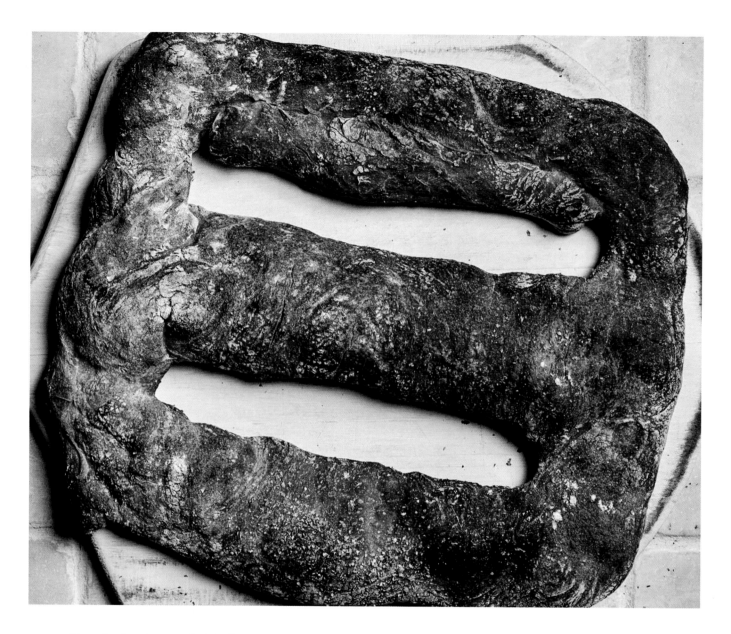

Turn the dough onto a lightly floured work surface and lightly pre-shape into a rounded shape. No need to divide this dough as we are making a large loaf. Let the dough rest for 15 minutes.

Flatten the dough and pat it down as thinly as possible. Using a knife or bench scraper, cut two long slits into the dough and spread the bread out into three parts. Place onto a piece of parchment paper and let proof for 3 hours at room temperature.

Place a baking stone or steel inside the oven and preheat to 500°F. Spray the oven and the loaf with water and add some ice in a baking pan placed on the bottom rack of the oven to create some steam. Lower the heat to 450°F and bake for 45 to 50 minutes, until the crust is a toasty, dark, and bold brown color

Cool on a wire rack before serving.

PAN DE PLÁTANO A LA PARRILLA

SOURDOUGH PREFERMENT

50 g (⅓ c + 1 Tbsp) all-purpose
   flour
25 g (3 Tbsp) whole wheat flour
25 g (3 Tbsp) bread flour
5 g (1 Tbsp) amaranth flour
100 g (¼ c + 3 Tbsp) warm water
50 g (¼ c) mature sourdough
   starter

DOUGH

4 small ripe plantains, or 2 large
   ones
725 g (3 c + 1½ Tbsp) water
200 g (scant 1 c) sourdough
   preferment
250 g (2 c + 1½ Tbsp) whole
   wheat flour
50 g (⅓ c + ½ Tbsp) sorghum
   flour
450 g (3½ c + 1½ Tbsp) bread
   flour
250 g (2 c) all-purpose flour
15 g (2 tsp) honey, plus extra for
   drizzling
20 g (2 Tbsp + ½ tsp) kosher
   salt
4 large banana leaf strips
Olive oil, for brushing
Sea salt, for sprinkling

One of my obsessions is grilling ripe plátanos, or plantains, because of the delicious flavor they take on when compared to other cooking methods. Eating plátano was a big part of my upbringing, although my mom did prefer to make tajadas with unripe, green ones. As I got older, my appreciation for the ripe variety increased. I'm no stranger to making bread with plátanos, but putting them on the grill takes things to a new level. A hot grill allows the flames to kiss the skin, creating a blistered cover for the tender plátano inside. When grilling, I like to char the outside completely, until the skin starts to burst and caramelize.

I wanted to create a fun, pull apart bake with this recipe so that you can get larger chunks of plátano in each bite. Of course, this loaf wouldn't be complete if it wasn't baked on a banana leaf so make sure you have some handy to give it a little kiss of flavor while it is in the oven.

SOURDOUGH PREFERMENT

In a tall jar or large container with a lid, mix the all-purpose flour, whole wheat flour, bread flour, amaranth flour, water, and mature sourdough starter with your hand or a fork. Ensure that no dry flour remains at the bottom of the jar.

Cover the container and let it rest at room temperature (ideally between 70° and 80°F) for 4 hours. It should double in size and have a firm, bubbly structure on the top. Once the preferment is ready to use, you can start baking straight away or place it in your fridge for later use (up to 2 days).

DOUGH

Grill the plantains over high heat with the skin on, directly on the flame, until the skin is completely black and starts to burst. Let cool at room temperature, then transfer to the fridge.

In a large mixing bowl, combine 675 g (2¾ c + 2 Tbsp) of the water with the sourdough preferment and mix until roughly dissolved. Add the whole wheat flour, sorghum flour, bread flour, all-purpose flour, and honey and mix with both hands until there is no dry flour left. Let the dough rest for 5 minutes.

Add 25 g (1 Tbsp + 2 tsp) of the water to the dough and squeeze together until the water incorporates, 5 to 6 minutes. Let the dough rest for 10 minutes.

Add the salt and the remaining water. Incorporate once again with your hands by squeezing the dough until the surface smooths out and there are no streaks of water in the mixing bowl. Transfer to a clean, lightly oiled bowl and cover. Let the dough rest for 30 minutes. Stretch the dough and fold into the middle a few times to develop strength during the bulk fermentation phase. Cover and let the dough ferment for 3½ additional hours.

Flour a work surface, dump out the dough, and fold loosely into a cylinder. Place the dough on a sheet pan, brush it with olive oil, and cover with plastic wrap. Put the dough in the fridge overnight and let proof for a minimum of 12 hours.

After the cold fermentation, let the dough rest at room temperature for 2 hours. Using a bench scraper, divide into 6 horizontal pieces. Take each piece and gently stretch it until it is the width of the sheet pan and set aside. Place the banana leaves on the sheet pan so that the entire surface area is covered. If you don't have banana leaf, grease the same sheet pan with olive oil and place the dough strips on it. Let the dough rest for 1 hour.

Preheat the oven to 425°F.

Remove the plantains from the fridge and peel. Slice in half, lengthwise, then slice each of those pieces into 3 chunks (if using 2 large plantains, that is a total of 12 chunks) . On each strip of dough, add a few chunks of plantains and push into the dough. Drizzle with honey and sprinkle with sea salt.

Place the sheet pan in the oven and bake the loaves for 25 minutes or until the crust takes on a nice brown coloring. You should see the plantains get a little more caramelized after the bake.

BLUE MASA SOURDOUGH

Makes
2 LOAVES

There are several common additions that bakers today have up our sleeves to bring fresh energy to the classic sourdough loaf. Cranberry-walnut, olive-polenta, you name it. This is my version, incorporating a connection to my heritage by using corn in three different ways. It pays respect to an ingredient that was worshiped in this part of the world, maíz, and makes a loaf that is extraordinary and delicious.

I am fortunate to live in Queens, New York, where high-quality flour *and* high-quality fresh masa are both easily accessible. Masa comes in many colors, forms, and textures—and here, I choose blue masa because of the extra nutty flavor that it packs while also complementing the deeply savory qualities of stone ground whole grain flour.

I began making blue masa sourdough in loaf pans to slice for sandwich bread, but one day I spied a bin of dried corn husks under my work bench, and instinctively plopped my dough directly on them before the bake. Not only does the husk impart a fun aesthetic, it also creates steam during the bake and lends its own flavor to the crust of the loaf. The final element came a few bakes later, when I struggled to score the highly hydrated dough; I rubbed it down with toasted corn flour to get a nice clean score before the bake. The toasted corn flour adds a golden brown contrast to the loaf. The husk, the masa, and the toasted corn flour are a beautiful trio, creating a very special bread.

NOTE: Try to find fresh blue masa, if possible, but you can also order blue masa harina and make the masa yourself: combine 150 g (1⅓ c) blue masa harina with 150 g (⅓ c + 5 Tbsp) warm water.

SOURDOUGH PREFERMENT

In a tall jar or large container with a lid, mix the bread flour, whole wheat flour, water, and mature sourdough starter with your hand or a fork. Ensure that no dry flour remains at the bottom of the jar.

Cover the container and let it rest at room temperature (ideally between 70° and 80°F) for 4 hours. It should double in size and have a firm, bubbly structure on the top. Once the preferment is ready to use, you can start baking straight away or place it in your fridge for later use (up to 2 days).

DOUGH

In a large mixing bowl, combine 720 g (3 c + 1 Tbsp) of the water with the sourdough preferment and dissolve. Add the bread flour, amaranth flour, all-purpose flour, and whole wheat flour and use both of your hands to mix until most of the flour is absorbed and you have a roughly incorporated dough. Let rest for 30 minutes.

(CONTINUED)

SOURDOUGH PREFERMENT

50 g (⅓ c + 1 Tbsp) bread flour
50 g (scant ½ c) whole wheat flour
75 g (¼ c + 2 Tbsp) warm water
50 g (¼ c) mature sourdough starter

DOUGH

820 g (3½ c) water
200 g (1 scant c) sourdough preferment
350 g (2¾ c + 1 Tbsp) bread flour
50 g (½ c) amaranth flour
300 g (2⅓ c + 1 Tbsp) all-purpose flour
300 g (2½ c) whole wheat flour
300 g (1¼ c) fresh blue masa
20 g (2 Tbsp + ½ tsp) kosher salt

FOR BAKING

Toasted corn flour, for dusting
2 dried corn husks

*If using masa harina in lieu of fresh masa, start by combining the masa harina and water in a mixing bowl and mix until it reaches a smooth, Play-Doh consistency. Cover with a damp towel and set aside.

*If you can't find toasted corn flour, place corn flour in a dry skillet over medium heat. Stir occasionally until you smell a nutty, toasted aroma, about 5 minutes. Set aside.

Add 100 g (⅓ c + 1½ Tbsp) of the fresh blue masa and 35 g (2½ Tbsp) of the water. Squeeze the mix until homogenous. If you are hand mixing, don't expect to see an even distribution of the masa into the dough; that is okay. If you are using a stand mixer with the dough hook attached, you will see a more even distribution of the masa during the mixing process.

Repeat the previous step adding another 100 g (⅓ c + 1½ Tbsp) of the fresh blue masa and 35 g (2½ Tbsp) of the water. Squeeze the mix until homogenous. And repeat one more time, adding the remaining fresh blue masa and the remaining water. At the very end of the mixing process, add the salt and squeeze together until the dough smooths out. The dough should be slightly sticky, but smooth to the touch. Transfer to another clean, lightly oiled bowl or container. Let the dough rest for 30 minutes.

Fold the dough over itself from each side of the bowl and into the middle of the dough. Cover and let rest for another 30 minutes. Repeat the fold one more time. Cover and let ferment for an additional 3½ hours at an ideal room temperature of 75° to 80°F.

After the initial fermentation, flour a work surface, dump out the dough, and divide in half. Gently pre-shape the dough into two rounds and let rest for 45 minutes. To apply the final shape after this rest period, flip each dough round over and fold the top and bottom sides of the dough into the middle. Press down to apply tension and rotate the dough 45 degrees. Roll the dough pieces into 2 cylinders while applying tension to create a seam on each one.

It is time to let the dough rest before baking, and ideally you will want to use proofing baskets so that the dough holds its shape. Dust two proofing baskets with toasted corn flour and place the loaves into the baskets with the seams facing up. (If you don't have proofing baskets, put them seam side down on a cornmeal-dusted cutting board and cover with a cloth.) Dust the seam side with more toasted corn flour and place in the fridge for a minimum of 12 hours.

After the overnight fermentation period, place a baking stone, steel, or cast-iron skillet inside the oven and preheat to 500°F.

Place 1 dried corn husk along the seam of each loaf.

Load into the oven depending on your baking vessel of choice. If using a cast-iron skillet, cut out a piece of parchment that fits the bottom of the skillet and place the loaves on it, seam side down. Slash the loaves with a knife or blade, cover, and place the hot skillet back in the oven.

If you are using a baking stone or steel, place a piece of parchment on a loading peel, place the loaves on it, and slash them with a knife or blade. Load onto the stone, add ice to a baking pan placed at the bottom of the oven, and spray the surface of the loaves and the inside of the oven with water.

Lower the heat to 475°F or 450°F depending on how hot your oven gets. Bake the loaves for 20 minutes before releasing the steam.

Let the steam out by uncovering the cast-iron skillet or simply opening the oven door if on a stone or steel. Bake for 25 more minutes. I like to bake dark, so sometimes I go a little extra, and I finish my bake with the oven door open to let all the moisture out during the last couple of minutes.

Cool on a wire rack before slicing or eat warm out of the oven.

PAN DE MOLDE CON AJONJOLÍ

SOURDOUGH PREFERMENT

50 g (⅓ c + 1 Tbsp) bread flour

50 g (scant ½ c) whole wheat flour

100 g (¼ c + 3 Tbsp) warm water

25 g (2 Tbsp) mature sourdough starter

DOUGH

300 g (2⅓ c + 1 Tbsp) all-purpose flour

150 g (1¼ c) whole wheat flour

50 g (⅓ c + 1 Tbsp) bread flour

200 g (1 scant c) sourdough preferment

315 g (1⅓ c) water

15 g (1 Tbsp) olive oil

15 g (1 Tbsp + 2 tsp) kosher salt

50 g (6 Tbsp) sesame seeds, soaked overnight

25 g (3 Tbsp) pumpkin seeds, soaked overnight

Sesame seeds, for topping

Ajonjolí, or sesame seeds, are often used to top baked goods in Latin America and around the world. They are especially delicious to use for a molded sandwich bread. By "de molde," we refer to the baking pan being the mold for the shape of the bread. This loaf includes toasted sesame and pumpkin seeds in the dough for extra texture and an added jolt of flavor. This simple but flavorful loaf can be sliced and frozen for later use if you don't eat it all in the first sitting. Note that this recipe yields 2 loaves when using a standard 8½ × 4½ × 2¾ loaf pan.

NOTE: Soak your seeds in water overnight so that they don't absorb the water in the dough mix.

SOURDOUGH PREFERMENT

In a tall jar or large container with a lid, mix the bread flour, whole wheat flour, water, and mature sourdough starter with your hand or a fork. Ensure that no dry flour remains at the bottom of the jar.

Cover the container and let it rest at room temperature (ideally between 70° and 80°F) for 8 hours. It should double in size and have a firm, bubbly structure on the top. Once the preferment is ready to use, you can start baking straight away or place it in your fridge for later use (up to 2 days).

DOUGH

In the bowl of a stand mixer with a dough hook attachment, combine the all-purpose flour, whole wheat flour, bread flour, sourdough preferment, and 295 g (1¼ c) of the water. Mix on low speed until a rough dough forms, about 3 minutes.

Switch the mixer to medium speed and slowly add in the olive oil until it combines evenly into the dough. Next add the salt and trickle in the remaining water and switch the mixer to high speed (being careful not to splash everywhere!).

Mix the dough for 4 to 5 minutes on high speed or until the dough is smooth and elastic. Transfer the dough to a lightly oiled bowl. Strain the soaked sesame and pumpkin seeds completely, dry them, and add half of them to the surface of the dough. Fold the sides of the dough over the middle and flip the dough over. Spread the other half of the seeds on the dough and stretch it one more time. Cover and let ferment for 4 hours at room temperature.

(CONTINUED)

After the initial fermentation, line a sheet pan with a clean, wet kitchen towel and have a large bowl full of sesame seeds handy. On a floured work surface, divide the dough in half and shape each one into a tube, using tension to create a seam.

Gently grabbing the dough from the seam, rock the smooth side of the dough back and forth on the wet towel and then dip into the bowl of seeds. Place each piece of dough, seam side down, into two greased loaf pans. Let the loaves proof at room temperature for 30 minutes and then transfer to the fridge for an overnight fermentation, about 12 hours.

After the cold fermentation, remove from the fridge and let rest at room temperature for 1 hour. Preheat the oven to 500°F.

Slash the loaves with a blade or a knife and bake for 40 to 45 minutes, or until they spring up and have a nice, toasted color. Remove immediately from the pans when done baking and cool on a wire rack.

Makes
2 LOAVES

PAN DE MOLDE
100% Integral

This sourdough section cannot be complete without a delicious, hearty 100 percent whole grain loaf, and making it "de molde" is a good way to increase the amount of water in the dough without requiring deep baking expertise when shaping the dough. Any shaping issues that come from the high-hydration dough are forgiven by the loaf pan. Using high amounts of whole grain flour means we can use a higher amount of water, but the key is to add the water in increments and to pay attention to the rest times as instructed. Be patient with this one! Note that this recipe yields 2 loaves when using a standard 8½ × 4½ × 2¾ loaf pan.

SOURDOUGH PREFERMENT

In a tall jar or large container with a lid, mix the flour, water, and mature sourdough starter with your hand or a fork. Ensure that no dry flour remains at the bottom of the jar.

Cover the container and let it rest at room temperature (ideally between 70° and 80°F) for 4 hours. It should double in size and have a firm, bubbly structure on the top. Once the preferment is ready to use, you can start baking straight away or place it in your fridge for later use (up to 2 days).

DOUGH

In a large mixing bowl, combine the whole wheat flour with 315 g (1⅓ c) of the water and mix thoroughly with both hands for 5 minutes. Cover and let rest for 1 hour.

Add the sourdough preferment and 25 g (1 Tbsp + 2 tsp) of water. Mix thoroughly with both hands until it is smooth. Transfer it to a work surface and slap it down on the table to strengthen it, if needed, just make sure not to add any more water until it is completely smooth. Let rest for 15 minutes and repeat this step 3 more times, with 15 minute rests between each one, adding the salt with the last 25 g (1 Tbsp + 2 tsp) of water.

Once the dough has incorporated all ingredients and is smooth and not falling apart, transfer to a clean, lightly oiled bowl and cover. Let ferment at room temperature for 3 to 3½ hours. With no white flour, this will ferment faster than most doughs.

Once the dough has roughly doubled in size, dump onto a floured work surface and divide in half. Shape each piece tightly into a log, applying tension as you go and creating a seam.

SOURDOUGH PREFERMENT

100 g (¾ c + 1½ Tbsp) whole wheat flour
100 g (¼ c + 3 Tbsp) warm water
50 g (¼ c) mature sourdough starter

DOUGH

500 g (4 c + 2½ Tbsp) whole wheat flour
415 g (1¾ c) water
200 g (1 scant c) sourdough preferment
15 g (1 Tbsp + 2 tsp) kosher salt

Grease two loaf pans and place the loaves in them. Let sit at room temperature for 30 minutes and then transfer to the fridge for an overnight fermentation, about 12 hours.

After the overnight fermentation, preheat the oven to 500°F, remove the loaves straight from the fridge, slash them with a knife or razor, and bake for 40 to 45 minutes or until the top is dark and boldly baked.

Remove immediately from the pans and cool on a wire rack before serving.

ROLES DE PIMIENTO ASADO

SOURDOUGH PREFERMENT

50 g (⅓ c + 1 Tbsp) bread flour
50 g (scant ½ c) whole wheat flour
100 g (¼ c + 3 Tbsp) warm water
25 g (2 Tbsp) mature sourdough starter

DOUGH

350 g (1½ c) water
400 g (3 c + 3 Tbsp) all-purpose flour
100 g (¾ c + 1½ Tbsp) whole wheat flour
10 g (1 Tbsp) kosher salt
200 g (1 scant c) sourdough preferment
1 whole red bell pepper, roasted, seeded and skinned
1 whole jalapeño pepper, roasted, seeded and skinned
1 whole hatch or banana pepper, roasted, seeded and skinned
15 g (6 Tbsp) chopped fresh cilantro

To round out this chapter full of rustic, savory sourdough bakes, I wanted to enhance the taste of the bread eaten alone as well as complement any sandwich made from it. I decided to roast peppers and cilantro to add a savory flavor profile that is suitable for any time of day and any number of fillings, toppings, or accompaniments. The aroma from the oven during this bake is divine. If you are one of those people who don't like cilantro, this loaf might change your mind!

SOURDOUGH PREFERMENT

In a tall jar or large container with a lid, mix the bread flour, whole wheat flour, water, and mature sourdough starter with your hand or a fork. Ensure that no dry flour remains at the bottom of the jar.

Cover the container and let it rest at room temperature (ideally between 70° and 80°F) for 8 hours. It should double in size and have a firm, bubbly structure on the top. Once the preferment is ready to use, you can start baking straight away or place it in your fridge for later use (up to 2 days).

DOUGH

In a large mixing bowl, combine 295 g (1¼ c) of the water, the all-purpose flour, and whole wheat flour and mix until it comes together and there is no dry flour at the bottom of the bowl. Cover and let the dough rest for 30 minutes.

Add the salt, sourdough preferment, and the remaining water to the dough and squeeze it together until it incorporates, about 5 minutes. The dough should not have any streaks of water on the surface and should return to a smooth consistency. Transfer the dough to a lightly oiled bowl and let it rest for another 30 minutes.

In a large mixing bowl, add the red bell pepper, jalapeño pepper, hatch pepper, and cilantro and mix well, Spread half this mixture on top of the dough and stretch the sides of the dough over the mixture. You will do this 3 to 4 times and then flip the dough upside down. Let the dough rest for another 30 minutes.

Spread the remaining pepper mixture on the dough and repeat the stretching and folding of the dough. Let the initial rise continue for 3 more hours on the countertop at room temperature, for a total fermentation period of 4 hours.

On a floured work surface, divide the dough into 8 pieces and round into balls. Place on a parchment-lined sheet pan, 2 by 4, and wrap with plastic wrap. Place in the fridge for an overnight proof, between 10 to 12 hours.

The next day, preheat the oven to 450°F and bake the loaves for 30 minutes, or until the rolls turn a nice deep golden brown. Let cool on a wire rack before enjoying.

FUGAZZA

Well after colonization, between 1870 and 1960, there was an influx of Italians to Argentina that helped mold some of the culinary traditions that remain beloved there today. Many Argentines that I have met have told me about their Italian heritage, and they make this known to me the most when they bring up their unique pizza culture.

Fugazza is not a pizza or a focaccia (they are all flatbreads to me anyway), but a third kind of baseline item: a crisp, chewy dough topped with lots and lots and lots (and lots) of thinly sliced onions that have been tossed in oregano and olive oil. There is no sauce or cheese here, and it might remind you of a focaccia, which some say is where the name is derived from. Keep in mind that you will use this same dough base for all the Argentine-style pizzas that follow.

SOURDOUGH PREFERMENT

In a tall jar or large container with a lid, mix the all-purpose flour, whole wheat flour, bread flour, water, and mature sourdough starter with your hand or a fork. Ensure that no dry flour remains at the bottom of the jar.

Cover the container and let it rest at room temperature (ideally between 70° and 80°F) for 4 hours. It should double in size and have a firm, bubbly structure on the top. Once the preferment is ready to use, you can start baking straight away or place it in your fridge for later use (up to 2 days).

DOUGH

In a large mixing bowl, dissolve the sourdough preferment with 250 g of the water

Add the all-purpose flour, bread flour, and whole wheat flour and mix until a rough dough forms.

Spread the salt on the dough. Add the remaining splash of water and squeeze into the dough to incorporate. Once the dough has come back together and the salt and water are fully incorporated, turn the dough onto a lightly floured work surface and begin kneading.

Using your fingers to bring the dough into the middle and the palm of your hand to push the dough back and forward, knead until the dough is smooth and elastic. We really want to work this dough, so be patient as this will likely take around 10 minutes. If the dough starts tearing at any stage, it means it needs to rest and you have probably over kneaded it. Once this process is complete, add the dough to a lightly oiled bowl (preferably olive oil), cover, and let ferment at room temperature for 3½ hours.

After the initial fermentation, divide the dough into 2 or 4 pieces, depending on size preference. A cake pan will be used to bake these and they come in

SOURDOUGH PREFERMENT

50 g (⅓ c + 1 Tbsp) all-purpose flour
25 g (3 Tbsp) whole wheat flour
25 g (3 Tbsp) bread flour
100 g (¼ c + 3 Tbsp) warm water
100 g (½ c) mature sourdough starter

DOUGH

175 g (heaped ¾ c) sourdough preferment
295 g (1¼ c) water
375 g (3 c) all-purpose flour
100 g (¾ c + 1 Tbsp) bread flour
25 g (3 Tbsp) whole wheat flour
15 g (1 Tbsp + 2 tsp) kosher salt

TOPPINGS

1 large white onion
Dried oregano, al gusto
30 g (2 Tbsp) olive oil
Flaky sea salt (optional)
Red pepper flakes (optional)

different sizes. The size and weight of each dough piece will depend on the pan used for baking. A large 12-inch cake pan fits a 500-g dough piece, and an 8- to 9-inch cake pan fits a 250-g dough piece. I prefer the 12-inch for making Argentine-style pizza because you get to feed more people with it!

Round each dough piece into a ball with plenty of tension on the bottom. Lightly oil the cake pans and place the dough balls in the cake pans. Splash some olive oil on the surface of the dough and cover very tightly with plastic wrap, making sure there are no gaps and that they are very snugly wrapped. Place the cake pans in the fridge for 24 hours. You have now made your dough base for all the Argentine-style pizzas found in this chapter.

The next day, take the dough out of the fridge 1 to 2 hours before baking. Preheat the oven to 500°F.

Once the dough has relaxed and warmed up, press and stretch it directly in the pan so that the dough reaches the edges. Now it is time for the toppings.

Finely slice the white onion and toss with the desired amount of oregano and the olive oil. Don't go too heavy on the olive oil as this can cause the final product to be greasy. Add a pinch of sea salt and red pepper flakes, if desired.

Spread the onions all over the dough. It might seem like a lot, but that's okay. Place the cake pans in the oven, lower the heat to 475°F, and bake the fugazza for 25 to 30 minutes, or until the onions are crisped and the dough takes on a nice brown coloring. Be mindful of the rack positioning so as not to burn the bottoms.

Remove from the pan using a wooden spatula and let cool on a wire rack before serving.

FUGAZZETA

〰〰〰〰〰〰〰

Makes
TWO 12-INCH PIZZAS

〰〰〰〰〰〰〰

1 batch Fugazza dough (page 120) shaped into 500, g dough balls
900 g (4 c) low-moisture mozzarella, cubed
2 large white onions, finely sliced
60 g (2 Tbsp) olive oil
9 g (½ Tbsp) kosher salt
6 g (1 Tbsp) dried oregano
6 g (½ Tbsp) red pepper flakes
3 g (½ Tbsp) dried parsley
2 cloves garlic, finely minced
16 black olives, pitted

I love a good simple fugazza but nothing gets me going like a fugazzeta. As the name suggests (at least in my brain) this is a more exciting, bigger, and badder situation than the plain predecessor. And what can make something more exciting than loads of cheese oozing off the sides of a thick slice of well-fermented dough?

While the specific cheeses used in Argentina (for example Muzza or Queso Cremoso) might be different than what we have readily available, you will still be able to get the full effect of the ridiculous cheese pull necessary to call something a fugazzeta. In order to achieve this, I like to use low-moisture mozzarella cheese cut into cubes. Be careful with fresh mozzarella, as you need to use a lot of cheese here and fresh cheese will give off so much liquid it can become problematic during the bake. To top it off, I like to add a "dry chimichurri" mixture that maximizes the flavor of every bite. I prefer to make these as 12-inch pizzas, so shape your dough mix into two dough balls of 500 g.

NOTE: See the Fugazza recipe (page 120) for the complete step-by-step instructions for the dough. Once you make the dough and it has fermented in the fridge, proceed to the instructions below.

〰〰

Take the fugazza dough out of the fridge and let it reach room temperature for 1 to 2 hours.

Preheat the oven to 500°F.

Once the dough has relaxed, press and stretch it in the pan all the way to the edges, ensuring it does not tear.

Use 450 g of cheese per fugazzeta. Spread the cheese over the dough and all the way to the edges. The amount of cheese called for is a guideline, so feel free to modify it if you want. The key is to make sure it is evenly distributed and there is not one spot of dough with a higher concentration of cheese than another.

Next, in a small bowl, toss the sliced onions with the olive oil, to lightly coat the slices. Spread the onions all over the top of the cheese, again looking for even distribution. A heaping amount of onion is welcome here, so don't be shy about using it all.

Place the fugazzeta in the oven, lower the heat to 475°F, and bake for 25 to 30 minutes, or until the cheese has melted, the onions are getting crispy (but not burnt), and the crust is taking on a nice brown coloring. Be aware of the oven rack positioning so as not to burn the bottom.

While the fugazzeta bakes, in a small bowl, toss the salt, oregano, red pepper flakes, parsley, and garlic.

Once baked, remove the fugazzeta from the cake pan with a wooden spatula, sprinkle the dry herb mixture evenly over it, and scatter the black olives on top (chop the olives in chunks or leave them whole—whatever you desire). If you want to get that iconic cheese pull, slice it up while it's hot and enjoy!

STUFFED FUGAZZETA

If you thought a fugazzeta couldn't get leveled up any further, well, you see the title to this recipe so you can expect and appreciate the greatness that is about to happen. If there is one common denominator among my Argentine friends, it's saying "more cheese and more onion"—so, here you go. Think of this fugazzeta with more dough and cheese on top, to create the perfect pocket of cheesy goodness with each bite. For this, we will use two doughs and add some fresh mozzarella and caramelized onion to the top of the fugazzeta for a little extra flavor. I prefer to make one 12-inch stuffed fugazzeta with this recipe, so make sure to shape your dough balls to 500 g when making the fugazza dough recipe.

Makes
1 TO 2 PIZZAS,
DEPENDING ON
SIZE PREFERENCE

1 batch Fugazza dough (page 120), shaped into one 500-g or two 250-g dough balls
500 g (16 oz) low-moisture mozzarella, cubed, al gusto
100 g (3½ oz) fresh mozzarella
1¼ large white onions, 1 finely sliced, ¼ finely sliced and caramelized
30 g (2 Tbsp) olive oil
4½ g (½ Tbsp) kosher salt
3 g (1 Tbsp) dried oregano
3 g (½ Tbsp) red pepper flakes
1½ g (½ Tbsp) dried parsley
1 clove garlic, finely minced

Take two pieces of the fugazza dough out of the fridge and let them come to room temperature for 1 to 2 hours.

Preheat the oven to 500°F.

Once the dough has relaxed, press and stretch the first piece in a cake pan all the way to the edges, ensuring it does not tear.

Spread the low-moisture mozzarella over the dough but NOT all the way to the edges this time. Leave about ½ inch of space all the way around to have room to later seal the dough on top. It's okay if the cubes of cheese are touching each other in the center of the dough.

Toss the finely sliced uncooked onion with the olive oil, to lightly coat it. Evenly distribute the onion slices on top of the cheese. A heaping amount is great, so don't be shy about using more than you think you need.

Add the remaining ¼ onion to a saucepan over medium heat, stir for 10 minutes until caramelized, and set aside.

Stretch the second piece of dough in a separate cake pan or on a work surface to get it to roughly the same size as the dough in the pan with the cheese and onion. Place this second piece of dough on top of the one in the pan and press the edges down. Twist the edge of the dough so that the bottom dough comes over the top and pinch it down. You basically want to create as tight of a seam as possible.

On top of the second piece of dough, add the fresh mozzarella, the caramelized onion, and a splash of olive oil.

Place the cake pan in the oven, lower the heat to 475°F, and bake for 25 to 30 minutes, or until the cheese has melted, the onions are crispy (but not burnt), and the crust takes on a nice brown coloring. Be aware of the oven rack positioning so as not to burn the bottom.

While the stuffed fugazzeta bakes, make the dry herb mixture by combining the salt, oregano, red pepper flakes, parsley and garlic.

Once the stuffed fugazzeta is ready, remove from the cake pan with a wooden spatula and top with the dry herb mixture. Slice it hot if you want to see the cheese ooze out, but don't let it go to waste.

FUGAZZETA DE VEGETALES

There is one last stop on the fugazzeta train and this one is, I suppose one could say, "healthier"...well, at least that's what I tell myself so I don't feel bad for eating this much cheese in one sitting. This fugazzeta is stuffed, but instead of adding raw onion, the onions are in a spinach mixture and sautéed, offering a bit of green freshness and texture to the cheesy inside. To prepare the spinach mixture, add whatever vegetables you want, there are no rules here. I like to go with spinach, bok choy, and green onion.

Take two pieces of fugazza dough out of the fridge and let them come to room temperature for 1 to 2 hours.

Preheat the oven to 500°F.

In a medium skillet over medium heat, add the white onion, bok choy, spinach, green onions, parsley, olive oil, salt, and black pepper. Sauté until the vegetables are translucent, but do not cook all the way down as they will cook more during baking. Remove from the heat and allow the mixture to cool completely.

Once the dough has relaxed, press and stretch the first piece in a cake pan all the way to the edges, ensuring it does not tear.

Spread the mozzarella over the dough but NOT all the way to the edges this time. Leave about ½ inch of space all the way around to have room to later seal the dough on top. It's okay if the cubes of cheese are touching each other in the center of the dough. The key is to make sure it is evenly distributed and there is not one spot of dough with a higher concentration of cheese than another, except for the edges, which should have no cheese. Add the sautéed veggies on top of the cheese.

Stretch the second piece of dough in a separate cake pan or on a work surface until it is roughly the same size as the dough in the pan with the cheese and veggies. Place the dough on top and press the edges down. Next, twist the edge of the dough so that the bottom dough comes over the top and pinch it down. You basically want to create as tight of a seam as possible.

Add the sliced red onion and a handful of cubed mozzarella on top of the second dough.

Place the pan in the oven, lower the heat to 475°F, and bake for 25 to 30 minutes, or until the cheese has melted, the onions are crispy (but not burnt), and the crust takes on a nice brown coloring. Be aware of the oven rack positioning so as not to burn the bottom.

While the stuffed fugazzeta bakes, make the dry herb mixture by combining the oregano, red pepper flakes, parsley, and garlic.

Once the stuffed fugazzeta is baked, remove from the cake pan with a wooden spatula and top with the dry herb mixture. Slice it hot if you want to see the cheese ooze out, but don't let it go to waste.

1 batch Fugazza dough (page 120), shaped into one 500-g or two 250-g dough balls
1 large white onion, finely sliced
2 baby bok choy
120 g (4 c) fresh spinach
60 g (1 c) green onions, finely chopped
½ bunch fresh parsley, finely chopped
30 g (2 Tbsp) olive oil
4½ g (½ Tbsp) kosher salt
4½ g (½ Tbsp) freshly ground black pepper
500 g (16 oz) low-moisture mozzarella, cubed, al gusto
¼ large red onion, sliced
3 g (1 Tbsp) dried oregano
3 g (1 Tbsp) red pepper flakes
1½ g (½ Tbsp) dried parsley
1 clove garlic, finely minced

PIZZA DE JAMÓN Y MORRONES

△△△△△△△△△△△△△△△

Makes
2 PIZZAS

⌄⌄⌄⌄⌄⌄⌄⌄⌄⌄⌄⌄⌄⌄⌄

1 batch Fugazza dough (page 120), shaped into two 500-g dough balls
10 roasted red bell peppers, cooled, skinned, and seeded
1 head garlic
60 g (2 Tbsp) olive oil
6 g (1 Tbsp) dried oregano
Pinch sea salt
One 1500-g (28 oz) can good quality, whole peeled tomatoes, crushed
750 g (7 oz) low-moisture mozzarella, cubed
12 large slices jamón cocido (cooked ham)
Pinch kosher salt
Freshly ground black pepper, al gusto
6 g (½ Tbsp) red pepper flakes
3 g (½ Tbsp) dried parsley
14 green olives, pitted

Stepping outside of the world of cheese and onion lands us in the new territory of the equally traditional and delicious jamón y morrones, one of the most commonly eaten pizzas in Buenos Aires. There are a couple of key points to making this the most delicious way possible: use freshly roasted red bell peppers and avoid anything from a jar or can; use jamón cocido, or cooked ham; parbake the crust and let it set before adding the sauce and cheese; and DO NOT use a pizza cutter when done—the toppings will get disoriented and unevenly distributed. Use a good large knife to make your cuts from the middle down to the crust. I also add a roasted garlic mixture on top at the end; it complements the traditional green olives that are added to each slice. As with all of the other pizzas, I prefer to shape 500-g dough balls and use a 12-inch cake pan, which yields two pizzas from one batch of the fugazza dough that you will need to make for this recipe.

〰️

Preheat the oven to 500°F.

Take the dough out of the fridge and let it come to room temperature for 1 to 2 hours.

Meanwhile, roast the red bell peppers in the oven for 35 minutes, or until they are blistered and soft. Cool them in ice water and peel. Set aside.

Cover the head of garlic tightly in foil and roast in the oven for 45 minutes, or until soft; remove and set aside to cool.

Once the dough has come to temperature, press and stretch it out to the edges of a cake pan. Reduce the heat to 450°F.

Top the dough with the olive oil, oregano, and sea salt and parbake for 12 minutes.

Remove the dough from the oven and take out of the cake pan. Let it cool completely and then transfer back into the pan. This will help the dough set as a light and airy dough before adding the toppings.

Add the crushed tomatoes and cheese, place in the oven, and bake for 8 minutes, or until the cheese is just melted.

Slice the roasted red pepper into strips, remove the pan from the oven, and top with the roasted red peppers strip and the ham. Return to the oven and bake for another 5 minutes.

Meanwhile, squeeze out the roasted garlic from the head into a bowl, add a pinch of salt and black pepper, and mix thoroughly.

Once the pizza is done, remove from the pan and top with the roasted garlic, red pepper flakes, and parsley. Using a large knife, cut the pizza into quarters starting from the center and pressing the blade down on the crust. Rotate and cut into the number of slices you need. Add a green olive to each slice and serve.

PIZZA AL MOLDE NAPOLITANA

Makes
2 PIZZAS
BAKED IN A 12-INCH
MOLD

The final installment in my interpretation of Argentine-style pizza is the classic napolitana al molde. Pizza napolitana, as the Italians prepare it, uses very specific ingredients and cooking methods. This style is a reimagining of that Italian technique into the Argentine "al molde" style. Fresh thick-sliced tomato and minced, sautéed garlic on top of melted mozzarella is the way to go here and it is nice and simple to make.

Preheat the oven to 500°F.

Take the dough out of the fridge and let it come to room temperature for 1 to 2 hours. Meanwhile, in a small skillet, sauté the minced garlic with the olive oil over medium heat, until just cooked and translucent, about 2 minutes, then set aside.

Once the dough has come to temperature, press and stretch it out to the edges of the mold. Top with a drizzle of olive oil, the oregano, and a pinch of salt and place the pan in the oven. Reduce the heat to 450°F, and parbake the dough for about 12 minutes. Remove from the oven and let cool on a wire rack to set.

Once cooled, top the dough with the cubed low-moisture mozzarella and the fresh mozzarella. A 50-50 ratio of the cheeses should be evenly spread over the dough all the way to the edges. It should be roughly a handful of each, but use your intuition and preference here.

Cover the cheese with as many tomato slices as possible, return to the oven, and bake for another 6 to 7 minutes, until the cheese is just melted and the tomatoes are slightly cooked.

Remove the pizza from the pan and sprinkle it with the sautéed garlic, red pepper flakes, and parsley. Use a large knife to cut from the middle, pressing down on the crust so as not to disrupt the tomatoes. Finish with a few green olives per slice and serve.

1 batch Fugazza dough (page 120), shaped into two 500-g dough balls
8 cloves garlic, minced
60 g (2 Tbsp) olive oil, plus extra for drizzling
6 g (1 Tbsp) dried oregano
Pinch kosher salt
500 g (16 oz) low-moisture mozzarella, cubed
100 g (3½ oz) fresh mozzarella, sliced
4 large beefsteak tomatoes, sliced
6 g (½ Tbsp) red pepper flakes
3 g (½ Tbsp) dried parsley
14 green olives, pitted

PAN TRENZA

During colonization, the Spanish planted wheat around Bogotá, the capital of Colombia, and neighboring areas where the climate was deemed suitable. This led to the creation of and advances in bread-baking techniques, although corn and corn-based food were still dominant. Corn arepas might take the crown in terms of consumption frequency in Colombia when compared to bread, but bakeries are found on every corner of big Colombian cities, making unique and delicious breads. One of my favorites is pan trenza, a braided bread that is soft, delicate, and balances sweet and savory elements to perfection. There are varieties with raisins added to the dough, some topped with a salty cheese, or even topped with sesame seeds.

SOURDOUGH PREFERMENT

In a tall jar or large container with a lid, mix the bread flour, whole wheat flour, water, and mature sourdough starter with your hand or a fork. Ensure that no dry flour remains at the bottom of the jar.

Cover the container and let it rest at room temperature (ideally between 70° and 80°F) for 4 hours. It should double in size and have a firm, bubbly structure on the top. Once the preferment is ready to use, you can start baking straight away or place it in your fridge for later use (up to 2 days).

DOUGH

In a large mixing bowl, combine the all-purpose flour, whole wheat flour, sourdough preferment, eggs, panela, sugar, water, oil, and salt and use your hands to mix thoroughly until everything is evenly incorporated and there is no dry flour left in the bowl. Turn the dough onto your countertop and knead until it is completely smooth and elastic, 8 to 10 minutes.

Once the dough has come together, transfer to a clean, lightly oiled bowl, cover, and let ferment for 5 hours at room temperature.

After the initial fermentation period, flour a work surface and divide the dough into 6 equal pieces. Loosely pre-shape them into round balls, not too tight, as we are going to extend them out. Cover and let them rest for 30 minutes.

Elongate each dough piece as thinly and long as possible, about 15 inches or so. Combine three of them at the tip and braid the dough by taking the piece on the left and putting it in between the middle and right piece. This is called the trenza, which means "braid" in Spanish. Now take the piece on the right and put it between the middle and left piece. Continue alternating between left and right until you have a braided dough. Let the dough proof on a parchment-lined sheet pan for 2 hours.

Preheat the oven to 375°F.

Brush the dough with water and top liberally with the sesame seeds and crumbled salty cheese. Bake for 35 minutes, or until the top is golden brown.

SOURDOUGH PREFERMENT
50 g (⅓ c + 1 Tbsp) bread flour
50 g (scant ½ c) whole wheat flour
100 g (¼ c + 3 Tbsp) warm water
50 g (¼ c) mature sourdough starter

DOUGH
450 g (3½ c + 1½ Tbsp) all-purpose flour
100 g (¾ c + 1½ Tbsp) whole wheat flour
200 g (1 scant c) sourdough preferment
2 large eggs
10 g (2 tsp packed) grated panela
65 g (⅓ c) granulated sugar
250 g (1 c + 1 Tbsp) water
15 g (1 Tbsp) vegetable oil
6 g (2 tsp) kosher salt
Sesame seeds, for topping
140 g (1 c) crumbled salty farmer's cheese, such as queso colombiano, for topping

MOGOLLA CHICHARRONA

△△△△△△△△△△△△

Makes
6 ROLLS

∿∿∿∿∿∿∿∿∿∿∿

In Colombia, a mogolla is a tender, slightly sweet roll that can take on several varieties, fillings, and flavor profiles, from sweet jams to savory meats. One of the most commonly eaten varieties is the chicharrona—I mean, what is better than soft, freshly baked bread stuffed with chicharrones (crispy pork rinds)? This dough is enriched with eggs and melted butter. It's important to melt the butter to release the water content, making an extremely soft, compact, and tender interior. When you've got a delicious, meaty bite of chicharrón in the center, it's important for the bread to complement the filling texturally, and be as pillowy-soft as possible. You can find fresh chicharrón at local Latin American supermarkets, bakeries, or restaurants. If you don't have any luck, substitute crispy pork belly.

SOURDOUGH PREFERMENT

In a tall jar or large container with a lid, mix the bread flour, whole wheat flour, water, and mature sourdough starter with your hand or a fork. Ensure that no dry flour remains at the bottom of the jar.

Cover the container and let it rest at room temperature (ideally between 70° to 80°F) for 4 hours. It should double in size and have a firm, bubbly structure on the top. Once the preferment is ready to use, you can start baking straight away or place it in your fridge for later use (up to 2 days).

DOUGH

In the bowl of a stand mixer with the dough hook attachment, combine the all-purpose flour, sourdough preferment, water, 1 of the eggs, the butter, panela, and salt and mix on low speed until the ingredients are fully incorporated, about 4 minutes. Switch the mixer to medium-high speed and mix for 5 to 6 minutes until the dough is smooth and elastic. Transfer to a clean, buttered bowl, cover, and let ferment at room temperature for 5 hours.

After the initial fermentation, divide the dough into 6 pieces, roughly 160 g each (about the size of a medium tomato), and flatten into a square. In the middle of each square, place a few chunks of chicharrón and seal by turning the corners of the dough into the middle and creating a seam. Flip the dough over and shape the dough ball until it is smooth and round. Place on a parchment-lined baking sheet and let proof for 3 hours.

Preheat the oven to 425°F.

Whisk together the remaining egg and a pinch of salt to create an egg wash. Brush the mogollas with the egg wash, place in the oven, and bake for 20 minutes, or until golden brown on the outside.

SOURDOUGH PREFERMENT

50 g (⅓ c + 1 Tbsp) bread flour
50 g (scant ½ c) whole wheat flour
100 g (¼ c + 3 Tbsp) warm water
50 g (¼ c) mature sourdough starter

DOUGH

500 g (4 c) all-purpose flour
150 g (scant ¾ c) sourdough preferment
250 g (1 c + 1 Tbsp) water
2 large eggs
50 g (3½ Tbsp) unsalted butter, melted
35 g (2½ Tbsp packed) grated panela
6 g (2 tsp) kosher salt, plus a pinch for egg wash
150 g chicharrón or crispy pork belly

MOGOLLA INTEGRAL

Another common way to make mogolla is with wheat bran, whole grain flour, and caramel to give a sweet balance to the dough. These mogollas make for great table bread or for general snacking. In general, the mogolla is designed to be a nourishing, handheld food so if you don't want to eat chicharrón (as on page 134), the whole grain variety is just as hearty and a bit more versatile.

∿

SOURDOUGH PREFERMENT

In a tall jar or large container with a lid, mix the bread flour, whole wheat flour, water, and mature sourdough starter with your hand or a fork. Ensure that no dry flour remains at the bottom of the jar.

Cover the container and let it rest at room temperature (ideally between 70° and 80°F) for 4 hours. It should double in size and have a firm, bubbly structure on the top. Once the preferment is ready to use, you can start baking straight away or place it in your fridge for later use (up to 2 days).

DOUGH

In the bowl of a stand mixer with the dough hook attachment, combine the all-purpose flour, whole wheat flour, wheat bran, sourdough preferment, water, 1 of the eggs, the melted butter, panela, and salt and mix on low speed until the ingredients are fully incorporated, about 4 minutes. Switch the mixer to medium-high speed and mix for 5 to 6 minutes until the dough is smooth and elastic. Transfer to a clean, buttered bowl, cover, and let ferment at room temperature for 5 hours.

After the initial fermentation, divide the dough into 6 pieces, roughly 160 g each (about the size of a medium tomato), and flatten into a square. Flip the dough over and round the dough ball until it is smooth and round. Place on a parchment-lined baking sheet and let proof for 3 hours.

Preheat the oven to 425°F.

Whisk together the remaining egg and a pinch of salt to create an egg wash. Brush the mogollas with the egg wash, place in the oven, and bake for 20 minutes, or until golden brown on the outside.

SOURDOUGH PREFERMENT

50 g (⅓ c + 1 Tbsp) bread flour

50 g (scant ½ c) whole wheat flour

100 g (¼ c + 3 Tbsp) warm water

50 g (¼ c) mature sourdough starter

DOUGH

250 g (2 c) all-purpose flour

250 g (2 c + 1½ Tbsp) whole wheat flour

50 g (⅓ c + 2 Tbsp) wheat bran

150 g (scant ¾ c) sourdough preferment

250 g (1 c + 1 Tbsp) water

2 large eggs

50 g (3½ Tbsp) unsalted butter, melted

35 g (2½ Tbsp packed) grated panela

6 g (2 tsp) kosher salt, plus a pinch for the egg wash

HALLULLAS

Hallullas are almost as popular in Chile as the marraqueta. Bread is so commonly eaten in Chile that it could even be referred to as "the tortilla" of the country, eaten with every meal. Hallulas are perfect for snacking or sandwiches, as the round, crisp texture can complement all sorts of fillings or spreads. This recipe is perfect to make in big batches for later use, by simply wrapping your sheet pan with plastic wrap and popping it into the freezer.

SOURDOUGH PREFERMENT

In a tall jar or large container with a lid, mix the bread flour, whole wheat flour, water, and mature sourdough starter with your hand or a fork. Ensure that no dry flour remains at the bottom of the jar.

Cover the container and let it rest at room temperature (ideally between 70° and 80°F) for 4 hours. It should double in size and have a firm, bubbly structure on the top. Once the preferment is ready to use, you can start baking straight away or place it in your fridge for later use (up to 2 days).

DOUGH

In the bowl of a stand mixer with the dough hook attachment, combine the all-purpose flour, sourdough preferment, milk, 80 g (⅓ c) of the water, sugar, and lard and mix on low speed until it comes together, about 5 minutes.

Add the salt and the remaining water, increase the speed to medium, and mix for 5 minutes, finishing the dough on high speed for 2 to 3 minutes or until smooth.

Transfer the dough to a clean, oiled bowl and cover. Let the dough rest at room temperature for 5 hours.

After the initial fermentation, turn the dough onto a floured work surface and dust with more flour. Use a rolling pin to roll the dough out to about 4 millimeters thick. Using a round cookie cutter, cut out 10 rounds from the flattened dough and place them on a parchment-lined sheet pan.

Brush with melted lard and let them rest at room temperature for 1 hour. Preheat the oven to 425°F.

Place the sheet pan in the oven and bake for 20 minutes, or until golden brown. Transfer to a cooling rack and brush with the honey and butter.

SOURDOUGH PREFERMENT

50 g (⅓ c + 1 Tbsp) bread flour
50 g (scant ½ c) whole wheat flour
100 g (¼ c + 3 Tbsp) warm water
50 g (¼ c) mature sourdough starter

DOUGH

500 g (4 c) all-purpose flour
200 g (1 scant c) sourdough preferment
205 g (⅔ c + 3 Tbsp) whole milk
95 g (¼ c + 2½ Tbsp) water
50 g (¼ c) granulated sugar
20 g (1½ Tbsp) lard, plus extra for brushing
10 g (1 Tbsp) kosher salt
Honey, for brushing
Unsalted butter, for brushing

GALLETAS DE CAMPANA

Makes
6 BISCUITS

Commonly eaten in Argentina, Uruguay, and the south of Brazil, galletas de campana are reminiscent of an American biscuit to the naked eye. Upon further inspection, the textures and flavors are quite different because it is not butter, but lard that is layered in a leavened dough. Instead of using the baking powder found in a biscuit, this dough typically uses commercial yeast. Considering the flavor profile is already going to be quite savory due to the lard, I felt that using sourdough would add an extra tang to the dough as well as contribute to the already unique texture.

SOURDOUGH PREFERMENT

In a tall jar or large container with a lid, mix the bread flour, whole wheat flour, water, and mature sourdough starter with your hand or a fork. Ensure that no dry flour remains at the bottom of the jar.

Cover the container and let it rest at room temperature (ideally between 70° and 80°F) for 4 hours. It should double in size and have a firm, bubbly structure on the top. Once the preferment is ready to use, you can start baking straight away or place it in your fridge for later use (up to 2 days).

DOUGH

In the bowl of a stand mixer with the dough hook attachment, combine the all-purpose flour, whole wheat flour, water, sourdough preferment, and sugar and mix on low speed for 3 to 4 minutes, until the dough combines. Switch the mixer to medium-high speed and add the 15 g (1 Tbsp) of lard and the salt. Mix for 5 minutes, until the dough is smooth, and transfer to a lightly oiled bowl. Cover and let ferment at room temperature for 4 hours, then transfer the dough to the fridge overnight, about 12 hours.

The next day, dump the dough on a floured work surface. Roll the dough out into a square and brush liberally with some of the melted lard. Fold the dough in half and roll out into a square again and brush the dough with more melted lard. Repeat this until the melted lard is gone, about 5 to 6 times. When you are on the last fold, don't roll the dough out too wide or long as it is time to cut it. You should aim for it to be around 12 inches wide and ½ inch thick.

Cut the dough into 6 squares, trimming any fat and uneven edges. Transfer to a parchment-lined sheet pan and let proof at room temperature for 3 hours.

Preheat the oven to 500°F, place the sheet pan in the oven, and bake the galletas for 20 to 25 minutes, or until golden brown and the layers start cracking open.

Let cool on a wire rack before serving.

SOURDOUGH PREFERMENT

25 g (3 Tbsp) bread flour
75 g (½ c + 2 Tbsp) whole wheat flour
75 g (¼ c + 1 Tbsp) warm water
50 g (¼ c) mature sourdough starter

DOUGH

400 g (3 c + 3 Tbsp) all-purpose flour
100 g (¾ c + 1½ Tbsp) whole wheat flour
300 g (1¼ c + 1 tsp) water
200 g (scant 1 c) sourdough preferment
25 g (2 Tbsp) granulated sugar
15 g (1 Tbsp) lard, for the dough, plus 100 g (⅓ c + 2½ Tbsp), melted, for the lamination
10 g (1 Tbsp) kosher salt

The Many Faces of Pan Dulce

After wheat was introduced to the Americas, there was the creation and evolution of rustic breads like bolillos, pan francés, or pan casero. The same was true of sweet, enriched breads as well. Although these new culinary traditions and techniques were introduced by the colonizers during the French occupation of México, it doesn't mean that they were instantly appreciated. After all, the Indigenous people in the lands of present-day México had distinct foodways heavily influenced by corn.

Why bring wheat in the first place, and how did its use become ingrained? It is thought that Christian Europeans needed wheat in order to make the Eucharist for religious celebrations, but that ritual was a completely foreign concept to the Indigenous peoples of the so-called New World. The lavish parties thrown by Maximilian "I" emphasized French food and created the perception that indigenous maíz-based food was for the poor. But it wasn't until simple white bread, possibly the Eucharist, was dipped in chocolate that it was enjoyed as something more complex and sweet than just the white bread itself. Soon enough, panaderías began popping up all over México with local bakers adapting European techniques into a "New World" product.

Combining European-style bread with native ingredients, such as piloncillo, vanilla, corn, chocolate, squash, and fruits like guava and pineapple, gave birth to the flavor, texture, and quality of what is now known as pan dulce. Creative forms of pan dulce arose regionally to honor traditions and holidays such as Pan de Muerto (page 175) and the Rosca de Reyes (page 177). Over time, these sweet baking traditions made their way throughout Latin America. Today, all sorts of renditions of pan dulce can be found, each adapted into its own unique expression given the ingredients, climates, and preexisting indigenous ways of the land.

CONCHA TRADICIONAL

With 25 million people living in Ciudad de México alone, one can only imagine how many bakers work to satisfy demand for the ever-popular pan dulce known as the concha. If I had to choose just one sweet bread that proves that Latin America is home to unique baking cultures, the concha would be high on the list. In fact, when it comes to pan dulce in general, it's possible that the concha mexicana is one of the genre's original starting points. Concha translates to "shell," and the crisp, sweet shell-like topping has become an iconic focal point of Latin American baking.

Using a sourdough preferment without added commercial yeast can be tricky with enriched dough, but this formula will leave you salivating once you smell them baking in the oven. My dear friends at Gusto Bread in Long Beach, California, inspire me when it comes to baking Mexican-style breads. When I first took a bite of their concha, I knew it was possible to create one that hit all the traditional qualities while using natural leavening for even more depth of flavor.

The key to making these is to have patience with the process and to make sure your sourdough starter is nice and active before building the preferment. Additionally, make sure you keep an eye on the temperature so that you can proof them as long as possible without losing the structure and bounciness before the bake.

*NOTE: If you do not have an adequate stand mixer, see page 24 for instructions on how to mix wet enriched doughs by hand.

SWEET SOURDOUGH PREFERMENT

In a tall jar or large container with a lid, mix the bread flour, whole wheat flour, sugar, water, and mature sourdough starter with your hand or a fork. Ensure that no dry flour remains at the bottom of the jar.

Cover the container and let it rest at room temperature (ideally between 73° and 80°F) for 4 hours. It should double in size and have a firm, weblike structure. Once the preferment is ready to use, you can start baking straight away or place it in your fridge for later use (up to 2 days).

DOUGH

In the bowl of a stand mixer with the dough hook attachment, combine the all-purpose flour, bread flour, whole wheat flour, milk, sugar, and sourdough preferment. Mix on low speed until the dough comes together and there is no dry flour at the bottom of the bowl, 2 to 3 minutes. Switch to medium speed and add the vanilla, egg, and egg yolk and mix until the eggs are fully incorporated.

(CONTINUED)

SWEET SOURDOUGH PREFERMENT

75 g (scant ⅔ c) bread flour
25 g (3 Tbsp) whole wheat flour
25 g (2 Tbsp) granulated sugar
50 g (¼ c) warm water
50 g (¼ c) mature sourdough starter

DOUGH

375 g (3 c) all-purpose flour
75 g (¾ c) bread flour
50 g (scant ½ c) whole wheat flour
338 g (1⅓ c) whole milk
150 g (¾ c) granulated sugar
215 g (1 c) sweet sourdough preferment
2 g (½ tsp) vanilla extract
1 large egg + 1 large egg yolk
113 g (1 stick) unsalted butter, softened
6 g (2 tsp) kosher salt

TOPPING

160 g (1⅓ c) powdered sugar
160 g (11½ Tbsp) unsalted butter
200 g (1½ c + 1½ Tbsp) all-purpose flour
1 to 2 g (¼ to ½ tsp) vanilla extract

Increase the mixer speed to medium-high and add the butter 50 g (3½ Tbsp) at a time and let it mix for a couple of minutes in between additions, making sure the dough comes back together and the butter is fully absorbed before adding more.

Once all the butter is incorporated, add the salt and mix for about 2 additional minutes, switching to the highest speed if necessary to get the dough to come together and smooth out.

Transfer the concha dough to a lightly oiled bowl, cover, and let ferment at room temperature for 4 hours. Transfer the dough to the fridge for an overnight fermentation, 8 to 10 hours, making sure your fridge is not too cold. Aim for a fridge temperature of about 40°F.

The next morning, divide the dough into thirteen 100-g pieces (about the size of small lemons) and place on a parchment-lined sheet pan.

To make the topping: In the bowl of a stand mixer with a paddle attachment, add the sugar and butter and mix for 3 minutes, until creamy. Add the flour and mix for 5 additional minutes. You are aiming for a Play-Doh-like consistency that can be balled up and pressed down without tearing.

Form thirteen 35-g balls and flatten them using a tortilla press or a rolling pin. Place a piece of topping over each dough ball and use a knife to cut your desired pattern on top. The traditional concha has a shell carved into the topping, but you can make any shape you like, or don't cut it at all for a natural crackling pattern.

Let the conchas proof for 3 to 4 hours at room temperature, or until they are nice and plump. They are ready to go into the oven when the topping breaks apart on top of the dough and the dough feels like a pillow.

Preheat the oven to 375°F, place the sheet pan in the oven, and bake the conchas for about 30 minutes, or until they are doubled in size and have a nice light brown coloring on the sides.

Cool on a wire rack before serving.

CONCHA DE CHOCOLATE Y JAMAICA

The concha form lends itself to many different expressions. The history of the concha being dipped into hot chocolate always has my wheels turning, trying to figure out the best way to combine the two; and México's love affair with flores de Jamaica (hibiscus flowers) is no secret. Instead of using food coloring to create a vibrant topping, I use cooled hibiscus tea, which creates a subtle pink hue. To create a decadent chocolate base for the concha, a mixture of semisweet chocolate and milk is added to the dough during the mixing process and it becomes perfectly chocolate colored and smooth.

NOTE: As in the Concha Tradicional recipe (page 143), it is important to use a stand mixer so that you can easily incorporate all the butter into the dough.

SWEET SOURDOUGH PREFERMENT

In a tall jar or large container with a lid, mix the bread flour, whole wheat flour, sugar, water, and mature sourdough starter with your hand or a fork. Ensure that no dry flour remains at the bottom of the jar.

Cover the container and let it rest at room temperature (ideally between 73° to 80°F) for 4 hours. It should double in size and have a firm, weblike structure. Once the preferment is ready to use, you can start baking straight away or place it in your fridge for later use (up to 2 days).

DOUGH

In a microwave-safe bowl, combine the chocolate and milk and heat for 2 to 3 minutes, until the chocolate is soft enough to melt when mixed. Let it sit at room temperature for 10 minutes.

After the brief rest, whisk the chocolate mixture. It will be liquid, and that is okay. The mixture is not supposed to be thick. Let the mixture cool for another 10 minutes.

In the bowl of a stand mixer with the dough hook attachment, combine the all-purpose flour, bread flour, chocolate and milk mixture, sugar, and sourdough preferment. Mix on low speed until the dough comes together and there is no dry flour at the bottom of the bowl, 2 to 3 minutes.

Add the egg and egg yolk and mix for another 2 to 3 minutes until combined.

Increase the mixer speed to medium-high and add the butter, 50 g (3½ Tbsp) at a time, letting it mix for a couple of minutes in between additions to make sure the dough comes back together and the butter is fully absorbed before adding more.

(CONTINUED)

SWEET SOURDOUGH PREFERMENT

75 g (scant ⅔ c) bread flour
25 g (3 Tbsp) whole wheat flour
10 g (1 Tbsp) granulated sugar
50 g (¼ c) warm water
50 g (¼ c) mature sourdough starter

DOUGH

113 g (¾ c) semisweet chocolate chunks
338 g (1⅓ c) whole milk
315 g (2½ c) all-purpose flour
185 g (1½ c) bread flour
100 g (½ c) granulated sugar
215 g (1 c) sweet sourdough preferment
1 large egg + 1 large egg yolk
113 g (1 stick) unsalted butter, softened
6 g (2 tsp) salt

TOPPING

150 g (5 oz) cooled hibiscus tea
160 g (1⅓ c) powdered sugar
160 g (11½ Tbsp) unsalted butter
1 to 2 g (¼ to ½ tsp) vanilla extract
235 g (1¾ c + 2 Tbsp) all-purpose flour

Once all the butter is incorporated, add the salt and mix for 2 minutes until the dough smooths out, switching to the highest speed if necessary.

Transfer the concha dough to a lightly buttered bowl, cover, and let ferment at room temperature for 4 hours. Transfer the dough to the fridge for an overnight fermentation, 8 to 10 hours, making sure your fridge is not too cold. Aim for a temperature of about 40°F.

The next morning, let the dough rest at room temperature for 1 hour before dividing. Divide the dough into thirteen 100-g pieces (about the size of small lemons) and place on a parchment-lined sheet pan.

To make the topping: In a medium saucepan over medium heat, reduce the hibiscus tea down to a thick, syrupy consistency by stirring on and off for 10 to 15 minutes, being careful not to let it burn. In the bowl of a stand mixer with a paddle attachment, add the sugar, butter, vanilla, and hibiscus tea syrup and mix for 5 minutes, until it is smooth and there is no dry powdered sugar left. Next, add the flour and mix for 5 more minutes. Aim for a Play-Doh-like consistency that can be balled up and pressed down without tearing.

Form thirteen 35-g balls and flatten using a tortilla press or a rolling pin. Place a piece of topping over each dough ball and use a knife to cut your desired pattern on top. The traditional concha has a shell carved into the top, but you can make any shape you like, or don't cut it at all for a natural crackling pattern.

Let the conchas proof for 4 hours at room temperature, or until they are nice and plump. You will know they are ready to go into the oven when the topping breaks apart and the dough feels like a pillow.

Preheat the oven to 375°F, place the sheet pan in the oven, and bake the conchas for about 30 minutes, or until they are doubled in size and have a nice light to dark brown coloring on the sides.

Cool on a wire rack before serving.

SEMITA DE YEMA INTEGRAL

Makes
12 ROLLS

Pan dulce migrated from México to other Latin American countries over time, with each culture making their own versions and giving them new names. In Honduras, the pan dulce of choice is a semita. There are a few different types, but one of the most popular is the semita de yema (yema is "egg yolk" in Spanish). Growing up, semitas de yema were one of the most classic treats that my parents would bring home. My mom told me stories of growing up in Honduras and having the most delicious, freshly baked semitas to share with her family. My parents would enjoy them in the afternoon with coffee quite frequently, and it was my go-to sweet bread. Not many of my classmates or friends knew what semitas were, but when I shared them, it was always met with a pleasant reaction of someone tasting the unknown and wondering how they had never had it before.

I decided to make a whole grain version because I had never seen one before. The flour mix is half whole wheat and half bread flour to ensure the semitas still have a nice, bouncy texture.

SWEET SOURDOUGH PREFERMENT

In a tall jar or large container with a lid, mix the bread flour, whole wheat flour, sugar, water, and mature sourdough starter with your hand or a fork. Ensure that no dry flour remains at the bottom of the jar.

Cover the container and let it rest at room temperature (ideally between 70° and 80°F) for 4 hours. It should double in size and have a firm, bubbly structure on the top. Once the preferment is ready to use, you can start baking straight away or place it in your fridge for later use (up to 2 days).

DOUGH

In the bowl of a stand mixer with the dough hook attached, combine the whole wheat flour, bread flour, milk, and sourdough preferment. Mix on low speed until it all comes together as a rough dough, 3 to 4 minutes.

Add the egg yolks and sugar and turn the mixer up to medium speed. Let the yolks and sugar mix for about 3 minutes until fully incorporated.

Turn the mixer up to medium-high speed and start adding the butter, 50 g (3½ Tbsp) at a time, ensuring that each time it fully incorporates before adding more.

Once all the butter has been incorporated, add the salt. Let the dough mix for 3 more minutes, or until silky smooth. Transfer the dough to a lightly oiled bowl, cover, and let rest at room temperature for 4 hours.

(CONTINUED)

SWEET SOURDOUGH PREFERMENT

- 50 g (⅓ c + 1 Tbsp) bread flour
- 50 g (scant ½ c) whole wheat flour
- 25 g (2 Tbsp) granulated sugar
- 50 g (¼ c) warm water
- 50 g (¼ c) mature sourdough starter

DOUGH

- 250 g (2 c + 1½ Tbsp) whole wheat flour
- 250 g (2 c) bread flour
- 338 g (1⅓ c) whole milk
- 215 g (1 c) sweet sourdough preferment
- 4 large egg yolks
- 150 g (¾ c) granulated sugar
- 113 g (1 stick) unsalted butter
- 6 g (2 tsp) kosher salt

TOPPING

- 160 g (1⅓ c) powdered sugar
- 160 g (11½ Tbsp) unsalted butter
- 200 g (1½ c + 1½ Tbsp) all-purpose flour
- 1 small bowl of granulated sugar, for dipping

After the initial fermentation, turn the dough out on a lightly floured work surface and divide into twelve 100-g pieces (about the size of small lemons) and shape into round balls. Place on a parchment-lined sheet pan.

To make the topping: In the bowl of a stand mixer with the paddle attachment, add the powdered sugar and butter and mix on medium speed until creamed together. Add the flour and mix for 5 minutes, until it comes together. You want something with a Play-Doh-like consistency, meaning not too wet and not crumbly.

Divide the topping into twelve 35-g (2 Tbsp) pieces and shape each into a round ball. Using a rolling pin or tortilla press, flatten the topping pieces and place on top of the dough balls. Roll the dough balls with the topping side down in the bowl of granulated sugar to create an extra layer of sugar coating on top.

Let the semitas proof at room temperature for 6 to 8 hours, or until the covering breaks naturally and they are visibly bouncy and pillowy soft. When you gently push the dough ball, it should bounce back slightly, and it should never collapse or tear. The window for proofing here is big because these can be quite sensitive and you want to push the proof as much as possible without ending up with dough that rips. Keep an eye on the dough around hour 4 and make an assessment based on how it feels.

Preheat the oven to 375°F, place the sheet pan in the oven, and bake the semitas for 30 minutes, or until they have a golden brown sheen and have doubled in size.

Cool on a wire rack before serving.

SEMITA HONDUREÑA DE MAÍZ

When I go to local bodegas and markets, it is easy to get lost in the pan dulce aisle trying to figure out what flavor I want to take home with me. This variation on the semita uses masa harina in the dough to create a more robust flavor as well as chewier texture. These are perfect for any time of day, but I like to get them to add to my breakfast plate. For this recipe, I toast the masa harina until it is golden brown to bring out even more of that nutty, slightly sweet corn flavor. The dough is cut with white flour to ensure that there is still a bouncy, fluffy texture in the final semita. Instead of using only butter, I use a half-and-half mixture of lard and butter to create a better balance for the addition of masa harina. Additionally, the honey in the dough and in the topping enhances the subtle sweet notes from the toasted corn flour.

SWEET SOURDOUGH PREFERMENT

In a tall jar or large container with a lid, mix the bread flour, sugar, water, and mature sourdough starter with your hand or a fork. Ensure that no dry flour remains at the bottom of the jar.

Cover the container and let it rest at room temperature (ideally between 70° and 80°F) for 4 hours. It should double in size and have a firm, bubbly structure on the top. Once the preferment is ready to use, you can start baking straight away or place it in your fridge for later use (up to 2 days).

DOUGH

In a medium skillet over medium heat, toast the masa harina until you smell the nutty, sweet notes and see the flour turning darker. Remove from heat and cool.

In the bowl of a stand mixer with the dough hook attachment, combine the cooled masa harina, bread flour, all-purpose flour, milk, and sourdough preferment and mix on low speed until the dough comes together, about 3 minutes. Add the sugar and eggs and mix for 3 more minutes, or until incorporated.

Increase the mixer speed to medium-high and add the lard and butter, one at a time, making sure the dough comes back together after adding one and before adding the other. It does not matter which one is added first.

Once all the fat is incorporated, add the salt and a splash of water and finish the mix on high speed, until smooth.

Transfer the semita dough to a lightly oiled bowl, cover, and let ferment at room temperature for 3 hours. Transfer the dough to the fridge overnight, about 12 hours.

The next morning, divide the dough into thirteen 100-g pieces (about the size of small lemons) and place on a parchment-lined sheet pan.

SWEET SOURDOUGH PREFERMENT

100 g (¾ c + 1 Tbsp) bread flour
25 g (2 Tbsp) granulated sugar
75 g (¼ c + 1 Tbsp) warm water
50 g (¼ c) mature sourdough starter

DOUGH

150 g (1⅓ c) masa harina
300 g (2⅓ c + 1 Tbsp) bread flour
50 g (⅓ c + 1 Tbsp) all-purpose flour
300 g (1¼ c) whole milk
215 g (1 c) sweet sourdough preferment
100 g (½ c) granulated sugar
2 large eggs
60 g (4½ Tbsp) lard
60 g (4 Tbsp) unsalted butter, softened
6 g (2 tsp) kosher salt
15 g (2 tsp) honey

TOPPING

200 g (1½ c + 1½ Tbsp) all-purpose flour
160 g (1⅓ c) powdered sugar
160 g (11½ Tbsp) lard or shortening
15 g (2 tsp) honey

To make the topping: In the bowl of a stand mixer with a paddle attachment, add the flour, sugar, lard, and honey and mix until just incorporated. If it is too creamy, add more flour. Aim for a Play-Doh-like consistency that can be balled up and pressed down without tearing.

Form thirteen 30-g (2 Tbsp) balls and use a tortilla press or a rolling pin to flatten the topping. Place a piece of topping over each dough ball and lightly press around the sides to seal it.

Let the semitas proof for 4 hours at room temperature, or until they are nice and plump. They are ready to go into the oven when the covering is completely separated and the dough feels like a pillow. When gently pushing the dough ball, it should bounce back slightly, and it should never collapse or tear. The window for proofing here is big because these can be quite sensitive, so push the proof as much as possible without ending up with dough that rips. Keep an eye on the dough around hour 4 and make an assessment based on how it feels.

Preheat the oven to 375°F, place the sheet pan in the oven, and bake the semitas for about 30 minutes, or until they are doubled in size and have a nice light to dark brown coloring on the sides.

Cool on a wire rack before serving.

SEMITA HONDUREÑA DE ARROZ

The final semita hondureña in this book is the popular semita de arroz, traditionally made with a blend of white rice flour and white wheat flour. Like other semitas, these are found in Honduran households as a staple to accompany a cup of coffee. It's all about having variety in your pan dulce! My version includes toasted brown rice flour to bring more bold, earthy flavor to the dough. Since these have a long final proof, the ideal timing when I make them is to have the initial fermentation done at night before bed, so that I can shape them and let them proof overnight.

SWEET SOURDOUGH PREFERMENT

In a tall jar or large container with a lid, mix the bread flour, sugar, water, and mature sourdough starter with your hand or a fork. Ensure that no dry flour remains at the bottom of the jar.

Cover the container and let it rest at room temperature (ideally between 70° and 80°F) for 4 hours. It should double in size and have a firm, bubbly structure on the top. Once the preferment is ready to use, you can start baking straight away or place it in your fridge for later use (up to 2 days).

DOUGH

In a medium skillet over medium heat, toast the brown and white rice flours until you smell the nutty, sweet notes and see the flour turning darker. Remove from the heat and let cool.

In the bowl of a stand mixer with the dough hook attachment, combine the toasted brown and white flours, the bread flour, milk, sourdough preferment, and water and mix on low speed until the dough comes together, about 3 minutes. Add the honey and eggs and mix for 3 more minutes, or until incorporated.

Increase the mixer speed to medium-high and add the butter,

Once all the butter is incorporated, add the salt and a splash of water and finish the mix on high speed, until smooth.

Transfer the semita dough to a lightly oiled bowl, cover, and let ferment at room temperature for 4 hours. After the fermentation period, divide the dough into ten 100-g pieces (about the size of small lemons) and place on a parchment-lined sheet pan.

To make the topping: In the bowl of a stand mixer with a paddle attachment, add the flour, sugar, lard, vanilla, and cinnamon and mix until just incorporated. If it is too creamy, add more flour. Aim for a Play-Doh-like consistency that can be balled up and pressed down without tearing.

SWEET SOURDOUGH PREFERMENT

100 g (¾ c + 1 Tbsp) bread flour
25 g (2 Tbsp) granulated sugar
75 g (¼ c + 1 Tbsp) warm water
50 g (¼ c) mature sourdough starter

DOUGH

50 g (⅓ c + 1 Tbsp) brown rice flour
100 g (¾ c) white rice flour
350 g (2⅓ c + 1 Tbsp) bread flour
100 g (⅓ c + 1½ Tbsp) whole milk
150 g (scant ¾ c) sweet sourdough preferment
200 g (½ c) water
50 g (2½ Tbsp) honey
2 large eggs
100 g (7 Tbsp) unsalted butter
6 g (2 tsp) kosher salt

TOPPING

200 g (1½ c + 1½ Tbsp) all-purpose flour
80 g (⅔ c) powdered sugar
60 g (4½ Tbsp) lard or shortening
1 to 2 g (¼ to ½ tsp) vanilla extract
1 to 2 g (½ to 1 tsp) ground cinnamon

Form ten 30-g (2 Tbsp) balls and flatten them using a tortilla press or a rolling pin. Place a piece of topping over each dough ball and press into the edges so that it covers the whole surface.

Let the semitas proof for 3 to 4 hours at room temperature, or until they are nice and plump. You will know they are ready to go into the oven when the covering is completely separated and the dough feels like a pillow. When gently pushing the dough ball, it should bounce back slightly, and it should never collapse or tear. The window for proofing here is big because these can be quite sensitive and you want to push the proof as much as possible without ending up with dough that rips. Keep an eye on the dough around hour 4 and make an assessment based on how it feels.

Preheat the oven to 375°F, place the sheet pan in the oven, and bake the semitas for about 30 minutes, or until they are doubled in size and have a nice light to dark brown coloring on the sides.

Cool on a wire rack before serving.

MALLORCA DE CHOCOLATE
with Guava Glaze

Mallorcas are a melt in your mouth, Puerto Rican treasure of a pan dulce. These soft, sweet rolls dusted liberally in powdered sugar are addictive. In my first book, *New World Sourdough*, I talked about my first experiences with mallorcas in college; my roommate was obsessed with them. Since creating a sourdough mallorca recipe, I've maintained my own obsession and have sought ways to make them with different ingredients and enjoy the pillowy soft texture. I realized that, as usual, you can't go wrong with chocolate. I began several tests: mallorca with chocolate chunks, mallorca with fudge, and both. But in reality, too much chocolate and too much texture can disrupt the experience of a mallorca. So I opted to go with a slurry of semisweet chocolate melted into milk. When added to the dough, the right amount of chocolatey flavor is imparted and the interior stays soft and smooth. Dusting the mallorca with powdered sugar, as is traditional, yields quite a tasty treat, but here I add a glaze. Guava, an indigenous staple fruit, is a natural choice.

SWEET SOURDOUGH PREFERMENT

In a tall jar or large container with a lid, mix the bread flour, whole wheat flour, sugar, water, and mature sourdough starter with your hand or a fork. Ensure that no dry flour remains at the bottom of the jar.

Cover the container and let it rest at room temperature (ideally between 70° and 80°F) for 4 hours. It should double in size and have a firm, bubbly structure on the top. Once the preferment is ready to use, you can start baking straight away or place it in your fridge for later use (up to 2 days).

DOUGH

In a microwave-safe bowl, combine the chocolate chips and milk and heat in the microwave for 2 to 3 minutes so that the chocolate starts to melt. Remove and let rest for 10 minutes. Whisk together to create a slurry. Note that this mixture will not be thick; it should be slightly runny.

In the bowl of a stand mixer with the dough hook attachment, add the chocolate mixture, all-purpose flour, bread flour, sugar, and sourdough preferment and mix on low speed until a rough dough forms, 3 to 4 minutes.

Increase the mixer to medium speed, add half of the softened butter, and mix for 2 to 3 minutes or until the butter gets fully incorporated. Add the remaining softened butter and mix again until the dough smooths out.

(CONTINUED)

SWEET SOURDOUGH PREFERMENT

75 g (scant ⅔ c) bread flour
25 g (3 Tbsp) whole wheat flour
25 g (2 Tbsp) granulated sugar
100 g (¼ c + 3 Tbsp) warm water
50 g (¼ c) mature sourdough starter

DOUGH

113 g (⅔ c) semisweet chocolate chips
300 g (1¼ c) whole milk
405 g (3¼ c) all-purpose flour
95 g (¾ c) bread flour
100 g (½ c) granulated sugar
215 g (1 c) sweet sourdough preferment
113 g (1 stick) unsalted butter, softened, plus 15 g (1 Tbsp) unsalted butter, melted, for the shaping stage
6 g (2 tsp) kosher salt
50 g (3½ Tbsp) water
1 large egg, for the egg wash
Pinch kosher salt, for the egg wash

GLAZE

50 g (2½ Tbsp) guava paste
113 g (1 stick) unsalted butter, softened
350 g (2¾ c + 3 Tbsp) powdered sugar, plus more for dusting
10 g (2 tsp) heavy cream

Add the salt, trickle in the water, switch the mixer to high speed, and mix for 3 to 4 minutes until all the water is incorporated and there's a smooth and elastic dough.

Transfer to a clean, lightly oiled bowl and cover. Let ferment at room temperature for 4 hours. After the initial fermentation period, divide the dough into twelve 100-g pieces (about the size of small lemons) and shape each piece into a tiny log. Cover and let the dough rest for 15 minutes.

To shape the mallorca, roll out each log to about 10 inches long and brush liberally with the melted butter. Roll the dough into a spiral shape and place on a parchment-lined sheet pan.

Let the dough proof at room temperature for 4 hours. The best way to proof them is to just leave them in the oven (not turned on, of course).

Remove the mallorcas from the oven before preheating, if you proofed them in the oven, and preheat the oven to 375°F.

In a small bowl, mix the egg and the pinch of salt, brush the mallorcas with the egg wash, place the sheet pan in the oven, and bake for 20 minutes.

To make the glaze: Heat the guava paste in a small saucepan on medium heat for about 5 minutes, or until it breaks down and has the consistency of thick jelly—be careful not to touch the guava when hot! Set aside briefly and let cool for 5 minutes. In the bowl of a stand mixer with the paddle attachment, add the guava paste, butter, powdered sugar, and heavy cream and mix on medium speed until creamed together and slightly runny.

When the mallorcas are baked, cool on a wire rack, glaze, dust with powdered sugar, if desired, and serve.

MEDIALUNAS

**SWEET SOURDOUGH
PREFERMENT**

75 g (scant ⅔ c) bread flour
25 g (3 Tbsp) whole wheat flour
25 g (2 Tbsp) granulated sugar
50 g (¼ c) warm water
**50 g (¼ c) mature sourdough
    starter**

DOUGH

750 g (6 c) all-purpose flour
250 g (2 c) bread flour
**100 g (7 Tbsp) unsalted butter,
    softened, plus 621 g (5½
    sticks) unsalted butter, for
    laminating**
**175 g (¾ c + 2 Tbsp) granulated
    sugar**
525 g (2¼ c) whole milk
**2 large eggs, plus 1 large egg
    and 1 large egg yolk for the
    egg wash**
**6 g (2 tsp) kosher salt, plus more
    for the egg wash**
**225 g (1 c + 1 Tbsp) sweet
    sourdough preferment**

GLAZE

150 g (¾ c) granulated sugar
155 g (⅔ c) water
Zest of ½ orange

With its Spanish and Italian influences, Buenos Aires has an undeniable European feel. Although the architecture might catch your eye, if you look at the signage of the many cafés lining the streets, you'll see one thing that is offered on every street corner: the medialuna. Upon first glance, it might be mistaken for a croissant. Flaky layers of butter laminated into dough and formed into that familiar crescent shape, known as a croissant, is a specialty that is originally Viennese, created during a period of conflict in Europe between the Habsburgs and the Ottoman Empire. The victory of the Habsburgs saw local bakers create a pastry in the crescent shape to mock the Ottoman flag and celebrate.

The complicated political state in Argentina was a perfect place for this pastry to arrive, as there are several pastries that revel in rebellion, like bombas and vigilantes. However, as with most European-origin baked goods that arrived in Latin America, there was a shift in technique and approach that culminated in a unique new product. Unlike croissants, the dough of medialunas includes egg for richness, and they are proofed and baked tightly together to create a moister interior and beautiful, soft, flaky layers as you pull them apart. To finish them off, they are drenched with syrup. My version of medialunas uses sourdough and a long overnight proof to create a deliciously funky flavor that is sure to have you going back for more. One of the most important tips I can give you when it comes to laminating in your kitchen is to make sure you get your air conditioning on to cool the ambient temperature down to somewhere between 65° and 70°F. Having a cool environment makes laminating your dough a breeze, but if it gets too warm and you start working the dough you will soon see butter ooze out of your dough. My final parting words are that if you aren't successful or find the sourdough component too challenging, add a pinch of fresh yeast to the dough, or use the conversion chart on page 19 to make a yeasted version and work your way up to making these with 100 percent sourdough.

SWEET SOURDOUGH PREFERMENT

In a tall jar or large container with a lid, mix the bread flour, whole wheat flour, sugar, water, and mature sourdough starter with your hand or a fork. Ensure that no dry flour remains at the bottom of the jar.

Cover the container and let it rest at room temperature (ideally between 73° and 80°F) for 4 hours. It should double in size and have a firm, bubbly structure on the top. Once the preferment is ready to use, you can start baking straight away or place it in your fridge for later use (up to 2 days).

(CONTINUED)

DOUGH

In the bowl of a stand mixer fitted with the dough hook attachment, combine the all-purpose flour, bread flour, 100 g (7 Tbsp) softened butter, sugar, milk, 2 of the eggs, the salt, and sourdough preferment and mix on low speed for 5 minutes.

Increase the speed to medium and mix for another 5 minutes. To avoid overworking the dough, a slow mix without using high speed is optimal. Once the dough is smooth, transfer to a work surface and knead with your hands for a couple of minutes to round it out. Put the dough into a lightly oiled bowl and let it ferment for 4 hours at room temperature.

After the initial fermentation period, flatten the dough out onto a lightly floured sheet pan so that it fits the shape of the sheet pan. It doesn't really matter what size, as you can adjust your lamination butter accordingly. Wrap the sheet pan and place in the fridge for 24 hours.

The next day, prepare the butter block by either using a large ziplock bag or two pieces of parchment paper. Place the remaining 621 g (5½ sticks) of butter in the middle and use a rolling pin to flatten it into a square that's about 10 millimeters thick. Try to make sure the butter block is the size of half of your sheet pan of dough to make the next steps easy. Place the butter in the fridge, wrapped tightly, until it firms up. Avoid using butter that has just been manipulated and warmed up because it will soften and leak out of the chilled dough. Let the butter block cool in the fridge for at least 30 minutes so that it can firm up, then remove from the fridge so that it becomes pliable. You want the consistency of the dough to match the consistency of the butter—it should be firm but bendable and should not break when you bend it.

On a lightly floured work surface, turn the dough out of the sheet pan, maintaining the rectangular shape. Check the size of the butter against the dough to make sure it can cover half of the dough and adjust the dough with your rolling pin accordingly.

Place the butter block onto half the dough and fold the other half on top as if closing a book. Slice the side of dough that is not exposed with a knife to relieve the pressure of the butter against the dough. Lightly flour the surface of the dough and use a rolling pin to begin elongating the dough.

Use the rolling pin from the center to gently push down and start rolling the dough forward. Once you feel any resistance, flip it around 180° and work the other side. Make sure to roll the dough out until it is about triple the original length. This is a rough estimate, and every dough will be different so try to learn how to use your senses. Also consider widening it a little so that it does not end up too narrow.

Always make sure to use a little flour on the work surface. It will be easier to dust off flour during the folding process than deal with dough that gets stuck on the counter and starts to tear. Flour is your friend and will prevent the dough from sticking. If there's any resistance or tearing, stop and let the dough rest in the fridge. If the butter begins to melt or explode out of the top or bottom, it is too warm. Cool it down in the fridge, but know that this imbalance in temperature may continue to disrupt the process. Don't throw the dough away, though. Power through, and then try again after finishing the whole process.

Once the dough is about tripled in length, trim the edges to create a uniform rectangle. These rounded edges most likely do not have any butter in them and will mess with the layering if not trimmed away.

(CONTINUED)

Fold the dough into thirds by bringing one side into the middle and the other side on top—this is one single fold. Place on a floured sheet pan, cover tightly with plastic wrap, and let the dough rest in the fridge for 30 minutes. After letting it cool repeat this process two more times, for a total of 3 single folds.

After completing 3 single folds, cover tightly with plastic wrap and let the dough rest in the fridge for 1 full hour.

Once it has rested after the third fold, it is now time to roll out and shape the medialunas. Flour a work surface and once again elongate the dough. I like to roll it out just until the dough starts to resist on either side. Don't go too thin here, but you should be able to get it down to about 4 milimeters. I find that a slightly thicker size to the dough can yield better layers in the case of using sourdough.

Trim the edges to create a uniform rectangle. Use a pizza cutter or a large chef's knife to cut the dough into 14 triangles.

Once the triangles are cut, elongate them a bit with your hand by holding the base and running your fingers up the back side of it. Cut a slit in the middle of the base of the triangle that will allow for a wider roll to create the familiar shape of a medialuna. Press the tip of the triangle into the surface, and then roll them up by starting at the base of the triangle. Once they've been rolled up tightly, fold the outside flaps into the middle, as if they were arms being crossed.

Place the medialunas on a parchment-lined sheet pan, making sure they are almost touching. One of the distinguishing features of a medialuna is the moist interior that is generated because of the way they are baked together.

The key to proofing these is a lot of patience and a stable room temperature environment. They need a solid 10 to 12 hours proofing at room temperature, so I find it best to do this overnight. Leaving the medialunas uncovered will dry them up, so take a large plastic bag and create a covered environment around the sheet pan. It will look weird, but it works. Just makes sure the bag doesn't touch the dough and allows for growth. Another option is to place the sheet pan in the oven while it is off, if the oven doesn't get a lot of draft that can dry the dough out, and leave it there overnight.

Before the next day, prepare the glaze so that it has time to cool down. In a medium saucepan over medium heat, combine the sugar and water until it simmers and the sugar disappears. Add the orange zest and stir. Remove from the heat and let the syrup cool overnight.

The next day, when checking on the medialunas, you should, first and foremost, notice an increase in volume/size and possibly a clearer definition of the layers. When shaking the sheet pan, the medialunas should wobble a bit. Note that with yeasted medialunas there is usually a noticeable wobble and size increase. That increase isn't as pronounced in this recipe. If there's butter leakage, it means that it was too warm for the proof. Go ahead and move into the bake stage, but it might not end up exactly as it should.

Once the medialunas are proofed and ready to go, preheat the oven to 400°F. Make an egg wash by whisking together 1 egg, 1 egg yolk, a splash of the glaze syrup, and a pinch of salt. Use a brush to paint the medialunas with this mixture, place the sheet pan in the oven, and bake for 5 minutes. Then lower the heat to 375°F and bake for 20 more minutes, rotating the pan halfway through. Make sure you bake on the highest rack to keep the bottoms from burning. I opt to bake them a little dark on top.

Once they are out of the oven, brush them liberally with the remaining glaze. Let them cool, and enjoy.

GOLFEADOS

One of the most popular baked goods in Venezuela and in Venezuelan communities around the world are sweet and salty golfeados. They are bound to have you eating more than just one at a time. The golfeado is said to originate from one of the pathways into the city of Caracas, in an area called Petare. Siblings Genaro and María Duarte baked them in a wood-fired oven and it did not take long for something so unique to catch on in the rest of the country, as the contrast between sweet piloncillo and crumbly semihard cheese makes for a treat like no other. Venezuela has the second largest Portuguese diaspora after Brazil, so it is no surprise that there was a wheat-based baking influence in the country that contributed to the evolution of the overall baking culture. These make for a great bake to bring to gatherings or to have around the house, and pair well with a thick slice of queso de mano. One thing to note is that traditionally, golfeados are not laminated, so these would be considered "Golfeados Hojaldradas"—flaky golfeados!

SWEET SOURDOUGH PREFERMENT

In a tall jar or large container with a lid, mix the bread flour, whole wheat flour, sugar, water, and mature sourdough starter with your hand or a fork. Ensure that no dry flour remains at the bottom of the jar.

Cover the container and let it rest at room temperature (ideally between 70° and 80°F) for 4 hours. It should double in size and have a firm, bubbly structure on the top. Once the preferment is ready to use, you can start baking straight away or place it in your fridge for later use (up to 2 days).

DOUGH

In the bowl of a stand mixer fitted with the dough hook attachment, combine the all-purpose flour, bread flour, 100 g (7 Tbsp) softened butter, sugar, milk, 2 of the eggs, the salt, ground anise seed, and sourdough preferment and mix on low speed for 5 minutes.

Increase the speed to medium and mix for another 5 minutes. To avoid overworking the dough, a slow mix without using high speed is optimal. Once the dough is smooth, transfer to a work surface and knead with your hands for a couple of minutes to round it out. Put the dough in a lightly oiled bowl and let it ferment for 4 hours at room temperature.

After the initial fermentation period, flatten the dough onto a lightly floured sheet pan so that it fits the shape of the pan. It doesn't really matter what size, since the butter lamination can be adjusted accordingly. Wrap the sheet pan and place in the fridge for 24 hours.

After the 24-hour cold fermentation period, prepare the butter block by either using a large ziplock bag or two pieces of parchment paper. Place the

SWEET SOURDOUGH PREFERMENT

75 g (scant ⅔ c) bread flour
50 g (scant ½ c) whole wheat flour
10 g (1 Tbsp) granulated sugar
50 g (¼ c) warm water
50 g (¼ c) mature sourdough starter

DOUGH

750 g (6 c) all-purpose flour
250 g (2 c) bread flour
100 g (7 Tbsp) unsalted butter, softened, for dough, plus 621 g (5½ sticks) unsalted butter, for laminating
175 g (¾ c + 2 Tbsp) granulated sugar
525 g (2¼ c) whole milk
2 large eggs, plus 1 large egg and 1 egg yolk for the egg wash
6 g (2 tsp) kosher salt, plus more for the egg wash
6 g (2 tsp) ground anise seed
225 g (1 c + 1 Tbsp) sweet sourdough preferment

FILLING AND TOPPINGS

1 piloncillo cone, chopped into rough cubes, for filling
200 g (1¾ + 1 Tbsp) shredded low-moisture cheese, such as queso de mano, for filling
14 slices queso de mano, for topping (optional)

MELADO SYRUP

1 piloncillo cone
295 g (1¼ c) water
1 cinnamon stick

(CONTINUED)

remaining 621 g (5½ sticks) butter in the middle and use a rolling pin to flatten it into a square that's about 10 millimeters thick. Try to make sure the butter block is half the size of the sheet pan with the dough to make the next steps easy. Place the butter block in the fridge, wrapped tightly, until it firms up. Avoid using butter that has just been manipulated and warmed up because it will soften and leak out of the chilled dough.

On a lightly floured work surface, turn the dough out of the sheet pan, maintaining the rectangular shape. Take the butter block out of the fridge and check it against the dough to make sure it can cover half of the dough, and adjust the dough with the rolling pin accordingly.

Place the butter block onto half the dough and fold the other half on top as if closing a book. Lightly flour the surface and use the rolling pin to elongate the dough.

Use the rolling pin from the center to gently push down and start rolling the dough forward. Once you feel any resistance, flip it around 180° and work the other side. Roll the dough out until it is about triple the original length.

Always make sure to use a little flour on the work surface. It will be easier to dust off flour during the folding process than deal with dough that's stuck on the counter and starts to tear. If there's any resistance or tearing, stop and let the dough rest in the fridge. If the butter is melting or exploding out of the top or bottom of the dough, the butter is too warm. Cool it down in the fridge, but know that this imbalance in temperature may continue to disrupt the process.

Once the dough is about tripled in length, trim the edges to create a uniform rectangle. These rounded edges most likely do not have any butter in them and will mess with the layering if not trimmed away.

Fold the dough into thirds, place on a floured sheet pan, cover tightly with plastic wrap, and let it rest in the fridge for 30 minutes. After letting it cool, repeat the elongation with the rolling pin. Aim for tripling the dough in length. Trim the edges just like last time. Fold one corner of the dough in, just slightly, about 5 inches. Fold the rest of the dough in toward that slight fold, and then close the whole thing like a book.

After completing this turn, let the dough rest in the fridge for 1 full hour.

Once it's rested, roll out and fill the golfeados. Flour a work surface and once again elongate the dough. I like to roll it out just until the dough starts to resist on either side. You don't want to go too thin here. A slightly thicker size to your dough can yield better layers when using sourdough.

Spread the chopped piloncillo and shredded cheese over the surface of the dough and roll the entirety of the dough into a tight log. Use a sharp chef's knife to cut the log into fourteen roughly 1-inch circles and place on a parchment-lined sheet pan. Feel free to cut them thicker, if desired. Proof in an environment around 74°F for 3 to 4 hours.

While the dough is proofing, make the melado syrup. In a small saucepan over medium heat, add the piloncillo cone, water, and cinnamon stick and cook until the cone has melted, about 10 minutes. Remove from the heat and set aside.

Preheat the oven to 375°F.

After proofing, in a small bowl, whisk the remaining egg and egg yolk with a pinch of salt and 1 Tbsp of the melado syrup and brush on the golfeados. Place the sheet pan in the oven and bake the golfeados for 15 minutes, or until dark brown. Remove from the oven and drizzle the golfeados liberally with the melado syrup. Add a slice of fresh queso de mano, if desired, and enjoy.

ROSCÓN DE AREQUIPE

Another extremely popular pan dulce is the roscón de arequipe, a delicious and soft sweet dough that is filled with arequipe, more commonly known as dulce de leche. In Bogotá, there are bakeries on almost every corner that have fresh breads and pastries; these roscones really stand out. In my visits I often noticed stacks of round, soft, perfectly golden rings of dough that had small slits around the edge with filling oozing out. The roscones, as they are called (meaning big round pastries), were filled with arequipe and other fruit jams as well—and my first bite was something special. The soft, buttery dough was perfectly fermented and effortlessly complemented the sweet filling of arequipe. I knew immediately I had to replicate this at home, and you can too!

SWEET SOURDOUGH PREFERMENT

In a tall jar or large container with a lid, mix the bread flour, sugar, water, and mature sourdough starter with your hand or a fork. Ensure that no dry flour remains at the bottom of the jar.

Cover the container and let it rest at room temperature (ideally between 73° and 80°F) for 4 hours. It should double in size and have a firm, bubbly structure on the top. Once the preferment is ready to use, you can start baking straight away or place it in your fridge for later use (up to 2 days).

DOUGH

In a bowl of a stand mixer with the dough hook attachment, combine the all-purpose flour, bread flour, sourdough preferment, vanilla extract, and lemon zest. Mix on low speed until a rough dough forms, 1 to 2 minutes. Add the sugar and 2 eggs to the dough, increase the speed to medium, and mix for about 3 minutes, or until the dough has completely come back together.

While the dough is mixing, start adding the butter in 50-g (3 Tbsp) increments, allowing it to be absorbed into the dough before adding more. With the last bit of butter, add the salt and increase the speed to high. Let the dough mix for 3 to 4 minutes, or until it is smooth and stays together.

Using wet hands, transfer the dough to a lightly oiled bowl and cover. Let the dough ferment at room temperature for 4 hours. Transfer the dough to the fridge for an overnight cold fermentation, between 8 and 12 hours. Always make sure the fridge is not too cold so that the dough does not become hard. Aim for a fridge temperature of 40°F and keep the bowl toward the front of the fridge as the back is usually colder.

The next day, take the dough out of the fridge and let it come to room temperature for 1 hour. Meanwhile, make the filling.

SWEET SOURDOUGH PREFERMENT

205 g (1⅔ c) bread flour
50 g (¼ c) granulated sugar
100 g (¼ c + 3 Tbsp) warm water
50 g (¼ c) mature sourdough starter

DOUGH

500 g (4 c) all-purpose flour
500 g (4 c) bread flour
350 g (1⅔ c) sweet sourdough preferment
4 g (1 tsp) vanilla extract or paste
Zest of ½ lemon
130 g (⅔ c) granulated sugar
2 large eggs, plus 1 large egg and 1 large egg yolk for the egg wash
150 g (10½ Tbsp) unsalted butter
7 g (2¼ tsp) kosher salt, plus more for the egg wash
500 g (2 c + 1½ Tbsp) whole milk
2 g (1 tsp) ground cinnamon

FILLING

400 g (1 c) dulce de leche
200 g (1½ c) powdered sugar

In the bowl of a stand mixer with the paddle attachment, add the dulce de leche and powdered sugar and mix on medium speed until a creamy paste forms, about 2 minutes. Set aside.

On a floured work surface, turn out the dough and use a rolling pin to flatten it into a rectangle, roughly 24 by 12 inches. Brush the surface of the dough with the dulce de leche mixture. Roll the dough tightly into a log and connect the edges, forming a circle. Pinch the edges together to make sure it seals and make the center circle as large as possible. Place on a parchment-lined baking sheet, cover, and let proof for 4 to 5 hours, or until the dough is bouncy and roughly doubled in size.

Preheat the oven to 375°F.

In a small bowl, add the remaining egg and egg yolk with a pinch of salt, mix, and brush the dough with this egg wash. Using scissors, make some shallow cuts around the edge of the dough, place it in the oven, and bake for 40 minutes, or until you see the filling oozing out and the color of the dough is a nice golden brown.

Cool the roscón on a wire rack before slicing and serving.

PAN DE COCO TRADICIONAL

Pan de coco is a special bread to me, my family, and my Honduran heritage. When you go to Honduras and want to eat bread, it is most likely going to be a freshly baked pan de coco. If you have followed my journey as a baker, you will know that I have made several different types of pan de coco ranging from sweet, to chocolatey, to earthy and seedy. But what I have not done yet is provide you with a recipe for an authentic-tasting pan de coco, similar to what one's grandmother would make for guests who come to the dinner table with an empty stomach. The kind of pan de coco that you dip into a delicious fish stew. I want you to make this your dinner table staple; your go-to recipe for the warm bread that you keep around the kitchen to snack on. I finally realized that the best way to make a delicious sourdough pan de coco is to make the preferment only with coconut milk, as opposed to relying on water. This adds a nice, funky, concentrated coconut flavor to your dough, as well as a creamy, even texture on the inside that is still quite fluffy. You can use this dough and bake as rolls or in a loaf pan, whichever you prefer. (And don't worry, I've got some fun, new, sweet versions for you later on in this chapter!)

SWEET SOURDOUGH PREFERMENT

In a tall jar or large container with a lid, mix the bread flour, coconut milk, sugar, and mature sourdough starter with your hand or a fork. Ensure that no dry flour remains at the bottom of the jar.

Cover the container and let it rest at room temperature (ideally between 70° and 80°F) for 4 hours, or until doubled in size. It should have a firm, bubbly structure on the top. Once the preferment is ready to use, you can start baking straight away or place it in your fridge for later use (up to 2 days).

DOUGH

Make sure your coconut milk is warm, but not hot, before using. I typically heat it up in the microwave briefly or in a microwave-safe bowl at a simmer.

In a large mixing bowl, combine the sourdough preferment, coconut milk, all-purpose flour, bread flour, and whole wheat flour. Mix and let rest for 10 minutes.

Add the sugar and coconut oil to the dough, using your hands to squeeze and incorporate into the dough, 5 to 6 minutes. Once fully incorporated, let the dough rest for 5 minutes and then add the salt and butter to the dough, using the same technique to squeeze and incorporate into the dough. With each addition, make sure it is fully incorporated and the dough becomes smooth again.

SWEET SOURDOUGH PREFERMENT

100 g (¾ c + 1 Tbsp) bread flour
100 g (⅓ c + 1½ Tbsp) full-fat coconut milk
25 g (2 Tbsp) granulated sugar
50 g (¼ c) mature sourdough starter

DOUGH

200 g (1 scant c) sweet sourdough preferment
300 g (1¼ c) full-fat coconut milk, warmed
300 g (2⅓ c + 1 Tbsp) all-purpose flour
100 g (¾ c + 1 Tbsp) bread flour
100 g (¾ c + 1½ Tbsp) whole wheat flour
30 g (2½ Tbsp) granulated sugar
50 g (scant ¼ c) coconut oil
6 g (2 tsp) kosher salt, plus more for the egg wash
50 g (3½ Tbsp) unsalted butter, softened
1 large egg, for the egg wash
100 g (1¼ c) shredded coconut, for topping

Turn the dough out onto a lightly floured work surface and knead until the dough is strong and smooth, about 5 minutes. Place in a lightly oiled bowl, cover, and let ferment for 6 hours at room temperature.

After the initial fermentation period, turn the dough onto a work surface and divide. If you want to make loaves, you can divide the dough in half, shape each piece into a tube with tension, and place them into oiled loaf pans. If you want to bake as rolls, divide the dough into 6 equal pieces, round them into balls, and place on a parchment-lined sheet pan, 3 by 2.

Whisk together the egg and a pinch of salt. Brush the dough with the egg wash and let proof for 3 hours at room temperature. During the last hour of the proof, preheat the oven to 375°F.

Brush again with the egg wash at the end of the proof and top liberally with the shredded coconut. Place in the oven and bake the pan de coco for 30 to 35 minutes, or until golden brown and the coconut flakes are nice and toasted.

ROASTED GINGER AND CARAMELIZED PINEAPPLE PAN DE COCO

Making variations of pan de coco has become a hobby of mine. It's easy to pursue considering how many ingredients combine well with coconut. I have only recently started using roasted ginger in my cooking, and when I thought about incorporating fresh ginger for baking (instead of the ground spice), I knew that roasting it before incorporating it into the dough would be the only way to go. This loaf has lots of different textures, with the caramelized pineapple offering a nice, soft, jam-like consistency throughout.

Pineapple makes me think of Honduras, although it is grown all over the world, because the first time I saw pineapple being harvested was on the side of a mountain on the way to Tegucigalpa from San Pedro Sula. I was shocked because I didn't realize they grew straight out of the ground! I also love caramelized pineapple because my mom used to make us delicious pastelitos de piña growing up (you can find my recipe on page 276). For now, enjoy another rendition of pillow-soft pan de coco.

SWEET SOURDOUGH PREFERMENT

In a tall jar or large container with a lid, mix the bread flour, whole wheat flour, pineapple, coconut milk, mature sourdough starter, and sugar with your hand or a fork. Ensure that no dry flour remains at the bottom of the jar.

Cover the container and let it rest at room temperature (ideally between 70° and 80°F) for 4 hours, or until doubled in size. It should have a firm, bubbly structure on the top. Once the preferment is ready to use, you can start baking straight away or place it in your fridge for later use (up to 2 days).

DOUGH

Preheat the oven to 450°F.

Keeping the skin on, wrap the ginger in aluminum foil, place in the oven, roast for 45 minutes, remove, and cool. Once completely cooled, remove the skin.

Next, remove the top and skin from the pineapple. Using the large holes of a grater, shred half the pineapple into a medium skillet. Turn the heat to medium and add the brown sugar. You can add less or more sugar, depending on your preference. Allow the mixture to bubble up while you stir it, 5 to 10 minutes.

Using the grater, grate the roasted ginger into the pineapple mixture. Once you have a nice bubbling caramelization, decrease the heat to low and simmer for 5 minutes. Transfer the caramelized pineapple mixture to a bowl or

SWEET SOURDOUGH PREFERMENT

- 50 g (⅓ c + 1 Tbsp) bread flour
- 50 g (scant ½ c) whole wheat flour
- 25 g (2 Tbsp) diced fresh pineapple chunks (not canned)
- 100 g (⅓ c + 1½ Tbsp) full-fat coconut milk
- 50 g (¼ c) mature sourdough starter
- 25 g (2 Tbsp) granulated sugar

DOUGH

- 100 g (3½ oz, or 3 knobs) fresh ginger
- ½ fresh pineapple
- 50 g (¼ c) packed brown sugar
- 405 g (3¼ c) all-purpose flour
- 95 g (¾ c) bread flour
- 50 g (scant ½ c) whole wheat flour
- 50 g (⅓ c + 1 Tbsp) coconut flour
- 250 g (1 c + 2 tsp) coconut milk, slightly warm
- 190 g (¾ c + 1 Tbsp) water
- 100 g (½ c) granulated sugar
- 50 g (3½ Tbsp) unsalted butter, softened
- 250 g (heaped 1 c) sweet sourdough preferment
- 75 g (scant 1 c) shredded coconut, plus more for topping
- 1 large egg
- Pinch kosher salt

container and cool for at least 30 minutes. You can place it into the freezer after the 30-minute mark to cool it down some more before adding into the dough, but do not freeze it. It should ultimately be at room temperature.

In a large mixing bowl, combine the all-purpose flour, bread flour, whole wheat flour, coconut flour, coconut milk, water, sugar, butter, and sourdough preferment. Mix with both hands until well combined and there is not much dry flour left in the bowl. Turn out onto a floured work surface and knead until the surface is smooth. Cover and let rest for 4 hours at room temperature.

After the fermentation period, turn the dough out onto a floured work surface and divide in two. Flatten down each dough piece into a small rectangle. Evenly spread the pineapple mixture and shredded coconut over the surface of the dough and roll into a log like a jelly roll. Place each loaf in a lightly greased loaf pan and let proof for 4 hours at room temperature.

Preheat the oven to 375°F.

After the proof, in a small bowl, combine the egg and pinch of salt, brush each loaf with the egg wash, and top with more shredded coconut. Place the loaf pans in the oven and bake the pan de coco for 30 to 35 minutes, until they are golden brown and the coconut is a dark brown, toasty color.

Cool on a wire rack before serving.

BANANA AND RUM RAISIN PAN DE COCO

A couple of years ago, I did a pop-up at Jim Lahey's Sullivan Street Bakery in Hell's Kitchen, New York. It was eye opening to work with such a clever baker. We were debating what to make, and naturally I wanted to make some form of pan de coco. In the past, Jim had made a version of a banana and date loaf, and so we had the answer: a date and banana pan de coco. We wrapped it up in banana leaves before baking and I still have dreams about it. For the recipe I share with you, instead of dates, we use rum-soaked raisins and shredded coconut inside the dough, with a topping of crumbled cashews and shredded coconut. Cashews are native to Honduras and add good texture and a complementary saltiness to each sweet bite. You definitely want to make sure you've got some banana leaves for this one; they impart such beautiful, earthy flavor in addition to adding some extra steam to your bake.

SWEET SOURDOUGH PREFERMENT

In a tall jar or large container with a lid, mix the bread flour, coconut milk, sugar, and mature sourdough starter with your hand or a fork. Ensure that no dry flour remains at the bottom of the jar.

Cover the container and let it rest at room temperature (ideally between 70° and 80°F) for 4 hours, or until doubled in size. It should have a firm, bubbly structure on the top. Once the preferment is ready to use, you can start baking straight away or place it in your fridge for later use (up to 2 days).

DOUGH

In a small saucepan over medium heat, combine the rum and raisins and cook while stirring until the raisins are plump, about 10 minutes. Remove from the heat and let them sit in the rum until ready for use.

In a large mixing bowl, combine the all-purpose flour, bread flour, whole wheat flour, coconut flour, wheat bran, coconut milk, water, and sourdough preferment. Mix with both hands until well combined and there is not much dry flour left in the bowl. Cover and rest for 30 minutes. At this point, drain any excess rum from the raisins as it is now time to add them to the dough.

Turn the dough onto a floured work surface and pat down to flatten. Add half of the raisins and half of the bananas to the surface of the dough, evenly spread out, and fold the sides, top, and bottom over them to seal them up. Flip the dough over and add the remaining raisins and bananas, folding the dough over again to seal it up. Round the dough into a ball (it's okay if chunks of bananas or raisins are falling out). Add to a lightly oiled bowl, along with

SWEET SOURDOUGH PREFERMENT

100 g (¾ c + 1 Tbsp) bread flour

100 g (⅓ c + 1½ Tbsp) full-fat coconut milk

5 g (1 tsp) granulated sugar

50 g (¼ c) mature sourdough starter

DOUGH

150 g (⅔ c) rum

150 g (1 c) raisins

405 g (3¼ c) all-purpose flour

95 g (¾ c) bread flour

50 g (scant ½ c) whole wheat flour

50 g (⅓ c + 1 Tbsp) coconut flour

25 g (¼ c + 2 Tbsp) wheat bran

250 g (1 c + 2 tsp) coconut milk, slightly warm

190 g (¾ c + 1 Tbsp) water

250 g (heaped 1 c) sweet sourdough preferment

150 g (1 c) chopped banana (roughly 1½ bananas)

1 large banana leaf, defrosted

1 large egg, for the egg wash

Pinch kosher salt, for the egg wash

60 g (¾ c) shredded coconut

50 g (⅓ c + 2 Tbsp) cashews

anything that's fallen out of the dough, cover, and let the dough ferment at room temperature for 4 hours.

After the initial fermentation period, turn the dough out onto a floured work surface and divide into 8 pieces. Round the dough pieces into tight balls and place on a sheet pan lined with banana leaves. In a small bowl, combine the egg and pinch of salt, brush the dough balls with the egg wash, and top with lots of shredded coconut and crumbled cashews. Let the dough rest at room temperature for 3 hours.

Preheat the oven to 375°F, place the sheet pan in the oven, and bake the rolls for 30 to 35 minutes, until they are golden brown and the coconut is a dark, brown toasty color. Cool on a wire rack before serving.

PAN DE MUERTO

On October 31, 2022, not long after I submitted the first draft of this book to my editor, my father passed away. After hanging up the phone and hearing this news, I was a bit frantic and needed to take a long walk and process everything, as well as call my siblings and my mom. I knew I would fly down to Honduras in a few days, but I was overcome with the need to bake bread to bring to him, and not just any bread. I wanted to honor my father with pan de muerto, as October 31 is also the beginning of the celebration known as el Día de los Muertos (The Day of the Dead). This is a time in México where friends and family gather to honor those who have passed away and to pay respect to their memories. Although my family is not Mexican, my heart felt the need to honor this tradition. I wish I had been able to bake for him more often, so I didn't want to miss this chance to put one more loaf of bread in his hands.

Pan de muerto is considered a pan dulce, and it is quite tasty. Not all pan de muerto is alike, with different varieties found throughout the states of México. You might find some filled with chocolate, topped with sesame seeds, sugar, or even pastry cream. One constant is the flavor of the dough, with hints of citrus and anise permeating the soft, chewy interior. The bread is shaped into a ball, but some of the dough is separated to layer on top with shapes of bones or a skull.

As I mentioned in this book's dedication, the first bread I ever baked in my life was a cinnamon raisin loaf for my dad. He loved it. It was both burnt and underbaked, but he ate the whole thing. Naturally, I made a cinnamon raisin dough because I knew that he would love it. I had never had to deal with the death of a close loved one before, and although it was not an easy time nor does it get easier to digest the fact that he is gone, I appreciate that baking bread connects me to him, and this tradition will live on forever. I will always go down to San Pedro Sula and honor his memory with pan de muerto.

If you ever want to find a way to celebrate the memory of a loved one, this delicious and delicately soft pan dulce is a good way to go.

SWEET SOURDOUGH PREFERMENT

In a tall jar or large container with a lid, mix the bread flour, whole wheat flour, sugar, anise, water, and mature sourdough starter with your hand or a fork. Ensure that no dry flour remains at the bottom of the jar.

Cover the container and let it rest at room temperature (ideally between 70° and 80°F) for 4 hours. It should double in size and have a firm, bubbly structure on the top. Once the preferment is ready to use, you can start baking straight away or place it in your fridge for later use (up to 2 days).

(CONTINUED)

SWEET SOURDOUGH PREFERMENT

50 g (⅓ c + 1 Tbsp) bread flour
50 g (scant ½ c) whole wheat flour
25 g (2 Tbsp) granulated sugar
2 g (1 tsp) ground anise
100 g (¼ c + 3 Tbsp) warm water
50 g (¼ c) mature sourdough starter

DOUGH

300 g (2⅓ c + 1 Tbsp) all-purpose flour
200 g (1½ c + 1½ Tbsp) bread flour
75 g (¼ c + 2 Tbsp packed) brown sugar
250 g (1 c + 2 tsp) whole milk, plus more for the egg wash
2 large eggs, plus 1 large egg for the egg wash
50 g (3½ Tbsp) unsalted butter
10 g (1 Tbsp + 2 tsp) ground anise
6 g (2 tsp) kosher salt, plus more for the egg wash
200 g (scant 1 c) sweet sourdough preferment
Zest of ½ large orange

TOPPING

Granulated sugar and sesame seeds, for dusting

DOUGH

In a large bowl, combine the all-purpose flour, bread flour, brown sugar, milk, 2 of the eggs, the butter, anise, salt, sourdough preferment, and orange zest and mix with your hands until there is no dry flour left in the bowl.

Turn the dough out onto the countertop and knead for 10 minutes, or until the dough smooths out. Transfer to a clean, lightly oiled bowl and let ferment at room temperature for 4 hours, covered. Transfer to the fridge for an additional 12 hours.

The next day, line a sheet pan with parchment paper and set aside. On a clean work surface dusted with all-purpose flour, turn out the dough and divide it into two equal pieces. From each piece, separate 50 g of dough (about the size of a small clementine) and set aside. Shape each large piece into a tight ball. Set aside.

From the smaller 50-g pieces, separate one 15-g piece (about the size of a gumball). You should now have two 15-g gumball-size pieces and two 35-g new-potato-size pieces.

Roll each of the 35-g pieces into as long a log as possible. Cut each log in half. Use your knuckles to roll each log back and forth, creating indentations in the dough. Shape each of the two 15-g pieces into a small ball.

On each large, rounded piece of dough, overlay two indented dough logs in an X, tucking the ends of the logs underneath the round. Then place one 15-g ball on top, where the logs cross.

Place your breads on the parchment-lined sheet pan and proof for 3 hours.

Preheat the oven to 375°F.

Whisk together the remaining egg, a splash of milk, and a pinch of salt. Brush each pan de muerto gently with the egg wash. Sprinkle one of them liberally with sesame seeds.

Place the sheet pan in the oven and bake for 25 to 30 minutes or until golden brown. When they come out of the oven, dust the plain loaf with the sugar. Cool on a wire rack before serving.

ROSCA DE REYES

Every year on January 6, Epiphany is celebrated across the globe as the twelfth day of Christmas. This holiday commemorates the Three Kings being led to the baby Jesus while bearing gifts. In modern times, the celebration of this day includes festivals, feasts, and of course delicious sweets.

There are different versions of the Three Kings cake that represents this history. In France, the galette des rois is made with thin, flaky puff pastry layers and a creamy frangipane filling. In New Orleans, king cake is a cinnamon sugar brioche–style dough that is filled with cream cheese and topped with colored sugar. The Mexican version is rosca de reyes, which translates to (you guessed it), kings' cake. In Spain, the traditional cake is roscón, and naturally this tradition made its way to the New World.

The adapted version of the rosca that you find in México includes figs, quince, candied cherries, and several other types of dried fruit. One thing that all of these cakes have in common is that there is traditionally a small, plastic figurine included that is sometimes hidden within the cake itself. Although this plastic doll represents baby Jesus, you don't have to be religious to enjoy a delicious slice—and in México, you might be on the hook to cook a meal for those with whom you are sharing the rosca.

SWEET SOURDOUGH PREFERMENT

In a tall jar or large container with a lid, mix the bread flour, sugar, water, and mature sourdough starter with your hand or a fork. Ensure that no dry flour remains at the bottom of the jar.

Cover the container and let it rest at room temperature (ideally between 70° and 80°F) for 4 hours. It should double in size and have a firm, bubbly structure on the top. Once the preferment is ready to use, you can start baking straight away or place it in your fridge for later use (up to 2 days).

DOUGH

In the bowl of a stand mixer with the dough hook attachment, combine the bread flour, all-purpose flour, orange blossom water or orange juice, sourdough preferment, vanilla, orange zest, and lemon zest. Mix on low speed until a rough dough forms, 1 to 2 minutes. Add the sugar and eggs to the dough, increase the speed to medium, and mix for about 3 minutes, or until the dough has completely come back together.

While the dough is mixing, start adding the butter in 100-g (7 Tbsp) increments, allowing it to be absorbed into the dough before adding more. With the last bit of butter, add the salt and increase the speed to high. Let the dough mix for 3 to 4 minutes, or until it is smooth and stays together.

(CONTINUED)

SWEET SOURDOUGH PREFERMENT

125 g (1 c) bread flour
25 g (2 Tbsp) granulated sugar
125 g (½ c + ½ Tbsp) warm water
50 g (¼ c) mature sourdough starter

DOUGH

290 g (2⅓ c) bread flour
710 g (5⅔ c) all-purpose flour
100 g (¼ c + 3 Tbsp) orange blossom water or orange juice
275 g (1¼ c + 1 Tbsp) sweet sourdough preferment
5 g (1 tsp) vanilla extract
Zest of ½ orange
Zest of ½ lemon
300 g (1½ c) granulated sugar
3 large eggs
300 g (21 Tbsp) unsalted butter, room temperature
8 g (2½ tsp) kosher salt

FILLING

50 g (3½ Tbsp) unsalted butter, melted
100 g (½ c) granulated sugar
Zest of ½ orange
Zest of ½ lemon
1 large egg, for the egg wash
Pinch salt, for the egg wash

TOPPING

200 g (1½ c + 1½ Tbsp) all-purpose flour
80 g (⅔ c) powdered sugar
60 g (4½ Tbsp) lard or shortening
1 to 2 g (¼ to ½ tsp) vanilla extract
8 thin slices guava paste
6 dried figs
100 g (heaped 1 c) sliced almonds
50 g (⅓ c + 1½ Tbsp) powdered sugar, for dusting

Using wet hands, transfer the dough to a lightly oiled bowl and cover. Let the dough ferment at room temperature for 4 hours. Transfer the dough to the fridge for an overnight cold fermentation, between 8 to 12 hours. Always make sure the fridge is not too cold so that the dough does not become hard. Aim for a fridge temperature of 40°F and keep the dough toward the front of the fridge as the back is usually colder.

The next day, take the dough out of the fridge and let it come to room temperature for 1 hour. On a floured work surface, turn out the dough and use a rolling pin to flatten it into a rectangle, roughly 24 by 12 inches.

To add the filling: Brush the dough with the melted butter and sprinkle with the sugar, orange zest, and lemon zest. Roll the dough tightly into a log and connect the edges, forming a circle. Pinch the edges together to make sure it seals and make the center circle as large as possible. Place on a parchment-lined baking sheet. Whisk together the egg and pinch of salt and brush the dough with the egg wash.

To make the topping: In a small bowl, combine the flour, powdered sugar, lard, and vanilla and mix until a slightly crumbly but pliable mixture is formed. Pinch off about 20 g (about the size of a big gumball) of the mixture and roll it into a tiny log, using flour on the work surface to help. You will want about 8 of these. Place them evenly around the dough, spacing them out to leave room for the other toppings.

Next, place a slice of guava paste in between the strips of the topping. Then add the dried figs in any empty spaces left and sprinkle with the sliced almonds. Cover and let proof for 4 to 5 hours, or until the dough is bouncy and roughly doubled in size.

Preheat the oven to 375°F, place the baking sheet in the oven, and bake the rosca for 40 minutes, or until it reaches an internal temperature of 200°F.

Cool the rosca on a wire rack and dust with the powdered sugar before slicing and serving. If you want to add a figurine, add it to the cooled rosca so as not to have baked a piece of plastic into your dough!

Makes
2 ROLLS

T'ANTA WAWA

In Perú and Bolivia, Spanish is not the only officially recognized language. Before the Spanish invaded and colonized the area, Quechua and Aymara were spoken by the Indigenous people of the land. Although the Spanish language is now dominant, there are areas where Quechua and Aymara traditions remain strong, including a special baked good in the Andean regions—the t'anta wawa (t'anta meaning "bread" and wawa meaning "child"). In other parts of Latin America, such as Ecuador, Colombia, and Argentina, this bread's name has been hispanicized to guagua de pan, or wawas de pan. This bread was traditionally offered as a gift in the memory of children who have passed on, but it is also consumed on All Souls' Day and shared with friends and family. The bread itself is shaped like an infant and is soft, slightly sweet, and sometimes contains fillings.

SWEET SOURDOUGH PREFERMENT

In a tall jar or large container with a lid, mix the bread flour, whole wheat flour, sugar, anise, water, and mature sourdough starter with your hand or a fork. Ensure that no dry flour remains at the bottom of the jar.

Cover the container and let it rest at room temperature (ideally between 70° and 80°F) for 4 hours. It should double in size and have a firm, bubbly structure on the top. Once the preferment is ready to use, you can start baking straight away or place it in your fridge for later use (up to 2 days).

DOUGH

In a large bowl, combine the all-purpose flour, bread flour, sugar, cloves, and salt. Mix until evenly distributed and set aside. In a separate bowl, whisk together the milk, 2 whole eggs and 1 egg yolk, the sourdough preferment, and the butter. Slowly pour the wet mixture into the dry mixture while mixing with your hand. Once it is all incorporated, mix with both hands until there is no dry flour left in the bowl. Turn the dough out onto the countertop and knead for 5 to 7 minutes, or until the dough smooths out and comes together without being too sticky. Transfer to a clean, lightly oiled bowl, cover, and let ferment at room temperature for 4 hours.

Line a sheet pan with parchment paper and set aside. On a clean work surface dusted with all-purpose flour, turn out the dough and divide it into two equal pieces. Shape each piece into an oval.

To create the figure of a small person, I like to use scissors to cut the sides to create "arms" and fold them across the dough. Using scissors, cut two diagonal slits on each side, but do not cut all the way through. The idea is to create two flaps, almost as if it was a penguin. Fold those two flaps across the rest of the dough as if the arms are folded.

SWEET SOURDOUGH PREFERMENT

50 g (⅓ c + 1 Tbsp) bread flour
50 g (scant ½ c) whole wheat flour
5 g (1 tsp) granulated sugar
2 g (1 tsp) ground anise
100 g (¼ c + 3 Tbsp) warm water
50 g (¼ c) mature sourdough starter

DOUGH

250 g (2 c) all-purpose flour
250 g (2 c) bread flour
80 g (¼ c + 2½ Tbsp) granulated sugar
8 g (1 Tbsp + 1 tsp) ground cloves
6 g (2 tsp) kosher salt, plus more for the egg wash
250 g (1 c + 2 tsp) whole milk, plus more for the egg wash
2 large eggs + 1 large egg yolk, 1 large egg for the egg wash
200 g (1 scant c) sweet sourdough preferment
50 g (3½ Tbsp) unsalted butter, melted
Sesame seeds, for topping
Food color gel, for decoration

Place the t'anta wawa on the lined sheet pan and proof for 3 to 4 hours, or until they double in size and jiggle.

Preheat the oven to 375°F.

Whisk together the remaining egg, a splash of milk, and a pinch of salt. Brush the rolls gently with the egg wash. Sprinkle lightly with sesame seeds.

Bake for 25 to 30 minutes or until golden brown. Use the food color gel to create a face at the top and any other designs desired.

ROLES DE CANELA
with Mango Cream Cheese Frosting

Nothing makes me smile more than a really delicious rol de canela, or cinnamon roll. Although not specific to any country in Latin America, you can often find freshly baked, jumbo-size roles in bakeries and cafés throughout the region. In this recipe I'm using a lot of panela to create a distinct sweetness and adding chunks of fresh mango and lemon zest for a creamy frosting.

SWEET SOURDOUGH PREFERMENT

In a tall jar or large container with a lid, mix the bread flour, whole wheat flour, sugar, water, and mature sourdough starter with your hand or a fork. Ensure that no dry flour remains at the bottom of the jar.

Cover the container and let it rest at room temperature (ideally between 70° and 80°F) for 4 hours. It should double in size and have a firm, bubbly structure on the top. Once the preferment is ready to use, you can start baking straight away or place it in your fridge for later use (up to 2 days).

DOUGH

In a large bowl, combine the all-purpose flour, bread flour, butter, sugar, milk, eggs, sourdough preferment,, salt, lemon zest, and orange zest and mix until it is all incorporated. Use your fingers to squeeze everything together.

Turn out the dough onto the countertop and use your palm to knead the dough until it is smooth. Place in a greased bowl and cover with plastic wrap. Let the dough sit on the countertop for 12 hours at room temperature. My kitchen is usually 70° to 75°F so adjust for your environment as needed.

FILLING

In a medium bowl, add the softened butter, brown sugar, and cinnamon and cream together. Then add the crushed pecans and mix until it is all evenly distributed.

After the bulk fermentation has concluded (usually overnight), dump the dough on a floured work surface. Lightly flour the surface of the dough and use a rolling pin to roll into a 36 by 12-inch rectangle.

Spread the filling onto the entirety of the dough rectangle.

From the top, longer side of the rectangle, roll into a tight log. Slice the log into 14 pieces that are about 2 inches thick.

Line a half sheet pan with parchment paper and place the rolls on it, 3 by 4, slightly touching.

Proof in a warm environment, like in the oven, turned off, with a pot of boiled water in it. The proof will take about 3 hours.

SWEET SOURDOUGH PREFERMENT

75 g (scant ⅔ c) bread flour

50 g (scant ½ c) whole wheat flour

30 g (2½ Tbsp) granulated sugar

100 g (¼ c + 3 Tbsp) warm water

50 g (¼ c) mature sourdough starter

DOUGH

500 g (4 c) all-purpose flour

500 g (4 c) bread flour

175 g (12½ Tbsp) unsalted butter

130 g (⅔ c) granulated sugar

500 g (2 c + 1½ Tbsp) whole milk

2 large eggs

300 g (1⅓ c) sweet sourdough preferment

7 g (2¼ tsp) salt

Zest of ½ lemon

Zest of ½ large orange

FILLING

150 g (10½ Tbsp) unsalted butter, softened

150 g (¾ c packed) brown sugar

25 g (¼ c) ground cinnamon

150 g (1¼ c) crushed pecans

FROSTING

226 g (8 oz) cream cheese

130 g (9½ Tbsp) unsalted butter

150 g (1¼ c) powdered sugar

Juice of 1 lemon

1 ripe mango, chopped

FROSTING

While the dough is proofing, in the bowl of a stand mixer with the paddle attachment, combine the cream cheese, butter, powdered sugar, lemon juice, and mango on low speed until the frosting is slightly thick and creamy. Add powdered sugar or water as needed. You can also mix by hand with a spatula and a whisk.

Preheat the oven to 375°F, place the sheet pan in the oven, and bake the rolls for 20 to 25 minutes or until golden brown. While the roles are hot, spread the frosting over the top of them before serving.

PAN DE YEMA

In the Mercado Central de Abastos in Oaxaca Centro, walking around can feel intimidating—there are so many different narrow pathways that lead to different artesanías, foods, spices, and peppers. When I stumbled into a large room full of pan de yema, I became intrigued by the history of this bread. Located in the Central Valleys region of Oaxaca, a small town named Santo Domingo Tomaltepec is thought to be the original home to the production of pan de yema, which translates to "egg yolk bread." Although in modern times this bread is produced in a more industrial way, traditionally this dough was worked and kneaded by hand in wooden containers until a strong dough was formed and then baked in adobe and brick ovens. Among the Zapotecs, the Indigenous people of Oaxacan land, there is the custom of making sure that visitors to one's home receive a loaf, usually accompanied by chocolate or coffee. Sometimes it is sliced and used to give consistency to some stews, such as mole, other times it is coated and fried to prepare capirotada.

My first bite of Oaxacan pan de yema was simply excellent—a tender, velvety interior with a nice soft crust and the beautiful complement of toasted sesame seeds. My recipe uses sourdough to leaven it and help create a delicious and complex flavor profile, and a good bit of egg yolk to ensure the bread bakes with the classic look that you might find in the streets of Oaxaca.

SOURDOUGH PREFERMENT

In a tall jar or large container with a lid, mix the bread flour, whole wheat flour, water, egg yolks, and mature sourdough starter with your hand or a fork. Ensure that no dry flour remains at the bottom of the jar.

Cover the container and let it rest at room temperature (ideally between 70° and 80°F) for 4 hours. It should double in size and have a firm, bubbly structure on the top. Once the preferment is ready to use, you can start baking straight away or place it in your fridge for later use (up to 2 days).

DOUGH

In the bowl of a stand mixer with the dough hook attachment, combine the all-purpose flour, bread flour, whole wheat flour, anise seeds, water, and preferment. Mix on low speed until a rough dough forms, about 3 minutes.

Increase the speed to medium and add half of the egg yolks and the brown sugar and mix until it all gets incorporated and the dough comes back together. Add the remaining egg yolks and half of the softened butter and increase the mixer's speed to medium-high. Let the dough mix until it incorporates and comes back together and add the remaining butter and the salt.

(CONTINUED)

SOURDOUGH PREFERMENT
50 g (⅓ c + 1 Tbsp) bread flour
50 g (scant ½ c) whole wheat flour
50 g (3½ Tbsp) warm water
2 large egg yolks
50 g (¼ c) mature sourdough starter

DOUGH
500 g (4 c) all-purpose flour
450 g (3½ c + 1½ Tbsp) bread flour
50 g (scant ½ c) whole wheat flour
8 g (4 tsp) whole anise seeds
550 g (2⅓ c) water
225 g (1 c) sourdough preferment
8 egg yolks
75 g (¼ c + 2 Tbsp packed) brown sugar
150 g (10½ Tbsp) unsalted butter, softened
20 g (2 Tbsp + ½ tsp) kosher salt
Sesame seeds, for sprinkling

Remove the dough from the mixing bowl and place in another lightly oiled bowl. Cover and let the dough ferment for 4 hours at room temperature.

After the initial fermentation, turn the dough onto a lightly floured work surface and divide into two equal pieces. Shape each one into a tube, applying tension to create a seam.

Brush the dough pieces with water and sprinkle with sesame seeds. Place them on a canvas baker's cloth dusted with wheat bran or flour, or a cutting board dusted with wheat bran or flour, seam side down, and proof at room temperature. I typically proof them in a large plastic bag or in a turned-off oven to prevent the draft in your kitchen from developing a skin over the top of the dough. Let the dough proof for 3 to 4 hours, or until bouncy and noticeably bigger in size.

Place a baking stone or steel inside the oven and preheat to 450°F. You can also use a cast-iron pot, like a combo cooker. If using a steel or stone, line a loading peel with parchment and turn the loaves onto it. (Note: If you can do 2 at a time, great. If you can only do 1 at a time, make sure you reheat the stone for 30 minutes in between bakes.)

Slash the loaves down the middle with a serrated knife or blade, load into the oven, and bake the loaves for 45 minutes, until they develop a nice dark brown crust. Cool on a wire rack before slicing.

PAN DE JAMÓN

During the holidays, Venezuelans absolutely must have pan de jamón around for the family to share. If you think you have had a satiating Christmastime bread, think again—the flavor combination, especially when homemade, is out of control. Pan de jamón consists of a decadent, buttery dough that encases fresh ham, a touch of bacon, raisins, and green olives. But what takes it to another level is the touch of melado de papelón, a thick, slightly sweet syrup made from fresh piloncillo.

With its origins in Caracas, supposedly at Gustavo Ramella's bakery around 1905, it came at a time where the baking traditions of Venezuela were still being established. Soon after Gustavo launched his pan de jamón, many other bakeries followed suit in the elaboration of this bread as the people of Venezuela quickly caught on to its deliciousness. There are different ways to achieve a beautiful decorative pattern on the top of the bread, but you can also just roll it up and maintain a simple, smooth top with no pattern. One tip to those who are bacon obsessed is to parcook your bacon before rolling it up if you prefer to have a crispier bacon sensation in each bite.

SOURDOUGH PREFERMENT

In a tall jar or large container with a lid, mix the bread flour, whole wheat flour, water, and mature sourdough starter with your hand or a fork. Ensure that no dry flour remains at the bottom of the jar.

Cover the container and let it rest at room temperature (ideally between 70° and 80°F) for 4 hours. It should double in size and have a firm, bubbly structure on the top. Once the preferment is ready to use, you can start baking straight away or place it in your fridge for later use (up to 2 days).

DOUGH

In the bowl of a stand mixer with the dough hook attachment, combine the bread flour, all-purpose flour, milk, 2 of the eggs, the panela, honey, half the butter, the vanilla, and sourdough preferment and mix for 3 to 4 minutes on medium-low speed until all of the ingredients are incorporated.

Switch the mixer to medium-high speed and add the remaining butter and the salt. Mix for 4 to 5 minutes until a smooth dough has formed. Transfer the dough to a lightly oiled bowl, cover, and let ferment at room temperature for 4 hours. After this period of fermentation, transfer the dough to the fridge for 12 hours of cold fermentation.

SOURDOUGH PREFERMENT

50 g (⅓ c + 1 Tbsp) bread flour

50 g (scant ½ c) whole wheat flour

100 g (¼ c + 3 Tbsp) warm water

50 g (¼ c) mature sourdough starter

DOUGH

250 g (2 c) bread flour

250 g (2 c) all-purpose flour

250 g (1 c + 2 tsp) whole milk

2 large eggs, plus 1 large egg for the egg wash

50 g (scant ¼ c packed) grated panela (or ¼ c granulated sugar)

20 g (1 Tbsp) honey

50 g (3½ Tbsp) unsalted butter

2 g (½ tsp) vanilla extract

300 g (1⅓ c + 1½ Tbsp) sourdough preferment

7 g (2¼ tsp) kosher salt, plus more for the egg wash

MELADO SYRUP

295 g (1¼ c) water

1 piloncillo cone, chopped into rough cubes

1 cinnamon stick

FILLING

20 g (1½ Tbsp) unsalted butter, melted

340 g (12 oz) honey ham, thinly sliced

3 slices thick-cut bacon

15 to 20 green olives, pitted

120 g (heaped ¾ c) raisins

(CONTINUED)

MELADO SYRUP

In a saucepan over medium heat, add the water, chopped piloncillo, and cinnamon stick. Stir constantly until the piloncillo breaks down completely and then simmer until the mixture has a thick, syrup-like consistency, about 10 minutes. Remove from the heat and cool.

FILLING

Take the dough out of the fridge and turn out onto a floured work surface. Pat the dough down into a rectangle, about 18 by 12 inches (basically the whole length of a half sheet pan). Brush the dough with the melted butter and then cover only the top two-thirds of the dough with the ham (so only 8 inches of the 12-inch sides of the rectangle, which should be to your left and right, are covered with ham, leaving the bottom 4 inches of dough exposed). Next, add the strips of bacon by placing one strip 2 inches from the top, one directly in the middle, and the other below, spaced out evenly on the ham, still leaving the bottom of the dough exposed.

Next, place the olives in a line right above the first strip of bacon at the top of the rectangle. This will ensure that every slice has an olive right in the center of it. Scatter the raisins over the ham and bacon and top with any extra or leftover green olives. Then drizzle liberal amounts of the melado syrup over the surface of the filling ingredients

This bread is shaped like a jelly roll. Roll the dough tightly from the top, being careful to keep the line of olives intact and applying tension to seal them up as you roll, going all the way to where the ham ends and then stop.

Using a knife, cut strips in the exposed dough that are roughly ¾ inch thick from side to side. To create a pattern on top of the roll, start on either side and pull a strip of dough diagonally over the top of the rolled surface and on to the other side. Pull a strip next to the first one and make an X over the dough, essentially going in the opposite direction. Repeat until you have several Xs over the dough.

Transfer the loaf and designed dough to a parchment-lined sheet pan. In a small bowl, combine the remaining egg and a pinch of salt, brush the rolled dough with the egg wash, and let proof at room temperature for 3 hours, until it is bouncy.

Preheat the oven to 375°F, place the sheet pan in the oven, and bake the pan de jamón for 45 to 50 minutes, making sure the rack is not too low, to prevent the bottom from burning.

Let the pan de jamón cool completely on a wire rack before slicing and serving.

PAN PAYASO

I first encountered the Mexican pan dulce called pan payaso (which hilariously translates to "clown bread") in a small market in Zimatlán de Álvarez, a town south of Oaxaca Centro. To be fair, it is found all over México, but I had not seen it until I stumbled into it stacked next to some beautiful pan de yema. I was in this small village getting to know some friends that I had met in the city who have a family bakery, and they wanted to show me around. Once I got back home, I realized that pan payaso is also available at many Latin American bakeries and bodegas in neighborhoods like Jackson Heights, New York.

The characteristics of pan payaso are fun, with a bright red or pink spiraled interior and the delicious sugary topping that is found on many types of pan dulce—a delightful treat to bring to a birthday party or gathering. It is usually baked as a long, free-formed loaf, but I opt for a loaf pan for ease of baking. My favorite version of this loaf has a bold red spiral, and food coloring is the only way to get such a concentrated, vibrant color. However, Jamaica (hibiscus) tea or beetroot powder can be substituted for a more muted pinkish color.

SWEET SOURDOUGH PREFERMENT

In a tall jar or large container with a lid, mix the bread flour, whole wheat flour, sugar, water, and mature sourdough starter with your hand or a fork. Ensure that no dry flour remains at the bottom of the jar.

Cover the container and let it rest at room temperature (ideally between 70° and 80°F) for 4 hours. It should double in size and have a firm, bubbly structure on the top. Once the preferment is ready to use, you can start baking straight away or place it in your fridge for later use (up to 2 days).

DOUGH

In the bowl of a stand mixer fitted with the dough hook attachment, combine the all-purpose flour, bread flour, eggs, sugar, sourdough preferment, and water and mix on low speed until all ingredients are incorporated into a rough dough, about 3 minutes. Switch to medium speed and start adding the butter, 50 g (3½ Tbsp) at a time.

Once all the butter is incorporated, switch to high speed and add the salt. Let the dough mix until it is smooth and elastic, about 4 minutes.

Take out the dough and cut it in half. Place half of the dough in a lightly oiled bowl and cover. Place the other half of the dough back in the stand mixer bowl, mix on medium speed, and add the food coloring slowly, letting the drops fully incorporate until the dough is completely red and homogenous, 1 to 2 minutes. You don't want to overmix this as it was already developed earlier. Remove the dough, place it in separate lightly oiled bowl, and cover.

SWEET SOURDOUGH PREFERMENT
- 50 g (⅓ c + 1 Tbsp) bread flour
- 50 g (scant ½ c) whole wheat flour
- 10 g (1 Tbsp) granulated sugar
- 100 g (¼ c + 3 Tbsp) warm water
- 50 g (¼ c) mature sourdough starter

DOUGH
- 250 g (2 c) all-purpose flour
- 250 g (2 c) bread flour
- 2 large eggs
- 130 g (⅔ c) granulated sugar
- 200 g (1 scant c) sweet sourdough preferment
- 250 g (1 c + 1 Tbsp) water
- 130 g (9½ Tbsp) unsalted butter
- 6 g (2 tsp) kosher salt
- 10 drops red food coloring

TOPPING
- 200 g (1½ c + 1½ Tbsp) all-purpose flour
- 80 g (⅔ c) powdered sugar
- 60 g (4½ Tbsp) lard or shortening
- 1 to 2 g (¼ to ½ tsp) vanilla extract

Let the dough ferment at room temperature for 4 hours and then put both bowls of dough in the fridge for 12 hours.

After the cold fermentation, remove from the fridge and let the dough come up to room temperature. On a floured work surface, divide each dough into 4 pieces and roll them out into rectangles with a rolling pin. Place one red dough halfway onto one white dough, vertically, and then fold the edges into the middle. Roll tightly into a log and place in a greased loaf pan.

In a medium bowl, add the all-purpose flour, powdered sugar, lard, and vanilla, mix well, and spread the topping over the dough. Cover and let proof at room temperature for 3 to 4 hours, or until it is just popping out of the loaf pan.

Preheat the oven to 375°F, place the pan in the oven, and bake the pan payaso for 35 to 40 minutes, until the topping becomes golden brown.

CH 5

DESSERTS AND PASTRIES

The introduction of wheat is not the only thing that sparked a baking revolution in Latin America; sugarcane also played a significant role. As much as I love to eat pan and pan dulce, there is something special about the depth of tradition in the pastries and desserts of the region.

Dutch entrepreneurs were big players in the conquering of the Brazilian northeast, the importation of enslaved people, and the establishment of sugar plantations, which ravaged fertile land in Brazil and Cuba. Since then, the Indigenous people of the land have worked very hard to adapt and make good use of the now prevalent industrialized crop.

When you think about cookies, cakes, and hand pies, what is the first thing that comes to mind? For me it's alfajores, the delicious, slightly crumbly cookies that are stuffed with dulce de leche and lined with coconut, or a tres leches cake that is slightly sweet and very moist from the three different milks that soak it. Or how about pastelitos de piña, a homemade jam wrapped in a buttery, crispy dough that my mom used to make for me every weekend? There are lots of avenues for the mind to wander when it comes to exploring the sweet treats that Latin America has to offer.

TRES LECHES TRADICIONAL

A moist, freshly prepared tres leches cake is easily one of the most popular desserts in Latin America, and is found in some form or another at many family celebrations. It is thought to have originated in Nicaragua or México, but there is also speculation that the rise of canned milk in the 1940s was responsible for the origin by printing a recipe on the label. Tres leches means "three milks," and as the name implies, one typically uses three different types of milk to soak a soft, moist, freshly baked cake: evaporated milk, sweetened condensed milk, and whole milk. When used in the right proportions, you end up with a soaked, moist cake that has the perfect flavor balance of sweet and fatty. To top it off, tres leches cakes are usually coated with a whipped frosting or cream of choice and sometimes fruit, often cherries.

Preheat the oven to 350°F, grease a 9 by 9-inch square cake pan with a light amount of vegetable oil, and set aside.

CAKE

In the bowl of a stand mixer with the whisk attachment, combine the flours, baking powder, and salt. Whisk together on low speed to form a homogenous mixture. Transfer to another bowl and set aside.

Clean the mixer bowl and switch to the paddle attachment. On medium speed beat 125 g (1 c) of the granulated sugar and the egg yolks until they are light and creamy, about 2 minutes. Add in the milks and vanilla and mix for another minute. Transfer this mix to another bowl and switch your mixer to the whisk attachment. Add the egg whites and beat until stiff peaks form, about 8 minutes.

Add half of the flour mixture to the batter and fold together until combined, about 2 minutes. Once all combined, add the rest of the flour mixture and mix until homogenous. Finally, fold the stiff egg whites into the batter until fully incorporated.

Pour the batter into the greased cake pan and bake in the preheated oven for 20 to 25 minutes. You should see the top crown slightly with no wobble, and a toothpick should come out clean if stuck in the middle.

Remove from the oven and set the cake pan on a wire rack. Let cool while you make the whipped cream and milk mixture.

TOPPING

In a large bowl, whisk the heavy whipping cream with the powdered sugar, vanilla, honey, and minced pineapple until stiff peaks form. Set aside.

Makes
ONE 9 BY 9-INCH CAKE

CAKE

160 g (1¼ c) all-purpose flour, sifted
20 g (2 Tbsp) spelt flour
10 g (2 tsp) baking powder
3 g (1 tsp) kosher salt
250 g (1¼ c) granulated sugar
6 large eggs, separated
100 g (½ c) whole milk
20 g (¼ c) coconut milk
5 g (1 tsp) vanilla extract

TOPPING

250 g (1 c) heavy whipping cream
25 g (3½ Tbsp) powdered sugar
3 g (¾ tsp) vanilla extract
3 g (½ tsp) honey
25 g (2½ Tbsp) minced pineapple
6 red cherries, sliced

TRES LECHES SOAKING LIQUID

213 g (¾ c + 2 Tbsp) evaporated milk
213 g (⅔ c + 1 tsp) sweetened condensed milk
213 g (¾ c + 2 Tbsp) whole milk
3 g (1½ tsp) ground cinnamon

TRES LECHES SOAKING LIQUID

In a small bowl, combine the evaporated milk, condensed milk, whole milk, and cinnamon and whisk together.

Use a fork to poke holes all over the surface of the cake (they're important because they'll allow the cake to absorb the milk). Pour the soaking liquid directly onto the cake while still in the cake pan, making sure to pour slowly to let the cake absorb it. Cover and let rest in the refrigerator for at least 3 hours or overnight.

Before serving, spread the whipped cream over the cake and top with the sliced cherries. Use a serving spoon to serve.

CHOCOLATE TRES LECHES DE COCO

It's not a good party without chocolate, right? It didn't take me long to stray in this direction when I began making tres leches cakes years ago, because few sweets can go wrong with the addition of chocolate. But chocolate isn't the only ingredient that I like to add when I'm experimenting with Latin American baked goods—if you haven't noticed already, I really like coconut! Adding shredded coconut to the batter really helps the inside texture come alive, and switching the whole milk to coconut milk is a great way to get immersed in that fatty flavor. For the topping, a simple meringue plus toasted coconut and cherries.

Preheat the oven to 350°F and grease a deep 9-inch cake pan with a light amount of vegetable oil. Set aside.

CAKE

In the bowl of a stand mixer with the whisk attachment, combine the flour, cocoa powder, baking powder, and salt. Whisk together on low speed. Set aside.

Switch from the whisk to the paddle attachment on medium speed and add the egg yolks with 100 g of the granulated sugar and beat until homogenous. Next, stir in the coconut milk and vanilla and mix until completely incorporated. Transfer this mix to another bowl and switch your mixer to the whisk attachment. Add the egg whites and beat until stiff peaks form, about 8 minutes. Halfway through this process, add the remaining sugar.

Add half of the flour mixture to the batter and fold together until combined, about 2 minutes. Once all combined, add the rest of the flour mixture and mix until homogenous. Finally, fold the stiff egg whites and shredded coconut flakes into the batter until fully incorporated.

Pour the batter into the greased cake pan and bake in the preheated oven for 20 to 25 minutes. The top should crown slightly with no wobble, and a toothpick should come out clean if stuck into the middle.

Remove from the oven and set the cake pan on a wire rack. Let cool while you make the meringue.

MERINGUE

Heat the sugar and water in a saucepan on the stove until it reaches a temperature of 240°F, stirring until you notice the mixture start to bubble up. In the bowl of a stand mixer with the whisk attachment, on medium-high speed, whisk the egg whites until they become frothy and form stiff peaks.

Once the sugar mixture reaches the right temperature, slowly pour it into

CAKE

175 g (1⅓ c) all-purpose flour, sifted

45 g (scant ½ c) cocoa powder

17 g (1 Tbsp + ¾ tsp) baking powder

3 g (1 tsp) kosher salt

200 g (¾ c + 1½ Tbsp) full-fat coconut milk

5 g (1 tsp) vanilla extract

6 large eggs, separated

200 g (1 c) granulated sugar

80 g (1 c) shredded coconut flakes

MERINGUE

240 g (1 c + 3½ Tbsp) granulated sugar

180 g (¾ c + 1 tsp) water

4 large egg whites

TRES LECHES SOAKING LIQUID

213 g (¾ c + 2 Tbsp) full-fat coconut milk

213 g (⅔ c + 1 tsp) sweetened condensed milk

213 g (¾ c + 2 Tbsp) evaporated milk

TOPPING

50 g (½ c) toasted coconut flakes

6 red cherries, sliced

the egg white mixture while the mixer is still on medium-high speed and mix for about 10 minutes, or until you get a creamy, firm mixture. If you stop the mixer and pull up the whisk attachment, you are looking for a stiff texture that holds its shape on the whisk. If it is runny and does not hold on to the whisk attachment, try mixing for 5 to 10 more minutes.

TRES LECHES SOAKING LIQUID

In a small bowl, combine the coconut milk, condensed milk, evaporated milk, and cinnamon and whisk together.

Use a fork to poke holes all over the surface of the cake to allow it to absorb the milk. Pour the soaking liquid directly onto the cake while still in the cake pan, making sure to pour slowly to let it absorb.

Place the meringue in a piping bag and pipe directly onto the top of the cake in your desired pattern. If you have a blow torch, torch the meringue to crystallize it and create a beautiful aesthetic. Finally, top with the toasted coconut and sliced cherries. Use a serving spoon to serve.

TORTA DE RICOTA

Makes
ONE 9-INCH CAKE

CRUST

422 g (⅓ c + ½ Tbsp) all-purpose flour

120 g (½ c + 1½ Tbsp) granulated sugar

40 g (2½ Tbsp) whole milk

226 g (2 sticks) unsalted butter, softened

1 g (¼ tsp) kosher salt, plus more for the egg wash

2 large eggs, plus 1 large egg for the egg wash

FILLING

4 large egg yolks

430 g (1¾ c + 2 Tbsp) ricotta

80 g (¼ c + 2½ Tbsp) granulated sugar

1 g (¼ tsp) vanilla extract

Zest of 1 lemon

Earlier in this book, we mentioned some delicious savory tortas, but the word torta also means cake, and it's time for you to make a delicious sweet torta known as the torta de ricota. If you like moist fillings and a buttery, crumbly crust, then the torta de ricota was made just for you. Translated as "ricotta cake," this torta seems to be a fusion of Italian and Argentine cultures, as its origins are not exactly known. However, this is one of Argentina's most popular desserts, and it has a refreshing hint of vanilla and citrus. The double shortbread crust helps the filling stand out since there are two layers of crumble to hold it together and keep it moist. There are tons of different dessert options in Argentina and a lot of them can include dulce de leche, which can be added on top of the bottom crust in a thin layer, if you so choose.

In the bowl of a stand mixer fitted with the paddle attachment, combine the all-purpose flour, sugar, milk, butter, salt, and 2 of the eggs and mix on low speed until a soft, crumbly dough forms and there is no dry flour left. Turn the dough out onto a lightly floured work surface and knead until smooth, being careful not to overwork the dough. Divide the dough in two equal portions, wrap them with plastic wrap, and refrigerate while making the filling.

Back in the stand mixer with the paddle attachment, combine the egg yolks, ricotta, sugar, vanilla, and lemon zest and mix on medium speed to evenly incorporate. Place the filling in the fridge to firm up, and take out the chilled dough.

Preheat the oven to 375°F and grease a 9-inch tart pan.

Roll each dough piece out to the size of the greased tart pan and place one of the dough layers on the bottom, molding it against the side of the pan.

Grab the filling from the fridge and spoon it all into the tart pan, evenly distributing it across the bottom dough layer. Cover with the second rolled out piece of dough. In a small bowl, whisk the remaining egg and a pinch of salt and brush the top piece of dough with the egg wash.

Place the tart pan in the oven and bake for 40 to 45 minutes. Cool on a wire rack before serving.

BIZCOCHO DE RON

In the Caribbean, there are several versions of rum cake, a dessert that has been perfected in this part of the world. It is thought that British colonists' soaked fruit pudding traditions inspired the evolution of indigenous traditions to create this cake. Food preservation proved to be difficult for the colonists, so they turned to using sugar and alcohol, thus the reason for soaking fruit with rum and infusing it into cakes.

Rum itself is thought to have originated in the West Indies on sugarcane plantations, although it is also suggested that the technique to ferment molasses on these plantations first occurred in Brazil and ultimately made its way to Barbados. Either way, rum and rum cake are Caribbean staples that are sought after all over the world.

To keep rum cake extra moist, instant pudding is added to the cake mix, which perhaps comes from the evolution of British puddings, and the cake is soaked with rum and finished with a glaze. Although most commonly eaten and gifted during the holidays, you can make and enjoy this delicious rum cake anytime.

Preheat the oven to 350°F and grease a bundt cake pan with butter. Add the crushed walnuts and coconut flakes, if desired, and set aside.

In a mixing bowl, whisk together the all-purpose flour, coconut flour, coconut cream powder, baking powder, baking soda, and salt and set aside.

In a separate mixing bowl, whisk together the sugar and butter until creamy, then add the eggs and vanilla. Whisk until incorporated. Next, add the whole milk, rum, and coconut milk while whisking until everything is evenly combined.

Fold the flour mixture into the wet mixture slowly until a thick batter forms. Pour into the bundt cake pan and bake for 55 minutes. You should see the top crown slightly with no wobble, and a toothpick should come out clean if stuck in the middle. Remove from the oven and set on a wire rack, still in the bundt cake pan.

To make the rum soak, in a small saucepan over medium heat, add the brown sugar, rum, and butter and stir until combined. Turn the heat up to high until the mixture starts to bubble and boil, about 5 minutes, and then immediately reduce to low heat. Let simmer for another 5 minutes and remove from the heat.

Using a toothpick or fork, poke holes all over the bottom of the cake, getting as deep as possible. Pour the rum soak over the surface a little at a time and let it absorb before adding more—since it is thick, it can take some time to fully absorb, so be patient. Cover with a plate and wait a few hours before inverting, slicing, and serving.

CAKE

- Handful crushed walnuts (optional)
- Handful coconut flakes (optional)
- 300 g (2⅓ c + 1 Tbsp) all-purpose flour, sifted
- 75 g (½ c + 1½ Tbsp) coconut flour
- 25 g (2 Tbsp + 2 tsp) coconut cream powder
- 6 g (1¼ tsp) baking powder
- 6 g (1 tsp) baking soda
- 3 g (1 tsp) kosher salt
- 200 g (1 c) granulated sugar
- 150 g (10½ Tbsp) unsalted butter, softened
- 3 large eggs
- 1 tsp (5 g) vanilla extract
- 200 g (¾ c + 1½ Tbsp) whole milk
- 150 g (⅔ c) white or dark rum
- 75 g (¼ c + 1 Tbsp) coconut milk

RUM SOAK

- 150 g (¾ c packed) brown sugar
- 75 g (⅓ c) white or dark rum
- 50 g (3½ Tbsp) unsalted butter, melted

MANTECADA CON MASA MADRE

Mantecadas are one of the staples of Mexican baking, and you'll most likely find them in your local panadería or mercado. You could think of them as a really delicious cousin to the muffin. They're moist, and some of them are flavored with chocolate or lemon zest. But along with the baking powder there is some yeast in the batter, which gives them a fluffy texture and greater rise than the baking powder alone. The yeast would technically make them a pan dulce, but because there is no fermentation time, and the dough mix is akin to a batter, I feel they belong with other quick, sweet treats.

OPTIONAL: To give these even more of a pop, make a simple glaze with lemon juice and powdered sugar. Dip the mantecada tops in the glaze and finish with lemon zest.

Preheat the oven to 350°F and grease the muffin pan or a 6-ounce pastry mold with a light amount of vegetable oil. Add the muffin liners and set aside.

In the bowl of a stand mixer with the whisk attachment, combine the flour, orange zest, instant yeast, sugar, baking powder, and salt. Whisk together on low speed to form a homogenous mixture.

Switch from the whisk to the paddle attachment and add the milk, eggs, vanilla, and melted butter and mix on medium speed until a thick batter forms. Finally, slowly pour in the sourdough discard until fully incorporated and the batter thins out.

Pour the batter evenly into the muffin molds and bake for 15 to 20 minutes. You should see the top crown with no wobble, and a toothpick should come out clean if stuck in the middle. Cool on a wire rack before serving.

Makes
6 MANTECADAS
IN A 6-OZ MUFFIN PAN

150 g (1 c + 3 Tbsp) all-purpose flour, sifted
Zest of ½ orange
4 g (1¼ tsp) instant yeast
100 g (½ c) granulated sugar
10 g (2¼ tsp) baking powder
3 g (1 tsp) kosher salt
100 g (⅓ c + 1½ Tbsp) whole milk
2 large eggs
4 g (¾ tsp) vanilla extract
50 g (3½ Tbsp) unsalted butter, melted
100 g (½ c) sourdough discard, or mature sourdough starter

AREPA DULCE DE MAÍZ

200 g (1⅓ c) masarepa
200 g (¾ c + 1½ Tbsp) coconut milk
200 g (¾ c + 1½ Tbsp) whole milk
150 g (¾ c packed) brown sugar
75 g (5½ Tbsp) unsalted butter
100 g (⅔ c) raisins
6 cinnamon sticks
5 g (1½ tsp) kosher salt

When most people hear the word *arepa*, the savory Venezuelan classic probably comes to mind. In the Dominican Republic, an arepa is quite different, with the only similarity being the use of the precooked corn flour masarepa (you'll learn more about this in the next chapter). Instead of cooking the precooked corn flour on a griddle and stuffing it with savory fillings or cheeses, as the word *dulce* might suggest in the name of the dish, the Dominican version makes it into a sweet cake. Traditionally, this was made in a large pot with hot coals on top as it slowly cooked on the stove with heat coming from both directions. Today, it is typically started on the stove and then transferred to a bundt cake pan and finished in the oven. This recipe is relatively simple to prepare and delicious to share with your loved ones.

Preheat the oven to 350°F.

In a large saucepan over medium heat, add the masarepa, coconut milk, whole milk, sugar, butter, raisins, cinnamon sticks, and salt and stir until combined. Increase the heat to medium-high and continue to mix, allowing the mixture to come to a boil and start to thicken.

Once the mixture becomes a thick batter, lower the heat and stir for 2 more minutes, making sure it never sticks to the bottom of the pan.

Transfer to a lightly oiled bundt cake pan and bake for 45 minutes. Allow to cool before inverting, slicing, and serving.

BIZCOCHO DE NARANJA

This citrus-infused quick bread is popular in Colombia and simple to make. Chunks of chopped orange, a little fresh squeezed juice, and a good helping of zest makes this sweet bread perfect for a morning treat with a cup of coffee. (I choose to finish this off with a simple cream cheese icing to add some texture and bite that complements the citrusy flavor. If you feel like this might be too much of an orange punch, scale back the amount you use to get it just right for your preference.)

OPTIONAL: Top with a simple glaze of powdered sugar and a splash of milk and finish with the zest of 1 orange.

200 g (1½ c + 1½ Tbsp) all-purpose flour
50 g (scant ½ c) whole wheat flour
9 g (2 tsp) baking powder
3 g (1 tsp) kosher salt
100 g (½ c) granulated sugar
25 g (2 Tbsp) vegetable oil
3 large eggs
5 g (1 tsp) vanilla extract
Juice of 1 orange
2 oranges, zested, peeled, and cubed

Preheat the oven to 350°F.

In a large mixing bowl, add the all-purpose flour, whole wheat flour, baking powder, and salt and whisk until combined.

In the bowl of a stand mixer fitted with the paddle attachment, on medium speed, cream the sugar, vegetable oil, eggs, vanilla, and orange juice until combined and smooth.

With the mixer running, add half of the flour mixture slowly and let it incorporate. Then add the remaining flour mixture and mix until just combined. Transfer the batter to another bowl and fold in the zest of 1 orange and cubed orange flesh.

Pour the batter into a greased and parchment-lined loaf pan and bake for 40 minutes. Cool on a wire rack before slicing and serving.

DULCE DE CAMOTE

Camote is a word used in Latin America to identify sweet potatoes and yams, which are used in a variety of ways. One of the most delicious preparations is creating dulce de camote, a sweet, thick puree. It can be chunky or fully mashed; I prefer it smooth and jam-like in consistency. It can be stored in the fridge for a few days. My favorite ways to use it are as the filling for Alfajores (page 218) and stuffing it into Masa Hojaldre (page 272) for a quick, flaky pastry.

500 g (2½ c) cubed sweet potato (from about 2 to 3 medium sweet potatoes)
850 g water, or just enough to cover the sweet potatoes
50 g (3½ Tbsp) unsalted butter
200 g (1 c) granulated sugar
4 cinnamon sticks

In a medium pot over medium-high heat, add the cubed sweet potatoes and enough water to cover them, and boil until tender. Strain and add to a large saucepan on medium heat with the butter and sugar. Use a masher to mash and combine the sweet potatoes until you have a creamy mixture. Add the cinnamon sticks and let the puree simmer while stirring until it is thick, about 10 minutes. Store your dulce de camote in the fridge after it cools and use to make pastelitos, alfajores, or however you like.

DULCE DE PAPAYA

Papaya is one of the staples of Caribbean and Latin American fruit culture and is perfect for a jam. This process is very simple and yields the right amount of jam for you to use immediately to make alfajores, a sweet pastelito, or to have simply on a piece of toast!

Makes
ABOUT 2 CUPS

300 g (scant 2 c) papaya, finely
   sliced or cubed
150 g (¾ c) granulated sugar
Juice of ½ lemon

///

In a medium saucepan over medium heat, combine the papaya, sugar, and lemon juice. Stir constantly until the mixture starts to bubble up, and then reduce the heat to medium-low. Make sure that the chunks of papaya break down while you are stirring.

Stir the mixture for about 15 minutes until a thick jam forms, then let it simmer on low for 5 minutes and remove from the heat.

Let cool before using. Store in the fridge for up to 1 week.

DULCE DE LECHE

Makes
ABOUT 1½ C

1500 g (6¼ c) whole milk
310 g (1½ c) granulated sugar
½ tsp baking soda
1 small cinnamon stick (optional)
10 g (2 tsp) fresh vanilla bean, scraped with seeds, or vanilla paste

One of the most common sweet fillings in South America, dulce de leche is an unforgettable and irresistible treat: similar to caramel, but creamier and richer. Although you can find it ready-made in the stores, the best flavor is homemade. All you need is a few ingredients and the patience to stir and keep an eye on the mixture throughout this whole process. One thing to note is that this recipe comes out much, much better if you use fresh vanilla bean or at least vanilla paste when compared to using extract. If all you can find is extract, that will make do. I also like to add a small cinnamon stick during the beginning of the process to add a touch of aromatic to the dulce. This filling is the star of the dulce show, and you will find so many incredible uses for it, specifically when it comes to making traditional alfajores (page 213).

Combine the milk, sugar, baking soda, and cinnamon stick, if using, in a saucepan over medium heat. Stir until well combined. Let the mixture come to a simmer while continuing to stir, about 4 minutes.

Once it is simmering, set the heat to low and let it simmer for 2½ hours, uncovered, while stirring occasionally. You want to stir if you feel like it is starting to stick to the pan, but I would say about every 15 to 20 minutes should be fine. Halfway through this process, add the vanilla and continue to stir.

Once you get near the end of the 2½ hours, the mixture will start to thicken rapidly and may require more frequent stirring. You are looking for a beautiful mahogany color and a thickness that is slightly runny. You don't want it to get too thick, as it will thicken more when it cools. Be very careful not to touch this with your bare hands. It is extremely hot.

Let the dulce de leche cool and transfer it to a jar. Once completely cooled, you can refrigerate it for a few weeks. This is going to be your best friend, and is the star of the show when it comes to making alfajores and other sweet delights.

From Al-Hasú to Alfajor

The alfajor, the dulce de leche–stuffed confection that assumes the identity of both cookie and candy, embodies a tradition of culinary craftsmanship that spans centuries—and continents. Born from the historic kitchens of the Middle East, the journey of alfajores to becoming a beloved staple in various countries in South America is rich, layered, and nuanced, just like the cookie itself. Crafting an alfajor demands a balance of precision and artistry, from the tender crumb of the cookies to the rich sweetness of the filling.

The story of the alfajor begins with its name, derived from the Arabic word *al-hasú* (which translates to "filled" or "stuffed"). In Arabic culinary practices, there is a history of sweets, such as Ma'amoul, that have been filled with dates and various nuts. When the Moorish empire expanded into Spain, these confections evolved to incorporate new ingredients like honey, almonds, hazelnuts, sesame seeds, and different spices. The Spanish rendition of the alfajor set the stage for its eventual journey across the Atlantic via the eventual colonizers of the Americas. Each bite of an alfajor is a journey through time, from the ancient markets of the Middle East to the vibrant landscapes of South America.

South American bakers evolved the alfajor into what may be considered the most popular version of the cookie. Local ingredients like dulce de leche, a caramel-like filling made from sweetened milk and a touch of vanilla, and corn flour/starch began to play starring roles in the alfajor's composition. The result was a treat that now bridged cultures and histories with its sweet, layered flavors. Alfajores de Maicena (page 214) lead the pack as the most commonly found version of the alfajor, with a high percentage of cornstarch in the dough leading to a cookie that crumbles ever so smoothly in your mouth with each bite.

In Argentina and Uruguay, where the alfajor almost feels like a national treasure, it is not merely a sweet treat but a cultural icon, enjoyed from the cosmopolitan streets of Buenos Aires to the beautiful beaches of Montevideo. It is hard to turn the corner in either of these countries without seeing bundles of perfectly baked, sometimes bite-sized, alfajores in the windows of cafés and bakeries. In Chile, you'll find Alfajores Chilenitos (page 213), which are thought to be one of the original renditions of the cookies that South America has seen. In Perú, you'll find them made with a thick chancaca syrup, which is different from the ones that are more commonly found filled with rich dulce de leche. While there are several different types found throughout South America, the love for them remains the same.

The allure of the alfajor begins with its texture. The goal is a cookie that's tender yet sturdy enough to sandwich a rich filling without cracking. These cookies will crumble when eaten, but the crumble has to be just right—a tender, soft crumble that flows into the filling while the majority of the cookie still remains intact. This balance hinges on the ratio of fat, flour, and cornstarch as well as the method of mixing. Traditional recipes often call for cornstarch (maicena) alongside regular flour, which contributes to the cookie's characteristic tender, melt-in-your-mouth qualities. The technique of creaming butter and sugar together until just combined, then gently folding in the dry ingredients, prevents the development of much gluten, ensuring the cookies remain delicate and soft.

The baking process itself requires careful attention to temperature and timing. Overbaking can lead to dry, hard cookies, while underbaking results in an alfajor too fragile to fill. Achieving the perfect bake ensures the cookies retain their moisture and tenderness, creating the ideal foundation for the filling. Once assembled, alfajores are often left to rest, allowing the flavors to meld and the moisture from the dulce de leche to slightly soften the cookies, enhancing their texture. These also keep quite well in the fridge for days—even weeks in my experience—but unless they are chocolate dipped, freezing them can result in a freezer-burned taste, so I avoid that.

ALFAJORES CHILENITOS

Makes
8 COOKIES,
OR 4 ALFAJORES

125 g (1 c) all-purpose flour
3 large egg yolks
60 g (4 Tbsp) unsalted butter,
   softened
1 g (¼ tsp) white vinegar
250 g (1 c) Dulce de Leche (page
   210), for filling
Powdered sugar, for topping
   (optional)

What makes the alfajor chilenito so special? How could you resist a heaping tablespoon of dulce de leche sandwiched between two thin, crunchy cookies that become slightly bubbly when baked? These are unleavened, which makes them quick and simple to make. The addition of a small amount of white vinegar helps give them their appealing crackly top.

Preheat the oven to 350°F.

In the bowl of a stand mixer fitted with the paddle attachment, combine the all-purpose flour, egg yolks, butter, and white vinegar and mix on low speed for 1 minute, until crumbly. Turn the mixer to medium speed and beat until the mixture becomes more homogenous. If necessary, add small splashes of water to make sure the dough is smooth.

Remove the dough from the mixer once it is smooth and wrap in plastic wrap. Place in the fridge for at least 30 minutes before rolling out.

Roll out the dough to about ⅛ inch thick (the cookies should be quite thin). Use your cookie cutter to cut out the cookie rings and place on a parchment-lined baking sheet. Use a fork to poke holes in the cookie rounds and bake for 15 minutes, until golden brown.

Let cool completely on a wire rack.

Once completely cooled, take two cookies and assemble your Alfajor Chilenito. Using a piping bag, pipe the dulce de leche onto one cookie and lightly press another cookie on top. Top with powdered sugar, if desired, and enjoy.

ALFAJORES DE MAICENA

One of the most popular alfajores in South America is the alfajor de maicena. Maicena refers to cornstarch, which gives these alfajores an interesting texture: a crumbly yet soft interior that pairs perfectly with creamy dulce de leche. You can find these at most Latin American bakeries and grocery stores in major US cities. The key to cooking an alfajor de maicena is that you can see the layers on the edge, almost like a flaky biscuit dough.

In a mixing bowl, combine the all-purpose flour, cornstarch, whole grain flour, baking powder, orange zest, and salt. Whisk together to evenly incorporate and set aside.

In the bowl of a stand mixer with the paddle attachment on medium speed, cream the butter granulated sugar, and brown sugar. Once those are incorporated, add the egg and egg yolks, one at a time, allowing each to incorporate. Finally, add the vanilla. Once all these ingredients are creamed together, slowly add the flour mixture and mix until you have a firm dough with no dry flour left in the bowl.

Remove the dough from the mixer and knead lightly. The dough should be soft but slightly crumbly. Wrap the dough with plastic wrap and place in the fridge to rest for at least 30 minutes.

Preheat the oven to 350°F.

Flour a work surface and use a rolling pin to roll out the dough to about ½-inch thickness. Use cookie cutters to cut the dough into round shapes. Place on a parchment-lined sheet pan, place the pan in the oven, and bake for 15 minutes.

Remove the cookies and let them rest on a wire rack. Once they are cool, take one cookie and pipe a heaping tablespoon of dulce de leche onto its center. Top with another cookie and roll the sides in a bowl with the shredded coconut. Serve and enjoy.

185 g (½ c) all-purpose flour
140 g (1 c) corn starch
15 g (2 Tbsp) whole grain flour
14 g (1 Tbsp) baking powder
1 tsp orange zest
5 g (1½ tsp) kosher salt
113 g (1 stick) unsalted butter, softened
80 g (¼ c + 2½ Tbsp) granulated sugar
20 g (1½ Tbsp packed) brown sugar
1 large egg plus 2 large egg yolks
5 g (1 tsp) vanilla extract
Dulce de Leche (page 210), for filling
Shredded coconut, for finishing

ALFAJORES BLANCOS Y NEGROS
with Dulce de Papaya

▲▲▲▲▲▲▲▲▲▲▲▲▲

Makes
**14 COOKIES,
OR 7 ALFAJORES**

⌣⌣⌣⌣⌣⌣⌣⌣⌣⌣⌣⌣⌣

DOUGH AND FILLING

180 g (1½ c) all-purpose flour
130 g (¾ c + 3 Tbsp) cornstarch
15 g (2 Tbsp) whole grain flour
14 g (1 Tbsp) baking powder
2–3 g (1 tsp) orange zest
110 g (1 stick) unsalted butter, softened
100 g (½ c) granulated sugar
1 large egg plus 2 large egg yolks
5 g (1 tsp) vanilla extract
Dulce de Papaya (page 209), for filling

CHOCOLATE COVERING

250 g (1¼ c) semisweet chocolate, chopped into chunks
250 g (1¼ c) white chocolate, chopped into chunks

It's not hard to see why these are popular in parts of South America, like Argentina and Uruguay, because who does not like crisp, delicious cookies dipped in chocolate?

DOUGH AND FILLING

In a mixing bowl, combine the all-purpose flour, cornstarch, whole grain flour, baking powder, and orange zest. Whisk together to evenly incorporate and set aside.

In the bowl of a stand mixer with the paddle attachment on medium speed, cream the butter and sugar. Once those are incorporated, add the egg and egg yolks one at a time, allowing each to incorporate before adding the next. Finally, add the vanilla. Once these ingredients are creamed together, slowly add the flour mixture and mix until a firm dough forms with no dry flour left in the bowl.

Remove the dough from the mixer and knead lightly. The dough should be soft but slightly crumbly. Wrap the dough with plastic wrap and place in the fridge to rest for at least 30 minutes.

Preheat the oven to 350°F.

After the dough rests, flour a work surface and use a rolling pin to roll the dough out to about ½-inch thickness. Use cookie cutters to cut the dough into round shapes. Place on a parchment-lined sheet pan and bake for 15 minutes. Remove the cookies from the oven and sheet pan and let them rest on a wire rack until cool.

CHOCOLATE COVERING

In a microwave-safe bowl, place the chocolates in 2 bowls and microwave for 5 minutes. Let the bowls sit for 10 minutes after removing from the microwave, and then whisk until smooth and glossy. Set aside. You can also use the double boil method if you do not have a microwave: place a heatproof bowl over a pot of boiled but simmering water and add the semisweet chocolate to the bowl. Whisk until it melts and then set aside. Repeat with the white chocolate.

Once the cookies are cool, dip the top side of the individual cookies in the dark or white chocolate. Place them on a wire rack to set. Once the chocolate has set, pipe a heaping tablespoon of dulce de papaya onto the center of a cookie coated with semisweet chocolate. Top with a cookie coated with white chocolate and, if you prefer, drizzle some more chocolate onto the top and let set once more. Serve and enjoy.

NATURALLY LEAVENED ALFAJORES CON DULCE DE CAMOTE

I couldn't resist including a recipe for alfajores that uses sourdough preferment instead of baking powder as a leavening agent. Any of these cookies could have been made with sourdough starter. But that funkier flavor pairs especially well with the subtle sweetness of the camote. Bumping up the whole grain flour adds to the cookie's depth of flavor. But instead of letting the dough rest for only thirty minutes in the fridge, you will have to survive three whole days without touching it before you bake them. The results are worth it.

∽

In a mixing bowl, combine the all-purpose flour, cornstarch, whole grain flour, orange zest, and salt. Whisk together to evenly incorporate and set aside.

In the bowl of a stand mixer with the paddle attachment on medium speed, cream the butter, granulated sugar, and brown sugar. Once those are incorporated, add the egg and egg yolks, one at a time, allowing each to incorporate. Finally, add the sourdough preferment and vanilla. Once these ingredients are creamed together, slowly add the flour mixture and mix until you have a firm dough with no dry flour left in the bowl.

Remove the dough from the mixer and knead lightly. The dough should be soft but slightly crumbly. Wrap the dough with plastic wrap and place in the fridge to rest for at least 3 days.

Once the dough has sufficiently fermented in the fridge, preheat the oven to 350°F. Flour a work surface and use a rolling pin to roll it out to about ½-inch thickness. Use cookie cutters to cut the dough into round shapes. Place on a parchment-lined sheet pan, put in the oven, and bake for 15 minutes.

Remove the cookies from the oven and the pan, and let them rest on a wire rack until cool.

Once they are cool, take one cookie and pipe a heaping tablespoon of dulce de camote onto its center. Top with another cookie, serve, and enjoy.

Makes
14 COOKIES, OR 7 ALFAJORES

- 170 g (1⅓ c + ½ Tbsp) all-purpose flour
- 135 g (1 c) cornstarch
- 25 g (3 Tbsp) whole grain flour
- 2 g (1 tsp) orange zest
- 113 g (1 stick) unsalted butter, softened
- 80 g (¼ c + 2½ Tbsp) granulated sugar
- 20 g (1½ Tbsp packed) brown sugar
- 1 large egg plus 2 large egg yolks
- 100 g (½ c) mature sourdough preferment
- 5 g (1 tsp) vanilla extract
- Dulce de Camote (page 208), for filling
- 5 g (1½ tsp) kosher salt

ALFAJORES DE MIEL

It was only a matter of time before anise made its appearance in one of my alfajor recipes, as it's quite common in sweet Latin American cookies and pan dulce. In this recipe I use ground anise seed, but you could keep it whole for a pop of texture that adds a little mystery to these sweet, sticky sandwich cookies. Although "miel" means honey, I'm here to tell you that no honey actually makes an appearance in this recipe. There are many variations and names given to panela (or piloncillo) when it is reduced into a syrup-like consistency. In Perú, chancaca reigns supreme.

A lot of traditional chancaca "miel" recipes use vinegar instead of cornstarch as a thickener; both work, but I get more consistent results with cornstarch. If you wish to try vinegar instead, use one teaspoon instead of the tablespoon of cornstarch and mix it in after the syrup is dissolved and simmering, just before you remove it from the heat.

DOUGH

120 g (1 c) all-purpose flour
2 large egg yolks
75 g (¼ c + 2 Tbsp) granulated
  sugar
60 g (4½ Tbsp) lard
2 g (1 tsp) ground anise seed
1 g (¼ tsp) baking powder

FILLING

150 g (¾ c + 1½ Tbsp) panela,
  chopped into rough pieces
100 g (¼ c + 3 Tbsp) water
9 g (1 Tbsp) cornstarch
2 cinnamon sticks
1 g (½ tsp) ground anise seed

DOUGH

Preheat the oven to 350°F. In the bowl of a stand mixer fitted with the paddle attachment, combine the all-purpose flour, egg yolks, sugar, lard, ground anise seed, and baking powder and mix on low speed for one minute, until crumbly. Turn the mixer to medium speed and beat until the mixture becomes more homogenous. If necessary, add small splashes of water to make sure the dough is smooth.

Remove the dough from the mixer once it is smooth and wrap in plastic wrap. Place in the fridge for at least 30 minutes before rolling out.

To make the chancaca syrup: While the dough is chilling, in a medium saucepan over medium heat, add the panela, water, and cornstarch. Use a whisk to stir together. Reduce the heat to low. Add the cinnamon sticks and anise seed and simmer. Once the panela is dissolved completely and almost boiling, about 10 minutes, remove from the heat. It should have a thick, syrupy consistency.

Remove the dough from the fridge and roll it out using a rolling pin to about a ½-inch thickness. Use a cookie cutter to cut out the cookie rings and place on a parchment-lined baking sheet. Place the sheet in the oven and bake for 15 minutes, until golden brown.

Let cool completely on a wire rack. Once completely cooled, take two cookies and assemble your Alfajores de Miel. There is no need to use a piping bag here. Using a large spoon, scoop the chancaca filling onto one cookie and place another on top.

PUDÍN DE PAN

Many cultures have their own versions of bread pudding, created as a way to eliminate the waste of old bread. "Old bread" does not necessarily mean that it has gone bad or is moldy. I'm simply referring to bread that is a day or two old and has gotten dry, which makes it the perfect vehicle to soak up the sweet milk and egg mixture and create a very moist texture once it comes out of the oven. You can feel free to use dairy-free alternatives like almond, soy, oat, or coconut milk instead of the whole milk and heavy cream.

300 g (10½ oz) day-old bread or pan dulce, cubed and shredded
400 g (1⅔ c) whole milk
5 large eggs
100 g (½ c packed) brown sugar
2 g (1 tsp) ground cinnamon
1 g (1 tsp) ground nutmeg
100 g (⅔ c) raisins
75 g (¾ c) shredded coconut, plus more for topping
50 g (⅓ c) semisweet chocolate chips
100 g (½ c) granulated sugar
50 g (3½ Tbsp) unsalted butter
40 g (3 Tbsp) heavy cream
5 g (1 tsp) vanilla extract
Dark rum al gusto

Cube up the old bread or pan dulce. I like to then take each cube and shred it as finely as possible.

In a large bowl, add the milk, eggs, brownj sugar cinnamon, and nutmeg and whisk together until it's blended well. Add the cubed bread into this mixture and incorporate until all the bread is moist. There should be more moisture than bread, which is good because the bread will begin to absorb it. If it feels too dry, make adjustments accordingly.

Add the raisins and shredded coconut into the mixture and mix again until they are evenly distributed. Cover the mixture and put in the fridge overnight (8 to 12 hours), or transfer to a baking pan and let it sit for at least 30 minutes before baking.

Once ready to bake, preheat the oven to 375°F.

Pour the mixture into a loaf pan or cake pan and top with the chocolate chips. Add more shredded coconut on top so that it develops a nice, toasty flavor. Place the pan in the oven and bake the bread pudding for about 35 minutes.

Meanwhile, in a small saucepan over low heat, combine the granulated sugar, butter, and heavy cream and whisk until the sugar is just about dissolved. Aim for a relatively thick consistency. If necessary, let it reduce for 5 minutes. Once the desired consistency has been achieved, add the vanilla and as much rum as desired and whisk together. Set aside until the pudding is done.

Let the bread pudding cool for about 15 minutes before slicing. Serve warm and pour rum sauce on top.

CHAMPURRADAS

Makes
20 COOKIES

250 g (2 c + 1½ Tbsp) all-purpose flour
64 g (heaped ½ c) masa harina
16 g (1 Tbsp + ½ tsp) baking powder
5 g (1½ tsp) kosher salt
113 g (1 stick) unsalted butter, softened
75 g (⅓ c) granulated sugar
1 large egg
2 g (½ tsp) vanilla extract
Sesame seeds, for topping

Champurradas are not your ordinary round cookies—these bad boys are made with masa harina in addition to flour, which adds a beautiful hint of sweet and savory at the same time, and they feature a crispy texture, a buttery kick, and a generous coating of sesame seeds on top. Champurradas are a traditional Guatemalan cookie that has been enjoyed for generations. The exact history of the cookie is not known, but it is believed to have originated in the early twentieth century. Today, they fly off the shelves in the local Guatemalan panaderías. So grab a cup of coffee or a hot chocolate and treat yourself to this heavenly sweet.

Preheat oven to 350°F.

In a large bowl, add the all-purpose flour, masa harina, baking powder, and salt and whisk until evenly combined. Set aside.

In the bowl of a stand mixer fitted with the paddle attachment on medium speed, cream the butter and sugar until evenly combined and then add the egg. Add in the flour mixture, half at a time, and mix until a smooth, thicker dough forms.

Place the dough on a lightly floured work surface and, using a rolling pin, roll it out until it is about 3 millimeters thick. Cut 20 cookies with a cookie cutter. Place on a parchment-lined baking sheet. Top with the sesame seeds, place in the oven, and bake for 20 minutes, or until the cookies have a nice golden color and the sesame seeds are toasted.

TORTA ROGEL

Torta Rogel is a popular traditional Argentine dessert, and its history almost feels like folklore. It started in 1928 with Rogelia Iglesias, who arrived in Buenos Aires from Spain, where she ended up taking baking courses at the request of the family she began working for. She then became known for a special pastry called the Alfajor Rogel, propelling her to the status of a renowned baker within the nearby communities, as well in the world of entertainment figures, politicians, and journalists. As time passed, a family with the name Balbaini visited the area and were enamored of the quality of the baked goods—so much so, they returned to their home town of Recoleta and attempted to create something equally delicious. The Balbainis used a recipe with Dutch heritage but replaced the filling between multiple layers of cookie with dulce de leche as opposed to fruit candy. Word got around to them that the equipment used by Rogelia Iglesias became available, but their recipe had not been properly patented. As such, the Balbainis have been selling what is now known as torta Rogel ever since. Over the years, torta Rogel became a staple at celebrations across Argentina. The recipe has been passed down from generation to generation, and many families have their own variations on the classic dessert. Here's my interpretation.

In a large bowl, combine the flour and salt. Whisk together until homogenous and set aside.

In the bowl of a stand mixer with the paddle attachment on medium speed, cream the butter and sugar, then add 3 of the egg yolks. Once incorporated, add the remaining 3 egg yolks, vanilla, and milk. Once the yolks are fully incorporated, slowly add half of the flour mixture and mix until a dry dough forms. With the mixer on low speed, add the water and milk until the dough turns into a thick batter. Add the remaining flour mixture and increase the speed to medium until the everything comes together and forms a smooth dough. Turn it out onto a work surface and knead briefly. Place on a sheet pan, cover, and let rest for 20 minutes in the fridge.

Preheat the oven to 400°F.

After the dough has rested, turn out onto a floured work surface and cut into 10 equal pieces. Roll each piece into a 10-inch circle and place on a parchment-lined sheet pan. You should be able to bake two of these on one sheet pan, so you'll need to rotate a fresh batch into the oven when the first batch is done.

Bake for 10 minutes or until the top is golden brown.

Let the baked shells cool completely on a wire rack while you make the meringue topping.

In a small saucepan over medium heat, add the sugar and water and stir until it reaches a temperature of 240°F.

In the bowl of a stand mixer with the whisk attachment, whisk the egg

DOUGH

685 g (5½ c) all-purpose flour
7 g (2¼ tsp) kosher salt
175 g (12½ Tbsp) unsalted butter, softened
75 g (¼ c + 2 Tbsp) granulated sugar
6 egg yolks
5 g (1 tsp) vanilla extract
150 g (⅔ c) water
75 g (¼ c + 1 Tbsp) whole milk

TOPPING

240 g (1 c + 3½ Tbsp) granulated sugar
180 g (¾ c + 1 tsp) water
4 large egg whites

FILLING

500 g (1½ c) Dulce de Leche (page 210)

whites on medium-high speed until they become frothy and form stiff peaks.

Pour the sugar mixture slowly into the egg white mixture and mix for about 10 minutes, or until the texture becomes creamy and firm. If you stop the mixer and pull up the whisk attachment, there should be a stiff texture that holds its shape on the whisk.

Once the shells are cooled, pipe each one around the edge and in the middle with the dulce de leche. Stack them on top of each other and pipe the meringue on top in a design of your choice.

SUSPIROS

4 large egg whites
150 g (¾ c) granulated sugar
Juice of ½ lime

Suspiros are a heavenly meringue dessert found in Costa Rica and other parts of Latin America. They are one of several baked goods born by marrying colonizers' techniques with Indigenous innovation. In Ecuador, fluffy, sweet suspiros are often served with fresh fruit or ice cream, while in Costa Rica, they're usually enjoyed on their own as a sweet treat. The original recipe consisted of whipped egg whites and sugar, but over time, variations were added. In Costa Rica, for example, some recipes include sweetened condensed milk, which gives the meringue a richer flavor and creamier texture. In Ecuador, some recipes call for cinnamon or vanilla extract to enhance the flavor. Some recipes even incorporate fruit flavors like passionfruit or guava.

In the bowl of a stand mixer with the whisk attachment, beat the egg whites on medium speed until the peaks are almost stiff. Slowly add in the granulated sugar while the mixer is running. Ensure that the sugar is thoroughly incorporated, and then add the lime juice. Continue to mix thoroughly, about 3 minutes.

Preheat the oven to 175°F.

Place heaping spoonfuls of the egg white mixture on a parchment-lined sheet pan, 3 by 4. Place in the oven and bake for 2 hours.

After the two hours have elapsed, open the oven door and turn the oven off. Allow the suspiros to cool completely while still in the oven before removing and serving.

COYOTAS

The coyota is a cookie that originated in the state of Sonora, in northern México. Its name is believed to come from the word *coyote*, as these cookies were a common food for hunters who went out to hunt coyotes in the desert. The exact year when coyotas were invented is not known as they have been a part of the culinary tradition of northern México for centuries. With the arrival of the Spanish and the introduction of refined wheat flour, the coyota evolved and each region of México began making their own adaptations. In Sonora, they are filled with piloncillo and jam, while other regions include nuts, chocolate, cheese, or coconut. You'll enjoy this version with a delicious piloncillo syrup and a perfectly crisp cookie.

200 g (¾ c + 2 Tbsp packed) grated piloncillo
100 g (¼ c + 3 Tbsp) water
455 g (3½ c + 2 Tbsp) all-purpose flour
5 g (2½ tsp) ground cinnamon
50 g (scant ½ c) whole wheat flour
200 g (¾ c + 2 Tbsp) lard or shortening
10 g (2¼ tsp) baking powder
1 large egg, for the egg wash
3 g (1 tsp) kosher salt, plus more for the egg wash
100 g (½ c) cinnamon sugar

To make the piloncillo syrup: In a small saucepan over medium heat, add half of the the piloncillo and half of the water. Stir until combined and turn the heat to low. Once the piloncillo is dissolved completely, about 10 minutes, remove from the heat and let cool.

To make the filling: In a small mixing bowl, combine the remaining piloncillo with 5 g (2 tsp) of the all-purpose flour and the cinnamon. Mix until evenly incorporated and set aside.

Preheat the oven to 375°F.

In a large mixing bowl, combine the remaining all-purpose flour, the whole wheat flour, lard, piloncillo syrup, baking powder, and salt. Use your hands to mix well, ensuring the lard is completely and evenly combined. Transfer the dough to a work surface and knead until smooth, 4 to 5 minutes.

Flour the work surface and use a rolling pin to flatten the dough until it is roughly 3 to 4 millimeters thick. With a cookie cutter, cut out an even number of cookies, as each of these is composed of two circles of dough, so you should have 24 circles to make 12 cookies.

On half of the circles, place a spoonful of filling (not too close to the edge) and on the other half, brush the edges lightly with water. Top the dough pieces with filling with the brushed ones and use a fork to crimp them closed and seal them.

In a small bowl, whisk together the egg and a pinch of salt, brush the top of the coyotas with the egg wash, and poke a few holes with a fork in the center of each coyota. Dust with the cinnamon sugar and bake for 15 minutes, until golden brown.

GALLETAS DE BODA

Makes
24 COOKIES

200 g (1½ c + ½ Tbsp) all-purpose flour
100 g (1 c) almond flour
3 g (1½ tsp) ground cinnamon
3 g (1 tsp) kosher salt
200 g (1⅔ c) powdered sugar
226 g (2 sticks) unsalted butter, room temperature
2 g (½ tsp) vanilla extract

Galletas de boda, also known as Mexican wedding cookies, have a history that dates back centuries. The exact origin of the cookies is unclear, but it is believed that they were first made in medieval Arab countries and then brought to Europe during the Crusades. From there, the cookies were introduced to México by Spanish colonizers during the sixteenth century. Galletas de boda were called "polvorones," which comes from the Spanish word *polvo*, meaning "dust." This name referred to the cookie's crumbly and powdery texture. Over time, the cookies became a popular treat for special occasions, such as weddings, hence the name "galletas de boda." You'll find this recipe to be super simple and extra delicious, so make sure you treat someone to these on their special day!

Preheat the oven to 350°F.

In a small mixing bowl, combine the all-purpose flour, almond flour, cinnamon, and salt and mix until evenly incorporated. Set aside.

In the bowl of a stand mixer fitted with the paddle attachment, combine 100 g (¾ c + 1½ Tbsp) of the powdered sugar with the butter and vanilla and mix on low speed until fluffy and creamy, about 5 minutes.

Increase the mixer to medium speed and slowly add the flour mixture until combined. Remove from the mixer and divide the dough into roughly 24 pieces. Roll each piece of dough into a ball and place on a parchment-lined sheet pan. Slightly flatten them, place in the oven, and bake for 20 minutes.

Once they finished baking, remove from the oven and let cool on a wire rack for 5 minutes. Toss them in the remaining powdered sugar and serve.

CHURROS TRADICIONALES

Churros are a crispy and delicate fried treat made from a thick, light batter containing flour, sugar, water, and eggs. After the batter is heated and cooled, it gets piped into hot oil and fried. If you don't have piping bags, just use a ziplock bag and cut off a bottom corner—but be aware that you won't get the classic star shaped aesthetic. The churros are then tossed in a cinnamon and sugar mixture after they're cooked and dipped into chocolate, so you really aren't going to go wrong when you make this quick recipe.

There are a few theories at play about the origin of churros, most notably that Portuguese explorers imitated a Chinese technique of frying batter when back on the Iberian coast. The distinct Spanish churro was born and spread like wildfire when introduced in Latin America. One thing that helped evolve this tradition was the native cacao in Latin America, used to create the very popular chocolate churro dipping sauce, although many people might prefer cajeta sauce, a delicious and sweet caramel-style dip that complements churros quite perfectly. If you've been to México, it's not a secret where you can find a good churro. It's not a matter of *if* you are going to have some, it's a matter of *how many* and *how often*.

DOUGH

In a small saucepan over medium heat, combine the water, butter, brown sugar, and vanilla and stir until it is almost boiling. Once at the boiling point, remove from the heat and add the flour and salt to the saucepan. Mix thoroughly until it turns into a cohesive dough. Let the dough cool for 15 minutes.

CHOCOLATE DIPPING SAUCE

In a microwave-safe bowl, add the dark chocolate, coconut milk, and whole milk and heat for 2 to 3 minutes. Let it sit for 10 minutes and then stir with a whisk. Set aside.

CINNAMON SUGAR

In a bowl, add the sugar and cinnamon, mix well and set aside.

CHURROS

In a large, deep pan or pot over medium heat, heat the canola oil until it reaches between 350° and 400°F. It shouldn't be too hot.

In the bowl of a stand mixer with the paddle attachment, combine the dough and the eggs and mix on medium speed until the eggs are fully incorporated and form a smooth, thick batter.

Makes
12 CHURROS

CHURRO DOUGH

150 g (⅓ c + 5 Tbsp) water
50 g (3½ Tbsp) unsalted butter
38 g (3 Tbsp packed) brown sugar
2 g (½ tsp) vanilla extract
100 g (¾ c + 1 Tbsp) all-purpose flour
4 g (1¼ tsp) kosher salt
2 large eggs

CHOCOLATE DIPPING SAUCE

200 g (1⅓ c) dark chocolate chunks
100 g (⅓ c + 1½ Tbsp) coconut milk
100 g (⅓ c + 1½ Tbsp) whole milk

CINNAMON SUGAR

100 g (½ c) granulated sugar
15 g (2½ Tbsp) ground cinnamon
Canola oil, for frying

If you have a piping bag, prepare it with a star tip and place in a tall jar with the edges folded over and add the batter. If you don't have a piping bag, put the batter in a ziplock bag and cut off a bottom corner. Don't make too big of a cut or you'll end up with uncooked blobs.

Cut a rectangle of parchment paper and pipe the churros onto the paper in thick, straight lines that are roughly 6 inches long.

Once the oil is heated, slide the parchment paper directly into the oil. Cook for about 2 minutes, remove the parchment from the oil, and fry the churros for 4 to 5 minutes, turning with tongs if needed to evenly cook them. Once done cooking, transfer them to a wire rack over a sheet pan lined with paper towels to allow the excess oil to drip off and then toss them in the cinnamon sugar mixture. Serve immediately with the chocolate dipping sauce.

CHOCOLATE CHURROS

Why reduce yourself to dipping churros in chocolate when you can actually have a chocolate churro? I first encountered these in Oaxaca Centro and I've never looked back. All the outdoor vendors served two types of churros, but the chocolate ones stood out to me. Elegant and made with local, fresh chocolate, it was hard to not eat more than one. This recipe is similar to the traditional churro, but with the addition of cocoa powder. Keep an eye on the fry time, as it is slightly harder to tell when exactly they are done since the dough is darker.

DOUGH

In a small saucepan over medium heat, combine the water, butter, brown sugar, and vanilla and stir until it is almost boiling. Once at the boiling point, remove from the heat and add the flour, cocoa powder, and salt to the pan. Mix thoroughly until it turns into a cohesive dough. It might feel a little runny, but that is okay. Let the dough cool for 15 minutes.

CINNAMON SUGAR

In a bowl, add the sugar and cinnamon, mix well, and set aside.

CHURROS

In a large pan or pot over medium heat, heat the canola oil until it reaches between 350° and 400°F. It shouldn't be too hot.

In the bowl of a stand mixer with the paddle attachment, add the dough and the eggs and mix on medium speed until the eggs are fully incorporated and form a smooth, thick batter.

If you have a piping bag, prepare it with a star tip and place into a tall jar with the edges folded over and add the batter. If you don't have a piping bag, put the batter int a ziplock bag and cut off a bottom corner. Don't make too big of a cut or you'll end up with uncooked blobs.

Cut a rectangle of parchment paper and pipe your churros onto the sheet in thick, straight lines that are roughly 6 inches long.

Once the oil is heated, slide the parchment paper directly into the oil. Cook for about 2 minutes, remove the parchment from the oil, and fry the churros for 4 to 5 minutes, turning with tongs if needed to evenly cook them. Once done cooking, transfer them to a wire rack set over a paper towel–lined sheet pan to allow the excess oil to drip off and then toss them in the cinnamon sugar mixture. Serve immediately.

CHURRO DOUGH

150 g (⅔ c) water
50 g (3½ Tbsp) unsalted butter
2 g (½ tsp) vanilla extract
38 g (3 Tbsp packed) brown sugar
100 g (¾ c + 1 Tbsp) all-purpose flour
10 g (2 Tbsp) cocoa powder
3 g (1 tsp) kosher salt
1 large egg
Canola oil, for frying

CINNAMON SUGAR

100 g (½ c) granulated sugar
15 g (2½ Tbsp) ground cinnamon

CHURROS DE MASA MADRE

I couldn't make churro variations without incorporating some mature sourdough starter, also known as sourdough discard. The fun part about these is that you don't need to add any extra flour or water since the sourdough starter already has equal parts of flour and water. These are easy to make, and have a nice, funky flavor that is complementary to the sugary coating. Make sure you are not using a sourdough preferment that is ready to make bread rise, or you might end up with something more reminiscent of a tempura batter.

MASA

In a small saucepan over medium heat, combine the butter, vanilla, sourdough starter, salt, and sugar and stir until it begins to thicken, about 5 minutes. Once at the point where it is becoming thick and forming a dough-like consistency, remove from the heat, add the flour, and mix together until combined. Let the masa rest for 15 minutes.

CINNAMON SUGAR

In a bowl, add the sugar and cinnamon, mix well, and set aside.

CHURROS

In a large pan or pot over medium heat, heat the canola oil until it reaches between 350° and 400°F. It shouldn't be too hot.

In the bowl of a stand mixer with the paddle attachment, add the dough and the egg and mix on medium speed until the egg is fully incorporated and forms a smooth, thick batter.

If you have a piping bag, prepare it with a star tip and place into a tall jar with the edges folded over and add the batter. If you don't have a piping bag, put the batter in a ziplock bag and cut off a bottom corner. You don't want to make too big of a cut or you'll end up with uncooked blobs.

Cut a rectangle of parchment paper and pipe the churros onto the sheet in thick, straight lines that are roughly 6 inches long.

Once the oil is heated, slide the parchment paper directly into the oil. Cook for about 2 minutes, remove the parchment paper from the oil, and fry the churros for 4 to 5 minutes, turning with tongs if needed to evenly cook them. Once done cooking, transfer them to a wire rack on a parchment-lined sheet pan to allow the excess oil to drip off and then toss them in the cinnamon sugar mixture. Serve immediately.

CHURRO MASA

50 g (3½ Tbsp) unsalted butter
2 g (½ tsp) vanilla extract
100 g (½ c) sourdough starter
50 g (⅓ c) all-purpose flour
38 g (3 Tbsp packed) brown sugar
3 g (1 tsp) kosher salt
Canola oil, for frying
1 large egg

CINNAMON SUGAR

100 g (½ c) granulated sugar
15 g (2½ Tbsp) ground cinnamon

PICOS

Picos, sweet Nicaraguan tarts filled with a spectacular sugar and cheese mixture, have been a staple of Nicaraguan cuisine for many years, and they have a rich history. While there are various theories regarding their origin, many believe that they were first created in the city of León, which has a long tradition of baking and pastry-making. The tart consists of a buttery pastry crust and is filled with a sweet and creamy custard made from condensed milk, eggs, and vanilla. In Nicaragua, it is common for families to bake picos at home for special, life-changing events such as baptisms or weddings, and they are often decorated with colorful frosting or fruit to make them even more festive.

In the bowl of a stand mixer with the paddle attachment on medium speed, cream the butter, sugar, yeast, milk, and eggs. Once combined, add the flour, baking powder, and salt. Once the dough comes together, turn out onto a lightly floured work surface and knead lightly until smooth. Cover and let the dough rest for 1 hour.

Preheat the oven to 400°F.

In a medium bowl, add the condensed milk, vanilla, granulated sugar, brown sugar, queso fresco, and quesillo, and mix well. Set aside.

Divide the dough into 10 equal portions. Using a rolling pin, create flattened, rounded dough circles and place a heaping tablespoon of the filling in the middle. Fold the dough into a triangle shape and top with a little extra cheese. Place the picos on a parchment-lined sheet pan.

In a small bowl, combine the egg and a pinch of salt, brush the tarts with the egg wash, place in the oven, and bake for 20 minutes, or until golden brown.

DOUGH

113 g (1 stick) unsalted butter, softened
65 g (⅓ c) granulated sugar
6 g (2 tsp) instant yeast
25 g (1 Tbsp + 2 tsp) whole milk
3 large eggs plus 1 large egg yolk for the egg wash
200 g (1½ c + 1½ Tbsp) all-purpose flour
6 g (1¼ tsp) baking powder
1 g (¼ tsp) kosher salt, plus more for the egg wash

FILLING

30 g (4 tsp) condensed milk
5 g (1 tsp) vanilla extract
150 g (¾ c) granulated sugar
50 g (¼ c packed) brown sugar
100 g (⅔ c + 1 Tbsp) crumbled queso fresco
100 g (¾ c + 1½ Tbsp) pulled quesillo

ROSQUILLAS

Makes
20 COOKIES

250 g (2¼ c) masa harina
250 g (1¾ c) crumbled queso fresco
2 large eggs
100 g (½ c) granulated sugar
100 g (⅓ c + 1½ Tbsp) mantequilla rala (crema hondureña)
10 g (1 Tbsp) kosher salt

Rosquillas are round, perfectly crunchy Honduran cookies with a distinct taste, unlike anything in the world that I have ever eaten (but that might be my nostalgia talking...). And I have to warn you: they are addictive. The crunch will cause you to eat more than a handful, and the unique flavor will have you taking bite after bite as you analyze and appreciate their complexity. They are spectacular when dunked into a cup of coffee—and dunking baked goods into coffee really warms my heart. If you want a small taste of what it was like for me growing up, rosquillas are it—so enjoy and appreciate to the fullest.

In a large bowl, add the masa harina, queso fresco, eggs, sugar, mantequilla rala, and salt and mix until lumpy. Turn out onto a work surface and knead until it comes together. The dough will feel a bit coarse and dry, so add splashes of water as needed until it comes together. Let the dough rest on the counter for 1 hour at room temperature.

Divide the dough into 20 pieces and roll each into a ball. Let the balls of dough rest for 20 minutes.

Preheat the oven to 375°F.

Roll each ball into a small log, and then shape into a circle. Place on a sheet pan lined with parchment paper and bake the rosquillas for 20 to 25 minutes or until golden. Enjoy these alone or soaked in coffee.

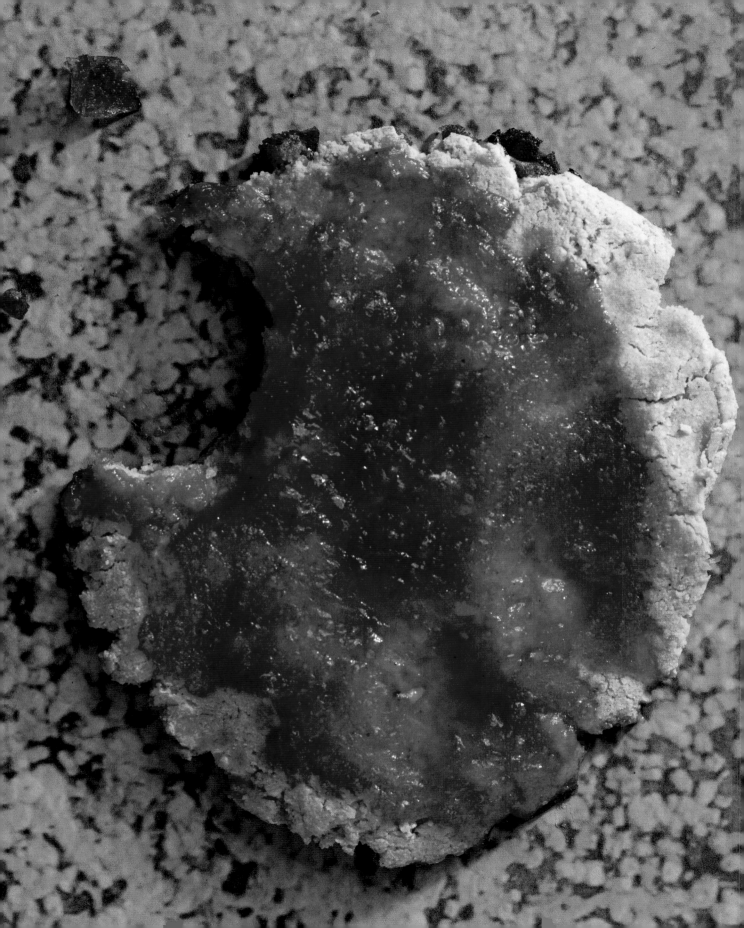

TUSTACAS

Makes
20 COOKIES

250 g (2¼ c) masa harina
240 g (1¾ c) crumbled queso
 fresco
2 large eggs
100 g (½ c) granulated sugar
100 g (⅓ c + 1½ Tbsp)
 mantequilla rala (crema
 hondureña)
10 g (1 Tbsp) kosher salt
1 pound (455 g) block of panela,
 shredded

Tustacas are one of the most delicious and iconic Honduran snacks. Like rosquillas, these crispy, golden-brown cookies are a staple of Honduran cuisine, with the main difference being the grated panela that goes into the center to add even more of a sweet kick to the final flavor. The origins of tustacas are not entirely clear, but they are believed to have come from the Indigenous communities of Honduras. The word *tustaca* comes from the Lenca language and means "little round bread." The Lencan people were one of the largest Indigenous groups in Honduras, and they used to make a similar snack called "ataole," which was made from ground cornmeal and water. The Spanish colonizers introduced wheat flour to the region in the sixteenth century, which led to the development of tustacas as we know them today.

In a large bowl, combine the masa harina, queso fresco, eggs, sugar, mantequilla rala, and salt and mix until lumpy. Turn out onto a work surface and knead until it comes together. The dough will feel a bit coarse and dry, so add splashes of water as needed until it comes together. Let the dough rest on the counter at room temperature for 1 hour.

Divide the dough into 20 pieces and roll them into balls. Let the balls of dough rest for 20 minutes.

Preheat the oven to 375°F.

Flatten each dough ball and cover liberally with the shredded panela. Place the tustacas on a parchment-lined sheet pan.

Place in the oven and bake the tustacas for 20 to 25 minutes or until golden.

Enjoy them alone or soaked in coffee.

FLAN DE COCO

200 g (1 c) granulated sugar
15 g (1 Tbsp) water
3 whole eggs plus 3 large egg yolks
One 14-oz can sweetened condensed milk
One 12-oz can evaporated milk
100 g (⅓ c + 1½ Tbsp) coconut milk
5 g (1 tsp) vanilla extract
2 g (½ tsp) kosher salt
15 g (1 Tbsp) rum

Flan is a dessert with versions and variations found in cultures around the world. The origins of flan can be traced back to ancient Rome, where the dish was known as "custardum" and made with milk, eggs, and honey. In the Middle Ages, flan evolved into a dish that was popular in Spain and other parts of Europe, where it was often flavored with cinnamon, lemon zest, and other spices. The Spanish brought flan to the Americas during colonization, and it became a staple dessert in Latin America, adapted to local tastes, techniques, and ingredients. In México, for example, flan is often made with condensed milk, while in France it is known as crème caramel and made with cream and caramelized sugar. In the Philippines, a popular version of flan is known as "leche flan" and is made with condensed milk and egg yolks.

I wanted to do something that suited my taste, which is coconut heavy, but without reinventing the texture. So, adding coconut milk was my way of making this recipe fun for me, and I hope for you!

Preheat the oven to 300°F.

In a small saucepan over medium heat, add the sugar and water and cook until it begins to brown, about 5 minutes. Stir lightly and allow the caramel to form and thicken. Once thick and deep brown, remove from the heat and coat a baking pan with the caramel. Make sure to cover the sides as well.

In a medium mixing bowl, add the eggs and egg yolks and whisk lightly in one direction. Set aside.

Prepare a large vessel (big enough to fit your baking pan) with boiling water. Set aside.

In a medium saucepan over medium-low heat, add the condensed milk, evaporated milk, coconut milk, vanilla, salt, and rum and stir until the mixture reaches 170°F, about 5 minutes.

Remove the milk mixture from the heat and temper the eggs and milk carefully. Once the mixture has been fully combined, pour into the baking pan over the caramel. Place the baking pan into the vessel with boiling water and cover with aluminum foil. Bake for 45 to 60 minutes, or until it has begun to set and the center of the custard jiggles slightly. Remove from the oven and let cool at room temperature for 20 minutes, then cover the baking pan with plastic wrap and transfer to the fridge overnight before serving.

QUESADILLA ECUATORIANA

When I landed in Quito, nestled in the Andes Mountains at 9,350 feet, I was determined not to let the elevation affect my immediate desire to walk around the city and find the most delicious pastries I possibly could. I was with my close friend Carlos Vera, and he took me straight to the spots with his favorite quesadillas. Quesadilla ecuatoriana is a sweet pastry made with flour, butter, sugar, and eggs, and is typically filled with cheese, dulce de leche, or guava paste. It's then baked until it is golden brown and crispy, and it's one of the popular desserts in Ecuador served during special occasions such as weddings, birthdays, and holidays.

Preheat the oven to 350°F.

DOUGH

In the bowl of a stand mixer fitted with the paddle attachment, combine the flour, butter, sugar, milk, salt, and 1 of the eggs, and mix on low speed until a soft, crumbly dough forms and there is no dry flour left. Turn the dough onto a lightly floured work surface and knead until smooth. Divide the dough into 6 equal pieces and round them into small balls.

FILLING

In a small mixing bowl, sift together the all-purpose flour, whole wheat flour, white rice flour, baking powder, and salt. Set aside.

In the bowl of a stand mixer with the paddle attachment, cream the sugar, milk, butter, eggs, and egg yolk. Once creamy, add the cream cheese and mix until fully incorporated and smooth. Next, add the flour mixture and mix until just combined and smooth.

Use a rolling pin to flatten each dough piece into a circle. Place a generous tablespoon of filling onto the dough, using the back of the spoon to spread it out, just shy of the edges.

To shape the quesadilla, fold the sides of the dough inward about ½ inch, forming a hexagonal shape.

Place on a parchment-lined baking sheet. Make an egg wash by combining the egg yolk and a pinch of salt, then brush the sides of the dough and bake for 30 minutes, until the filling is very slightly browned but the sides have a nice golden crust. Cool on a wire rack before serving.

DOUGH

- 211 g (1⅔ c) all-purpose flour
- 113 g (1 stick) unsalted butter, softened
- 60 g (¼ c + 1 Tbsp) granulated sugar
- 20 g (1 Tbsp + 1 tsp) whole milk
- 1 g (¼ tsp) kosher salt, plus more for the egg wash
- 1 large egg, plus 1 large egg for the egg wash

FILLING

- 85 g (⅔ c) all-purpose flour
- 15 g (2 Tbsp) whole wheat flour
- 20 g (2½ Tbsp) white rice flour
- 8 g (1¾ tsp) baking powder
- 3 g (1 tsp) kosher salt
- 75 g (¼ c + 2 Tbsp) granulated sugar
- 75 g (¼ c + 1 Tbsp) whole milk
- 40 g (3 Tbsp) unsalted butter, room temperature
- 2 large eggs, plus 1 large egg yolk
- 135 g (9½ Tbsp) cream cheese

BRAZILIAN BOMBOCADO

The bombocado is believed to have originated in Brazil during the colonial period, which began in 1500 when the Portuguese first arrived in Brazil. During this time, the Portuguese introduced many of their traditional foods and recipes to Brazil, including the pastel de nata, a Portuguese egg custard tart that is still popular in Portugal today. The Indigenous cooks began to adapt the recipe for the pastel de nata to include local ingredients such as coconut milk and cornmeal, which eventually led to the creation of the bombocado.

Preheat the oven to 350°F.

In a small mixing bowl, combine the eggs, egg yolks, condensed milk, coconut, Parmesan, butter, flour, baking powder, and salt and mix with a wooden spoon until evenly incorporated.

Heavily grease or line 6-ounce baking molds and add the mixture to the molds until about three-quarters filled. Bake for 12 minutes, or until lightly browned on the top.

Let cool for 15 minutes and then flip over to make removing easier before serving.

2 large eggs, plus 2 large egg yolks

One 14-oz can sweetened condensed milk

150 g (1¾ c + 2 Tbsp) grated coconut

75 g (1⅓ c) finely grated Parmesan cheese

25 g (2 Tbsp) unsalted butter, softened

15 g (2 Tbsp) all-purpose flour

5 g (1 tsp) baking powder

3 g (1 tsp) kosher salt

335 g (heaped 1 c) sweetened
    condensed milk
100 g (7 Tbsp) unsalted butter
25 g (¼ c + 1 Tbsp) cocoa
    powder
300 g chocolate sprinkles

BRIGADEIROS

There is a lot more than meets the eye when it comes to these rich, sweet chocolate fudge bombs. It is thought that these sweet confections were first created during the presidential campaign of a Brazilian brigadier general named Eduardo Gomes, which was the first time that women were able to cast a vote in an election. The popularity of the brigadeiro skyrocketed, and they are found all over the country—and even in other parts of the world due to Brazilian migration. There are not too many ingredients needed to make a delicious brigadeiro, and their simplicity is what makes them desirable for gatherings of all kinds.

In a medium saucepan over medium heat, add the sweetened condensed milk, butter, and cocoa powder, stir to combine, and continue stirring for 7 to 8 minutes until the mixture becomes thick and concentrated in the middle of the pan.

Once a thick, fudge-like consistency has been reached and the mixture is not touching the sides of the pan, transfer to a plate and let it rest for 10 minutes. Next, cover with plastic wrap (it's okay if it is still hot, the plastic wrap will not affect it) and place in the fridge for 45 minutes.

In a small bowl add the chocolate sprinkles.

After the resting period, remove the plastic wrap and scoop some of the mixture into your hands to form into the size of a golf ball. Aim to make about 14 balls from this mixture. Roll each ball in the sprinkles so that the whole brigadeiro is covered and enjoy immediately or freeze for up to 2 weeks for later!

CURAU DE MILHO

The origins of curau de milho can be traced back to the northeastern region of Brazil, which has a long history of corn cultivation. The dish was likely first created by Indigenous communities in this region, who would grind corn kernels into a paste and cook it over a fire to make a simple porridge. After the Portuguese arrived in Brazil in the sixteenth century, they brought with them new culinary techniques and ingredients such as sugar and cinnamon, which were then incorporated into the traditional corn pudding to create the recipe we know today as curau de milho.

Use a knife to cut the kernels off the ears of corn and place them all in a blender with the coconut milk. Blend until smooth.

Use a strainer or cheesecloth to strain out the liquid and separate the chunks of corn flesh, keeping the liquid in a bowl.

In a large saucepan, combine the liquid with the condensed milk, butter, and salt. Cook over medium heat, stirring constantly, for 30 minutes, being careful not to let it boil over.

Once the mixture thickens, remove it from the heat and serve in a small bowl or cup, dusted with cinnamon.

4 ears of corn
500 g (2 c + 1½ Tbsp) coconut milk
205 g (⅔ c) sweetened condensed milk
75 g (5½ Tbsp) unsalted butter
3 g (1 tsp) kosher salt
Ground cinnamon, for dusting

CUCAS

Cucas are an extremely distinct round and crunchy cookie–like dessert that has origins in the Valle del Cauca in Colombia. Within Colombia, whether cucas are actually considered cookies or not, is debated—but what's not debatable is just how delicious they are. Made with panela, cinnamon, and cloves, cucas are an excellent choice when it comes to baking a simple and sweet crowd pleaser.

Preheat the oven to 375°F.

To make the dough syrup: In a small saucepan over medium heat, add the panela, ground cloves, and water. Stir until combined and reduce the heat to low. Once it is dissolved completely, about 7 minutes, remove from heat and let cool.

To make the dough: In a large mixing bowl, combine the all-purpose flour, butter, the dough syrup, baking powder, baking soda, salt, cinnamon, and ginger. Use your hands to mix well, ensuring the butter is completely and evenly combined. Transfer the dough to a work surface and knead until smooth, 2 to 3 minutes.

Next, flour the work surface and use a rolling pin to flatten the dough until it is roughly 3 to 4 millimeters thick. With a cookie cutter, cut out an even number of cookies and place them on a parchment-lined sheet pan.

Bake in the oven for 20 minutes or until golden brown.

200 g (¾ c + 2 Tbsp packed) grated panela
8 cloves, ground
100 g (¼ c + 3 Tbsp) water
315 g (2½ c) all-purpose flour
200 g (14 Tbsp) unsalted butter, room temperature
10 g (2 tsp) baking powder
5 g (1 tsp) baking soda
3 g (1 tsp) kosher salt
5 g (2½ tsp) ground cinnamon
5 g (2½ tsp) ground ginger

CHOCOTORTA

Chocotorta is a popular Argentine dessert that consists of layers of chocolate cookies and a dulce de leche–infused cream filling. The cookies, though, are the star of the show. The ones traditionally used in Argentina are a brand called Chocolinas—but don't worry, we will make some cookies similar to those in this recipe. It's a delicious cake that has become a staple of the Argentine dessert world; one of the reasons for its popularity is its simplicity. The preparation is straightforward and so easy to modify that many families have their own variation of the recipe, with some using different types of cookies or additional ingredients.

COOKIE

In a large bowl, sift the flour, cocoa powder, baking powder, and salt into a bowl. Whisk together and set aside.

In the bowl of a stand mixer fitted with the paddle attachment on medium speed, cream the butter, granulated sugar, and brown sugar. Once combined, add the eggs one at a time and finish with the vanilla.

Remove the mixing bowl with the wet mixture from the mixer and add half of the dry ingredients to this bowl. Mix and fold in with a spatula. Once combined, add the rest of the dry mixture and fold again until completely combined.

Divide into 2 pieces, wrap with plastic wrap, and refrigerate for 2 hours. Once chilled, preheat the oven to 350°F.

Roll the dough out with a rolling pin and cut into about four or five 8 by 4-inch rectangles. Place each rectangle on a parchment-lined baking sheet and bake for 10 to 12 minutes. Let the cookies cool completely and set aside.

CREMA FILLING

In the bowl of a stand mixer with the paddle attachment, add the cream cheese and powdered sugar and beat together on medium speed. Once smooth, remove the bowl from the mixer and fold in the dulce de leche with a spatula until combined. Set aside.

CHOCOTORTA

Line an 8 by 4-inch loaf pan with plastic wrap.

Pour the brewed coffee and milk onto a sheet pan and dunk each cookie in this mixture—you don't want to soak it so heavily the cookie falls apart. If you have a bowl large enough to fit the cookie, that works too, but I usually just use a sheet pan.

Add a soaked cookie to the loaf pan as the base layer. Each cookie should be roughly the size of the loaf pan, but make adjustments as needed for them to fit.

CHOCOLATE COOKIE

325 g (2½ + 1½ Tbsp) all-purpose flour
115 g (1⅓ c) cocoa powder
8 g (1¾ tsp) baking powder
2 g (½ tsp) kosher salt
200 g (14 Tbsp) unsalted butter
150 g (¾ c) granulated sugar
150 g (¾ c packed) brown sugar
2 large eggs
5 g (1 tsp) vanilla extract

CREMA FILLING

340 g (1½ bricks) cream cheese
100 g (¾ c + 1½ Tbsp) powdered sugar
250 g (⅔ c + 2 Tbsp) dulce de leche

COOKIE SOAK

175 g (¾ c) brewed coffee, cooled
175 g (⅔ c + 1 Tbsp) whole milk

CHOCOLATE FROSTING

113 g (¾ c) chopped chocolate
75 g (⅓ c) heavy cream

Next, use an offset spatula or the back of a spoon to spread a few tablespoons of the crema filling evenly over the cookie. Top with another soaked cookie, spread more crema filling, and repeat 4 more times. Make sure to save leftover crema filling to pipe onto the top during the final assembly.

Once the top cookie has been placed, wrap the loaf pan completely with plastic and place the chocotorta in the fridge for 24 hours (you can also freeze this for longer-term storage, up to two weeks to avoid a freezer burned taste).

CHOCOLATE FROSTING

In a microwave-safe bowl, add the chopped chocolate and heavy cream and microwave for 3 to 4 minutes. Let sit at room temperature for 10 minutes and then whisk together until thick and creamy.

Take the chocotorta out of the fridge and invert onto a plate (this means the first layer you put in the loaf pan will actually be the top layer).

Remove the plastic wrap and spread the chocolate frosting on the top (and the sides, if desired). Pipe the remaining crema filling in dollops over the frosting, if desired. Cut and serve.

PASTAFROLA

Pastafrola is a traditional Argentine dessert that consists of a shortbread crust filled with quince paste, dulce de leche, or sweet potato jam. The top of the pie is often decorated with a lattice pattern and makes for a delicious, simple bake if you are craving something like a pie or a tart. The origins of pastafrola can be traced back to the Middle Ages, when it was known as "pastel de frutas" (fruit pie) in Spain. The recipe was brought to Argentina by Spanish immigrants in the late nineteenth and early twentieth centuries and quickly became a popular dessert in the country.

Preheat the oven to 350°F.

CRUST

In the bowl of a stand mixer fitted with the paddle attachment, combine the flour, butter, sugar, milk, salt, and 2 of the eggs and mix on low speed until a soft, crumbly dough forms and there is no dry flour left in the bowl.

Turn the dough out onto a lightly floured work surface and knead until smooth, being careful not to overwork the dough. Divide the dough into two equal portions, wrap the dough with plastic wrap, and refrigerate while making the filling.

FILLING

In a saucepan over medium heat, add the cubed quince paste, orange juice, and lemon zest and stir until a thick paste forms, about 6 minutes. Set aside to cool completely.

PASTAFROLA

Roll out one piece of the dough into a circle with a rolling pin on a lightly floured work surface. Press into a 9-inch tart pan and add the filling on top. Roll out the other half of the dough and cut into 1-inch strips.

Create a lattice pattern by taking half of the strips and laying them out vertically parallel to one another, spaced evenly across the filling. Then weave each of the remaining strips horizontally through the vertical strips, spacing each of them equally as you go.

In a small bowl, whisk the remaining egg and a pinch of salt to make an egg wash. Brush the lattice with the egg wash, place the pan in the oven, and bake for 45 minutes. You should see the quince filling bubbling up and thickened, as well as a nice golden brown on the crust toward the end of the bake.

Let the pastafrola cool for an hour before serving.

CRUST

420 g (⅓ c + ½ Tbsp) all-purpose flour

226 g (2 sticks) unsalted butter, softened

120 g (½ c + ½ Tbsp) granulated sugar

40 g (2½ Tbsp) whole milk

2 g (½ tsp) kosher salt, plus more for the egg wash

2 large eggs, plus 1 large egg for the egg wash

FILLING

500 g (17½ oz) quince paste, cubed

25 g (1 Tbsp + 2 tsp) orange juice

Zest of ½ lemon

VOLCÁN DE DULCE DE LECHE

Makes
4 LAVA CAKES

Unsalted butter, for greasing
500 g (1½ c) Dulce de Leche (page 210)
3 large eggs plus 2 large egg yolks
40 g (2½ Tbsp) whole milk
70 g (heaped ½ c) all-purpose flour
5 g (1 Tbsp) cocoa powder
Powdered sugar, for dusting

I'm sure you've heard of a lava cake and most probably have enjoyed one at some point in your life. But in Latin America, the molten lava that flows is none other than the ruler of the land: dulce de leche. It's unbelievable how versatile this ingredient is and how prevalent it is in several unique dishes. This dessert is quite simple to make, with only a few ingredients and a very short bake time, which helps the middle stay gooey. Make sure you check out the recipe for homemade Dulce de Leche (page 210), but if you don't have time to make it, your local grocery store should have it in stock. For this recipe, you will need 3- to 4-inch muffin molds or ramekins.

Preheat the oven to 400°F and grease 4 cups of a muffin mold with butter.

In a mixing bowl, add the dulce de leche, eggs, and egg yolks and whisk together until combined and creamy. Next, whisk in the milk until the consistency becomes creamy again. Finally, add the flour and cocoa powder and whisk vigorously to avoid any clumps.

Pour the batter into the greased muffin mold and bake for 6 minutes. You are looking for the center to wobble considerably. Be aware that it will set slightly when you remove them from the oven while they cool, so don't overcook them if you want to get that gooey center when you cut into it.

Remove from oven, let cool until you are able to remove from the mold. Top with powdered sugar and serve immediately.

QUESADILLA HONDUREÑA/ SALVADOREÑA

Makes
1 QUESADILLA

200 g (1 c) granulated sugar
200 g (1½ c + 1½ Tbsp) all-purpose flour
100 g (¾ c) sesame seeds
113 g (1 stick) unsalted butter, room temperature
3 large eggs, room temperature
225 g (¾ c + 3 Tbsp) crema hondureña
75 g (½ c + 2 Tbsp) grated queso hondureño
25 g (3 Tbsp) whole wheat flour
15 g (1 Tbsp) baking powder
5 g (1½ tsp) kosher salt

One of the first baked goods I ever tasted was my mom's quesadilla. When most people hear the word quesadilla, they immediately think about the savory Mexican dish that is widely consumed in North America. In Central America, however, quesadilla is sweet and salty cake—one of the marquee desserts of the region.

My mom baked this for us on special occasions. There is some debate over whether this version is Honduran or Salvadorean, but no matter the origin, the salty and sweet combination is one of the most delightful desserts. The batter is made with salty cheese and Honduran crema, yielding a moist interior and slightly crispy exterior topped with sesame seeds. I'm hoping to do my mom proud with this one!

Like so many simple cakes, you can easily embellish this by giving it a different topping than sesame seeds, ranging from powdered sugar to jam to dulce de leche and beyond.

Preheat the oven to 350°F and spray a 9-inch cake pan with nonstick cooking spray.

In a small bowl, add 10 g (1 Tbsp) of the granulated sugar, 5 g (2 tsp) of the all-purpose flour, and the sesame seeds and mix well. Powder the bottom and sides of the cake pan with a tablespoon of the sesame mixture and reserve the rest.

In the bowl of a stand mixer fitted with the paddle attachment on medium speed, beat together the remaining granulated sugar and the butter until creamy, about 2 minutes. Add the eggs one at a time, mixing well after each addition.

In a small bowl, mix the queso and crema together and set aside briefly.

In another bowl, whisk together the remaining all-purpose flour, whole wheat flour, baking powder, and salt.

Add the flour mixture alternately with the queso mixture to the batter in the stand mixer, beginning and ending with the flour. Mix well until the batter is smooth.

Pour the batter into the prepared pan and top liberally with the remaining sesame seed mixture.

Place in the oven and bake until the quesadilla is golden brown and mostly set but still jiggles in the middle, about 45 minutes. Remove from the oven. Let cool slightly on a wire rack before serving.

COCADAS

Cocadas are a popular sweet treat in Bolivia and many other Latin American countries. They are extremely easy to make by mixing grated coconut with sugar and egg whites, then baking or cooking the mixture until it becomes firm. The origin of cocadas is believed to be from the coastal regions of Latin America, where coconut trees are abundant. The exact history in Bolivia is not well documented, but it is known that they have been a part of Bolivian cuisine for many years. In Bolivia, cocadas are associated with the city of Cochabamba, where they are a popular snack food.

150 g (1¾ c + 2 Tbsp) grated unsweetened coconut
50 g (heaped ⅓ c) slivered almonds
2 large eggs
100 g (⅓ c) sweetened condensed milk

Preheat the oven to 400°F.

In a medium bowl, combine the coconut, almonds, eggs, and condensed milk and mix until evenly combined. Scoop heaping teaspoons onto a parchment-lined sheet pan.

Bake for 15 to 20 minutes or until the cocadas have a golden-brown bottom and they are not wobbly but firm.

SEMITA DE PIÑA

In El Salvador, the word semita signifies something quite different than the Honduran counterpart (page 152). This dough is a hybrid shortbread-style dough but with a pinch of yeast and whole grain flour to give it a soft, airy texture. This particular style has the dough covering a whole sheet pan and is filled with pineapple jam, then topped again with more dough to create the perfect sandwich of a bite.

In a mixing bowl, combine the all-purpose flour, whole grain flour, baking powder, instant yeast, and salt until evenly incorporated. Set aside.

In the bowl of a stand mixer with the paddle attachment at medium speed, cream the butter, sugar, 2 of the eggs, and the vanilla.

Switch to the dough hook attachment and slowly add the flour mixture and mix until a smooth dough forms, 3 to 4 minutes.

Let the dough rest, covered, on the countertop for 30 minutes.

To make the jam filling, add the pineapple cubes to a saucepan with the brown sugar and lemon juice.

Allow the mixture to bubble up while you stir it, 5 to 10 minutes. Once you have a nice bubbling caramelization, reduce the heat to a simmer. After 5 minutes, transfer the jam to a bowl and let cool completely.

Preheat the oven to 350°F and line a sheet pan with parchment paper.

Portion out 200 g of dough from the whole dough (a bit less than ¼ of the dough) and set aside. Divide the larger portion of the dough into two equal portions. Thinly roll each dough portion out to the size of the sheet pan and place onto the prepared pan. Spread the pineapple jam onto the dough and top with the second piece of dough.

Divide the smaller portion of dough into thin strips and stretch them as long as possible. Layer them into a lattice pattern, diagonally, over the top layer of dough. Let the semita rest for 30 minutes.

In a small bowl, whisk the remaining egg and a pinch of salt to make an egg wash. Brush the latticed top layer of the dough with the egg wash, sprinkle with granulated sugar, and bake for 35 minutes until golden brown.

Ingredients

300 g (2⅓ c + 1 Tbsp) all-purpose flour
300 g (2½ c) whole grain flour
10 g (2¼ tsp) baking powder
4 g (1¼ tsp) instant yeast
3 g (1 tsp) kosher salt, plus more for the egg wash
113 g (1 stick) unsalted butter
100 g (½ c) granulated sugar, plus more for sprinkling
2 large eggs, plus 1 large egg for the egg wash
5 g (1 tsp) vanilla extract
200 g (⅔ c + 3 Tbsp) cold water
1 fresh pineapple, cubed
150 g (½ c packed) brown sugar
Juice of ½ lemon

PICARONES

Picarones are an iconic Peruvian delight, and one of the most unique batters that I have ever made. Softened sweet potato and squash are pureed into a creamy consistency, with yeast, anise, and flour added before being deep fried to perfection and topped with a classic chancaca syrup. This is an interesting dough to work with, as the traditional way to make it is to grab some dough directly from the fermented bulk and quickly form a round shape with a hole in the center. I find the key is to have slightly wet hands and to work with confidence and speed. The addition of sourdough discard is a great way to use up extra starter for an extra funky flavor and a nice pop in the fryer.

DOUGH

200 g (1 c) roasted or boiled
   squash
200 g (1 c) roasted or boiled
   sweet potato
250 g (2 c) all-purpose flour
100 g (½ c) sourdough discard
10 g (1 Tbsp) instant yeast
8 g (1 Tbsp + 1 tsp) anise seed
Canola oil, for frying

CHANCACA SYRUP

250 g (1 c + 1 Tbsp) water
200 g (¾ c + 2 Tbsp packed)
   grated panela
Zest of 1 orange

In a large mixing bowl, combine the cooked squash and sweet potato and use a spoon to mix well. Add the flour, sourdough discard, instant yeast, and anise seed and mix until the ingredients are completely combined. The dough should be relatively soft but not too creamy. If it feels too loose, add more flour. Cover and let ferment at room temperature for 1 hour.

While the dough is resting, make the chancaca syrup. In a medium saucepan over medium heat, combine the water, panela, and orange zest and boil until the panela dissolves and becomes thick, about 8 minutes. Stir the syrup until it has a molasses-like consistency, about 30 minutes. Remove from the heat and let cool.

Heat a pot of canola oil to 375°F.

With wet hands, grab a chunk of the dough, lightly shape it into a ball, quickly poke a hole into it, and drop it into the pot. Fry for 3 to 4 minutes, flipping every 30 seconds or so to color both sides, and remove from pot,.Place on a paper towel–lined plate. Repeat with the remaining dough.

When the picarones are done, drench them with the syrup and serve.

MASA HOJALDRE

△△△△△△△△△△△△

Makes
ENOUGH DOUGH
FOR 6 PASTELITOS

▽▽▽▽▽▽▽▽▽▽▽▽

What would a pastry chapter be without a recipe for a dough that puffs up to create crisp, golden layers that can be stuffed with a number of sweet or savory fillings?

Masa hojaldre is what puff pastry is called throughout Latinoamerica. Originally, it was only popular among the wealthy and in high-end bakeries, as butter was expensive. But a culture of pastelerías grew to keep up with the demands of the rich to make these decadent desserts. Over time, puff pastry became more widely available and affordable, and it spread beyond the upper classes to become a staple in Mexican bakeries and households. Today, it is commonly used in a variety of sweet and savory dishes, like pastelitos and orejas. This dough is not leavened, but is thinly laminated several times in order to create the distinct layers.

This recipe calls for four different types of flour: all-purpose, bread flour, cake flour, and a bit of whole grain flour. You can certainly use only all-purpose flour, if that's what you've got, but I think this mix of flours brings the right tenderness, flavor, and strength to make pastries.

You'll also want to make sure to use good butter—look for brands that have a high butterfat content.

People think of puff pastry as something limited to the professional kitchen. There is a lot of lore about how your hands need to be cold, you have to work the dough on marble, and so on. Sure, those things will help. But you can also just give it a shot with what you've got at home. Why hold yourself back from something this delicious? Masa hojaldre is buttery and flaky, and while you could spend years trying to achieve mastery over this art, it's also pretty hard to mess up.

The margin for error before baking is minimal—this is not a yeasted dough, so you don't have to worry about the dough being under- or over-proofed. Even if you can't get the dough super thin on each lamination turn, you're still going to end up with a delicious pastry.

When I go through the labor of laminating dough, I want to keep some extra in the fridge. That's why I usually double this recipe: that way, I can use half and save the other half tightly wrapped in plastic in the freezer for a month or so, and pull it out the next time I'm looking to make a delicious pastelito.

DOUGH

125 g (1 c) all-purpose flour
100 g (¾ c plus 1 Tbsp) bread flour
50 g (scant ½ c) cake flour
25 g (3 Tbsp) whole grain flour
62 g (4 Tbsp) unsalted butter, cold
3 g (1 tsp) kosher salt
120 g (½ c) ice-cold water, plus a few more Tbsp as needed

BUTTER BLOCK

227 g (2 sticks) unsalted butter, room temperature
31 g (¼ c) bread flour

DOUGH

In the bowl of a stand mixer with the dough hook attachment on low-medium speed, combine the all-purpose flour, bread flour, cake flour, whole grain flour, butter, salt, and 75 g (¼ c + 1 Tbsp) of the cold water and mix until the dough comes together, about 4 minutes. Switch the mixer to medium-high speed and slowly drizzle in the remaining water. If the dough is still feeling dry, drizzle in additional tablespoons as needed until the dough smooths out completely and feels slightly elastic. Mix until you have a nice, smooth dough, about 3 minutes. Wrap the dough in plastic wrap and let chill in the fridge for at least 30 minutes.

BUTTER BLOCK

In a medium bowl, add the room-temperature butter and bread flour and mix until combined. Spread into a rectangle about the size of a normal piece of paper and about ½ inch thick onto a piece of parchment paper. Take care to square off the edges as best you can, then cover the butter block and refrigerate until it is firm but pliable (65° to 70°F). It should be able to gently bend without breaking.

LAMINATION

On a lightly floured surface, roll out the dough to twice the width of the butter block. Be sure to keep the edges straight and squared off (you can use a bench scraper to help with this). Remove the butter block from the parchment and place on one side of the dough. Fold the dough over the butter, pressing firmly to seal the edges all the way around by using your thumbs and pressing down along the edges of the book of dough and butter.

Flour your work surface and use a rolling pin to roll out the dough into a long rectangle that is about 24 to 30 inches long and ½ inch thick. Position the dough so that one of the shorter sides of the rectangle is facing you, if it isn't already. Fold the dough into thirds by folding the top portion of the dough about three-quarters of the way over the dough and folding the bottom portion over the other part of the dough. Wrap and refrigerate for 30 minutes so that it can cool down and firm up.

Repeat the folds and rest period 3 more times for a total of 4 folds. After the final fold, the dough should be tightly wrapped in plastic wrap and refrigerated for at least 12 hours (and up to 2 days) before using. For longer storage, it can be frozen for up to 3 months (just thaw overnight in the refrigerator before using).

PASTELITOS DE GUAYABA Y QUESO

GUAVA JAM

200 g (7 oz) guava, peeled and quartered (about 4 guavas)
100 g (1 c) granulated sugar
Juice of ½ lemon
1 g (1 tsp) lime zest, optional

PASTELITOS

1 recipe Masa Hojaldre (page 272), chilled
180 g (9 Tbsp) guava jam (see above or store-bought)
90 g (6½ Tbsp) cream cheese
1 large egg, for the egg wash
Pinch salt, for the egg wash

I love the crisp, creamy crunch of a Cuban-style pastelito. Cuban pastelitos are distinct from other forms of pastelitos or empanadas in Latin America—flaky, airy, and light puff pastry dough is the key to getting it right. There are a few different ideas about the exact origin of the tradition of making these incredibly delicious pastelitos. Was it a group of enslaved Cubans in the sugar mills? Perhaps a Lebanese immigrant trying to replicate baklava? No matter the origin, I am thankful that they exist, as I genuinely consider Cuban pastelitos to be some of the best baked goods on the planet. Pastelito culture on the streets of Miami, for example, is akin to pizza culture in New York City—you can get them anywhere, everyone talks about them, and you can find several versions of them on any corner.

You can find good quality guava pastes and jams at the grocery store, but not all are great (I avoid guava jams that are deep, dark red in color and opt for the ones with a pinker hue). If you are in an area where you can find fresh, ripe, pink guava, then go ahead and make the jam yourself. But truthfully, when I'm making these pastelitos, I often reach for the stuff I buy at the local shop.

GUAVA JAM (IF NOT USING STORE-BOUGHT)

In a saucepan over medium heat, combine the guava with equal parts water and bring to a boil. Cook for 20 minutes or until the guava is completely tender and able to be mashed. Pass the mixture through a sieve, using a spoon to press the flesh through, and remove the seeds.

Return the guava mixture to the saucepan and add the sugar, lemon juice, and lime zest, if using. Stir constantly over medium heat until the mixture starts to bubble up, and then reduce the heat to medium-low and cook, stirring constantly, for about 15 minutes until a thick jam forms. Let it simmer on low heat for 5 more minutes. Remove from the heat, let cool, and store in the refrigerator.

PASTELITOS

Preheat the oven to 400°F.

Roll out the chilled masa hojaldre so it's 2 to 3 millimeters thick, about 10 inches by 15 inches. If you roll too thin, you won't get flaky layers; if you go too thick, it might underbake and come out gummy. Cut the dough into 5 by 5-inch squares totaling around 6 pieces.

Add a heaping dollop of guava jam (about 1½ Tbsp or 30 g) to the center of each square of masa hojaldre and about half that amount of cream cheese (15 g or 1 Tbsp). Fold the dough in half diagonally to form a triangular-shaped pastry. Repeat for the remaining squares.

Line a baking sheet with parchment paper and transfer the pastries onto the sheet.

In a small bowl, whisk together the egg and a pinch of salt to make the egg wash. Brush the egg wash all over the top of each pastry. Place the baking sheet in the oven and bake for 20 minutes, or until puffed up and golden brown.

PASTELITOS DE PIÑA

Makes
8 PASTELITOS

½ fresh pineapple, cubed
100 g (½ c packed) brown sugar
Juice of ½ lemon
½ recipe Masa Hojaldre (page 272)
1 large egg, for the egg wash
Pinch salt, for the egg wash

Every weekend for the longest time while growing up, delicious aromas arose from the kitchen throughout the day. My mom would always make sure to prepare her best sweet and savory dishes for us on the weekend, and there was nothing that would get me and my siblings more excited than the pastelitos de piña we would get to have for dessert, with freshly made pineapple jam enclosed in a crisp, flaky crust and baked to perfection. The smell of these was unmistakable, and the flavor was always a delight. In the version here, I thought it would be fun to make these with the masa hojaldre to get even more flaky, buttery bites as opposed to the traditional shortbread crust.

In a saucepan over medium heat, add the cubed pineapple, brown sugar, and lemon juice and stir until the mixture bubbles up, 5 to 10 minutes. Once there's a nice bubbling caramelization, reduce the heat to a simmer and cook for 5 minutes. Transfer the caramelized pineapple mixture to a medium bowl and let cool completely before filling the pastelitos.

Preheat the oven to 375°F.

Flour a work surface and roll the masa hojaldre into a 10 by 16-inch rectangle. You should be able to cut 8 disks out of the dough depending on the size of your cutter. I used some mini tart pans as my cutting device. A cookie cutter or plastic cup will do as well.

Place 1½ Tbsp of the filling into the center of each disk. Close the disk into a half-moon shape by taking the top side and bringing it over the filling onto the bottom side. Use a fork to seal the edges of the pastelito and place on a parchment-lined sheet pan.

In a small bowl, whisk the egg with a pinch of salt to make an egg wash. Brush each pastelito generously with the egg wash.

Bake the pastelitos for 20 to 25 minutes, or until golden brown.

PASTELITOS DE CAMOTE Y MOLE

Here's another pastelito variation that you can easily prepare using the Dulce de Camote that you learned how to make on page 208, as well as the flaky Masa Hojaldre (page 272). I'm lucky enough to live by a Mexican grocery that sells two types of fresh mole: one sweet and one spicy. I tend to get the sweet variety for this pastelito as it pairs well with the camote flavor. If you don't live by a Mexican grocer, most national grocery chains carry some form of mole in a jar that will work just fine.

Preheat the oven to 400°F.

Roll out the chilled masa hojaldre so it's 2 to 3 millimeters thick. If you roll too thin, you won't get flaky layers; if you go too thick, it might underbake and come out gummy. Cut the dough into 6 equal squares.

Add a heaping dollop of dulce de camote and mole to the center of each square of masa hojaldre. Fold the dough in half diagonally to form a triangle-shaped pastry. Repeat with the remaining squares and place on a parchment-lined baking sheet.

In a small bowl, whisk together the egg and a pinch of salt to make the egg wash. Brush the egg wash all over the top of each pastry. Bake for 20 minutes, or until puffed up and golden brown.

1 batch Masa Hojaldre (page 272), chilled
200 g (about ¾ c) Dulce de Camote (page 208)
200 g (about ¾ c) store-bought mole
1 large egg, for the egg wash
Pinch salt, for the egg wash

PASTELITOS DE PAPAYA Y QUESO

1 recipe Masa Hojaldre (page 272), chilled
200 g (about ¾ c) Dulce de Papaya (page 209)
100 g (7 Tbsp) cream cheese
1 large egg, for the egg wash
Pinch salt, for the egg wash

It's time to show some love to papaya and use the Dulce de Papaya you made on page 209. The final pastelito in this chapter uses this ever-present and delicious fruit that you'll always find in Latin American and Caribbean communities. It's kind of a play on the guava and cheese pastelito, but using a different fruit.

In pastelitos, I like to go heavier on the jam than the cream cheese, but you could switch up the ratio to whatever you prefer.

Preheat the oven to 400°F.

Roll out the chilled masa hojaldre so it's 2 to 3 millimeters thick. If you roll too thin, you won't get flaky layers; if you go too thick, it might underbake and come out gummy. Cut the dough into 5 by 5-inch squares; you should have around 6.

Add a heaping dollop of dulce de papaya and about half that amount of cream cheese to the center of each square of masa hojaldre,. Fold the dough in half diagonally to form a triangular-shaped pastry. Repeat for the remaining squares and place them on a parchment-lined baking sheet.

In a small bowl, whisk together the egg and salt to make an egg wash. Brush the egg wash all over the top of each pastry. Bake for 20 minutes, or until puffed up and golden brown.

10 g (1 Tbsp + 2 tsp) ground
cinnamon
100 g (½ c) granulated sugar
1 recipe Masa Hojaldre (page
272)

OREJAS

Orejas are a type of Mexican pastry where the puff pastry dough is rolled and folded to create many layers, then sliced and baked, resulting in a cookie with a distinctive shape and flaky, crisp texture. The name "orejas" means "ears" in Spanish, so the name of these cookies is derived from their shape, which resembles a pair of ears or a butterfly. Orejas are believed to have originated in France, where they are known as "palmiers."

Preheat the oven to 400°F.

In a small bowl, combine the cinnamon and sugar and mix well. Set aside.

Roll out the masa hojaldre until it is about 3 millimeters thick and cut it into 1-inch strips. From both ends of the strip, fold the dough inward on top of itself until they meet in the middle and form the shape of a heart. Dip generously in the cinnamon sugar mixture and place on a parchment-lined baking sheet.

Bake for 15 minutes, or until golden brown.

PASTELITOS CRIOLLOS

Makes
8 PASTELITOS

1 recipe Masa Hojaldre (page 272)
Canola oil, for frying
200 g (½ c + 2 Tbsp) Dulce de Leche (page 210)
Powdered sugar, for dusting

Pastelitos criollos are a traditional Argentine pastry that originated in Buenos Aires during the colonial period. The pastry was originally made by Spanish nuns who lived there in the eighteenth century, from a recipe brought from Spain and adapted to the local ingredients. The pastry dough is usually made with flour, lard, and a small amount of sugar and salt. The filling is typically made with quince paste, sweet potato, or dulce de leche, a caramelized milk-based filling.

Roll out the masa hojaldre until it is about 3 millimeters thick and cut it into squares that are 3 inches by 3 inches. Layer two squares on top of each other, in a staggered fashion so that the corners do not overlap. Place into the palm of your hand and press down gently into the middle to form a divot. Press the edges of the squares together. Place these on a parchment-lined sheet pan and refrigerate while the oil heats up.

In a large pot or pan over medium heat, heat the canola oil to 375°F.

Add the dough squares, two or three at a time, to the oil and fry until flaky and crispy, light to medium brown, about 4 minutes.

Fill each pastelito with the dulce de leche, sprinkle with powdered sugar, and serve.

CH 6

SAVORY AND GLUTEN-FREE

Some of my favorite baked goods are gluten-free, but that's not because I'm trying to keep up with the latest trends. In South America, cassava flour, amaranth, sorghum, and maíz (corn) have been used for thousands of years to create mesmerizing baked goods and savory treats.

While wheat has become a huge part of Latin American baking traditions, corn remains king. The cultural staples made with corn masa are often talked about as the "real" bread of Latin America. This section takes you beyond the strict definition of what it means to "bake" as you will use your stovetop to make things like arepas, tortillas, and pastelitos. Be prepared to feel dough that is much different than the yeasted, strong-gluten-network doughs of the previous chapters, although there are still some wheat flour–based savory treats for you waiting here. In addition to these staple food items, there are several gluten-free baked goods that use Indigenous grains that are healthy and delicious—as well as my formula for a gluten-free sourdough starter.

The Real "Bread" of Latin America

Corn was the basis for Mesoamerican spirituality because this nutritious kernel represented the connection and responsibility that human beings have with the earth—as evidenced by the fact that Mesoamericans actually talked to corn sprouts, prayed to the gods of corn, and viewed their harvest as something to nourish themselves. It is even believed by some that human beings were created by corn! A Mayan creation myth told the story of the patriarchal gods struggling to create humans from various materials before finding that only corn could produce the perfect human being. The gods turned to the goddess Grandmother Xmucane. According to Paula Morton's *Tortillas: A Cultural History:*

> "She picked up a jug and walked to the mountain stream where she mixed the clear water with kernels scraped from corn grown inside the sacred mountain. Then she knelt before the grinding stone to massage the corn into a coarse dough. Now the gods had the life force of corn to work with and they molded the dough into four men and four women made of flesh, perfect in their own image." This is why the Mayans were called "the men of corn."

These creation myths detail the still unchanged ancient process that required Mesoamerican women to spend up to six hours a day on their knees grinding corn using ametate, a slightly sloped grinding stone made of volcanic rock. This mythology only emphasizes the way in which corn is deeply ingrained in the history of Central America and México.

Early Mesoamerican women made dough by way of grinding, and as such, corn tortillas have been the cornerstone of Central American and Mexican diets for thousands of years. Ancient Aztec and Mayan creation myths both feature gods who brought forth human life by grinding corn and making it into masa. From that masa, the gods formed the first humans and from there rose the Aztec and Mayan empires. The history of corn tortillas is the story of the rise and fall of civilizations in Mesoamerica. The great civilizations of Mesoamerica were often warring and divided, but the people were united by a simple and humble grain: corn. Corn in ancient Mesoamerica was considered a sacred and life-giving force. There was no country without corn, "Sin maíz no hay país."

In several countries that I have visited, there is always someone who comments on how corn-based staples are the "bread" of Latin America. This makes sense because of how important it was for the Aztec, Zapotec, and Mayan people. The actual origin of corn tortillas has not exactly been determined, as their existence goes back thousands of years. Each civilization had a different name for the dough, but the Spanish ultimately took charge to name it what we know it as today: masa. The reality is that corn influenced cultural and societal change from these ancient times until now.

The three names for this nourishing and life-giving dough are markers of the importance of the corn tortilla on this peninsula. Many empires rose and fell on the

Mesoamerican peninsula and yet the humble corn tortilla remains. Would it surprise you to hear that calcium hydroxide, slaked lime, or cal is essential to making the perfect corn tortilla? Calcium hydroxide is added to dried white corn kernels mixed in water. The corn is cooked and soaked in an alkaline solution created by the slaked lime. Essentially, the hull is loosened and detaches from the inside part of the kernel, thereby releasing nutrients to create a nutritious end product. While this sounds like a process cooked up in a lab by modern food scientists, it is in fact the ancient Mesoamerican practice called nixtamalization invented more than 3,500 years ago.

The secret to great corn tortillas begins in the flour, and fresh corn ground in the metate is but one component to achieving the best corn flour for tortillas. Nixtamalization is said to bring forth the flavor and essence of fresh corn. It was initially called *nahuatl* by the Aztec, which was derived from the words *tamalli* and *nextli*, meaning "corn dough" and "ashes," respectively. The Spanish simply called it nixtamal.

The narrative around early Mesoamerican life is often based on the accounts of colonizers who had every incentive to paint these technologically advanced societies as barbaric. However, it was Mesoamerican women who experimented and developed the process of nixtamalization by calculating and standardizing the exact measurements needed.

The nutritional value of the mixture was unexpectedly enhanced because the lime-infused masa (corn dough) increased the human digestive system's ability to access niacin, six amino acids, and calcium. The reality of Mesoamerican ingenuity cannot be denied. "So superior is nixtamalized maize to the unprocessed kind that it is tempting to see the rise of Mesoamerican civilization as a consequence of this invention, without which the peoples of México and their southern neighbors would have remained forever on the village level," argues anthropologist Sophie Coe.

Masa has evolved in several ways since ancient times. In the 1940s, a company called Maseca created the first commercialized, instant masa flour, also known as masa harina. Commercial brands are widely used in Latin American households. Growing up, my mom, uncles, and aunts used this type of masa harina to create really delicious tortillas de maíz for us. If you are not able to access dried corn and cal to nixtamalize, or simply do not have the time, I strongly recommend keeping some masa harina in your kitchen so that you can whip up your own version of the delicious food staples of Latin America. Corn tortillas are still front and center in Mexican and Central American cooking, and are the primary component of several traditional dishes, such as chilaquiles, enchiladas, tacos dorados, tostadas, and quesadillas. The quality of tortillas in Latin America is very high compared to most found in the United States, as the streets are riddled with tortillerías that take the utmost pride in upholding tortilla tradition. From using instant masa harina to using commodity corn and finding the most artisanal and flavorful corn varieties, it does not look like the tradition and staple of tortillas de maíz is going anywhere anytime soon.

TORTILLAS DE MAÍZ

Makes
8 TORTILLAS

120 g (heaped 1 c) masa harina
5 g (1½ tsp) kosher salt
100 g (¼ c + 3 Tbsp) warm
water, plus more if the masa
is too dry

While I wish everyone at home had a metate and other resources to nixtamalize corn every time they want a corn tortilla, I believe it is best to give a simple, widely used method of making corn tortillas at home using readily available masa harina. My mom loved making these for us every now and then, although her preferred tortilla was a coconut milk–based flour tortilla, which you can learn about on page 296. I love to eat these for breakfast with eggs and a little refried beans and cheese, but of course you can do just about anything with them. The process is quite simple. The key to success here is making sure you hydrate the masa harina enough—even though there are just three ingredients, it can be easy to end up with something a little too dry and crumbly, so you must be patient to make sure your masa is smooth and pliable.

In a mixing bowl, combine the masa harina and salt and mix well. Next, pour in 80 g (⅓ c) of the water and mix with your hands until all the flour is absorbed. Slowly add the remaining water with one hand while mixing with the other, ensuring you are evenly incorporating it to avoid any clumps. The masa should be smooth and shouldn't crumble or crack on the edges when picked up and squeezed or bent. If you find that the masa is too dry for whatever reason, slowly add small amounts of water to it while mixing until you feel it loosen up and become more pliable. Cover and let the dough rest for 10 to 20 minutes.

Divide the dough into your desired tortilla size. I find roughly 20 to 30 g (about 2 Tbsp) is the perfect size for most standard tortilla presses. If you don't have a tortilla press, you can simply use wet hands to press the dough together and flatten it. When pressing a tortilla, aim to get it to be as thin as possible as this will help with the extensibility when using.

Heat up a cast-iron skillet over medium-high heat, until you see it start to smoke a little bit. Reduce the heat to medium, and cook the tortilla on each side for 3 to 4 minutes. Look for nice brown spots to appear on the tortilla on each side, pressing down on them with a spatula to create air bubbles and ensure you have a nice, light tortilla. Once your tortillas are cooked, they are best eaten warm. You can put them on a plate, wrapped in a clean kitchen cloth, or in a tortilla warmer while you prepare the rest of your meal.

TORTILLAS DE HARINA DE TRIGO

Makes
12 TORTILLAS

400 g (3 c + 3 Tbsp) all-purpose
 flour
6 g (2 tsp) kosher salt
205 g (¾ c + 1 tsp) warm water
60 g (¼ c) lard

The introduction of wheat into Latin America, and México specifically, changed the cuisine forever. It was not just the influx of new baked goods and breads that created change, but a shift in the iconic tortilla culture that permeates the country. Tortillas, historically made with nixtamalized corn, started to be made with wheat flour as a way to continue to nourish communities and utilize the new and ever-present crop that Europeans forced upon the land. As a result, flour tortillas are an original and authentically Mexican creation—contrary to the belief that they were born in the United States.

While the tortilla de maíz (corn tortilla) dominates street corners and dinner tables across México, the flour tortilla is very commonly eaten in Northern México, where the terrain is much more suited to growing wheat than the rest of the country. With this simple recipe, you'll have fresh tortillas in under an hour and will be able to fill them with beans, cheeses, meats as you see fit. One of the key ingredients is the lard, as this is what keeps the tortillas soft and pliable on the inside, so that you get the perfect bite and chew when eating while maintaining an elastic gluten structure. One of my favorite ways to have this type of tortilla? A little butter and a pinch of salt.

NOTE: You can make tortillas by hand or with a stand mixer. The stand mixer can help the fat incorporate better.

In a bowl, combine the flour and salt and mix to incorporate. Next, add the water and mix until there is no dry flour left in the bowl. Don't knead the dough yet. Let it rest for 5 minutes.

After the period of rest, spread the lard on the dough and then squeeze it in. This might take about 5 minutes. It is important to let the gluten relax before adding the fat to get a strong dough network. You will know the fat is incorporated when the dough does not feel too slimy and returns to its original, smooth texture.

Once the fat is incorporated into the dough, turn it out onto a work surface and use the palm of your hand to push the dough forward, and your fingers to fold it back into the middle. When kneading, it is okay to break apart the gluten network as it will come back stronger. Repeat the kneading process for about 7 minutes, or until the dough is slightly sticky but smooth. Cover and let rest for at least 20 minutes. Don't skip this resting period as it lets the dough relax and become even more elastic.

Elongate the dough into a log shape. It should be silky and offer no resistance at this point but be strong enough to stretch out. Divide into 12 pieces

and shape into round balls. Cover, preferably with a moist paper towel, and let rest another 10 to 15 minutes.

Using a tortilla press or a rolling pin and a little bit of flour, stretch out or press your tortilla.

Heat up a cast-iron skillet over high heat, until it becomes very hot and slightly smoky, then decrease the heat to low. Wait 5 minutes before cooking the tortillas. High heat is important, but avoid it getting too high during the entire cooking process.

Cook the tortillas, one at a time, for about 3 minutes per side, with an additional minute per side after each side has cooked. Look for the tortilla to bubble up and develop those familiar caramel brown spots evenly on each side.

Have a clean towel handy and place the cooked tortillas in the towel, bundling them up as you continue to cook the others. This will keep the tortillas warm and soft before serving.

TORTILLAS DE HARINA INTEGRAL

Makes
12 TORTILLAS

215 g (1¾ c + 1 Tbsp) whole wheat flour
155 g (1¼ c) all-purpose flour
30 g (¼ c + 1 Tbsp) amaranth flour
Pinch baking powder
255 g (1 c + 1 Tbsp) water
30 g (2 Tbsp) lard

Tortillas are no exception to my style of wanting a whole grain variety in my staple doughs, and make no mistake, tortillas are a staple in my household no matter what time of year or city I'm living in. I wanted a recipe that included over 50 percent whole grain while maintaining the flexibility and texture of a classic flour tortilla. Using amaranth flour adds an earthiness to the flavor, in addition to the inherent health benefits of using more whole grain. You'll be able to use these tortillas for anything you'd use a regular, white flour tortilla for, so long as you are patient during the mixing process and let the dough rest for the suggested times.

In a large bowl, combine the whole wheat flour, all-purpose flour, amaranth flour, and baking powder and mix to incorporate. Next, add 235 g (1 c) of the water and 15 g of the lard. Mix until there is no dry flour left in the bowl. Let the dough rest for 5 minutes.

Add the rest of the lard to the dough and use both hands to squeeze it in. This might take about 5 minutes. Once the fat is incorporated into the dough, add 10 g of water and squeeze it in. This should take another few minutes. Once the dough is smooth again, let it rest for 5 minutes. Then repeat the process with the remaining 10 g of water.

Once the dough is smooth again, turn it out onto a work surface and use the palm of your hand to push the dough forward, and your fingers to fold it back into the middle. Repeat the kneading process for 6 to 7 minutes, or until you have a slightly sticky but smooth dough. Cover and let rest for at least 20 minutes. Don't skip this resting period as it lets the dough relax and become even more elastic.

Elongate the dough into a log shape; it should be silky and offer no resistance at this point, but be strong enough to stretch out. Divide into 12 pieces and shape into round balls. Cover, preferably with a moist paper towel, and let rest for another 10 to 15 minutes.

Using a tortilla press or a rolling pin and a little bit of flour, stretch out/press your tortilla.

Heat up a cast-iron skillet on high, until it becomes very hot and slightly smokey, then reduce the heat to low. Wait 5 minutes before cooking the tortillas. High heat is important, but avoid it getting too high during the entire cooking process.

Cook each tortilla on the heated cast-iron skillet for about 3 minutes per side, with an additional minute per side after each side has cooked. Look for the tortilla to bubble up and develop those familiar caramel brown spots evenly on each side.

Have a clean towel handy and place the cooked tortillas in the towel, bundling them up as you continue to cook the others. This will keep the tortillas warm and soft before serving.

MY MOM'S TORTILLAS DE HARINA

The first dough that I ever learned how to knead was tortilla dough, and it was not just any old tortilla dough. It was my mom's! In the words of one of my uncles (and several other people in and around my family), "No one can make the tortillas like Herling can." I've found that this statement is 100 percent accurate. It makes sense that they are so good, as my mom grew up eating tortillas three times a day in Honduras. There was always a piping hot comal outside ready for the tortillas, she recalls, with a constant supply of delicious beans always at the ready as well.

As time went on, she perfected this family recipe and there is a (not so) secret ingredient that really makes them stand out: coconut milk. When the aroma of coconut milk permeated our house growing up, I knew it meant we were having Baleadas (page 301) for lunch, the national dish of Honduras. For now, buckle up and get your hands ready to knead the most delicious, mouthwatering tortillas you'll ever have. In the past I have made versions of this with sourdough starter, discard, and whole grain flour, but this time I want to come as close as possible to those childhood memories.

Makes

12 TORTILLAS

400 g (3 c + 3 Tbsp) all-purpose flour
6 g (2 tsp) kosher salt
Pinch baking powder (I mean the *slightest* pinch!)
100 g (¼ c + 3 Tbsp) warm water
125 g (½ c) full-fat coconut milk
40 g (3 Tbsp) vegetable oil
1 large egg

Mom helping out at my first NYC bakery pop-up

In a large bowl, combine all-purpose flour, salt, and pinch of baking powder and mix to incorporate. Next, warm up the coconut milk in a saucepan over medium heat. This part is important for the dough (because my mom said so!), so make sure you are not using cold coconut milk. Don't let it reach a boil, but make sure it's a little bit past warm.

Add the water, coconut milk, and half the oil to the bowl with the dry ingredients and mix until there is no dry flour left. Let the dough rest for 5 minutes. Add the rest of the oil and squeeze it into the dough. This might take about 5 minutes.

Once the oil is incorporated, turn the dough out onto a lightly floured work surface and use the palm of your hand to push the dough forward, and your fingers to fold it back into the middle. Repeat the kneading process for about 7 minutes, or until the dough is slightly sticky but smooth. Cover and let rest for at least 20 minutes. Don't skip this resting period as it lets the dough relax and become even more elastic.

Elongate the dough into a log shape. It should be silky and offer no resistance at this point but be strong enough to stretch out. Divide into 12 pieces and shape into round balls. Cover, preferably with a moist paper towel, and let rest for another 10 to 15 minutes.

To stretch these tortillas, use the technique that my mom showed me with a large plate that is lightly oiled. Place a tortilla ball onto the center of the plate and, using oiled hands, flatten the dough ball using your fingertips until it is a medium-sized tortilla. Heat up a cast-iron skillet on high, until it becomes very hot and slightly smokey, then reduce the heat to low. Wait 5 minutes before cooking the tortillas. High heat is important, but avoid it being too high during the entire cooking process.

Cook each tortilla on the heated cast-iron skillet for about 3 minutes per side, with an additional minute per side after each side has cooked. Look for the tortilla to bubble up and develop those familiar caramel brown spots evenly on each side.

Have a clean towel handy and place the cooked tortillas in the towel, bundling them up as you continue to cook the others. This will keep your tortillas warm and soft before serving.

SOURDOUGH DISCARD TORTILLAS

Makes
12 TORTILLAS

340 g (1⅔ c) sourdough discard
100 g (¼ c + 3 Tbsp) water
400 g (3 c + 3 Tbsp) all-purpose
   flour
15 g (1 Tbsp + 2 tsp) kosher salt
Pinch baking powder (optional)
30 g (2 Tbsp) lard or vegetable
   oil

There has most certainly been a craze about using leftover mature sourdough starter, also known as sourdough discard, as of late. Typically, when feeding a sourdough starter, one must "discard" a portion of the existing starter and replace it with fresh flour and water so that it will activate and grow. There are several fun ways to use discard, including pancake batter, muffins, biscuits—essentially anything that can be baked can be infused with discard if only to add flavor (as its leavening power is spent). It almost seems like common sense to use this discard to make flour tortillas. In this recipe, I include baking powder for a nice, quick puff, but it is optional. For optimal flavor, I use a sourdough starter that is roughly 50 percent whole grain. If you have a sourdough starter made of just white flour, you won't get as much of the flavor benefit.

In a bowl, combine the sourdough discard and water and mix until it is dissolved. It is okay if there are some chunks of starter still floating around, just make sure it is frothy and evenly distributed.

Add the flour, salt, and baking powder (if using) into the bowl and use one hand to squeeze and mix until you have a shaggy dough with not much dry flour left. It is important to make sure you don't have any clumps of flour here, so really squeeze and turn the dough to break up any clumps of flour.

Finally, add 15 g (1 Tbsp) of the lard on top of the dough and spread it around the surface. Once again, squeeze it into the dough to help the fat incorporate. Once the dough smooths out again, add the rest of the oil and repeat the process. Look for an elastic, smooth dough that does not feel wet or moist.

Turn the dough out onto a work surface and use the palm of your hands to push the dough away from you, then pull it back into the middle with your fingers. Repeat until you have a smooth, silky round ball. Cover and let the dough rest for 20 minutes at room temperature. I typically use a moist paper towel and lay it over the dough so that it does not dry out and develop a skin.

After the rest period, divide the dough into 12 pieces and round them into tight dough balls. Once again, let the dough rest for 20 minutes. This helps the gluten relax so that the tortillas can be stretched out without resisting.

Heat a cast-iron skillet on high, until it becomes very hot and slightly smoky, then reduce the heat to low. Wait 5 minutes before cooking your tortillas. High heat is important, but avoid it being too high during the entire cooking process.

Using a tortilla press or a rolling pin and a little bit of flour, stretch out/press your tortilla.

Cook on the heated cast-iron skillet for about 3 minutes per side, with an additional minute per side after each side has cooked. The tortilla should bubble up and develop those familiar caramel brown spots evenly on each side.

Have a clean towel handy and place the cooked tortillas in the towel, bundling them up as you continue to cook the others. This will keep the tortillas warm and soft before serving.

BALEADAS

▲▲▲▲▲▲▲▲▲▲▲▲▲

Makes
12 BALEADAS

〜〜〜〜〜〜〜〜〜〜

60 g (4 Tbsp) unsalted butter
1 white onion, diced
20 g (3 Tbsp) cumin seeds
15 g (2 Tbsp) cracked black
   pepper
360 g (2 c) dry red kidney beans,
   soaked overnight
940 g (4 c) water
2 bay leaves
3 g (1 tsp) kosher salt
1 batch of My Mom's Tortillas de
   Harina (page 296)
Crumbled queso hondureño, al
   gusto
Crema hondureña, al gusto
1 avocado, sliced (optional)
Scrambled eggs (optional)
Chorizo (optional)
Carne asada (optional)

Waking up and knowing I'm going to eat a baleada is a childhood memory that stands above every other food memory that I have. Whether it was before or after school, a weekend lunch, or just a snack, it was always a good time to have baleadas and get together as a family.

The baleada is one of the most famous dishes from Honduras, and in my opinion, it is a national treasure. Creamy, perfectly refried beans, crema hondureña, and a heavy dose of crumbled queso duro stuffed into a silky smooth tortilla is an irresistible combination that can also be spruced up by carne asada, avocado, eggs, or chorizo. Baleadas are thought to have originated on the North Coast of Honduras, possibly in La Ceiba, where a woman had been selling some of the best street food around. Legend has it that she, or someone around her food vending site, was gunned down and after this happened, locals wanted to go and eat "adonde la baleada" (which translates roughly into "where they shot her"). As seemingly tragic as this story is, there is no doubt that those baleadas are delicious, if people still want to go to that spot!

〰〰

In a large pot over medium heat, add 30 g (2 Tbsp) of the butter and half of the white onion. While the onion sautés, grind the cumin seeds with a mortar and pestle. Add 2 Tbsp of the ground cumin to the butter and onion mixture. Next, add the cracked pepper and the soaked beans. Stir the beans for about 1 minute then reduce the heat to low and add the water. Add the bay leaves and let the beans cook for 4 to 6 hours. Once the beans are cooked, strain, remove the bay leaves, and let them cool completely before moving on to the refrying step.

In a large skillet over low heat, add the remaining butter and the remaining onion. Cook until translucent, about 3 minutes. Add the cooked beans and use a potato masher to mash the beans into a creamy paste. Add the salt, more cracked black pepper, if desired, and the remaining cumin. Once the beans are mashed and creamy, allow them to simmer for about 1 hour so that they lose as much moisture as possible. They should be the consistency of a thick paste. You can probably get away with whisking or blending them, but the masher is the way I prefer and enjoy. Remove from the heat. The frijoles fritos hondureños are done!

On one of the tortillas, spread a thick, even layer of beans. Top generously with crumbled queso hondureño and a heavy dose of crema. This is called a baleada sencilla, and it is my preferred way to eat them. However, you can also add avocado, scrambled eggs, chorizo, or carne asada, depending on what part of the day you are in and how much sustenance you need!

SALSA ROJA

Makes
ABOUT 1 QUART

30 g (2 Tbsp) olive oil
4 medium tomatoes, quartered
1 large white onion, halved
3 cloves garlic
1 large green bell pepper,
    jalapeño, poblano, or serrano
    pepper, halved
235 g (1 c) chicken broth
10 g (¼ c) chopped cilantro
Kosher salt, al gusto
Freshly ground black pepper, al
    gusto

My mom often made a nice salsa roja for my family when serving savory dishes, such as chuletas fritas and enchiladas de carne molida. Her preference is to use green bell peppers as opposed to other spicy pepper varieties to create a salsa with balanced, mild flavor. Most Honduran cooking—indeed, most cooking in Latin America outside of México—is not driven by the spicy heat of chile peppers. There are of course dozens if not hundreds or thousands of kinds of salsas that range in intensity and in their method of preparation. Feel free to use any type of pepper to get to the spice level that you want for your salsa—this is a good basic place to start.

Heat a heavy skillet over high heat. The pan should be so hot a little smoke comes off its surface. Once the pan is very hot, carefully add the olive oil and let that heat up for a minute or two. Then add the tomatoes, onion, garlic, and pepper, placing them all face down.

Let everything char in the pan for about 5 minutes, or until black blisters form on the side of the vegetables touching the bottom of the pan. Once they're nice and charred, flip them over to allow the other side to char as well. Let the veggies sear for another 5 to 7 minutes until they are noticeably tender. Remove from the heat and set aside until slightly cooled.

Add the charred veggies to a blender with the chicken broth and cilantro and blend just until a smooth mixture forms. Add back into the skillet over medium heat, season with salt and pepper to your liking, and let simmer for 20 minutes. Remove from the heat until ready to serve.

Encurtido al Lago de Yojoa

On one family trip back to Honduras in 2010, my Tío Lenchito, my mother's brother, wouldn't stop talking about a magical fish shack at the edge of el Lago de Yojoa. He claimed this was the place to get the most delicious fried fish and encurtido, a classic pickled vegetable condiment that is rarely absent from the Honduran table. So one morning, we loaded into his car and set out for lunch.

The lake is the largest in Honduras, formed by volcanoes, and the area around it is full of biodiversity. Like many areas in Honduras, and Latin America more broadly, its tranquility is threatened by the encroachment of deforestation and development. But the drive along the lake was breathtaking, the water calm and motionless, almost frozen in time. I noticed the local cooks bringing freshly caught fish into their kitchens just a few steps from the water's edge, and I could see why my tío loved to get away from his home in San Pedro Sula to enjoy the peace of the lago.

We finally pulled up to our destination: an unnamed lakeside vendor selling a single perfect platter of whole fried red snapper with crisp fried plantains, black beans, coconut rice, red chile salsa, and fresh limes. Tío Lenchito had been raving about the food for days, so I was eager for a taste.

But in all his praise, he had neglected to mention the encurtido: jars of pickled beets, onions, carrots, and peppers on every table. My little sister nearly started eating her fish without adding a proper spoonful to her plate, but my mom stopped her, "¡Mira, hay que poner el encurtido, mama!"

Mom was right. The encurtido's tangy, crisp bite was as perfect as the fish.

There are many variations of encurtido (or curtido) found throughout Latin America and, in some ways, it is a reflection of many nations' common bonds. Lots of recipes for the condiment/side dish of pickled vegetables include cabbage and carrot, while others are beet or onion based. There is frequently (but not always) some level of spicy heat, often provided by jalapeños. So many traditional Latin American foods—think Salvadoran pupusas, Honduran baleadas, or Mexican tacos—feature soft textures and salty, fatty flavors. A scoop of crisp encurtido adds crucial fresh, bright acidity to lift every bite. Each cook's recipe adds its own special touch, like a sprinkle of dried thyme or a balancing scoop of sugar.

Home in New York, I often head back to the Bronx, the neighborhood of my birth, to reconnect with the flavors of my culture. One of my favorite restaurants is Seis Vecinos. The name, which translates to "six neighbors," is an homage to six countries—México, El Salvador, Nicaragua, Costa Rica, Guatemala, and Honduras. These countries share geographic proximity and a common diaspora partially due to the United States' banana industry of the nineteenth century, in which the United Fruit Company was granted huge swaths of Central American land and enslaved workers from the local region as well as Africa and the West Indies.

Look around Seis Vecinos and you'll notice diners spooning encurtido on everything from plátano to chula frita (a pan-fried pork chop) to cut the fatty meat. With its vinegar punch and satisfying crunch, it's no wonder this prize of the Honduran kitchen has a ubiquitous spot on home and restaurant tables. Once you understand the general technique—simmer tough vegetables like beets and carrots until tender, then add quick-cooking ones like onions to a boiling vinegar brine—it's easy to make and adjust to your taste. It will keep for weeks in the fridge, but once you start using it, you'll want to keep it out on the table.

CURTIDO

½ head green cabbage,
  shredded
235 g (1 c) white vinegar
100 g (½ c) granulated sugar
35 g (¼ c) kosher salt
2 medium carrots, peeled and
  sliced
½ medium white onion, sliced
1 large serrano chile, sliced
1 garlic clove, sliced
30 g (¾ c) cilantro, chopped

Curtido, also known as encurtido, is a delicious pickled accompaniment that adds a bright crunchy texture to savory dishes in Latin America from breakfast to dinner. Although there are a great many variations, its simplest form is a lightly fermented, thinly sliced cabbage and pepper mixture pickled with vinegar, salt, and a bit of sugar. In Honduran encurtido, beets are used instead of cabbage, and other vegetables such as cauliflower are often included. Here, you could include beets as an optional addition, which will give this curtido a purple hue.

In a medium saucepan over medium heat, add water and bring it to a simmer, then add the green cabbage and blanch for 1 minute. Drain and squeeze out as much moisture as possible, using a clean cloth or paper towel to press down on the cabbage while it is in the strainer.

In a small pot over medium heat, add the vinegar, sugar, and salt. Bring to a simmer, stirring occasionally, just until the solids have dissolved, 1 to 2 minutes. Remove from the heat and set aside.

In a large bowl, toss the cabbage, carrots, onion, chile, garlic, and cilantro and place in a large mason jar. Pour the vinegar mixture over the cabbage mixture. Cover with a lid and refrigerate for at least 2 hours, though a full day before serving is best. Keep chilled in the fridge for 3 to 4 weeks.

CHIMICHURRI

Makes
ABOUT 2 C

½ bunch parsley, roughly
   chopped
4 cloves garlic, peeled
15 g (1 Tbsp) white vinegar
15 g (1 Tbsp) red wine vinegar
6 g (1 Tbsp) red pepper flakes
3 g (1 Tbsp) dried whole oregano
   leaves
3 g (1 tsp) kosher salt
220 g (1 c) olive oil

I love this stuff. A few years ago I went through a phase where I made
chimichurri several times a week for dinner. I'd roast a whole chicken, cook up
some coconut rice and black beans, and spoon the bright, herbaceous sauce
all over it. While I don't claim to make a traditional Argentine-style chimichurri,
I have a friend from Argentina who seems to have enjoyed it when I made it for
him, so I'll take that. I've also gotten into the habit of using this as a finisher for
my fugazzeta slices—this is life-changing stuff!

In a blender or food processor, combine the parsley, garlic, white vinegar, and
red wine vinegar. Blend until a relatively smooth consistency forms. You don't
want the parsley to be drenched in vinegar, but lightly coated and slightly
clumped together.

   Remove from the blender and place in a mortar and pestle. Add the red
pepper flakes, oregano leaves, and salt. Mash together until everything is evenly
incorporated. To finish off the chimichurri, add this mixture to a small bowl
and pour the olive oil over it until the parsley mixture is completely submerged.
Without disturbing or mixing, let the chimichurri rest for a few hours. This will
allow the flavors to infuse into the oil and develop more quickly. When ready to
serve, mix it up and spoon it over your favorite foods.

AREPAS DE QUESO COLOMBIANAS

△△△△△△△△△△△△△

Makes
10 AREPAS

∿∿∿∿∿∿∿∿∿∿∿

300 g (2 c) yellow masarepa
6 g (2 tsp) kosher salt
500 g (2 c + 2 Tbsp) water
150 g (heaped 1 c) crumbled
    queso colombiano, or queso
    fresco
200 g (1⅔ c) shredded or cubed
    mozzarella cheese

While I was in Medellín working with a bakery, one of the bakers told me that
although they sell and consume a lot of bread, the arepa is "the real bread"
of Colombia. At the time I wasn't familiar with the Colombian arepa, but I
befriended them pretty quickly. Every breakfast, lunch, and dinner I had was
accompanied by fresh, cheesy, and perfectly cooked arepas. In pre-Colombian
times, the Indigenous populations made and consumed various preparations of
corn as it was believed to be a gift to their land from the Gods.

From an origin perspective, although it is hard to know for sure, Colombia
may be where the arepa originated before also being adapted in what is
now known as Venezuela. Some parts of the Caribbean and Central America
prepare arepas as well. There are several variations of arepas in Colombia, and
my favorite is the classic arepa de queso. These simple and delicious arepas will
make a great addition to your dinner table.

In a large bowl, combine the masarepa and salt and mix briefly. Slowly add the
water with one hand and mix with the other. Do not add all the water at once,
but in 3 to 4 increments, mixing in between.

Once a smooth, soft dough has formed, add the crumbled queso colombiano
or queso fresco and gently mix it in until it is evenly incorporated. Cover the
dough and let it rest for 10 minutes at room temperature.

With lightly oiled hands, divide the dough into 90-g pieces (about the size of
small lemons) and round each piece into a smooth ball.

Place dough ball in the palm of one hand and with the knuckles of the other
hand, indent the ball into a small, bowl-like shape.

Place 15 g (2 Tbsp) of mozzarella into each dough ball and pinch the ends
together to seal it. Now, gently pat the dough ball into a flat disk by using a
clapping motion, rotating it to keep it as round as possible.

Heat up a cast-iron skillet or a griddle on medium-high heat and lightly
grease with a neutral oil. Once hot enough that you see a little smoke, add the
arepas to the skillet and reduce the heat to medium-low. Don't cook these too
hot to get a nice even dark brown coloring on both sides. After about 4 minutes,
flip the arepas and cook the other side. Some cheese may melt out and that is
okay. Cook for another 4 minutes and flip again. Finish the arepas by cooking
for another minute on each side.

Cool slightly and serve warm.

AREPAS REINA PEPIADA

I lived in Miami for a while, and that's when I started to eat a lot of arepas. I found myself eating more Venezuelan arepas than Colombian because I loved that they are stuffed with different meats and cheeses. After a while, I found a specific arepa spot with the most wonderful reina pepiada. This arepa has a very refreshing feel; it's filling but doesn't make you feel too full. The crunch from the peppers and onions combined with the moistness of the shredded chicken and the creaminess of the avocado offers a very delightful bite. I had to start making these, and in my quest, I've come up with a filling mixture that really hits the spot.

In a large bowl, combine the masarepa and salt and mix together briefly until just incorporated. Slowly add the water with one hand while mixing with the other. Do not add all the water at once, but in 3 to 4 increments, mixing in between. Cover the dough and let it rest for 10 minutes.

Next, using lightly oiled hands, divide the dough into 10 pieces and round each piece into a smooth ball. Place the dough ball in the palm of one hand and gently pat it into a flat disk by using a clapping motion, rotating it to keep it as round as possible.

Heat a cast-iron skillet or a griddle on medium-high heat and lightly grease with a neutral oil. Once hot enough that you see a little smoke, add the arepas and reduce the heat to medium-low. Don't cook these too hot to get a nice even dark brown coloring on both sides. Cook for about 4 minutes, flip the arepas, and cook the other side for another 4 minutes. Flip the arepas and finish by cooking for another minute on each side. Let cool while making the filling.

In a large bowl, combine the chicken, red onion, white onion, bell pepper, garlic, cilantro, avocados, mayonnaise, salt, paprika, and red pepper flakes and mix well until there's an even coloring. Using a flat knife, slice into the side of each arepa three-quarters of the way and use the knife to create a pocket. Be careful not to tear the arepa.

Fill each arepa with about 1 cup of the filling. Top with fresh avocado and cheese, if desired, and enjoy!

AREPA DOUGH

300 g (2 c) masarepa (either yellow or white)
6 g (2 tsp) kosher salt
500 g (2 c + 2 Tbsp) water

REINA PEPIADA FILLING

2 chicken breasts, boiled, cooled, and shredded (this will yield roughly 350 g, or 3 c, of shredded chicken)
¼ red onion, diced (about ½ c)
¼ white onion, diced (about ½ c)
½ red bell pepper, diced (about ½ c)
3 cloves garlic, minced
1 bunch cilantro, stems removed, minced
1 to 2 avocados, sliced (if you prefer to mash them, add 2 tsp lemon juice to prevent browning), plus more for serving (optional)
230 g (1 c) mayonnaise
2 g (½ tsp) kosher salt
1 g (½ tsp) paprika
1 g (½ tsp) red pepper flakes
200 g queso llanero, queso fresco, or mozzarella cheese

PUPUSAS DE FRIJOL CON QUESO

Makes
14 PUPUSAS

470 g (2 c) warm water
450 g (4 c) masa harina
2 g (½ tsp) kosher salt (optional)
120 g (1 c) finely chopped chicharrón (fried pork rind)
50 g (¼ c) chopped tomato
35 g (¼ c) chopped onion
35 g (¼ c) chopped bell pepper
230 g (1 c) refried kidney beans or small red beans
120 g (1 c) grated quesillo (Salvadoran cheese)
Oil or rendered pork fat, for cooking
Salsa Roja (page 302)
Curtido (page 305)

In Central America, masa harina is not only used to make corn tortillas, but also used to make delicious stuffed treats called pupusas. Commonly eaten in Central America, specifically El Salvador, Nicaragua, Honduras, and Guatemala, you can find several different fillings and types. In fact, there are many different pupuserías, places that focus specifically on making and perfecting pupusas. These are staples that nourish families and bring people together, and one of my favorite things to seek out when I'm traveling to new cities both domestically and abroad—a good roadside pupusa made on a hot comal can put a smile on anyone's face. When it comes to the chicharrón, do not use the stuff that comes in a bag! I would just omit this if you can't find real chicharrón in your neighborhood. In terms of the cheese, if you can't find a good quesillo, you can use queso fresco or mozzarella.

In a large mixing bowl, combine the water and masa harina and knead while incorporating the salt. Make sure the dough is moist but not sticky. If the dough feels hard add more water. If the masa is too sticky add more harina. Cover the bowl with plastic wrap and let the masa rest for 15 minutes at room temperature.

While the masa rests, start on the filling by adding the chicharrón, tomato, onion, and bell pepper to a food processor and mix. Remove the mixture and set aside. In the same food processor add the beans and blend until smooth and creamy.

In a bowl, add the chicharrón paste and blended red beans with the cheese.

To assemble the pupusas, wet your palms and grab a mound of masa about the size of a baseball. Flatten the masa into a palm-size circle. Add 1 to 2 Tbsp of the filling to the middle and wrap the masa around the filling, enclosing it and rolling together to make a smooth ball. Flatten the ball of masa and filling until about ¼ inch thick and do not allow the filling to leak.

Heat a comal, cast-iron skillet, or heavy skillet over medium-high heat until hot. Brush lightly with the oil. Place the pupusas on the comal, then turn and press them as necessary until crisp brown markings appear (filling might bubble out!). You want to cook them for 3 to 4 minutes per side. Remove from the heat and serve immediately with the salsa roja and curtido.

You can prepare the pupusas 2 hours before cooking them. They can be chilled, covered with plastic wrap. Pupusas can be kept warm in a 250°F oven, if cooking many batches in a row. If the pupusas cool, reheat on the comal for 1 minute per side before serving.

The Empanada

Empanadas are shaped like half-moons, can be savory or sweet, and can be filled with just about anything. In Latin America, empanadas are made with various doughs and fillings that differ from country to country.

When Spanish colonizers arrived in México in the sixteenth century, they brought their empanada recipe to the Aztecs and the Maya. The Spanish empanadas were made with wheat and the Indigenous recipe with corn masa. During the Spanish colonial era in México, Hernán Cortés exemplified the excesses of the colonial ruling class with his fabled banquets. One night in 1538, Cortés threw an extravagant banquet in Ciudad de México. As the evening came to a close, all the ladies were invited to complete a special task: to break open the enormous empanadas presented at the end of the banquet. As the ladies cracked the empanada crusts open, a menagerie of live rabbits and birds burst out!

Spanish cuisine is greatly influenced by Arabic recipes. The empanada in particular is considered a variation on samosas. In Spanish, the verb *empanar* means to fold dough or bread around the filling. Empanadas first popped up in medieval Iberia (Spain) and Portugal when the Moors invaded. In 1529 Spanish chef Ruperto de Nola, who served as cook to King of Naples Ferdinand I, published *Llibre del Coch* (Cook Book). *Llibre del Coch* was the first cookbook published in Catalan that featured a variety of Catalan, French, Arabic, and Italian recipes including several for empanadas. One of his most elaborate recipes was called *Empanada en asador de gallina asada* (Empanada of Roast Hen on a Spit). This recipe required the whole chicken on a spit to be completely encased in the dough. De Nola instructed medieval chefs as follows: "And thin the said dough with the milk; if you have no milk, take rosewater and a little pot-broth, and mix it all together. And then, with some hen feathers, spread the said dough over the hen and rub it. And anoint it, and be careful that you do not thin it too much because it will not be able to cling to the flesh of the hen. And anoint it enough times that this dough or sauce forms a crust on the hen as thick as the crust of an *empanada*...and turn the spit in such a manner that the said dough stays upon the hen."

In case you're looking for a non-medieval way to make your empanadas, the traditional fold-over method is best.

MASA DE EMPANADAS

The mark of a good empanada is a crisp, fluffy crust that has enough strength to hold the filling, but enough softness in the dough to provide a tender bite and a slight chew. There are several types of empanadas in Latin America, and I wanted to create a recipe that would allow you to fill it several different ways according to different cultures. With this dough, you will be able to achieve the perfect empanada. Make it in bulk, and then focus on using several unique fillings and shaping techniques.

In a large bowl, combine the flour and butter and use your fingers to break the butter apart into the flour until there's a crumbly texture and no large butter chunks. Slowly add the ice-cold water with one hand while mixing with the other.

Once it comes together and there isn't much dry flour left in the bowl, turn it out onto a work surface and knead it until it is smooth, about 5 minutes. Let the dough rest in the fridge, covered with plastic wrap, for at least 30 minutes before using.

Follow the instructions for rolling and cutting the dough in each of the following empanada recipes in this chapter.

383 g (3 c + 1½ Tbsp) all-purpose flour
141 g (10 Tbsp) unsalted butter, chilled and cubed
113 g (scant ½ c) ice-cold water
8 g (2½ tsp) kosher salt
1 large egg plus 1 large egg yolk

MASA DE EMPANADAS INTEGRAL

For these whole grain empanadas, we will be using 66 percent whole wheat flour and sourdough discard to add a significant amount of flavor. I absolutely love the nutty flavor that comes through to complement the salty fillings of empanadas, so this version of the dough has become a staple in my household. You can use this dough recipe for any of the empanadas in this section that call for a flour-based empanada dough.

In a large bowl, combine the whole wheat flour, all-purpose flour, salt, and butter and use your fingers to break the butter apart into the flour until there's a crumbly texture and no large butter chunks.

Slowly add the ice-cold water with one hand while mixing with the other. Once it comes together and there isn't much dry flour left in the bowl, add the sourdough discard. Mix until it begins to come together and then turn it out onto a work surface and knead it until it is smooth, about 5 minutes.

Wrap the dough with plastic wrap and let rest in the fridge for at least 30 minutes before using.

Follow the instructions for rolling and cutting the dough in each of the following empanada recipes in this chapter.

200 g (1⅔ c) whole wheat flour
100 g (¾ c + 1 Tbsp) all-purpose flour
113 g (1 stick) unsalted butter, cold and cubed
50 g (3½ Tbsp) ice-cold water
75 g (⅓ c + ½ Tbsp) sourdough discard, chilled
5 g (1½ tsp) kosher salt
1 large egg

MASA DE EMPANADAS/ PASTELITOS DE MAÍZ

Makes
DOUGH FOR
10 PASTELITOS/
EMPANADAS

200 g (1¾ c) masa harina or
(1⅓ c) masarepa
8 g (2½ tsp) kosher salt
200 g (⅔ c + 3 Tbsp) water, plus
50 g (3½ Tbsp) more if using
masarepa

Sometimes in Latin America the words *empanada* and *pastelito* are used interchangeably, especially when it comes to fried versions. The one thing that is for certain is that a corn-based dough is widely used and stuffed with an incredible variety of fillings. This dough can be made with either masa harina or masarepa, depending on the flavor profile and country the final product originates from. You want to make sure that you hydrate the flour enough so that you don't end up with a crumbly dough. I love to add a little bit of paprika or achiote to this recipe to add color and flavor directly into the dough, which is typical in a Honduran variety called Pastelitos de Perro (page 335). Feel free to add or subtract seasonings to this dough to give your fried empanadas/ pastelitos your own twist.

If you use masarepa instead of masa harina, you will need to add a little more water. In countries like Venezuela and Colombia, the precooked corn flour known as masarepa is used instead of masa harina for cooking.

In a large bowl, combine the masa harina, salt, and any spices desired and mix to homogenize.

Slowly add the water in 3 increments with one hand and mix with the other hand.

Once the dough comes together and is sticky and soft, but pliable, cover and let it rest for 10 minutes.

Divide the dough into 80-g (⅓ c) dough balls and round them with your hands. Let them rest for 5 minutes before filling and frying them according to each recipe.

EMPANADAS DE PINO

≈≈≈≈≈≈≈≈≈≈≈

Makes

ABOUT 8 EMPANADAS

⌣⌣⌣⌣⌣⌣⌣⌣⌣⌣⌣

½ medium yellow onion, chopped
2 cloves garlic, minced
5 g (1 tsp) neutral oil
½ cube beef bouillon
120 g (½ c) water
225 g (8 oz) ground beef
1 g (½ tsp) ground cumin
3 g (1 tsp) paprika
1 tsp (3 g) chili powder
1 tsp (3 g) kosher salt
1½ tsp (3 g) freshly ground black pepper
1 recipe Masa de Empanadas (regular, page 315, or whole grain, page 317)
2 large eggs-cooled completely, quartered horizontally
16 black olives (2 per empanada), pitted
15 g (1½ Tbsp) raisins
1 large egg, for the egg wash
Pinch kosher salt, for the egg wash

In Chile, this is the most traditional and commonly eaten empanada, which I first learned about when I lived with Chilean roommates studying abroad in New Orleans. They would frequently cook dishes and bake casseroles made with pino, a filling of immaculately seasoned ground beef, raisins, black olives, and boiled egg. I was intrigued by pino, but even more intrigued once we started putting it into flaky dough and baking empanadas.

The word *pino* is derived from the the word *pinu* (meaning chunks of cooked meat) of the Indigenous language Mapudungen spoken by the Mapuche. Naturally, during the Spanish conquest there were new ingredients available for the Indigenous and local cooks, who created quite a thing of beauty with these empanadas, which also have a distinct-looking fold to seal the edges—a unique and tasty tradition.

In a large skillet over medium heat, sauté the onion and garlic in the oil for a couple of minutes, until the onion becomes translucent. Add the bouillon and water, and stir until homogenous.

Add the ground beef, cumin, paprika, chili powder, salt, and pepper and stir. Break the ground beef up into small, even pieces.

Increase the heat to medium-high and let the mixture cook until the ground beef is no longer pink, 2 to 3 minutes. Reduce the heat to medium and let simmer for 5 more minutes, stirring occasionally, until the meat is cooked all the way through. Set aside and let the mixture cool completely.

Preheat the oven to 400°F.

Lightly flour a work surface and roll out the empanada dough. Use a bowl, knife, or cookie cutter to cut it into 8 round pieces that are roughly 6 inches in diameter.

Add a heaping tablespoon (20 g) of the ground beef mixture to the middle of each empanada disk, one slice of boiled egg, 2 olives, and 4 to 5 raisins.

To seal the empanada de pino, close the empanada into a semicircle. Next, fold the top down about 3 centimeters so that the top side now becomes a straight line. Finally, fold the sides over to achieve a trapezoid shape. Place the empanadas on a parchment-lined sheet pan.

Whisk together the egg and pinch of salt to make the egg wash. Brush each empanada with the egg wash and bake for 20 minutes until lightly golden brown.

EMPANADAS DE CARNE CORTADA AL CUCHILLO

The regionality of Argentina's empanada scene is quite mind-blowing. The different provinces in the country offer unique varieties of this culinary staple, ranging from empanadas stuffed with llama to a variety stuffed with milk-soaked rice. If there is one thing that should be on your bucket list, it's a road trip in Argentina to try all these baked treats. One of the most well-known and widely consumed empanadas, hailing from the Tucumán province, uses chopped cuts of beef instead of ground meat, with onion, peppers, and spices. The key is to make sure the meat is tender and juicy for an empanada bite that will surely be unforgettable.

Chop the meat into cubes, roughly ½ inch by ½ inch (smaller than what a pair of dice would be, for reference.) Heat a large skillet over medium heat with a bit of oil or butter.

In a bowl, toss the beef with the cumin, paprika, salt, and pepper. Add to the hot skillet, stirring and cooking until browned, about 4 minutes. Once the cubes of meat have all taken color and a little bit of char, remove from the skillet and set aside in a bowl to cool completely.

Leave the skillet on the heat and add the onion and garlic and stir until the onion is translucent, 3 to 4 minutes. Next, add the beef broth and white wine and cook until it starts to slightly thicken, about 6 minutes. Make sure to scrape all the bits off the side of the skillet while stirring.

Remove from the heat and let cool completely. Once the meat and the sauce have both cooled, mix in a bowl, wrap, and refrigerate overnight. You want just enough liquid to cover the meat but still have a thick consistency.

The next day, add the chopped egg and green onions to the mixture and stir to incorporate evenly.

Preheat the oven to 400°F.

Roll out the empanada dough and cut into circles roughly 6 to 7 inches in diameter.

Place a heaping spoonful of the filling into the center of the dough circles and close into a half moon. Crimp the dough with your fingers by starting on one corner and pulling up a small piece of the dough and folding it right back onto the top, with a slight twisting motion. Alternatively, use a fork to crimp it closed. See page 328 for empanada shaping tips. Place on a parchment-lined baking sheet.

In a small bowl, whisk the egg and pinch of salt to make an egg wash. Brush the empanadas with the egg wash and bake for 20 minutes or until golden brown.

---

455 g (16 oz) bife de lomo, or filet mignon
30 g (2 Tbsp) unsalted butter or neutral oil
4 g (1½ tsp) ground cumin
3 g (1½ tsp) paprika
3 g (1 tsp) kosher salt
2 g (1 tsp) freshly ground black pepper
½ onion, chopped
4 cloves garlic, minced
120 g (½ c) beef broth
120 g (½ c) dry white wine
2 hard-boiled eggs, finely chopped
75 g (½ c) green olives, pitted and roughly chopped
30 g (½ c) green onions, chopped
1 recipe Masa de Empanada (page 315), replacing butter with lard
1 large egg, for the egg wash
Pinch kosher salt, for the egg wash

TIP: Make the empanada dough and filling a day in advance and let both chill in the fridge overnight.

EMPANADAS JUGOSAS DE POLLO

Makes
6 TO 8 EMPANADAS

Another staple of Argentine empanadas is the empanada jugosa de pollo, and there are plenty of reasons why this is such a popular treat. Who doesn't want an extremely juicy bite of chicken wrapped in a perfectly crisp exterior? In fact, a friend of mine from Argentina told me that they are sometimes called empanadas de piernas abiertas, which means "legs open"—so juicy that when you eat them you've got to spread your legs to avoid a mess on your clothing. Alright, alright, that is a bit much, but the point is, with this recipe you will be able to make an irresistible and exceptionally juicy empanada.

The key here is to create your own umami-filled chicken caldo, or broth, roasting a chicken with flavor-packed veggies and spices. That caldo is then blended with all the veggies before smothering the shredded chicken.

NOTE: Make sure you have your Masa de Empanadas from page 315 handy! This dough can be chilled in the fridge ahead of time.

TIP: Make the empanada dough and filling a day in advance and let both chill in the fridge overnight.

1 whole chicken
7 g (1 Tbsp) flaky sea salt
2 g (1 tsp) freshly ground black pepper, or al gusto
15 g (1 Tbsp) olive oil
30 g (2 Tbsp) unsalted butter
½ yellow onion, chopped
½ red onion, chopped
½ leek, chopped from the lighter side
2 garlic cloves, whole
2 g (1 tsp) smoked paprika
2 g (1 tsp) garlic powder
2 g (1 tsp) ground cumin
1 bay leaf
470 g (2 c) chicken broth
1 recipe Masa de Empanadas (regular, page 315, or whole grain, page 317)
150 g (1 c) whole, pitted black or green olives
1 large egg, for the egg wash
Pinch kosher salt, for the egg wash

Preheat the oven to 475°F.

Rub the whole chicken with the flaky salt, pepper, and olive oil. Set aside.

In a pot or Dutch oven over medium heat, add the butter, yellow and red onions, leek, and garlic cloves, stirring until tender and translucent, about 5 minutes.

Add the paprika, garlic powder, cumin, and bay leaf to the pot and stir until just combined. Add the chicken broth and let simmer for 5 minutes.

Add the whole chicken to the pot, and immediately place into the preheated oven.

Let the chicken roast for a total of 1½ hours, basting the top with the broth. Let it cook until the skin is nice and browned and the bones fall off with ease.

Remove the pot from the oven and place the chicken onto a sheet pan. Do not discard the remaining broth! Once the chicken cools down, shred all the meat and remove the bones.

Add the broth to a blender. Remove the bay leaf. Blend until you create a nice, homogenous sauce.

In a large mixing bowl, add the shredded chicken and sauce, cover, and place in the fridge, ideally overnight.

The next day, roll out the masa de empanadas and cut into rounds, ideally 6 to 7 inches in diameter.

Preheat the oven to 400°F.

Remove the mixture from the fridge. It should be nice and congealed. Place a heaping tablespoon of the mixture in the center of the dough round along with two olives. Fold over and seal the dough.

There are several ways to seal an empanada. For these, you can do three crimps, a repulgue, or simply use a fork. (See page 328 for empanada shaping guidance.)

Place the empanadas on a parchment-lined sheet pan.

In a small bowl, whisk the egg and pinch of salt to make an egg wash. Brush each empanada with the egg wash and bake for about 20 minutes or until golden brown.

EMPANADAS SALTEÑAS

Although there are origins in Salta, Argentina, the empanadas known as salteñas are undoubtedly an integral part of Bolivian food culture. Salteñas are in a class of their own. The dough, with a slight sweetness, is also spiced, which gives it a unique color when compared to the dough of other oven-baked empanadas. The crust is slightly thicker, with a texture that ensures that it can stand on its own and hold the filling.

What might that filling be? Easily one of the most delicious things I've ever tasted! The soupy stew filling in salteñas is called jigote and is a gelatin-rich stew of either chicken or beef that is cooled and added to the dough. When that jigote cools, it creates a delicious layer of gelatin that is important because when the salteñas bake it releases the juices into the inside to create that soupy filling we are craving. When you are eating these, you must take care to not spill or waste any of the filling. My first time eating a salteña, even under the guidance of experienced Bolivians, still ended up in a mess all over my shirt! I have definitely gotten better over time and I've worked on creating a recipe that can replicate all of the familiar textures and flavors that make salteñas a worthy staple in any household. I decided to braise a half chicken with beer and chicken broth to get an extremely juicy and tender flavor.

FILLING

In a Dutch oven over medium-high heat, add the butter, garlic, habanero pepper, and onion and cook until fragrant, about 3 minutes. Add the cumin, salt, pepper, garlic powder, and bay leaves and stir for 2 minutes until homogenous. Finally, add the beer and the broth, stirring until simmering, then add the chicken. Reduce the heat to its lowest setting and cook for 3 to 4 hours. (Make sure you use skin-on chicken because it helps create that nice, fatty gelatin that is needed when it is cooled down overnight.) Once the chicken is cooked, tender, and falling off the bone, let it cool completely, uncovered, before covering and transferring to the fridge overnight.

DOUGH

This dough is quite special because it needs to be strong enough to stand upright, and uses achiote to give it that special, deep color familiar in salteñas. In a small saucepan over low heat, melt the lard then add the achiote powder, stir until incorporated, and remove from the heat. Let this cool completely.

In a large mixing bowl combine and evenly incorporate the flour, salt, and sugar. Add the water and egg, mixing with your hands until a rough dough is formed without much dry flour left in the bowl. Add the cooled lard and achiote mixture to the flour mixture and mix until the fat is incorporated into the dough.

FILLING

55 g (½ stick) unsalted butter
2 garlic cloves, minced
1 habanero pepper, diced
½ white onion, chopped
Ground cumin, al gusto
Kosher salt
Freshly ground black pepper, al gusto
Garlic powder, al gusto
2 bay leaves
1 beer, preferably an ale or wheat beer
470 g (2 c) chicken broth
½ whole chicken (about 4 lbs), skin on
75 g (⅓ c) diced, cooked white potato, from about 1 small potato
40 g (⅓ c) cooked green peas
3 hard-boiled eggs, sliced
12 green olives, pitted

DOUGH

80 g (6 Tbsp) lard
20 g (3 Tbsp + 1 tsp) achiote powder (not the paste)
300 g (2⅓ c + 1 Tbsp) all-purpose flour
6 g (2 tsp) kosher salt
25 g (2 Tbsp) granulated sugar
90 g (⅓ c + 1 Tbsp) water
1 large egg, for the egg wash
Pinch kosher salt, for the egg wash

(CONTINUED)

Transfer to a work surface and knead the dough for 5 to 10 minutes, with the palm of your hands pushing out and your fingertips bringing it back into the middle. Rotate, and repeat until the dough is smooth. This dough needs to be strong, so don't skip the kneading process! Wrap the dough in plastic wrap and let it rest in the fridge overnight.

ASSEMBLE THE SALTEÑAS

Divide the dough into six pieces and round them into balls. Cover them with a damp paper towel and let them rest for 10 minutes.

After the rest period, flour the dough balls lightly and use a rolling pin to flatten them into disks about 6 inches in diameter.

Take the cold chicken mixture out of the fridge, add the potatoes and peas and mix until there's a good proportion in each spoonful. Add a heaping spoonful (roughly 60 g) of the jigote, the gelatinous chicken mixture, to the center of a dough disk. Then add a sixth of the sliced boiled eggs and two olives. Fold the dough over as if it was a turnover, and pinch together both sides to create a seam. At this point you can let your salteña stand upright.

To finish off the assembly process, perform the *repulgue,* which is the process of braiding the seam to create that familiar look. Use your thumb and index finger to pull back one of the corners and fold it back in, pressing down. Slide over slightly and repeat this process throughout the whole seam of the salteña to create the braided look.

Once the salteñas are assembled, place them on a parchment-lined sheet pan. In a small bowl, whisk the egg and a pinch of salt to make the egg wash. Brush the salteñas with the egg wash and bake for 15 to 20 minutes, or until they turn a nice golden yellow. You don't want to overbake them and risk the soupy goodness flowing out.

Let the salteñas cool for 5 to 10 minutes and eat by nibbling off one of the ends and sucking out the soup first. Then take a big bite!

EMPANADAS DE JAMÓN Y QUESO

Makes
8 EMPANADAS

400 g (14 oz) cooked ham, sliced into 4 by ½-inch strips
400 g (2¾ c) cubed mozzarella cheese
2 g (1 tsp) paprika
2 g (1 tsp) garlic powder
1 recipe Masa de Empanadas (regular, page 315, or whole grain, page 317)
1 large egg, for the egg wash
Pinch kosher salt, for the egg wash

Ham and cheese is easily one of the most popular filling combinations in the history of things being made with dough. Rounding off your trip through Argentina's most commonly eaten empanadas, these are the quickest and simplest empanadas to make, and are equally delicious because you cannot go wrong with melted cheese. You can experiment with different ham cuts and cheese combinations to get to your desired place, but I opt to keep it simple with a classic cooked ham and gooey mozzarella cheese.

Preheat the oven to 400°F.

In a large bowl, combine the ham, cheese, paprika, and garlic powder and mix until evenly distributed.

Roll out the chilled masa de empanadas and cut into eight 6-inch circles. Place roughly 2 Tbsp of filling in the middle of each dough circle. Fold over into a semicircle and pinch the ends together to form a crescent shape. Place on a parchment-lined sheet pan.

In a small bowl, whisk the egg and pinch of salt to make the egg wash. Brush each empanada with the egg wash and bake for 20 minutes or until golden brown.

EMPANADAS DE PABELLÓN CRIOLLO

1 batch Masa de Empanadas/
  Pastelitos de Maíz (page 318)
680 g (1½ lbs) flank steak
Kosher salt, al gusto
Freshly ground black pepper, al
  gusto
1 red bell pepper, diced
½ medium white onion, diced
2 cloves garlic, minced
6 g (2½ tsp) onion powder
6 g (2½ tsp) garlic powder
5 g (2½ tsp) ground cumin
1 g (1 tsp) oregano
3 g (1½ tsp) smoked paprika
200 g (¾ c + 1½ Tbsp) beef
  broth
20 g (1 Tbsp + 1 tsp) tomato
  paste
Canola oil, for frying
2 ripe plantains, pan-fried until
  golden brown, cooled
150 g (1 c) cooked black beans
Crumbled queso fresco or queso
  duro, al gusto

The national dish of Venezuela, pabellón criollo, is an exemplary plate of food that has all the necessary components to leave one feeling extremely satisfied: immaculately slow-cooked flank steak, sweet and soft plantains, and a serving of perfectly cooked rice and black beans. I have had pabellón criollo in arepas and on its own, but I was pleasantly surprised to discover that this dish can be enjoyed in empanada form using a crispy corn-based dough. I mean, seriously, I just had to take a shot at achieving a perfectly fried crust while maintaining the juiciness of the meat and plantains—effectively creating the perfect balance of pabellón in just a few bites.

Sprinkle the flank steak with salt and pepper, to taste, on both sides and sear in a medium skillet over high heat for 3 minutes per side, until a crust forms. Place in a Dutch oven. Add the bell pepper, onion, garlic, onion powder, garlic powder, cumin, oregano, smoked paprika, tomato paste, and broth.

Reduce the heat to medium-low, cover, and cook for 3 hours. Once the meat is cooked and shredding apart, set aside to cool.

Divide the masa de empanadas/pastelitos de maíz into about 10 dough balls.

In a large pot, heat the canola oil to around 375°F. The oil should be around 1½ inches deep.

Flatten each dough ball. I like to use plastic wrap and a cutting board, as most tortilla presses are too small for the size we are going for. Lay down one sheet of plastic wrap, place the dough ball on it, and overlay another sheet of plastic wrap. Use a cutting board to smash the dough ball down until achieving a nice sized circle, about 8 inches in diameter.

Cut the cooked plantains lengthwise 4 times and horizontally in half to yield a total of 10 strips of plantains.

Place a heaping spoonful of steak, with a tiny bit of the juices, in the center of the dough, followed by a plantain strip and a tablespoon of black beans and crumbled cheese.

Fold over the dough and press down the edges to crimp and create a handpie shape.

Place the empanadas in the pot with the canola oil, 3 or 4 at a time, and fry for 7 to 8 minutes, or until golden brown, flipping every 2 to 3 minutes to achieve an even color. Remove from the oil and place on a paper towel–lined plate.

Serve the empanadas with the consomé (broth) from the cooked steak. It makes a great dipping sauce!

PASTELITOS DE PERRO

If this dish's name has given you some pause, it's understandable, but don't worry—it's just a funny name! It is said that the name comes from the fact that at some point in time, leftover rice, meat, and potatoes were commonly fed to dogs. These pastelitos are a quintessential street food found all over the Honduran capital, Tegucigalpa, and they are served with pickled onions, cabbage, and a slightly sweet, spicy salsa. If you need a good, quick dish for a party or gathering, look no further than this Honduran staple.

In a large skillet over medium-high heat, sauté the onion, bell peppers, and garlic for about 4 minutes, until translucent.

Add the ground beef, cilantro, garlic powder, sazón, salt, and pepper. Using a wooden spoon, break the ground beef up and evenly incorporate the seasoning and onion mixture. Cook for 2 minutes while stirring.

Add the beef stock, reduce the heat to low, and simmer until the meat is cooked through and the liquid is reduced, about 7 minutes. Once the meat is cooked, set aside and let it cool.

Combine the cooled meat with the cubed cooked potato and cooked rice until evenly mixed.

Next, divide the masa de empanadas into 10 pieces. Lay down one sheet of plastic wrap, place a dough ball on it, and overlay another sheet of plastic wrap. Use a tortilla press to flatten, but if you don't have one, use a cutting board to smash the dough ball down until achieving a flat and nice sized circle, about 6 inches in diameter.

In a large pot or cast-iron skillet over medium heat, add the canola oil, about 1½ inches deep, and heat until it reaches 375°F for the fry.

In the center of each dough disk, place roughly 2 spoonfuls of the filling. Fold the dough disk over and crimp it closed by pressing down the edges.

Fry in the canola oil for 7 to 8 minutes, or until golden brown, flipping every 2 to 3 minutes.

Once the pastelitos are crispy and golden brown, remove from the oil and place them on a cooling rack.

After they cool, plate them and top with chopped cabbage, pickled onions, salsa, and queso fresco.

FILLING

⅛ white onion, diced
¼ green bell pepper, diced
¼ red bell pepper, diced
1 garlic clove, chopped
180 g (6½ oz) ground beef
Handful chopped cilantro
5 g (2 tsp) garlic powder
5 g (1½ tsp) sazón
Kosher salt, al gusto
Freshly ground black pepper, al gusto
100 g (¼ c + 3 Tbsp) beef stock
170 g (6 oz) small gold potato, cooked and cubed
75 g (½ c) cooked white rice
Canola oil, for frying
1 recipe Masa de Empanadas/ Pastelitos de Maíz, prepared with the addition of 10 g of achiote powder (page 318)

TOPPINGS

Chopped green cabbage, al gusto
Pickled red onion, or Curtido (page 305), al gusto
Salsa Roja (page 302), al gusto
Crushed queso fresco or queso duro, al gusto

TEQUEÑOS

Makes
12 TEQUEÑOS

500 g (4 c) all-purpose flour
15 g (1 Tbsp + 2 tsp) kosher salt
80 g (5½ Tbsp) unsalted, cold
   and shredded
1 large egg
150 g (⅓ c + 5 Tbsp) water
150 g (½ c + 2 Tbsp) whole milk
50 g (¼ c) sourdough discard
Canola oil, for frying
454 g (16 oz) block of low-
   moisture mozzarella, sliced
   into twelve 5 by ½-inch strips

It is said that at some point in the nineteenth century, a very wealthy family would take vacations in the city of Los Teques in the state of Miranda, named after the Indigenous Aractoeques Carabs tribe. During these stays, the cooks used leftover pastry dough to wrap around some of the cheeses available to them and fry them into tequeños, the golden, crunchy delights that are now seen and eaten everywhere in Venezuela.

You can't have a party or gathering in Venezuela without tequeños, so if you are ever hosting a gathering and want a cheesy snack that everyone will enjoy, make these. I make the dough akin to a rough puff pastry with the addition of sourdough discard to give it a slight tang without having to undergo any fermentation.

In a large mixing bowl, combine the flour and salt and mix until incorporated. Add the shredded cold butter and use your hands to incorporate into the flour, pressing the butter between your fingertips to smooth it into the flour.

Add the egg, 25 g (1 Tbsp + 2 tsp) of the water, 25 g of the milk, and the sourdough discard. Mix until all the water is incorporated then add a bit more. You want just enough for the dough to come together and smooth out. I would recommend adding the water and milk in 25-g increments.

Dump the dough onto a floured work surface and knead lightly for a couple of minutes until the surface of the dough is smooth. Dust with flour and let rest at room temperature for 30 minutes.

While the dough is resting, in a large pot, add enough canola oil to fill up your pot three-quarters of the way and heat to about 375°F.

Roll the dough out as thinly as possible and cut out 12 strips that are roughly ½ inch thick by 18 inches long. Roll the dough over each cheese strip using a diagonal pattern and making sure each dough layer overlaps with the other.

Fry the tequeños a few at a time for about 5 minutes, or until golden brown.

Let cool briefly and serve while the cheese is still melty.

SOPA PARAGUAYA

△△△△△△△△△△△

Makes
1 LARGE SOPA

▽▽▽▽▽▽▽▽▽▽▽

30 g (2 Tbsp) unsalted butter
½ medium white onion, sliced
30 g (3 Tbsp) shallots, diced
15 g (¼ c) chopped green onions
275 g (1 c + 2 Tbsp) whole milk
9 g (2 tsp) baking powder
300 g (1¾ c + 2 Tbsp) fine
   cornmeal
50 g (¼ c) granulated sugar
2 g (1 tsp) red pepper flakes
3 g (1½ tsp) smoked paprika
1 g (½ tsp) cayenne pepper
5 g (2 tsp) garlic powder
8 g (2½ tsp) kosher salt
3 large eggs
50 g (⅓ c + 1 Tbsp) cottage
   cheese
227 g (1½ c) cubed cheese,
   preferably queso Paraguay or
   queso fresco
Corn shaved from 1 full cob

The Indigenous Guaraní people of Paraguay were contacted by Spanish colonists in search of gold and silver, which ultimately led them to introducing dairy and eggs to the diet of the Guaraní. Before being colonized, the Indigenous food tradition consisted of mostly corn, sweet potato, and cassava that was maintained by the women in the tribe while the men hunted and fished for meat.

At some point in the nineteenth century, a cook was tasked with making soup for the Paraguayan president Carlos Antonio López and was unfortunately left with more of a pasty consistency when attempting to cook the soup. This most likely happened because the cook didn't balance the amount of corn flour with the amount of liquid, ending up with a thick batter-like consistency as opposed to that of a soup. Ultimately, the cook used intuition and baked it before serving it. To the delight of the cook, the president liked it so much that it was shortly thereafter declared the national dish of Paraguay.

Sopa paraguaya is a moist, cheesy cornbread-style baked good with onions. I like to add some extra spices and shallots to push the flavor a little more to my preference. It is a simple, quick dish that is perfect for your dinner table to accompany any meal.

Preheat the oven to 350°F.

In a small skillet over medium heat add the butter and sauté the onion, shallots, and green onions until translucent. Set aside and cool.

In a large mixing bowl, cream the milk with the baking powder and corn meal until it forms a thick paste.

Add the sugar, red pepper flakes, paprika, cayenne, garlic powder, salt, eggs, and cottage cheese. Mix until creamy. Add the onion mixture, cubed cheese, and corn and mix until evenly incorporated.

Pour into a greased bundt cake pan and bake for 35 minutes, or until the center is firm.

Turn out of the cake pan and let cool before serving.

SALT COD PÂTÉ HAÏTIEN

Makes
ABOUT 8 PATTIES

225 g (8 oz) salted cod
30 g (2 Tbsp) neutral oil
½ red bell pepper, chopped
1 scotch bonnet pepper, finely diced
½ small yellow onion, chopped
2 cloves garlic, chopped
2 g (1 tsp) freshly ground black pepper
2 g (1 tsp) garlic powder
2 g (1 tsp) paprika
5 g (2 Tbsp) minced parsley
Juice of ½ lime
1 recipe Masa Hojaldre (page 272)
1 large egg, for the egg wash
Pinch kosher salt, for the egg wash

What makes a Haitian patty different than an empanada? They are similar in that both are baked or fried parcels of dough containing deeply seasoned fillings. You can eat them out of hand and they are richly satisfying. But the details make the difference. The soft, flaky crust is a bigger player in the game.

In the Caribbean, salted fish is a big part of the culinary tradition, found in many homes across the region. The Salt Cod Pâté Haïtien is filled with delicious, flaky white fish cooked with peppers and wrapped in a buttery puff pastry. What I love about this particular patty's filling is that it includes the heat of a scotch bonnet pepper, which highlights the historic relationships between Caribbean and Latin American cooking and the traditions and produce of West Africa.

One thing you must remember to do is desalt the cod by soaking it in water overnight; otherwise your dish will be entirely too salty. For this filling, it is also important to shred and chop everything a little on the thicker side so that you get the distinct textures in each mouthful after the puff pastry shatters.

In a large bowl, soak the salted cod in water covering it by an inch and put in the fridge overnight. In the morning, change out the water and let it soak again until you are ready to make your patties.

In medium pot filled with fresh water over medium heat, bring the water to a boil. Dry off the cod with a paper towel. Reduce the heat to medium-low and add the cod to the water. Cook at a bare simmer until the cod starts to flake apart and soften, about 10 minutes. Don't overcook or it will become mushy. So keep a close eye on the cod after 6 to 7 minutes. Once the fish is done, transfer to a clean bowl and shred it apart. Let it rest until it is completely cooled.

In a medium sauté pan over medium heat, add the neutral oil of your choice and, once it's heated, add the bell pepper, scotch bonnet pepper, onion, and garlic and sauté until they are translucent, about 5 minutes. Let cool completely.

Add the cooled onion mixture to the fish and add the black pepper, garlic powder, paprika, parsley, and lime juice. Stir gently until the mixture is flakey and the seasonings are distributed evenly.

Preheat the oven to 425°F and line a baking sheet with parchment paper.

Roll out the masa hojaldre into a big rectangle, until it is just 1 to 2 millimeters thick—as thin as possible without tearing. Aim for a big rectangle about 20 inches by 10 inches. The dough should be relaxed enough in the fridge so there is no butter leaking and it should have a good amount of strength to handle the rolling pin.

Using a sharp paring knife, cut the dough into eight 5-inch squares. Divide each square in half vertically so there are a total of sixteen 2½ by 5-inch rectangles.

Place one rectangle of dough on the baking sheet, add a few spoonfuls of the cod mixture in the center, drape another rectangle of dough on top, and press the edges of the top and bottom pieces of dough together to seal. Repeat for the remaining patties.

In a small bowl, whisk the egg and pinch of salt to make an egg wash. Brush the pastries liberally with the egg wash and bake for 15 minutes, or until golden brown on the top and bottom. Let cool on a wire rack and serve.

PASTELITOS DE CARNE

Of all the tasty, flaky baked goods that come out of Cuban bakeries, my favorite savory pastry is the pastelito de carne. This pastelito is an absolute treat, full of tradition and class. When it comes to the meat in between two layers of buttery, crispy crust, nothing beats a Cuban-style picadillo. Picadillo is a traditional ground meat dish that is one of the staples of Cuban cuisine, consisting usually of ground meat, tomato, raisins, and spices. If you want a meat pastry, you want a filling that can stand by itself without anything else, like cheese, to do the umami job for it.

I used to eat one of these at least once a week in Miami, and my preferred destination was a gas station near where I worked as a soccer coach. I'd stop by and get a bag full of pastelitos and a colada (a Cuban espresso whipped together with sugar) for the coaches to sip on as our pre-session energizer. I make these square because this place made them like that, but most classic versions are round. I recommend making as many of these as you can and freezing them right after they are filled so that you can bake them anytime, to savor with a cafecito in the morning or as a mid-afternoon snack.

In a large skillet over medium-high heat, add the neutral oil with the onion, bell pepper, and garlic. Sauté until translucent, about 4 minutes, then add the white wine. Next, add the ground beef, garlic powder, sazón, cumin, salt, and pepper and cook until the beef is no longer pink, about 5 minutes.

After the meat and onion/pepper mixture has cooked through, add the raisins, olives, capers, and tomato paste and cook for an additional 5 minutes to let the flavors meld. Reduce the heat to medium-low and let simmer for 5 minutes. After everything has cooked down and been incorporated, turn off the heat and let cool completely.

Preheat the oven to 425°F.

Roll out the masa hojaldre until it is almost paper thin, about 12 inches by 16 inches. The dough should be relaxed yet cool enough that there is no butter leaking and it should have a good strength to handle the rolling pin.

Using a bowl and a sharp paring knife, cut the dough into twelve 4 by 4-inch squares. Wrap the leftover dough tightly and save it in the fridge. You can use this with different doughs, such as any pan dulce, to add an extra buttery flavor as well as avoid waste.

Lay down one square of dough on a parchment-lined baking sheet and add two spoonfuls of the picadillo. Brush the outside edges of the dough with water and top with another square of dough. Gently press down to seal the pastelito. Repeat with the rest of the dough pieces and picadillo.

In a small bowl, whisk the egg and a pinch of salt to make an egg wash. Brush the pastries liberally with the egg wash and bake for 15 minutes, or until golden brown on the top and bottom. Let cool on a wire rack and serve.

Ingredients:

- 30 g (2 Tbsp) neutral oil, like grapeseed or canola
- ¼ yellow onion, diced
- ¼ medium red bell pepper, diced
- 2 garlic cloves, minced
- 60 g (¼ c) dry white wine
- 225 g (8 oz) ground beef
- 3 g (1½ tsp) garlic powder
- 3 g (1½ tsp) sazón
- 3 g (1½ tsp) ground cumin
- Kosher salt, al gusto
- Freshly ground black pepper, al gusto
- 35 g (¼ c) raisins
- 35 g (¼ c) green olives stuffed with pimento
- 20 g (2 Tbsp) capers
- 225 g (8 oz) can tomato paste
- 1 recipe Masa Hojaldre (page 272)
- 1 large egg, for the egg wash

PASTELITOS DE GANDULES Y HONGOS

Makes
8 PASTELITOS

225 g (8 oz) portabello mushrooms, chopped
30 g (2 Tbsp) unsalted butter
¼ yellow onion, diced
2 garlic cloves, minced
112 g (4 oz) gandules, cooked and drained (canned or boxed is fine!)
3 g (1 tsp) garlic powder
3 g (1 tsp) sazón
3 g (1 tsp) ground cumin
Kosher salt, al gusto
Freshly ground black pepper, al gusto
1 recipe Masa Hojaldre (page 272)
1 large egg, for the egg wash

Although not exactly a combination that can be commonly found at Cuban bakeries, I thought it would be nice to have a vegetarian option for a savory pastelito. I have recently come to enjoy preparing mushrooms in more complex ways that allow them to satiate me the same way meat does. The biggest tip I've picked up along the way is to make sure they hit dry heat first, before adding any oils or moisture! Gandules, or pigeon peas, are one of the most commonly eaten foods in the Caribbean and they add nice texture and extra protein to this mixture.

In a medium skillet over medium-high heat, add the mushrooms. Stir for 2 minutes until they begin to take on a little color and release moisture. Add the butter, onion, garlic, gandules, garlic powder, sazón, cumin, salt, and pepper and sauté until the mushrooms, onions, and gandules are tender, about 3 minutes.

Preheat the oven to 425°F.

Roll out the masa hojaldre dough until it is almost paper thin, about 10 inches by 20 inches. The dough should be relaxed but cool enough so that there is no butter leaking and it should have a good strength to handle the rolling pin.

Using a knife, cut the dough into 8 squares. Wrap the leftover dough tightly and save in the fridge. You can use this with different doughs, pan dulce, to add an extra buttery flavor as well as avoid waste.

Divide each square in half vertically so you have sixteen 2½-by-5-inch rectangles.

Lay down one square of pastry dough on a parchment-lined baking sheet, add two spoonfuls of the mushroom mixture to the center, brush the outside edges with water, and top with another piece of dough. Gently press down to seal the pastelito. Repeat with the remaining dough squares and filling.

In a small bowl, whisk the egg and a pinch of salt to make an egg wash. Brush the pastelitos liberally with the egg wash and bake for 15 minutes, or until golden brown on the top and bottom. Let cool on a wire rack and serve.

PÃO DE QUEIJO

Makes
10 CHEESE BREADS

450 g (4 c) tapioca flour
138 g (1 c) whole milk
120 g (8½ Tbsp) unsalted butter
5 g (1 tsp) kosher salt
3 large eggs
85 g (¾ c) shredded white
cheddar cheese
150 g (2¾ c) finely grated
parmesan cheese

There are several versions of delicious, gluten-free cheese breads throughout Latin America, which highlights just how important cassava flour truly is, as it is a common ingredient found no matter which country you are in. Before wheat was introduced, there were several staple goods baked and consumed, and pao de queijo is one of the most recognizable. Long before the arrival of colonizers, the Indigenous Guaraní utilized cassava to make bread. However, when enslaved people arrived with the Portuguese, and they were unable to successfully plant wheat, cassava processing increased. (In order to actually consume cassava, it must be processed in a labor-intensive way as it contains cyanide.) The by-product, what is essentially tapioca flour, was used by enslaved people to supplement their diet and was baked in small balls.

After the abolition of slavery, the state of Minas was rich with farmland. Over time, eggs and fresh cheese were added to this mixture. Today, you can find pão de queijo all over the United States in Brazilian communities, or even frozen at grocery stores—but nothing beats the smell of these coming fresh out of your oven at home.

In a large mixing bowl add the tapioca flour and set aside.

In a microwave-safe bowl, add the milk, butter, and salt and microwave on high until the butter is fully melted, about 2 minutes. Let the mixture cool for 1 minute and then pour into the bowl with the tapioca flour. Using a spatula or wooden spoon, mix until there's a dry, stiff dough.

Add the eggs and mix with your hands until a thick, creamy batter forms. Then fold in the cheddar cheese and Parmesan until there's a thick mixture than can be manipulated without sticking to your hands.

Preheat the oven to 400°F.

Form the dough into roughly 10 balls. Place on a parchment-lined sheet pan and bake for 15 minutes, until they take on a slight color and the cheese has some dark spots.

Cool briefly and enjoy!

CUÑAPÉS

Makes
12 CUÑAPÉS

50 g (3½ Tbsp) unsalted butter
40 g (2½ Tbsp) whole milk
150 g (1⅓ c) tapioca flour
1 g (¼ tsp) baking powder
1 large egg
260 g (1¾ c + 2 Tbsp) crumbled
**   queso fresco**

In Ecuador, these are called pan de yuca, but you might be more familiar with the Brazilian version pão de queijo. In Paraguay and Argentina they are known as chipas, and in Bolivia they are known as cuñapés. High in the mountains of Ecuador, I encountered a delightful pan de yuca on a bus en route to Otavalo. I hope you will experience intense happiness when your kitchen is full of this aroma and you share the cuñapés with friends and family.

Preheat the oven to 400°F and line a sheet pan with parchment paper.

In a small saucepan over medium heat, add the butter and milk and heat without it reaching a boil. Aim for a simmer here. Remove from the heat and set aside.

In a large mixing bowl, combine the flour, baking powder, and milk mixture and add the egg and queso fresco. Mix vigorously with your hands until there's a uniform and smooth mixture. Cover and let the mixture rest for 10 minutes.

Divide the mixture into twelve 60-g (about ¼ c) pieces, then line them up, 3 by 4, on the sheet pan. Line more of them together, if desired, just be aware they might touch, which can affect the bake.

Bake for 20 minutes, or until golden brown and you see some of the cheese pop out and ooze a little bit. Cool them on a wire rack before serving.

PANDEBONO

150 g (1 c) masarepa
75 g (⅔ c) tapioca flour
15 g (1 Tbsp + 1 tsp) granulated sugar
270 g (1¾ c + 3 Tbsp) crumbled queso fresco
2 large eggs
80 g (⅓ c) whole milk, warm

It's hard to be in Colombia and not think about eating pandebono at every waking moment. From street vendors, to restaurants, to hotel breakfasts, pandebono is everywhere and always fresh. The taste for these warm, cheesy bites grew on me over time—I was so busy eating arepas that I didn't explore the pandebono scene as often as I probably should have while I was there. Thankfully, at the time I was living in Miami so I didn't have to look too hard to find pandebono back home.

There is an art to making these light, cheesy, and fluffy. Unlike pão de queijo, pandebono includes precooked corn flour, also known as masarepa. Given this, it can be easy to make these a little too dense, so using the right amount of water and cheese is important.

In a mixing bowl, combine the masarepa, tapioca flour, and sugar and mix until homogenous, making sure to evenly incorporate the masarepa to avoid any clumps.

Add the queso fresco, eggs, and warm milk. You can warm the milk in the microwave or the stovetop, just make sure it does not get hot. Add the milk 40 g (2½ Tbsp) at a time, squeezing and kneading lightly between additions.

After all the milk has been added, mix with both hands and turn out onto a work surface. Lightly knead the dough, just to get it together, cover with a damp paper towel or cloth, and let rest for 20 minutes.

Preheat the oven to 400°F.

Divide the dough into ten 60-g (about ¼ c) pieces. Shape the pandebono into balls or rings, depending on your preference. Place them on a parchment-lined sheet pan and bake for 20 minutes, until golden brown.

Let them cool on a wire rack and then serve. These are best eaten as is, perhaps with a cup of coffee or simply as a snack.

GLUTEN-FREE SOURDOUGH STARTER

Makes
200 GRAMS OF SOURDOUGH STARTER

To make the gluten-free bread recipes that follow, begin with this amaranth sourdough starter.

200 g (1¾ c + 3 Tbsp) amaranth flour, for all days of starter creation
200 g (⅔ c + 3 Tbsp) water, for all days of starter creation

Developing a gluten-free sourdough loaf has become more interesting to me as I use more Indigenous Latin American grains like amaranth as an addition to yeasted and sourdough breads. The more I taste amaranth, the more I realize how perfect it is to make healthy, nutritious bread. Its nutty, sweet, yet deeply earthy qualities are the ideal base for a gluten-free preferment. As the name gluten-free suggests, there may not be much structure in this dough, as fermentation and dough development work much differently, but I have found a way to make this a great alternative to regular bread with only the addition of psyllium husk, the fibrous powder made from the plant *Plantago ovata*.

On the first day, in a medium jar, mix 50 g (½ c) of the amaranth flour and 50 g (3½ Tbsp) of the water and cover. Make sure there is no dry flour left in the jar. Let this mixture sit at room temperature for 2 days. Repeat this process 2 more times, discarding half of the mixture each time, meaning you will have a total of 3 feedings over the course of 7 days.

You might not see the exact type of rise and fall that you see with wheat flour sourdough, but you will definitely notice large bubbles, increased size, and a similarly funky aroma. This starter does not have much strength to it, and when punctured, it is very soft and crumbly.

Once you see an increase in size and bubbles throughout the mixture every time you feed it, then you will know that it is ready to incorporate into the gluten-free sourdough bread mixes.

Makes
6 BOLILLOS

GLUTEN-FREE BOLILLO

Of all the different bolillo types in this book, this was the most challenging to figure out. Bolillos are, in theory, light, airy, and crispy. Achieving these textures without the benefit of using a normal preferment and wheat flour that can create a gluten network is not easy. However, if you need to eat gluten-free and are craving a bolillo, this recipe will get you where you need to be.

One ingredient I suggest you get is psyllium husk. This acts as a binding agent that allows the dough to stay together during the mixing and shaping process. Additionally, the Gluten-Free Sourdough Starter (page 353) acts as the means of leavening and fermentation—but feel free to add a pinch of gluten-free baker's yeast to this mix for an extra rise, if necessary.

⁄⁄⁄

GLUTEN-FREE SOURDOUGH PREFERMENT

In a tall jar or large container with a lid, mix the brown rice flour, amaranth flour, sorghum flour, water, and mature sourdough starter with your hand or a fork. Ensure that no dry flour remains at the bottom of the jar.

Cover the container and let it rest at room temperature (ideally between 70° and 80°F) for 12 hours. It should roughly double in size and have a bubbly structure on the sides. Once the preferment is ready to use, you can start baking straight away or place it in your fridge for later use (up to 1 day).

DOUGH

Since there is no gluten development, the mixing process for the gluten-free bolillo is uncomplicated. In a small bowl, add the psyllium husk powder and 75 g (¼ c + 1 Tbsp) of the water and whisk to make a slurry. Let sit for 10 minutes.

In a large bowl, combine the white rice flour, brown rice flour, tapioca starch, gluten-free sourdough preferment, salt, fresh yeast, psyllium husk slurry, and 235 g (1 c) of the water and mix until all the water is absorbed. It will likely be quite dry. Try to avoid making a soupy mixture and flooding the flours with all the water at once. Add the remaining water in 40-g (3 Tbsp) increments, mixing and pressing down with your fist to make sure it all gets absorbed.

Turn out the dough onto a work surface and gently knead for just a few seconds, enough to get it together into a ball. Place the dough in a lightly oiled bowl, cover, and let ferment for 5 hours at room temperature.

After the fermentation period, turn the dough out onto a work surface and divide it into six 200-g pieces (about the size of large tomatoes). The dough will feel strange, with a bouncy, firm texture, and that is okay. To shape it, don't be as carefree as with a yeasted dough since there is not much keeping it together like a strong gluten network typically found after the bulk fermentation period

GLUTEN-FREE SOURDOUGH PREFERMENT

50 g (⅓ c + 1 Tbsp) brown rice flour
25 g (¼ c) amaranth flour
25 g (3 Tbsp) sorghum flour
100 g (¼ c + 3 Tbsp) warm water
50 g (¼ c) mature gluten-free sourdough starter

DOUGH

50 g (heaped ⅓ c) psyllium husk powder
370 g (1½ c + 1 Tbsp) water
250 g (1¾ c) white rice flour
200 g (1½ c + 1 Tbsp) brown rice flour
50 g (⅓ c + 2 Tbsp) tapioca starch
200 g (1 scant c) gluten-free sourdough preferment
15 (1 Tbsp + 2 tsp) kosher salt
5 g fresh yeast

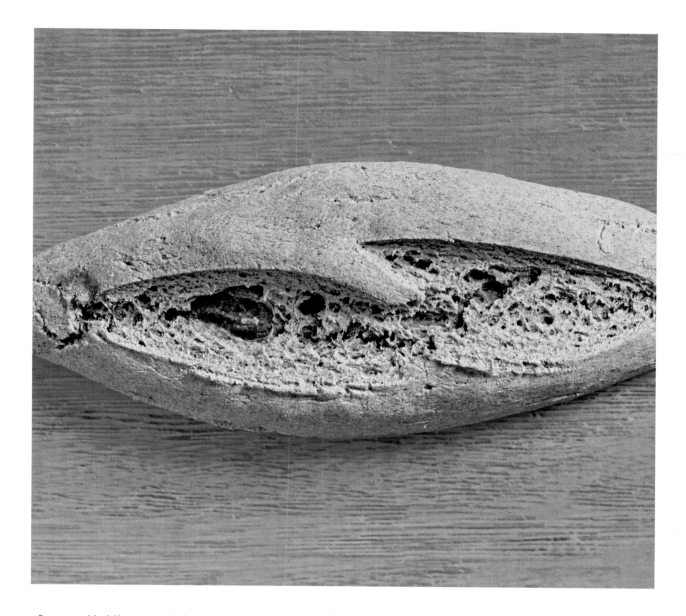

of a yeasted bolillo. Instead of tucking the dough into itself and creating tension, simply roll the dough into the familiar bolillo shape and point the edges.

Place the bolillos on a canvas cloth or cutting board and let proof at room temperature for 2 hours,

After the first hour, place a baking stone or steel inside the oven and preheat to 500°F.

Place the bolillos on a loading peel or thin cutting board lined with parchment paper and slash once down the middle with a knife or razor blade, mist them using a spray bottle of water, and load into the oven. Reduce the heat to 475°F and bake for 25 minutes, or until golden brown.

Let the bolillos cool completely for a couple of hours before tearing into them. Unlike yeasted bread, I find that this type of gluten-free bread needs to fully cool after baking to see maximum results in the inside texture.

PAN DE AMARANTO

This book would be incomplete without an homage to amaranto—a poem, a love song, or a recipe...take your pick. I am in love with amaranth and the qualities it brings to the table. It also happens to have the power to help end hunger in Latin America due to it being a complete protein with essential amino acids.

Learning how to bake with amaranth has been a benefit of writing this book, because I now know how much I have to learn about the sustainability and resilience of the grain—it has withstood the test of colonization; the Spanish outlawed growing it in Central America. Having Central American roots and using a grain that was supposed to be eradicated is a special feeling, and I am excited to share this naturally gluten-free loaf with you.

GLUTEN-FREE SOURDOUGH PREFERMENT

In a tall jar or large container with a lid, mix the amaranth flour, white rice flour, sorghum flour, water, and mature gluten-free sourdough starter with your hand or a fork. Ensure that no dry flour remains at the bottom of the jar.

Cover the container and let it rest at room temperature (ideally between 70° and 80°F) for 12 hours. It should roughly double in size and have a bubbly structure on the sides. Once the preferment is ready to use, you can start baking straight away or place it in your fridge for later use (up to 1 day).

DOUGH

In a large bowl, combine the amaranth flour, brown rice flour, cassava flour, psyllium husk, preferment, tapioca starch, honey, and 250 g (1 c + 1 Tbsp) of the water and mix until you have no dry flour left. It will feel like a clumpy paste.

Add the salt and the remaining water and mix until incorporated. You are aiming for a dough that feels like a soft paste, but with a slightly firm bounce to it. It will not have much strength. Cover and let ferment for 5 hours at room temperature.

After the bulk fermentation, the dough is going to be sticky and slightly paste-like, but should have a uniform consistency. Dump onto a work surface and gently form it into a cylinder.

Grease an 8 by 8-inch baking pan and place the dough inside. Brush water on the surface of the dough with a pastry brush and sprinkle liberally with the sesame seeds. Let the dough proof at room temperature for 2 hours.

During the last hour of the proof, preheat the oven to 500°F.

Slash the dough once or twice down the middle with a knife and bake for 40 minutes. Make sure the oven rack is in the middle to prevent burning the bottom.

Cool completely for 2 hours before slicing.

GLUTEN-FREE SOURDOUGH PREFERMENT

60 g (½ c + 1½ Tbsp) amaranth flour
50 g (⅓ c + ½ Tbsp) white rice flour
50 g (⅓ c + ½ Tbsp) sorghum flour
150 g (½ c) warm water
80 g (⅓ c + 1 Tbsp) mature gluten-free sourdough starter

DOUGH

350 g (3⅓ c + 1 Tbsp) amaranth flour
50 g (⅓ c + 1 Tbsp) brown rice flour
50 g (⅓ c + ½ Tbsp) cassava flour
25 g (3 Tbsp) psyllium husk powder
200 g (1 scant c) gluten-free sourdough preferment
50 g (⅓ c + 2 Tbsp) tapioca starch
15 g (2 tsp) honey
300 g (1¼ c + 1 tsp) water
10 g (2 tsp) salt
Sesame seeds, al gusto

PAN DE SORGO

Native to Africa, sorghum was introduced to the Americas roughly two hundred years ago, and it is now highly sought after for a variety of cuisines and nourishment. In the late 1960s and '70s, sorghum production doubled, and even tripled, in some countries in Central and South America. Oddly enough, most sorghum is used to feed animals or as a backup plan in case there is an issue with corn crops one day. That said, it is extremely healthy and rich with antioxidants and minerals, so using sorghum flour for a loaf of bread will give you a hearty canvas with which to accompany your meals or snack on by itself.

GLUTEN-FREE SOURDOUGH PREFERMENT

In a tall jar or large container with a lid, mix the brown rice flour, sorghum flour, water, and mature sourdough starter with your hand or a fork. Ensure that no dry flour remains at the bottom of the jar.

Make sure the container is covered and let it rest at room temperature (ideally between 70° and 80°F) for 12 hours. It should roughly double in size and have a bubbly structure on the sides. Once the preferment is ready to use, you can start baking straight away or place it in your fridge for later use (up to 1 day).

DOUGH

In a large bowl, combine the sorghum flour, white rice flour, tapioca starch, psyllium husk, 250 g (1 c + 1 Tbsp) of the water, and gluten-free sourdough preferment and mix until you have no dry flour left. It will feel like a clumpy paste, and that's okay.

Add the salt and the remaining water and mix until incorporated. Cover and let ferment for 4 hours at room temperature. Transfer to the fridge to ferment overnight, roughly 10 hours.

After the cold fermentation, the dough is going to be firm but it should have a uniform consistency. Dump it onto a work surface and gently form it into a cylinder. Since the dough is cold and slightly firm, you might need to work it a little bit more than usual to get it into the cylinder shape. It is okay if it tears a little bit or offers resistance. The most important thing is to get it into the pan.

Grease an 8 by 8-inch baking pan and place the dough inside. Brush water on the surface with a pastry brush and sprinkle liberally with the rolled oats. Let the dough proof at room temperature for 3 hours.

During the last hour of the proof, preheat the oven to 500°F.

Slash the dough once or twice down the middle with a knife and bake for 40 minutes. Make sure the oven rack is in the middle to prevent burning the bottom.

Cool completely for 2 hours before slicing.

GLUTEN-FREE SOURDOUGH PREFERMENT

110 g (¾ c + 1½ Tbsp) brown rice flour
50 g (⅓ c + ½ Tbsp) sorghum flour
150 g (½ c) warm water
80 g (⅓ c + 1 Tbsp) mature gluten-free sourdough starter

DOUGH

345 g (2½ c) sorghum flour
105 g (¾ c) white rice flour
50 g (⅓ c + 2 Tbsp) tapioca starch
25 g (3 Tbsp) psyllium husk powder
300 g (1¼ c + 1 tsp) water
200 g (1 scant c) gluten-free sourdough preferment
10 g (2 tsp) salt
Rolled oats, al gusto

CHOCOLATE QUINOA BREAD

Makes
1 LOAF

Quinoa is a staple in many areas of Latin America, and using flour ground from the seed can yield a spectacular gluten-free loaf. Its sweet and nutty flavor contrasts perfectly with dark chocolate. This loaf is packed with texture and flavor, and I enjoy it as is. However, it is also wonderful as a breakfast toast with butter and jam, or to dunk into a fresh cup of coffee. The blend of quinoa, tapioca, and rice flours offers a nice texture, as the tapioca helps bind, and the psyllium husk creates a pleasantly bready texture in the absence of gluten.

GLUTEN-FREE SOURDOUGH PREFERMENT

In a tall jar or large container with a lid, mix the brown rice flour, amaranth flour, sorghum flour, water, and mature gluten-free sourdough starter with your hand or a fork. Ensure that no dry flour remains at the bottom of a jar.

Cover the container and let it rest at room temperature (ideally between 70° and 80°F) for 12 hours. It should roughly double in size and have a bubbly structure on the sides. Once the preferment is ready to use, you can start baking straight away or place it in your fridge for later use (up to 1 day).

DOUGH

In a large bowl, combine the quinoa flour, brown rice flour, tapioca starch, psyllium husk powder, gluten-free sourdough preferment salt, yeast, and 300 g (1¼ + 1 tsp) of the water and mix well until the water is absorbed.

Add the remaining water in 25-g (1 Tbsp + 2 tsp) increments, mixing and pressing down with your fist to make sure it all gets absorbed. Once absorbed, add the cooked quinoa and chocolate to the dough and lightly fold them in.

Turn out onto a work surface and gently knead the dough for just a few seconds, enough to get it together into a ball. Place the dough in a lightly oiled bowl, cover, and let ferment for 5 hours at room temperature.

After the fermentation period, turn the dough out onto a work surface and roll into a cylinder shape. The dough will definitely feel strange, with a bouncy, firm texture, and that is okay. Place on a canvas cloth or cutting board and let proof at room temperature for 2 hours

During the last hour of proofing, place a baking stone or steel inside the oven and preheat to 500°F.

Place the loaf on a loading peel or thin cutting board lined with parchment paper and slash once down the middle, mist using a spray bottle of water, and load into the oven. Reduce the heat to 475°F and bake for 40 minutes, or until a deep brown crust has formed. Let cool completely before tearing in.

GLUTEN-FREE SOURDOUGH PREFERMENT

50 g (⅓ c + 1 Tbsp) brown rice flour
25 g (¼ c) amaranth flour
25 g (3 Tbsp) sorghum flour
100 g (¼ c + 3 Tbsp) warm water
50 g (¼ c) mature gluten-free sourdough starter

DOUGH

300 g (2¾ c) quinoa flour
150 g (1 c + 3 Tbsp) brown rice flour
50 g (⅓ c + 2 Tbsp) tapioca starch
25 g (3 Tbsp) psyllium husk powder
200 g (1 scant c) gluten-free sourdough preferment
15 g (1 Tbsp + 2 tsp) kosher salt
Pinch yeast (optional)
370 g (1½ c + 1 Tbsp) water
20 g (2 Tbsp) cooked quinoa
20 g (2 Tbsp) dark chocolate chunks

BEIJU DE TAPIOCA

Makes
4 BEIJUS

170 g (1½ c) tapioca starch
620 g (2⅔ c) water

Tapioca is one of the most celebrated and commonly consumed Indigenous ingredients in Brazil. Tapioca, naturally gluten-free, is derived from the cassava root. Because it does not have much, if any, flavor, it is the perfect canvas for both sweet and savory treats. Beiju de tapioca, also commonly just called tapioca, is a crepe-like treat. It is created by hydrating tapioca starch with water and pressing it out into a powder that cooks and binds itself when it hits a hot pan. These are a great snack to stuff with butter, cheese, coconut, or fruit and are a common street food in Brazil.

In a large, clear container, combine the tapioca starch and water, cover, and set in the fridge for 30 minutes to 1 hour.

After the resting period, remove from the fridge, drain the water, preserving the tapioca, and press it through a fine sieve and into a clean bowl—it will turn into a powder.

Heat a cast-iron skillet over medium heat until the skillet is hot. Using a spoon, sprinkle a spoonful of the powder into the hot skillet. The beiju will take the form of a crepe, as the heat will cause it to bind together and be extensible. Use the back of the spoon to press it down and spread it into a circular shape, trying to avoid leaving gaps or holes.

Flip after the beiju has solidified and you are able to move it without it falling apart, about 4 minutes. Let the other side cook for the same amount of time, and then add your desired filling (butter, coconut, condensed milk, fruit, or honey). Once filled, flip one side over, sealing it into a half-moon shape. Serve immediately, with any desired toppings.

INGREDIENT CONVERSIONS

VOLUME TO WEIGHT

FLOURS	
1 c all-purpose flour	125 g
1 c bread flour	125 g
1 c whole wheat flour	120 g
1 c amaranth flour	103 g
1 c brown rice flour	128 g
1 c sorghum flour	138 g
1 c cake flour	125 g
1 c masa harina (masaharina)	112 g
1 c masarepa	152 g
1 c white rice flour	142 g
1 c coconut flour	128 g
1 c tapioca flour or starch	113 g
1 c cassava flour	135 g
1 c quinoa flour	110 g

DRY INGREDIENTS	
1 tsp instant yeast	3 g
1 tsp kosher salt	3 g
1 c granulated sugar	200 g
1 c packed grated panela	228 g
1 c roughly chopped panela	180 g
1 tsp anise seed	2 g
1 c plain bread crumbs	105 g
1 tsp cayenne pepper	2 g
1 tsp dried oregano	1 g
1 Tbsp freshly ground black pepper	6 g
1 tsp cinnamon	2 g

1 tsp red pepper flakes / crushed red pepper	2 g
1 tsp dried parsley	1 g
1 c wheat germ	112 g
1 c powdered sugar	120 g
1 c wheat bran	64 g
1 tsp ground cloves	2 g
1 c crushed pecans	120 g
1 tsp baking powder	4½ g
1 tsp baking soda	5½ g
1 c cocoa powder	85 g
1 Tbsp coconut cream powder	9 g
1 c cornstarch	140 g
1 c almond flour	100 g
1 tsp paprika	2 g
1 c cornmeal	160 g
1 c psyllium husk powder	128 g

WET INGREDIENTS	
1 c [8 oz] water (or beer, tea, coffee, stock)	235 g
1 c chicha de jora	235 g
1 c sourdough starter, preferment, or discard	212 g
1 Tbsp butter	14 g
1 stick butter	113 g
1 Tbsp vanilla extract	14 g
1 large egg	50 g

1 c milk	240 g
1 c lard	210 g
1 c ricotta	240 g
1 c vegetable oil	220 g
1 c honey	340 g
1 c heavy cream	230 g
1 c dulce de leche	320 g
1 c coconut milk	240 g
1 c rum	225 g
1 c vanilla extract	225 g
1 c sweetened condensed milk	312 g
1 c evaporated milk	240 g
1 c mantequilla rala / crema hondureña	240 g
1 c jam	320 g
1 c mayonnaise	230 g
1 Tbsp tomato paste	15 g
1 c cottage cheese	130 g

OTHER INGREDIENTS

1 c cubed quesillo	145 g
1 c pulled/grated quesillo / 1 c grated queso hondureño	120 g
1 c crumbled queso fresco / farmer's cheese	140 g
1 c finely grated Parmesan	55 g
1 c chocolate chunks	150 g
1 c raisins	150 g
1 c sesame seeds	135 g
1 c pepitas	120 g
1 c chopped cilantro	40 g
1 c chopped jackfruit	150 g
1 c fresh spinach	30 g
1 c chopped green onion	60 g
1 c chocolate chips	170 g
1 Tbsp guava jelly	20 g
1 c shredded semi-hard cheese	110 g
1 c coconut oil	215 g
1 c shredded/grated coconut	80 g
1 c diced pineapple or guava	150 g
1 c minced pineapple or papaya	160 g
1 c whole cashews	113 g
1 c chopped bananas	150 g
1 c sliced almonds	90 g

1 c cooked squash or sweet potato	200 g
1 c diced onion	140 g
1 c chopped bell pepper	150 g
1 c chopped tomato	200 g
1 c refried beans	230 g
1 c chopped olives	150 g
1 c dry beans	180 g
1 c cooked beans	150 g
1 c cooked rice	150 g
1 c capers	160 g
1 c shredded cheddar cheese	110 g
1 c packed fresh masa	236 g
1 c slivered almonds	120 g

SIZES OF DOUGH BALLS (FOR *LEAVENED* BREAD)

a medium grapefruit	300 g
a large orange	250 g to 270 g
a large tomato	200 g
a medium tomato	150 g to 160 g
a medium lemon (a little smaller than a tennis ball, bigger than a golf ball)	120 g
a small lemon	90 to 100 g
a clementine	80 g
a small clementine	50 g
a new potato	35 g
a gumball	15 to 20 g

VEGETABLES

1 medium russet potato	150 g
1 large russet potato	200 g
1 c cooked spinach, pre-wringing	250 g
1 c cooked spinach that's been wrung out	80 g
1 c packed shredded lettuce	60 g
1 c chopped jalapeños	158 g
1 medium sweet potato	180 g

FURTHER READING

I am not a historian, just a baker, so I have relied on the expertise of others to help me develop my understanding of the history I share alongside the recipes in this book. If you are interested in diving deeper into this subject, I suggest starting with some of these sources.

César Morales, Julio. 2019. "Sin Mayonesa." *The Third Rail*, 19 Oct. 2019. thirdrailquarterly.org/sin-mayonesa/. Accessed 16 Jan. 2024.

Coe, Sophie D. 2015. *America's First Cuisines*. Texas: University of Texas Press.

Ducey, Michael T. 2017. "Douglas W. Richmond, Conflict and Carnage in Yucatán: Liberals, the Second Empire and Maya Revolutionaries, 1855–1876 (Tuscaloosa, AL: University of Alabama Press, 2015), pp. xv + 177, $49.95, Hb, E-Book." *Journal of Latin American Studies*, vol. 49, no. 2, (29 March): 392–394. https://doi.org/10.1017/s0022216x17000153. Accessed 11 July 2022.

Frens-String, Joshua. 2021. *Hungry for Revolution*. California: University of California Press. Accessed 11 July 2022.

Guzzo, Paul. 2018. "Ybor Institution Struggles to Find People Who Can Bake Cuban Bread like It's 1915." *Tampa Bay Times*, March 22, 2018, www.tampabay.com/news/business/Ybor-institution-struggles-to-find-people-who-can-bake-Cuban-bread-like-it-s-1915_166528175/. Accessed 16 Jan. 2024.

Hanna, Kathryn Abbey. 1954. "The Roles of the South in the French Intervention in México." *The Journal of Southern History*, vol. 20, no. 1: 3–21. www.jstor.org/stable/2954576, https://doi.org/10.2307/2954576. Accessed 6 July 2022.

Laperruque, Emma. 2018. "The Tricky, Twisty History of Flour Tortillas." *Food52*, March 3, 2018. food52.com/blog/21752-flour-tortillas-history.

Leonard, Thomas M. 2011. *The History of Honduras*. California: Greenwood.

Mahler, Scott. 2018 "The Real History of the Cuban Sandwich." *Sarasota Magazine*, October 26, 2018. www.sarasotamagazine.com/eat-and-drink/2018/10/the-true-history-of-the-cuban-sandwich.

Morton, Paula E. 2014. *Tortillas: A Cultural History*. New Mexico: University of New México Press. Accessed 11 July 2022.

Muntsch, Albert. 1961. "Xaibe: A Mayan Enclave in Northern British Honduras." *Anthropological Quarterly*, vol. 34, no. 2 (April): 121. www.jstor.org/stable/3317075, https://doi.org/10.2307/3317075. Accessed 26 June 2022.

Raichlen, Steven. 1993. "Sandwiches: The Cuban Connection." *Washington Post*, January 27, 1993. www.washingtonpost.com/archive/lifestyle/food/1993/01/27/sandwiches-the-cuban-connection/d8311781-3959-4401-8f15-05df88987854/. Accessed 16 Jan. 2024.

Ralat, Jose R. 2020. "Tex-Mexplainer: Nixtamalization Is the 3,500-Year-Old Secret to Great Tortillas." *Texas Monthly*, August 14, 2020. www.texasmonthly.com/food/tex-mexplainer-nixtamalization-is-the-3500-year-old-secret-to-great-tortillas/.

Richard, Analiese. 2022. "Chapter 4: 'Sin Maíz No Hay País': Citizenship and Environment in México's Food Sovereignty Movement." *Environment and Citizenship in Latin America*. New York: Berghahn Books, vol. 101 (December): 59–76. https://doi.org/10.1515/9780857457486-005. Accessed 11 July 2022.

Rooney, LW, and Sergio O Serna-Saldivar. 2015. *Tortillas: Wheat Flour and Corn Products*. Oxford, UK: Woodhead Publishing and AACC International Press.

Simmons, Erica S. 2016. *Sin Maíz No Hay País: The Mexican Tortillazo Protests*. Cambridge, UK: Cambridge University Press.

Smith, Jake. "Royal Menus—Emperor Maximilian—Mexi." *Royal Menus*. www.royal-menus.com/emperormaximillian-i-of-México-menu-1857. Accessed 16 Jan. 2024.

Spata, Christopher. 2021. "Actually, the Cuban Sandwich Was Not 'Invented' in Tampa, Says Historian." *Tampa Bay Times*, October 22, 2021. www.tampabay.com/life-culture/history/2021/10/22/actually-the-cuban-sandwich-was-not-invented-in-tampa-says-historian/. Accessed 16 Jan. 2024.

Travis, Helen Anne. 2015. "Business Still Booms at Cuban Bread's Birthplace: 100-Year-Old Florida Bakery." *The Guardian*, November 2, 2015. www.theguardian.com/us-news/2015/nov/02/cuban-bread-birthplace-100-year-old-florida-bakery-tampa. Accessed 16 Jan. 2024.

Wrigley, Colin W., et al. 2015. *Encyclopedia of Food Grains*. Massachusetts: Academic Press.

ACKNOWLEDGMENTS

This book was a heavy undertaking and I am honored to have been able to take the time to create it. I would like to send good energy to everyone who was involved in the making of this book and supported my work.

Thank you to my brother, Glen Ford, and my two sisters, Ariana Ford and Lizzie Ford-Madrid, who have been my best friends since day one.

Thank you to my wife, Bridget Kenna, who works tirelessly with me on our several businesses. I would not be the man that I am today without her daily love, hard work, and support. I cherish our relationship and dedicate my work to providing a nice life for us.

A very, very big thank you (and hug) to Michael Szczerban. I never knew an editor could be so kind, gentle, intelligent, caring, and lovely to work with. Throughout this process, it felt like we were old friends telling each other stories and having good conversation. You have been so great to work with and this book truly would not be what it is without you involved to guide me. Thank you, Michael.

To Lauren Ortiz, Jessica Chun, Gianella Rojas, Michael Noon, Nyamekye Waliyaya, Shubhani Sarkar, Cecilia Molinari, and the entire team at Voracious/Little, Brown, your patience and enthusiasm for my work has been so great and supportive. I am so glad you have chosen to help me bring to light the beauty of *Pan y Dulce*.

To Andrianna deLone, you have been such a strong addition to my career and have helped champion and support my ideas from start to finish. I look forward to continuing to work together!

To Brittany Connerly, Maeve Sheridan, Monica Pierini, Lizzie Ford-Madrid, and Amber Stauffer, thank y'all for making the most epic photo shoot of all time! Which translates into *Pan y Dulce* being quite the beautiful book. I definitely want to work together again and I want you to know how grateful I am that you took so much time to work on this project.

To Kathryn Pauline, you did such an amazing job helping out with the measurement conversions, and so many more people will be able to bake from this book thanks to your hard work!

Big thanks to Michelle de Vera for letting me use her awesome Mooshieware pottery in some of these fabulous pictures!

A big thank you to This Is Latin America for allowing us to use the beautiful artesanias in your store for some of the pictures in this book.

Finally, I would like to thank my ancestors. I hope my interpretation of these baked goods is met with positive energy.

INDEX

Note: Page references in *italics* indicate photographs.

A

achiote, 6
active dry yeast, 14
alfajores
    about, 212
    Alfajores Blancos y Negros with Dulce de Papaya, *216*, 217
    Alfajores Chilenitos, 213, *213*
    Alfajores de Maicena, 214, *215*
    Alfajores de Miel, *220*, 221
    Naturally Leavened Alfajores con Dulce de Camote, 218, *219*
almonds
    Cocadas, *266*, 267
    Galletas de Boda, 232, *233*
    Rosca de Reyes, 177–79, *178*
altitude, 27
amaranth (quihuicha), 4
    Chocolate Quinoa Bread, 360, *361*
    Gluten-Free Bolillo, 354–55, *355*
    Gluten-Free Sourdough Starter, 353
    Pan de Amaranto, 356, *357*

Pan Rústico de Sorgo y Amaranto Tostado, 106–7, *107*
anise and anise seeds, 8
    Alfajores de Miel, *220*, 221
    Pan de Cazuela, *94*, 95–96
    Pan Chapla, *104*, 105
    Pan Chuta, 90–91, *91*
    Pan de Muerto, *174*, 175–76
    Pan de Yema, *184*, 185–86
    Pan de Yema Peruano, *66*, 67
    Picarones, *270*, 271
    Sheca, 92–93, *93*
    T'anta Wawa, 180–81, *181*
Arepa Dulce de Maíz, 204, *205*
Arepas de Queso Colombianas, 308, *309*
Arepas Reina Pepiada, *310*, 311
avocados
    Arepas Reina Pepiada, *310*, 311
    Cemita Milanesa de Pollo, 76, 77

B

bacon
    Cachitos de Jamón, 72–74, *73*
    Pan de Jamón, 187–88, *189*
bake times, 26
baking pans, 9–10
baking stone or steel, 10

Baleadas, *300*, 301
Banana and Rum Raisin Pan de Coco, 172–73, *173*
beans
    Baleadas, *300*, 301
    Empanadas de Pabellón Criollo, 332, *333*
    Pupusas de Frijol con Queso, 312, *313*
    Torta Ahogada, *99*, 101
beef
    Empanadas de Carne Cortada al Cuchillo, 322, *323*
    Empanadas de Pabellón Criollo, 332, *333*
    Empanadas de Pino, *320*, 321
    Pastelito de Carne, *342*, 343
    Pastelitos de Perro, *334*, 335
    Tripleta on Pan Sobao, *63*, 65
Beiju de Tapioca, *362*, 363
bench scrapers, 10
birote
    about, 97
    Birote Salado, 98–100
Bizcocho de Naranja, *206*, 207
Bizcocho de Ron, 200, *201*
Blue Masa Sourdough, *110*, 111–12
bok choy
    Fugazzeta de Vegetales, 126, *127*
bolillos
    Bolillo, 34–36, *35*
    Bolillo Integral, 37–39, *38*

Gluten-Free Bolillo, 354–55,
355
Jalapeño Quesillo Bolillo, 40–
42, *41*
Bombocado, Brazilian, 250, *251*
bowls and tubs, 10
Brazilian Bombocado, 250, *251*
bread pudding
Pudín de Pan, 222, *223*
breads. *See also* gluten-free
breads and dishes; pan
dulce; sourdough breads;
tortillas; yeasted and
hybrid doughs
mixing, shaping, and baking,
20–25
Brigadeiros, *252,* 253
butter, 9

C

cabbage
Curtido, 305, *305*
Cachitos de Espinaca y Ricota,
70, 71
Cachitos de Jamón, 72–74, *73*
cake pans, 10
cakes
Bizcocho de Ron, 200, *201*
Chocolate Tres Leches de
Coco, 196–97, *197*
Chocotorta, 258–59, *259*
Mantecada con Masa Madre,
202, 203
Quesadilla Hondureña/
Salvadoreña, 264, *265*
Torta de Ricota, *198,* 199
Torta Rogel, 226–27, *227*
Tres Leches Tradicional, 194–95,
195
Volcán de Dulce de Leche, *262,*
263
cashews
Banana and Rum Raisin Pan de
Coco, 172–73, *173*
cassava, 4. *See also* tapioca flour
or starch

Pan de Amaranto, 356, *357*
Cemita Milanesa de Pollo, *76,* 77
Champurradas, *224,* 225
cheese
Arepas de Queso Colombianas,
308, *309*
Arepas Reina Pepiada, *310,* 311
Baleadas, *300,* 301
Brazilian Bombocado, 250, *251*
Cachitos de Espinaca y Ricota,
70, 71
Cemita Milanesa de Pollo, *76,*
77
Chocotorta, 258–59, *259*
Cuñapés, *348,* 349
Empanadas de Jamón y Queso,
330, 331
Empanadas de Pabellón Criollo,
332, *333*
Fugazzeta, 122, *123*
Fugazzeta de Vegetales, 126,
127
Golfeados, 163–64, *165*
Jalapeño Quesillo Bolillo,
40–42, *41*
Media Noche Sandwich, *60,* 61
Pandebono, 350, *351*
Pan Sarnita, 68, *69*
Pan Trenza, *132,* 133
Pão de Queijo, 346, *347*
Pastelitos de Guayaba y Queso,
274–75, *275*
Pastelitos de Papaya y Queso,
280, *281*
Picos, *240,* 241
Pizza al Molde Napolitana, 130,
131
Pizza de Jamón y Morrones,
128, 129
Pupusas de Frijol con Queso,
312, *313*
Quesadilla Ecuatoriana, *248,*
249
Quesadilla Hondureña/
Salvadoreña, 264, *265*
Roles de Canela with Mango
Cream Cheese Frosting,
182–83, *183*

Rosquillas, 242, *243*
Sopa Paraguaya, *338,* 339
Stuffed Fugazzeta, *124,* 125
Tequeños, 336, *337*
Torta de Ricota, *198,* 199
Tripleta on Pan Sobao, *63,* 65
Tustacas, *244,* 245
chemical leaveners, note on, 17
cherries
Chocolate Tres Leches de
Coco, 196–97, *197*
Tres Leches Tradicional,
194–5, *195*
chica de jora
Pan Chapla, *104,* 105
chicken
Arepas Reina Pepiada, *310,*
311
Cemita Milanesa de Pollo, *76,*
77
Empanadas Jugosas de Pollo,
324–25, *325*
Empanadas Salteñas, *326,*
327–28
chilies
Curtido, 305, *305*
Salsa Picante, 101
Salsa Roja, 302, *303*
Salt Cod Pâté Haïtien, 340–41,
341
Chimichurri, *306,* 307
chocolate, 8
Alfajores Blancos y Negros with
Dulce de Papaya, *216,* 217
Brigadeiros, *252,* 253
Chocolate Churros, *236,* 237
Chocolate Dipping Sauce, 234,
235
Chocolate Quinoa Bread, 360,
361
Chocolate Tres Leches de
Coco, 196–97, *197*
Chocotorta, 258–59, *259*
Concha de Chocolate y
Jamaica, *146,* 147–48
Mallorca de Chocolate with
Guava Glaze, *156,* 157–58
Pan de Cazuela, *94,* 95–96

Pudín de Pan, 222, *223*
Volcán de Dulce de Leche, *262,* 263
Chocotorta, 258–59, *259*
churros
    Chocolate Churros, *236,* 237
    Churros de Masa Madre, 238, *239*
    Churros Tradicionales, 234–35, *235*
cilantro
    Arepas Reina Pepiada, *310,* 311
    Curtido, 305, *305*
    Roles de Pimiento Asado, *118,* 119
    Salsa Roja, 302, *303*
    Torta Ahogada, *99,* 101
cinnamon (canela), 8
    Arepa Dulce de Maíz, 204, *205*
    Chocolate Churros, *236,* 237
    Churros de Masa Madre, 238, *239*
    Churros Tradicionales, 234–35, *235*
    Coyota, *230,* 231
    Cucas, *256,* 257
    Galletas de Boda, 232, *233*
    Orejas, *282,* 283
    Pan Chuta, 90–91, *91*
    Roles de Canela with Mango Cream Cheese Frosting, 182–83, *183*
    Roscón de Arequipe, 166–67, *167*
climate variables, 27
cloves
    Cucas, *256,* 257
    T'anta Wawa, 180–81, *181*
Cocadas, *266,* 267
coconut
    Alfajores de Maicena, 214, *215*
    Banana and Rum Raisin Pan de Coco, 172–73, *173*
    Bizcocho de Ron, 200, *201*
    Brazilian Bombocado, 250, *251*
    Chocolate Tres Leches de Coco, 196–97, *197*

Cocadas, *266,* 267
Pan de Coco Tradicional, 168–69, *169*
Pudín de Pan, 222, *223*
Roasted Ginger and Caramelized Pineapple Pan de Coco, 170–71, *171*
coconut milk, 9
    Banana and Rum Raisin Pan de Coco, 172–73, *173*
    Chocolate Tres Leches de Coco, 196–97, *197*
    Curau de Milho, 254, *255*
    Flan de Coco, 246, *247*
    My Mom's Tortillas de Harina, 296–97
    Pan de Coco Tradicional, 168–69, *169*
    Roasted Ginger and Caramelized Pineapple Pan de Coco, 170–71, *171*
coffee
    Chocotorta, 258–59, *259*
Concha de Chocolate y Jamaica, *146,* 147–48
Concha Tradicional, 143–44, *145*
cookies
    alfajores, about, 212
    Alfajores Blancos y Negros with Dulce de Papaya, *216,* 217
    Alfajores Chilenitos, 213, *213*
    Alfajores de Maicena, 214, *215*
    Alfajores de Miel, *220,* 221
    Champurradas, *224,* 225
    Coyota, *230,* 231
    Cucas, *256,* 257
    Galletas de Boda, 232, *233*
    Naturally Leavened Alfajores con Dulce de Camote, 218, *219*
    Orejas, *282,* 283
    Rosquillas, 242, *243*
    Tustacas, *244,* 245
corn (maíz), 4
    Curau de Milho, 254, *255*

Mayan creation myth, 288
nixtamalization process, 289
Sopa Paraguaya, *338,* 339
cornmeal
    Sopa Paraguaya, *338,* 339
corn tortillas
    historical importance of, 288–89
    origins of, 288
    Tortillas de Maíz, 290, *291*
Coyota, *230,* 231
creaming technique, 25
Cucas, *256,* 257
Cuñapés, *348,* 349
Curau de Milho, 254, *255*
curtido
    Curtido, 305, *305*
    variations of, 304

D

desserts
    list of recipes, viii
    and pastry techniques, 25–26
digital scale, 10–11
dough scrapers, 10
Dulce de Camote, 208, *208*
dulce de leche
    Alfajores Chilenitos, 213, *213*
    Alfajores de Maicena, 214, *215*
    Chocotorta, 258–59, *259*
    Dulce de Leche, 210–11
    Pastelitos Criollos, 284, *285*
    Roscón de Arequipe, 166–67, *167*
    Torta Rogel, 226–27, *227*
    Volcán de Dulce de Leche, *262,* 263
Dulce de Papaya, 209, *209*

E

eggs
    Empanadas de Carne Cortada al Cuchillo, 322, *323*

Empanadas de Pino, *320,* 321
Empanadas Salteñas, *326,*
    327–28
empanada dough
    Masa de Empanadas, 315, *315*
    Masa de Empanadas Integral,
        316, 317
    Masa de Empanadas/Pastelitos
        de Maíz, 318, *319*
empanadas
    about, 314
    Empanadas de Carne Cortada
        al Cuchillo, 322, *323*
    Empanadas de Jamón y Queso,
        330, 331
    Empanadas de Pabellón Criollo,
        332, *333*
    Empanadas de Pino, *320,* 321
    Empanadas Jugosas de Pollo,
        324–25, *325*
    Empanadas Salteñas, *326,*
        327–28
encurtido. *See* curtido
evaporated milk
    Chocolate Tres Leches de
        Coco, 196–97, *197*
    Flan de Coco, 246, *247*
    Tres Leches Tradicional, 194–
        95, *195*

F

fats, 8–9
figs
    Rosca de Reyes, 177–79, *178*
fish. *See* Salt Cod
Flan de Coco, 246, *247*
flax linen cloth, 11
flours
    all-purpose flour, 5–6
    bread flour, 6
    pastry and cake flour, 6
    rye flour, 6
    whole spelt flour, 6
    whole wheat or whole grain
        flour, 6
flour tortillas

My Mom's Tortillas de Harina,
    296–97
Sourdough Discard Tortillas,
    298–99, *299*
Tortillas de Harina de Trigo,
    292–93, *293*
Tortillas de Harina Integral
    (Whole Grain Flour
    Tortilla), 294–95, *295*
fresh yeast, 15
fruit. *See specific fruits*
Fugazza, 120–21, *121*
Fugazzeta, 122, *123*
Fugazzeta de Vegetables, 126, *127*

G

Galleta de Campana, *140,* 141
Galletas de Boda, 232, *233*
Gandules y Hongos, Pastelito de,
    344, 345
garlic
    Chimichurri, *306,* 307
    Pizza al Molde Napolitana, 130,
        131
    Pizza de Jamón y Morrones,
        128, 129
ginger
    Cucas, *256,* 257
    Roasted Ginger and
        Caramelized Pineapple
        Pan de Coco,
        170–71, *171*
gluten free breads and dishes
    Arepa Dulce de Maíz, 204, *205*
    Arepas de Queso Colombianas,
        308, *309*
    Arepas Reina Pepiada, *310,* 311
    Beiju de Tapioca, *362,* 363
    Brigadeiros, *252,* 253
    Chimichurri, *306,* 307
    Chocolate Quinoa Bread, 360,
        361
    Cocadas, *266,* 267
    Cuñapés, *348,* 349
    Curau de Milho, 254, *255*
    Curtido, 305, *305*

Dulce de Camote, 208, *208*
Dulce de Leche, 210–11
Dulce de Papaya, 209, *209*
Empanadas de Pabellón Criollo,
    332, *333*
Flan de Coco, 246, *247*
Gluten-Free Bolillo, 354–55,
    355
Gluten-Free Sourdough Starter,
    353
Masa de Empanadas/Pastelitos
    de Maíz, 318, *319*
Pan de Amaranto, 356, *357*
Pandebono, 350, *351*
Pan de Sorgo, *358,* 359
Pão de Queijo, 346, *347*
Pastelitos de Perro, *334,* 335
Pupusas de Frijol con Queso,
    312, *313*
Rosquillas, 242, *243*
Salsa Roja, 302, *303*
Sopa Paraguaya, *338,* 339
Suspiros, 228, *229*
Tortillas de Maíz, 290, *291*
Tustacas, *244,* 245
gluten-free and savory recipes, list
    of, ix
Golfeados, 163–64, *165*
grains, 4–6
guava
    Mallorca de Chocolate with
        Guava Glaze, *156,* 157–58
    Pastelitos de Guayaba y Queso,
        274–75, *275*
    Rosca de Reyes, 177–79, *178*

H

Hallullas, 138, *139*
ham
    Cachitos de Jamón, 72–74, *73*
    Empanadas de Jamón y Queso,
        330, 331
    Media Noche Sandwich, *60,* 61
    Pan de Jamón, 187–88, *189*
    Pizza de Jamón y Morrones,
        128, 129

Tripleta on Pan Sobao, *63,* 65
herbs. *See* cilantro; oregano;
    parsley
hibiscus tea
    Concha de Chocolate y
        Jamaica, *146,* 147–48
humidity, 27

I

ingredient conversions, 366–67
instant yeast, 14

J

Jalapeño Quesillo Bolillo, 40–42,
    41

L

laminating technique, 26
lard, 8–9
leavening, 14–17
loading peel, 11
loaf pans, 9–10

M

Mallorca de Chocolate with Guava
    Glaze, *156,* 157–58
Mango Cream Cheese Frosting,
    Roles de Canela with, 182–
    83, *183*
Mantecada con Masa Madre, *202,*
    203
Marraquetas, 102–3, *103*
masa, lime-infused, about, 289
Masa de Empanadas, 315, *315*
Masa de Empanadas Integral, *316,*
    317
Masa de Empanadas/Pastelitos de
    Maíz, 318, *319*

masa harina, 4
    Blue Masa Sourdough, *110,*
        111–12
    Champurradas, *224,* 225
    first commercialized, 289
    Masa de Empanadas/Pastelitos
        de Maíz, 318, *319*
    Pupusas de Frijol con Queso,
        312, *313*
    Rosquillas, 242, *243*
    Semita Hondureña de Maíz,
        152–53, *153*
    Tortillas de Maíz, 290, *291*
    Tustacas, *244,* 245
Masa Hojaldre, 272–73
masarepa, 4
    Arepa Dulce de Maíz, 204, *205*
    Arepas de Queso Colombianas,
        308, *309*
    Arepas Reina Pepiada, *310,* 311
    Masa de Empanadas/Pastelitos
        de Maíz, 318, *319*
    Pandebono, 350, *351*
meat. *See* beef; pork
Medialuna, 159–62, *160*
Media Noche Sandwich, *60,* 61
meringues. *See* Suspiros
milk, 9. *See also* coconut milk;
    evaporated milk;
    sweetened condensed milk
    Dulce de Leche, 210–11
    Tres Leches Tradicional,
        194–95, *195*
mixing technique, 25
Mogolla Chicharrona, 134, *135*
Mogolla Integral, *136,* 137
Mole y Camote, Pastelitos de, *278,*
    279
mushrooms
    Pastelito de Gandules y
        Hongos, *344,* 345

N

nixtamalization, 289
nuts. *See* almonds; cashews;
    pecans

O

olive oil, 9
olives
    Empanadas de Carne Cortada
        al Cuchillo, 322, *323*
    Empanadas de Pino, *320,* 321
    Empanadas Jugosas de Pollo,
        324–25, *325*
    Empanadas Salteñas, *326,*
        327–28
    Fugazzeta, 122, *123*
    Pan de Jamón, 187–88, *189*
    Pastelito de Carne, 342, *343*
    Pizza al Molde Napolitana, 130,
        131
    Pizza de Jamón y Morrones,
        128, 129
    Stuffed Fugazzeta, *124,* 125
onions
    Fugazza, 120–21, *121*
    Fugazzeta, 122, *123*
    Fugazzeta de Vegetables, 126,
        127
    Stuffed Fugazzeta, *124,* 125
orange
    Bizcocho de Naranja, *206,* 207
    Pan de Muerto, *174,* 175–76
    Rosca de Reyes, 177–79, *178*
oregano
    Chimichurri, *306,* 307
    Fugazza, 120–21, *121*
    Fugazzeta, 122, *123*
    Pizza al Molde Napolitana, 130,
        131
    Stuffed Fugazzeta, *124,* 125
Orejas, *282,* 283

P

Pan Casero, 82–84, *83*
Pan Casero Integral, 85–87, *86*
Pan de Cazuela, *94,* 95–96
Pan Chapla, *104,* 105
Pan Chuta, 90–91, *91*
Pan Cubano, 56–58, *57*
Pan de Amaranto, 356, *357*

Pandebono, 350, *351*
Pan de Cemita, 75–77, *76*
Pan de Coco Tradicional, 168–69, *169*
Pan de Jamón, 187–88, *189*
Pan de Media Noche, 59–61
Pan de Molde 100% Integral, 116–17, *117*
Pan de Molde con Ajonjolí, 113–15, *114*
Pan de Muerto, *174*, 175–76
Pan de Plátano a la Parrilla, 108–9, *109*
Pan de Sorgo, *358*, 359
Pan de Tres Puntas, 88–89, *89*
Pan de Yema, *184*, 185–86
Pan de Yema Peruano, *66*, 67
pan dulce (sweet breads)
    about, 142
    Banana and Rum Raisin Pan de Coco, 172–73, *173*
    Concha de Chocolate y Jamaica, *146*, 147–48
    Concha Tradicional, 143–44, *145*
    Golfeados, 163–64, *165*
    Mallorca de Chocolate with Guava Glaze, *156*, 157–58
    Medialuna, 159–62, *160*
    Pan de Coco Tradicional, 168–69, *169*
    Pan de Muerto, *174*, 175–76
    Pan Payaso, 190–91, *191*
    Roasted Ginger and Caramelized Pineapple Pan de Coco, 170–71, *171*
    Roles de Canela with Mango Cream Cheese Frosting, 182–83, *183*
    Rosca de Reyes, 177–79, *178*
    Roscón de Arequipe, 166–67, *167*
    Semita de Yema Integral, 149–50, *151*
    Semita Hondureña de Arroz, 154–55, *155*
    Semita Hondureña de Maíz, 152–53, *153*

T'anta Wawa, 180–81, *181*
panela, about, 7
pan francés, about, 32–33
Pan Michita, 43–45, *44*
Pan Mojicón, 53–54
Pan Payaso, 190–91, *191*
Pan Rústico de Sorgo y Amaranto Tostado, 106–7, *107*
Pan Sarnita, 68, *69*
Pan Sobao, 62–64
Pan Trenza, *132*, 133
Pão de Queijo, 346, *347*
Pãozinho, 48–49, *49*
papaya
    Alfajores Blancos y Negros with Dulce de Papaya, *216*, 217
    Dulce de Papaya, 209, *209*
    Pastelitos de Papaya y Queso, 280, *281*
parchment paper, 11
parsley
    Chimichurri, *306*, 307
Pastafrola, 260, *261*
pastelito dough
    Masa de Empanadas/Pastelitos de Maíz, 318, *319*
    Masa Hojaldre, 272–73
pastelitos
    Pastelito de Carne, 342, *343*
    Pastelito de Gandules y Hongos, *344*, 345
    Pastelitos Criollos, 284, *285*
    Pastelitos de Camote y Mole, *278*, 279
    Pastelitos de Guayaba y Queso, 274–75, *275*
    Pastelitos de Papaya y Queso, 280, *281*
    Pastelitos de Perro, *334*, 335
    Pastelitos de Piña, 276, *277*
pastries
    list of recipes, viii
    techniques for, 25–26
Pâté Haïtien, Salt Cod, 340–41, *341*
Pebete, 51, *52*
pecans

Roles de Canela with Mango Cream Cheese Frosting, 182–83, *183*
peppers. *See also* chilies
    Jalapeño Quesillo Bolillo, 40–42, *41*
    Pizza de Jamón y Morrones, *128*, 129
    Roles de Pimiento Asado, *118*, 119
    Salsa Picante, 101
    Salsa Roja, 302, *303*
Picarones, *270*, 271
Picos, *240*, 241
pie. *See* Pastafrola
pineapple
    Pastelitos de Piña, 276, *277*
    Roasted Ginger and Caramelized Pineapple Pan de Coco, 170–71, *171*
    Semita de Piña, 268, *269*
    Tres Leches Tradicional, 194–95, *195*
piping bag with tips, 11
Pirujos, 46–47, *47*
pizza
    Fugazza, 120–21, *121*
    Fugazzeta, 122, *123*
    Fugazzeta de Vegetales, 126, *127*
    Pizza al Molde Napolitana, 130, *131*
    Pizza de Jamón y Morrones, *128*, 129
    Stuffed Fugazzeta, *124*, 125
plantains
    Empanadas de Pabellón Criollo, 332, *333*
    Pan de Plátano a la Parrilla, 108–9, *109*
pork. *See also* bacon; ham
    Media Noche Sandwich, *60*, 61
    Mogolla Chicharrona, 134, *135*
    Pupusas de Frijol con Queso, 312, *313*
    Torta Ahogada, *99*, 101
    Tripleta on Pan Sobao, *63*, 65

potatoes. *See also* sweet potatoes
    Empanadas Salteñas, *326,* 327–28
    Pastelitos de Perro, *334,* 335
preferments, 15–17
pudding
    Curau de Milho, 254, *255*
    Pudín de Pan, 222, *223*
Pudín de Pan, 222, *223*
Pupusas de Frijol con Queso, 312, *313*

Q

Quesadilla Ecuatoriana, *248,* 249
Quesadilla Hondureña/ Salvadoreña, 264, *265*
quince
    Pastafrola, 260, *261*
quinoa
    about, 4–5
    Chocolate Quinoa Bread, 360, *361*

R

raisins
    Arepa Dulce de Maíz, 204, *205*
    Banana and Rum Raisin Pan de Coco, 172–73, *173*
    Empanadas de Pino, *320,* 321
    Pan de Cazuela, *94,* 95–96
    Pan de Jamón, 187–88, *189*
    Pastelito de Carne, 342, *343*
    Pudín de Pan, 222, *223*
rice (arroz)
    about, 4
    Pastelitos de Perro, *334,* 335
rice flour
    Chocolate Quinoa Bread, 360, *361*
    Gluten-Free Bolillo, 354–55, *355*
    Pan de Amaranto, 356, *357*
    Pan de Sorgo, *358,* 359

Semita Hondureña de Arroz, 154–55, *155*
rimmed sheet pans, 10
Roles de Canela with Mango Cream Cheese Frosting, 182–83, *183*
Roles de Pimiento Asado, *118,* 119
rolling pin, 11
Rosca de Reyes, 177–79, *178*
Roscón de Arequipe, 166–67, *167*
Rosquillas, 242, *243*
rum
    Banana and Rum Raisin Pan de Coco, 172–73, *173*
    Bizcocho de Ron, 200, *201*
    Flan de Coco, 246, *247*
    Pudín de Pan, 222, *223*

S

Salsa Picante, 101
Salsa Roja, 302, *303*
salt, 9
Salt Cod Pâté Haïtien, 340–41, *341*
sandwiches
    Cemita Milanesa de Pollo, *76,* 77
    Cuban sandwich origin story, 55
    Media Noche Sandwich, *60,* 61
    Torta Ahogada, *99,* 101
    Tripleta on Pan Sobao, *63,* 65
sauces. *See also* Salsa
    Chimichurri, *306,* 307
    Chocolate Dipping Sauce, 234, *235*
savory and gluten-free recipes, list of, ix
scale, 10–11
Semita de Piña, 268, *269*
Semita de Yema Integral, 149–50, *151*
Semita Hondureña de Arroz, 154–55, *155*
Semita Hondureña de Maíz, 152–53, *153*
sesame seeds
    Champurradas, *224,* 225

Pan de Cemita, 75–77, *76*
Pan de Molde con Ajonjolí, 113–15, *114*
Pan de Yema, *184,* 185–86
Pan de Yema Peruano, *66,* 67
Quesadilla Hondureña/ Salvadoreña, 264, *265*
T'anta Wawa, 180–81, *181*
Sheca, 92–93, *93*
Sopa Paraguaya, *338,* 339
sorghum (sorgo), 5
    Chocolate Quinoa Bread, 360, *361*
    Gluten-Free Bolillo, 354–55, *355*
    Pan de Amaranto, 356, *357*
    Pan de Plátano a la Parrilla, 108–9, *109*
    Pan de Sorgo, *358,* 359
    Pan Rústico de Sorgo y Amaranto Tostado, 106–7, *107*
sourdough and yeasted recipes, converting between, 18–19
sourdough breads. *See also* pan dulce; pizza
    baking timeline, 80
    Birote Salado, 98–100
    birote, about, 97
    Blue Masa Sourdough, *110,* 111–12
    Galleta de Campana, *140,* 141
    Gluten-Free Sourdough Starter, 353
    Hallullas, 138, *139*
    history of baking with sourdough, 79
    Marraquetas, 102–3, *103*
    Mogolla Chicharrona, 134, *135*
    Mogolla Integral, *136,* 137
    Pan Casero, 82–84, *83*
    Pan Casero Integral, 85–87, *86*
    Pan de Cazuela, *94,* 95–96
    Pan Chapla, *104,* 105
    Pan Chuta, 90–91, *91*
    Pan de Jamón, 187–88, *189*

Pan de Molde 100% Integral,
116–17, *117*

Pan de Molde con Ajonjolí, 113–
15, *114*

Pan de Plátano a la Parrilla,
108–9, *109*

sourdough breads (*cont.*)

Pan de Tres Puntas, 88–89,
89

Pan de Yema, *184,* 185–86

Pan Rústico de Sorgo y
Amaranto Tostado, 106–7,
107

Pan Trenza, *132,* 133

Roles de Pimiento Asado, *118,*
119

Sheca, 92–93, *93*

Torta Ahogada, *99,* 101

sourdough discard recipes

Churros de Masa Madre, 238,
239

Mantecada con Masa Madre,
202, 203

Masa de Empanadas Integral,
316, 317

Picarones, *270,* 271

Sourdough Discard Tortillas,
298–99, *299*

Tequeños, 336, *337*

sourdough preferment

preparing, 16

Sample Sourdough Preferment
Mix, 17

spatulas, 11

spinach

Cachitos de Espinaca y Ricota,
70, 71

Fugazzeta de Vegetales, 126,
127

squash

Picarones, *270, 271*

stand mixer, 11

Stuffed Fugazzeta, *124, 125*

sugar, story of, 7

Suspiros, 228, *229*

sweetened condensed milk

Brazilian Bombocado, 250, *251*

Brigadeiros, *252,* 253

Chocolate Tres Leches de
Coco, 196–97, *197*

Cocadas, *266, 267*

Curau de Milho, 254, *255*

Flan de Coco, 246, *247*

Tres Leches Tradicional, 194–95,
195

sweet potatoes

Dulce de Camote, 208, *208*

Naturally Leavened Alfajores
con Dulce de Camote, 218,
219

Pastelitos de Camote y Mole,
278, 279

Picarones, *270, 271*

T

T'anta Wawa, 180–81, *181*

tapioca flour or starch

Beiju de Tapioca, *362, 363*

Cuñapés, *348, 349*

Pandebono, 350, *351*

Pão de Queijo, 346, *347*

tarts and pies

Pastafrola, 260, *261*

Picos, *240,* 241

techniques

converting between yeasted
and sourdough recipes,
18–19

leavening, 14–17

mixing, shaping, and baking
bread, 20–25

pastry and dessert techniques,
25–26

temperature, climate, and
altitude, 27

temperature variables, 27

Tequeños, 336, *337*

thermometers, 11

tomatoes

Pizza al Molde Napolitana, 130,
131

Pizza de Jamón y Morrones,
128, 129

Salsa Roja, 302, *303*

tools, 9–11

Torta Ahogada, *99,* 101

Torta de Ricota, *198,* 199

Torta Rogel, 226–27, *227*

tortillas

Baleadas, *300, 301*

historical importance of, 288–89

My Mom's Tortillas de Harina,
296–97

origins of, 288

Sourdough Discard Tortillas,
298–99, *299*

Tortillas de Harina de Trigo,
292–93, *293*

Tortillas de Harina Integral
(Whole Grain Flour
Tortilla), 294–95, *295*

Tortillas de Maíz, 290, *291*

Tres Leches Tradicional, 194–95,
195

Tripleta on Pan Sobao, *63,* 65

tubs and bowls, 10

Tustacas, *244, 245*

V

vanilla, 8

vegetables. *See specific
vegetables*

Volcán de Dulce de Leche, *262,*
263

W

water, 9

weight conversions, 9

wheat (trigo), 5–6

wheat bran

Banana and Rum Raisin Pan de
Coco, 172–73, *173*

Mogolla Integral, *136,* 137

white chocolate

Alfajores Blancos y Negros
with Dulce de Papaya,
216, 217

Whole Grain Flour Tortilla (Tortillas de Harina Integral), 294–95, *295*

Y

yeasted and hybrid doughs
Bolillo, 34–36, *35*
Bolillo Integral, 37–39, *38*
Cachitos de Espinaca y Ricota, *70,* 71
Cachitos de Jamón, 72–74, *73*

Cemita Milanesa de Pollo, *76,* 77
Jalapeño Quesillo Bolillo, 40–42, *41*
Pan Cubano, 56–58, *57*
Pan de Cemita, 75–77, *76*
Pan de Media Noche, 59–61
Pan de Yema Peruano, *66,* 67
Pan Michita, 43–45, *44*
Pan Mojicón, 53–54
Pan Sarnita, 68, *69*
Pan Sobao, 62–64

Pãozinho, 48–49, *49*
Pebete, 51, *52*
Pirujos, 46–47, *47*
Tripleta on Pan Sobao, *63,* 65
yeasted and sourdough recipes, converting between, 18–19
yeasted preferments
liquid, 15
sourdough, 16
stiff, 15
yeasts, 14–15

ABOUT THE AUTHOR

BRYAN FORD is an award-winning baker "leading a sourdough revolution" (*Food and Wine*) whose first book, New World Sourdough, "brings the joy back to bread" (*Epicurious*). He has judged Netflix's *Blue Ribbon Baking Championship*, hosted Magnolia Network's *Baked in Tradition* and *The Artisan's Kitchen*, and guest starred on *Waffles + Mochi*. He co-created *The Flaky Biscuit Podcast* with his wife, Bridget Kenna, and together they run Pan y Café in New York City, a manifestation of this book in bakery form.

@artisanbryan
artisanbryan.com